D1474660

Childhood in nineteenth-century France

CHILDHOOD IN NINETEENTH-CENTURY FRANCE

Work, health and education among the 'classes populaires'

COLIN HEYWOOD

*Lecturer in History,
University of Nottingham*

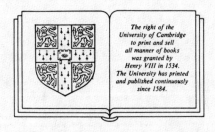

The right of the
University of Cambridge
to print and sell
all manner of books
was granted by
Henry VIII in 1534.
The University has printed
and published continuously
since 1584.

CAMBRIDGE UNIVERSITY PRESS

Cambridge
New York   New Rochelle   Melbourne   Sydney

Published by the Press Syndicate of the University of Cambridge
The Pitt Building, Trumpington Street, Cambridge CB2 1RP
32 East 57th Street, New York, NY 10022, USA
10 Stamford Road, Oakleigh, Melbourne 3166, Australia

First published 1988

Printed in Great Britain at Redwood Burn Ltd, Trowbridge, Wiltshire

British Library cataloguing in publication data
Heywood, Colin
Childhood in nineteenth-century France:
work, health and education among the *classes populaires*.
1. France. Children. Employment, 1800–1900
I. Title
331.3'1'0944

Library of Congress cataloguing in publication data
Heywood, Colin.
Childhood in nineteenth-century France: work, health and
education among the *classes populaires* / Colin Heywood.
p.   cm.
Bibliography.
Includes index.
ISBN 0 521 35038 7
1. Children – France – Social conditions. 2. Children – Employment –
France – History – 19th century. 3. Labor and laboring classes –
France – History – 19th century. 4. France – Social conditions – 19th century.
I. Title.
HQ792.F7H39   1988
305.2'3'0944 – dc19   88-2619   CIP

ISBN 0 521 35038 7

CE

To Sophie and Joseph

Contents

PART TWO THE IMPACT OF INDUSTRIALIZATION

PART THREE THE STATE INTERVENES

Maps

Tables

Acknowledgements

First and foremost I should like to acknowledge my long-standing debt to Professor Olwen Hufton, who first launched me into historical research at Reading University, and who helped at strategic points with the writing of this book. I should also like to thank Roger Price, of the University of East Anglia, Alan Booth, of Loughborough University, and Lee Weissbach, of the University of Louisville, Kentucky, for thought-provoking discussions and comments on parts of the manuscript.

Financial support was generously provided by the Nuffield Foundation, the Economic and Social Research Council, the Twenty Seven Foundation and the Economics Department at Loughborough University. The staffs of various libraries and archives provided invaluable assistance, particularly in the Archives Nationales, and Departmental Archives at Lille, Rouen, Colmar, Troyes, Epinal, Privas and Valence. The typing I owe to Ms Lorraine Salter, Mrs Madge Lowe and especially Mrs Gloria Brentnall, and the two original maps to Mrs Anne Tarver, of the Geography Department, Loughborough University. I must also express my gratitude to the editor of the journal for allowing me to incorporate material from my article 'The Market for Child Labour in Nineteenth-Century France', *History*, 66 (1981), 34–49.

On a personal note, I should like to thank Mme and André Becherand, for lending me flats in Paris and Epinal. Last but not least, I should like to mention the efforts of my wife Olena, who read the entire manuscript, and provided moral support through thick and thin.

Introduction

Children from peasant and working-class backgrounds were highly visible in France during the nineteenth century. The street, the workshop and the farm were still very much part of their territory, where they mingled freely with the world of adults. Even the most haughty members of the bourgeoisie could hardly fail to notice several of their activities. Venturing out in a city, they risked being accosted by the local *gamins*: poor, scruffy children who would beg the odd coin, or offer to do little jobs, such as opening a carriage door or scraping mud off boots during bad weather. All around, they would feel the bustle of young people plying their trades. These included peasant girls on their way to food markets; hawkers shouting their wares; delivery boys doing the rounds for tradesmen; apprentice *couturières* and *blanchisseuses* shuffling back and forth between their customers and their 'sweatshops'; *saltimbanques* doing street-shows with other members of their families; and soot-blackened *petits savoyards* touting for business beside the chimney sweeps. Other sights were more disturbing for the bourgeoisie, but equally unavoidable. Passing near to a working-class *quartier*, they were bound to observe the spectacle of small groups of children playing in the streets. Almost invariably, these urchins would be shorter, paler and less robust than their own sons and daughters. And then there were the gangs of older lads, approaching adolescence, to be seen marauding the slums, or wandering through gardens and orchards on the outskirts of town. These were the 'vagabonds', viewed with considerable apprehension by middle-class observers. The *notables* were convinced that idleness in youth led inexorably to dissipation, vice, petty crime – and political subversion. Long after the ferment of 1830 had died down, they were haunted by the awful image of the revolutionary *gamin*, so vividly depicted by Delacroix and Victor Hugo.

This genteel perspective on children in the towns was necessarily a partial one: the vast majority of comfortable bourgeois had little idea of what went on behind the walls of a slum tenement or a workshop. The proletariat itself knew the realities of this existence all too well. Children made their presence felt in a rather different way at this level of society. Outside the home, the labouring classes were likely to think of the young above all as assistants at work. Many of them started their day in the company of their own or neighbours' children with a hurried walk to work. During the 1830s, Louis Villermé was struck by the appearance of mill hands he observed streaming into Mulhouse from outlying villages:

There are among them a multitude of women, pale, thin, walking barefoot through the mud, and being without umbrellas, pulling their underskirts over their heads to protect their faces and necks from the rain. There are even greater numbers of young children, no less dirty, no less drawn, covered in rags well greased by the machine-oil which splashes on them as they work.[1]

Once in the workshops, adults often worked closely with both male and female juveniles – the two sexes usually being employed interchangeably at this stage of life. The *canut* of Lyons needed his *lanceur* and his *tireur* beside him to operate a Jacquard loom; the potter used a *gamin* to turn his wheel; the mule spinner had his (or her) team of *bobineurs* and *ratta-cheurs*; the calico printer employed a *tireur* to prepare his dyestuffs and mordants; and the glassblower was served by his *gamins* and *porteurs*. At the end of the working day, the crowds of labourers formed up again to go home, families in the domestic workshops assembled for their meals, and the only refuge from the babble of children was the *cabaret* (bar) – exclusively adult male territory.

In rural areas, children were if anything drawn into the mainstream of communal life more quickly than in the towns. The younger villagers sometimes gave the impression of being less sharp than their urban counterparts, for they lacked the stimulus of a more commercial culture. At the beginning of the century, most still spoke a *patois* or dialect that would have isolated them from their compatriots, and there was always a certain reserve towards outsiders. Nonetheless, they were much in evidence around the farms and villages. Passing travellers would have seen youthful shepherds and shepherdesses scattered around the fields with their livestock, or at least heard them calling to each other with long, yodelling cries. From time to time, they were likely to meet a child on the road, leading a farm animal, or collecting dung for manuring the fields. And should they happen to arrive on a holiday, they would have observed the young joining in all forms of celebration: the mass, the feasting, the

[1] Dr Louis R. Villermé, *Tableau de l'état physique et moral des ouvriers employés dans les manufactures de coton, de laine et de soie* (2 vols., Paris, 1840), vol. 1, p. 26. All translations from the French, unless stated otherwise, are by the author. On the background to this passage, see W. M. Reddy, *The Rise of Market Culture* (Cambridge, 1984), pp. 178–80.

games and the dancing. In short, peasants regularly worked, ate and relaxed with their own or other peoples' children. The latter were taken on as farm servants, lodging with their employers in much the same way as apprentices and domestic servants did in the towns.

This whole régime for children did not go unchallenged. From the time of the French Revolution onwards, a populist stream began to emerge in educational thinking, canvassing for some form of instruction as the birthright of every citizen. In the 1820s and 1830s, the practice of child labour in industry came under fire from various quarters, appalled by revelations of conditions in the manufacturing centres. A new domestic ideology, associated with the middle classes, also began to make an impact. The ideal here was for women and children to remain at home, away from the corrupting influence of the workplace. Eventually, a profound transformation of the rôle of children from the *classes populaires* took place. Over the course of the nineteenth century, they slowly abandoned their work in the fields and workshops, in order to move, definitively, to the school benches. Henceforth they were destined for an existence more segregated from society at large: a change that had already begun to occur among middle-class children a century or so before.[2] The emphasis would be on developing basic skills and character within the institutional framework of the school, rather than *sur le tas*, in an adult world now deemed unsuitable for the young.

The transition from work to school was never a complete one. During the eighteenth century, the work expected from children was not always exacting: young shepherds had plenty of time for play while out in the fields with their flocks, and, in the domestic workshops, the younger members of the family usually only put in a few hours beside their parents each day. At the same period, the *petites écoles* of the Catholic Church had attempted to bring some instruction to the *menu peuple*, while priests often ran classes for their parishioners. However, if the commitment of the ruling élites to the education of their own children was never in doubt, that of the lower orders was another matter. The Church was principally interested in the religious instruction of the population, and even in Enlightenment circles, there was no suggestion that peasants and artisans should have the same educational opportunities as members of the middle and upper classes.[3] The provision of schools was therefore very uneven

[2] This is a thesis, much contested in various areas, associated with the name of Philippe Ariès, and his *Centuries of Childhood* (Harmondsworth, 1973).

[3] James A. Leith, 'Modernisation, Mass Education and Social Mobility in French Thought, 1750–1789', in R. F. Brissenden (ed.), *Studies in the Eighteenth Century* (Toronto, 1973), vol. 2, pp. 223–38; Harvey Chisick, *The Limits of Reform in the Enlightenment: Attitudes towards the Education of the Lower Classes in Eighteenth-Century France* (Princeton, NJ, 1981), *passim*; Louis-Henri Parias (ed.), *Histoire générale de l'enseig-*

across the country, and the fact that the mass of the population had little or no time for school did not give rise to public concern.[4]

Latterly, during the second half of the twentieth century, the school system and the notion of a cloistered childhood have still not gained a total ascendency. Children have not been driven from playing in the streets entirely; truancy among those in the final years of compulsory education remains a problem; and even child labour itself flourishes in the 'black economy'. The law currently allows children to assist in a family enterprise, as long as school obligations are fulfilled, and to work part time during the holidays. An Enquiry in 1979 revealed the possibilities of abuse. Children were found working beside their parents on the land, in small shops, in *la biffe* (the rag-and-bone trade) and in domestic work-shops, where they assembled electric plugs, jewellery-boxes and various other knick-knacks. This could involve a heavy burden on their free time, with work expected before and after school, and on holidays. There were even examples of incitement to miss school.[5] Yet there is no escaping the fact that in the highly developed economy of post-war France, children have been removed from regular employment and their work relegated to marginal significance. Since 1967, the school-leaving age has been sixteen in France and families defying the law risk facing stiff penalties: infringe-ments have consequently been rare. A lingering resentment in some quarters over the prolonged period of compulsory attendance has not prevented the school being accepted as a useful source of skills and as a channel for social mobility. Complementing this bid to confine children to the classroom for much of their time, has been the growing desire to keep them in the home. The break-up of the old working-class communities by new housing developments in the twentieth century has encouraged the tendency for children to have their own room, their own toys and their own garden or play areas, away from the alleged dangers and 'promiscuity' of the slum street. The provision of crêches and *écoles maternelles* (nursery schools) has further helped this isolation during the early years.[6]

One can therefore talk of a sea change in the lives of peasant and

nement et de l'éducation en France, vol. 2, *De Gutenberg aux Lumières* (Paris, 1981), pp. 385–96.

[4] Yves Poutet, 'L'Enseignement des pauvres dans la France du XVIIe siècle', *XVIIe siècle*, 90–1 (1971), 87–110; Roger Chartier, Marie-Madeleine Compère and Domi.ique Julia, *L'Education en France du XVIe au XVIIIe siècle* (Paris, 1976), pp. 3–44; Maurice Gontard, *L'Enseignement primaire en France de la Révolution à la loi Guizot, 1789–1833* (Paris, 1959), pp. 5–68; Parias, *Histoire générale*, vol. 2, pp. 416–27.

[5] D. Rouard, 'Enfants au travail', *Le Monde de l'éducation*, 53 (1979), 9–18; Christiane Rimbaud, *52 millions d'enfants au travail* (Paris, 1980), p. 12.

[6] J. Gélis, M. Laget and M.-F. Morel, *Entrer dans la vie: naissances et enfances dans la France traditionnelle* (Paris, 1978), pp. 232–4.

working-class children, which for the latter in particular had its crucial stages during the nineteenth century. This is the focus of our study. Three key questions underpin its various sections. First, why did the employment of children, a custom that had been accepted without question for centuries, suddenly become a public issue during the second quarter of the nineteenth century, and decline in importance thereafter? Secondly, why did informal methods of educating the young in the family and the local community give way to the formal education system of the schools? And thirdly, how effective was the State in its efforts to promote the welfare of children? The existing historical literature has answers to these questions. The sufferings of factory children are after all as firmly implanted in the popular image of the Industrial Revolution as the steam engine, and the long struggle of the school system to establish itself has never lacked its historians. Yet the literature is not above criticism for its interpretations, nor is its coverage of the area at all comprehensive.

In reply to the first question, on child labour reform, a straight-forward pattern of challenge-and-response is presented.[7] The challenge came from the introduction of steam power and machinery into industry, which permitted a substitution of women and children for adult males. Employment in the mills is shown to have taken a heavy toll on the physical, moral and intellectual development of the young. Evidence can readily be marshalled on child 'martyrs' succumbing to tuberculosis or industrial accidents; deplorable military recruitment figures in manufacturing areas; widespread illiteracy among factory operatives; and the vice-ridden atmosphere of the workshops. Georges Dupeux provides a succinct, textbook summary:

Industrialists, above all in the textile industry, discovered that physical strength was not needed for certain simple tasks such as refastening broken threads, and even for starting up and watching over some of the machines. This led to the employment of female and child labour. Women were much cheaper to employ: they were paid between half and one-third less than men and children received

---

[7] We may cite two generations of historians here. The first appeared in the inter-war period: L. Guéneau, 'La Législation restrictive du travail des enfants: la loi française du 22 mars 1841', *Revue d'histoire économique et sociale*, 15 (1927), 420–503; Suzanne Touren, *La Loi de 1841 sur le travail des enfants dans les manufactures* (Paris, 1931); Simone Béziers, *La Protection de l'enfance ouvrière* (Montpellier, 1935); and F. Evrard, 'Le Travail des enfants dans l'industrie, 1780–1870', *Bulletin de la société d'études historiques, geographiques et scientifiques de la région parisienne*, 37 (1936), 1–14. Among post-war historians, see Edouard Dolléans and Georges Dehove, *Histoire du travail en France* (2 vols., Paris, 1953), vol. 1, pp. 148–9, 160–1; Maurice Bouvier-Ajam, *Histoire du travail en France depuis la Révolution* (Paris, 1969), pp. 90–2, 134–7; Claude Fohlen, 'Révolution industrielle et travail des enfants', *Annales de démographie historique* (1973), 319–25; Jean Sandrin, 'Le Travail des enfants au XIXe siècle', *Le Peuple français*, 21 (January–March 1976), 12–16, and 22 (April–June 1976), 27–30; and *idem*, *Enfants trouvés, enfants ouvriers, XVIIe–XIXe siècle* (Paris, 1982).

absurdly low wages ... The effect of this kind of work on the health of children was disastrous ... Their only apprenticeship was a precocious introduction to the sexual promiscuity of factory life.[8]

The response came in the form of child labour legislation. Some reference is usually made to new machinery making child workers redundant but the emphasis is more on the intervention of the State. The first *loi sur le travail des enfants*, indeed arguably the first piece of social legislation in France, was passed on 22 March 1841. Its failure to make much of an impact has been amply documented: Pierre Pierrard writes of the 'pourissement de la loi' in Lille; Roger Magraw describes it as 'virtually worthless'.[9] New laws and a more effective inspection system came in 1874 and 1892. At this point, the issue of child labour simply fades from the history books: none of the major texts concerned with the late nineteenth century can find much to say on the subject.[10] The impression is even given that the problem has been solved by the legislature: in the words of Suzanne Touren: 'Since 1874, the laws have succeeded each other, and the little worker has finally obtained reasonable protection. Today he has the right to have a real childhood before being harnessed to work, and the workshop has now been made human.'[11]

This interpretation undoubtedly gives a number of insights into the fate of child labour under industrial capitalism and the origins of the 1841 law. But it must still be asked whether the early nineteenth century really did bring a substantial change in the composition of the industrial labour force. The extent of the deterioration in the physical and intellectual condition of children is unclear. And it is still an open question whether it was the law or underlying conditions in the labour market that did most to pull children out of industrial employment.[12] We might accuse historians of following too closely the line taken by child labour reformers in the 1830s and 1840s.

There is the same fixation on the influence of the factory system, which naturally attracted early observers on account of its spectacular departure from earlier methods of production. Yet in 1851 the census found only 1.3 million people employed in 'manufacturing industry', dominated by

---

8 *French Society, 1789–1970* (London, 1976), p. 131.
9 Pierre Pierrard, *La Vie ouvrière à Lille sous le Second Empire* (Paris, 1965), p. 173; Roger Magraw, *France, 1815–1914: The Bourgeois Century* (London, 1983), p. 66.
10 The textbooks, of course, reflect the lack of published material in this area. See, for example, Fernand Braudel and Ernest Labrousse (eds.), *Histoire économique et sociale de la France*, vol. 4, *L'Ere industrielle et la société d'aujourd'hui, siècle 1880–1980* (Paris, 1979), part 1, pp. 454–534; and Pierre Sorlin, *La Société française* (2 vols., Paris, 1969), vol. 1, pp. 161–203.
11 Touren, *La Loi de 1841*, p. 133.
12 See, in the British context, Clark Nardinelli, 'Child Labor and the Factory Acts', *Journal of Economic History*, 40 (1980), 739–55.

mining, metallurgy and above all textiles, compared to 4.7 million in small-scale industry and commerce, not to mention 14.3 million in agriculture.[13] There is too the assumption that the health and morals of children were better in the countryside than in the town. Contemporaries took this for granted. In 1837, Villeneuve-Bargemont solemnly recommended young people to seek work in agriculture when they left school, on the grounds that its customs were purer, and its wages more secure.[14] Jules Michelet followed suit a decade later, asserting that in the countryside, the child was happy:

Almost naked, without clogs, with a piece of black bread, he keeps an eye on a cow or a few geese, he lives in the open air, he plays. The agricultural work with which he is gradually associated only serves to strengthen him. The precious years during which a man develops his body and his strength for the rest of his life are therefore passed in great freedom, in the gentle surroundings of the family.

In the factory areas, by contrast, Michelet alleged that children were weakened and often corrupted by their surroundings.[15] A plausible case can certainly be made out along these lines. But the risk of idealizing the peasant existence, or 'leading civilized man back to the charms of a primitive life', as George Sand put it during the 1840s, needs constantly to be borne in mind.[16] Correspondingly, there is the potential for overdoing the 'pathological' character of factory and city life. William Sewell has recently drawn attention to the prejudice evident in the much-quoted work of Louis Villermé. The emphasis in his study of the textile workers is very much on the poorest of the poor, the inhabitants of the dirtiest and most crowded slums, rather than on the more numerous urban craftsmen. The factory workers and the slum dwellers are highlighted, according to Sewell, because for middle-class observers like Villermé they seemed to epitomize the labour problem of the nineteenth century, and to provide an ominous pointer to the future of the working class as a whole. Furthermore, the moral degradation of the workers emerges as more shocking for Villermé than their physical degradation. Yet the moral lapses of the poor are often more a matter of conjecture than direct description. Sewell takes as an example the subtle imputation of incest among working-class

---

[13] Statistique de la France, *Territoire et population* (Paris, 1855), pp. xx–xxiv.
[14] *Economie politique chrétienne* (Brussels, 1837), p. 440.
[15] *Le Peuple* (Paris, 1974), pp. 103–4.
[16] George Sand, 'Notice' preceding *La Mare au diable* (Paris, 1962), p. 4, originally published in 1846 as one of her four *romans champêtres*. This theme is also discussed in Hervé Carrier, 'Le Manichéisme urbain–rural: quelques stéréotypes de la société heureuse', in Hervé Carrier and Emile Pin (eds.), *Essais de sociologie religieuse* (Paris, 1967), pp. 147–65; Marie-José Chombart de Lauwe, *Un monde autre: l'enfance* (Paris, 1971), *passim*; and, in the context of English literature, Raymond Williams, *The Country and the City* (London, 1973).

families in Lille. A careful reading of the text shows Villermé to be *assuming* that sexual promiscuity must logically have followed from the squalid conditions of slum housing, rather than to be relying on his own observations.[17]

The high moral tone that marked the discourse of child labour reformers during the mid-nineteenth century has also continued in the writings of many historians. F. Evrard, author of an early study in this area, contrasted the humanity of the 1841 law with the selfishness of employers, and concluded that 'The improvement of the destiny of working children posed a moral as much as an economic problem.' Suzanne Touren wrote of the 'egoism' and 'cynicism' of the bourgeoisie, and the 'greed' of working-class parents in her study of the 1841 law. During the 1970s, Jean Sandrin described working-class children being handed over to 'the ogres of industry' under the First Empire, and the heavy mortality they suffered as a consequence. And Douailler and Vermeren have taken a leaf from the polemics of Karl Marx, highlighting the 'immoral agreement' between fathers and employers of child workers, likening it to a contract between a slave-dealer and a slave-master.[18] There is no denying the moral dimension to the issue, and it is entirely right that historians make clear their abhorrence of the exploitation of children. The central rôle of self-interest in the workings of the capitalist system is also not in dispute. At the same time, it is all too easy to adopt a self-righteous attitude in our own, twentieth-century European society, where child labour has been reduced to tolerable proportions.[19] Moral judgements on the various interested parties should not be allowed to obscure the pressures they faced in their daily lives, for poverty was still endemic in French society during the early nineteenth century, and labour for the new textile mills difficult to recruit. The problem of finding alternatives to work for the children of the poor should also be considered, given the near-impossibility of supervising children in a slum, and the shortage of school facilities.

The second question posed in this book, concerning the transformation of educational methods, has attracted a great deal of attention from historians in the last few years. The outline answer is now clear. In the broadest context, historians have documented the shift from a 'popular' to a 'mass' culture: in other words, from a culture that was essentially oral, community-based and traditional to one that was more literate,

[17] William H. Sewell, *Work and Revolution in France* (Cambridge, 1980), pp. 223–32.
[18] Evrard, 'Le Travail des enfants', 14; Touren, *La Loi de 1841*, pp. 18, 65, 134; Sandrin, 'Le Travail des enfants', 12; S. Douailler and P. Vermeren, 'Les Enfants du capital', *Les Révoltes logiques*, 3 (1976), 25–6.
[19] This is a point made by Anna Davin, in 'Child Labour, the Working-Class Family, and Domestic Ideology in 19th Century Britain', *Development and Change*, 13 (1982), 650.

national and (formally at least) rational. They have all agreed that from the seventeenth century onwards, the popular culture was attacked from within and without. The post-tridentine Catholic Church and the centralizing State set out to 'civilize' the population, attempting to repress what they called 'superstition', 'ignorance' and 'disorder'. More insidiously, underlying changes in society, such as improved communications, the growth of the towns and the extension of market relations, caused many of the old beliefs to appear redundant. In the narrower context of educational practice, these upheavals discredited the traditional methods of transmitting skills and values through the family and the community, paving the way for a specialized institution: the school.[20] This is all very well, but in our view the nature of the transition is not always interpreted correctly. Two particular reservations may be suggested.

In the first place, the emphasis in most of the studies of cultural change is on a crisis, a rupture, a fundamental discontinuity during the nineteenth century. In his fine study of the peasantry, Eugen Weber presents an unflattering picture of the popular culture at the beginning of the century. An early chapter entitled 'The Mad Beliefs' on peasant 'superstition' gives a hint of the conclusion to come: 'Deprived of the support of élite thought, popular belief broke into a thousand subsystems unintegrated into a comprehensive view of the world. Popular wisdom was bitsy – a collection of recipes, ceremonies, rituals – and popular religion was little more.'[21] With a popular culture so moribund, the peasant in the nineteenth century is shown to be ripe for emancipation through the school system. Weber ends with the assertion that 'The rural convert to rationalism could throw away his ragbag of traditional contrivances, dodges in an unequal battle to stay alive, with the heady conviction that, far from being a helpless witness of natural processes, he was himself an agent of change.'[22] Robert Muchembled diverges from Weber in so far as he sees the school as a repressive agency, used to impose an alien culture on the masses: that of the dominant classes. But there is the same stress on the 'ideological gap' which opens up when the popular culture is 'assassinated' from above, leaving only 'the shameful survivals of old mentalities'.[23] Among the urban working class, the process of *déculturation* in the nineteenth century can be depicted even more spectacularly. Maurice Crubellier points to various mechanisms having this effect, notably

---

[20] Information from Peter Burke, *Popular Culture in Early Modern Europe* (London, 1978); Maurice Crubellier, *Histoire culturelle de la France, XIXe–XXe siècle* (Paris, 1974); *idem, L'Enfance et la jeunesse dans la société française, 1800–1950* (Paris, 1979); Yves Marie Bercé, *Fête et révolte* (Paris, 1976); Robert Muchembled, *Culture populaire et culture des élites dans la France moderne, XVe–XVIIIe siècles* (Paris, 1978).

[21] *Peasants into Frenchmen* (London, 1979), p. 495.   [22] *Ibid.*

[23] *Culture populaire, passim.*

migrations uprooting young people from the villages, slum housing weakening family relationships, and the dead weight of long hours of monotonous work in the factories. Despite extended sections on resistance from old forms, and on the rise of new innovations, he insists that during the nineteenth and early twentieth centuries the working class was 'culturally destitute'.[24] But can one really consign three or four generations of Frenchmen to some kind of 'cultural void', leaving them in limbo between two great systems: the traditional popular culture of the Medieval towns and villages on the one hand, and the mass culture (or 'pseudo-culture') of industrial capitalism on the other? This strains credibility, and rests on an unduly monolithic view of social and cultural change at this period. If one proposes instead that popular culture was highly adaptable to its changing environment, and that important elements of continuity allowed a smoother transition, this has major implications for the history of education.[25]

The long shadow of the struggle between the Catholic Church and the Republic for the 'soul of French youth' lay heavily over the work of earlier generations of historians in the field of education. The Republican interpretation began with the Revolutionary ideal of emancipating the people through education, and gradually built up to the climax of the 1880s, with the establishment of a free, compulsory and egalitarian primary school system. An element of what the British would call 'Whig history' inevitably crept in, the tendency being to denigrate anything outside the evolving State-run system. Catholic historians countered by emphasizing the achievements of Church Schools and teachers under the *ancien régime*. The Preface to one such work by the Abbé Allain, written during the 1880s, attacked the notion that it was the Revolution which invented primary instruction, thundering instead against 'the outrages the Revolution dared to commit against Christian primary instruction'. The author went on to assert a decline in teaching standards from the Republican influence. Under the *ancien régime*, he noted, the schools gave an important place to Christian teaching, whereas under the Third Republic religious instruction by means of the catechism had been dropped entirely:

It has been said, with reason, that the catechism is the philosophy of the people. Through it they became acquainted with the great rational and Christian truths which are the basis of our intelligence. A little reading and writing, a little

24 *Histoire culturelle, passim*; and his chapter on 'Les Citadins et leurs cultures', in Georges Duby (ed.), *Histoire de la France urbaine*, vol. 4, *La Ville de l'âge industriel: le cycle haussmanien* (Paris, 1983), pp. 359–470.
25 See the debate in the British literature: R. W. Malcolmson, *Popular Recreations in English Society, 1700–1850* (Cambridge, 1975); and H. Cunningham, *Leisure in the Industrial Revolution, c.1780–1880* (London, 1980).

arithmetic and grammar, a little geography and history, that is the curriculum for popular instruction today ... I was forgetting the gymnastics![26]

Now that the dust has begun to settle on this *lutte scolaire*, a more dispassionate account of events has emerged. Historians have come to recognize the common ground between the two sides, in their passion for education, and the elements of continuity running through the legislation of successive political régimes.[27]

The delicate problem remains of being able to record promising new developments in education, without undervaluing the contribution of earlier institutions. We now know, for example, that the future lay with purpose-built schools, teachers trained in *écoles normales* and full-time education into adolescence. But the makeshift classes run by an assortment of part-time or untrained teachers in their homes and workshops could be well adapted to the requirements of the poor, in the same way that para-medics today can be more appropriate than fully trained doctors in the villages of a less developed country. A recent work by Robert Gildea illustrates the difficulty. On the one hand, the author is prepared to override the criticisms made by reformers of *maîtres de pension*, artisan-teachers and 'dame schools' run by penniless spinsters, acknowledging their 'indispensable service at the margins of history at the beginning of the nineteenth century'. On the other hand, he occasionally adopts the full-blooded missionary fervour characteristic of an older Republican orthodoxy. In the Ile-et-Vilaine, for example, he asserts that until the Restoration, there was 'no real progress', the reason being that initiative was abandoned to 'charity and speculation'. And, in the same department, the Liberals of the July Monarchy are honoured as an 'exposed column of vanguard-fighters', who struggle against the 'nefarious influence of the parish clergy'.[28]

There remains too the problem of assessing the limits to the influence of the school. During the nineteenth century, Catholics and Republicans alike pinned their faith in the institution of the school, in their slightly desperate bids to produce good Christians or good citizens. Time-honoured methods of instruction within the family and the local commu-

---

[26] E. Allain, *L'Instruction primaire en France avant la Révolution* (Geneva, 1970; first publ. 1881). Preface by the Archevêque de Perga, coadjuteur de Bordeaux, pp. i–vi.

[27] See in particular Chartier *et al.*, *L'Education en France*, pp. 39–40; François Furet and Jacques Ozouf, *Reading and Writing* (Cambridge, 1982), pp. 1–4; Lous-Henri Parias (ed.), *Histoire générale de l'enseignement et de l'éducation en France*, vol. 3, *De la Révolution à l'école républicaine* (Paris, 1981), p. 297. Exemplary modern studies include Antoine Prost, *Histoire de l'enseignement en France, 1800–1967* (Paris, 1968); Gontard, *L'Enseignement primaire*; and *idem*, *Les Ecoles primaires de la France bourgeoise, 1833–1875* (Toulouse, 1957).

[28] *Education in Provincial France, 1800–1914* (Oxford, 1983), pp. 88–94, 172.

nity were not entirely dismissed, but the tendency to equate education with the formal instruction given in the schools began to emerge. Historians might be accused of following this lead rather too easily. The *Histoire générale de l'enseignement et de l'éducation en France* gives an authoritative and up-to-date survey of the present state of knowledge. Françoise Mayeur argues that any study of education in nineteenth-century France must be interested in the history of institutions for it was a period which believed strongly in the power of institutions.[29] But she also makes every effort to investigate the areas that escaped the school. Chapters on 'Childhoods' and 'Learning in Life' have excellent material on child-rearing practices during the early years, and on complementary institutions such as crêches, orphanages and apprentice schools. However, when it comes to investigating how peasant and working-class children learnt from those around them, Professor Mayeur is forced to rely on a handful of autobiographies and local studies. Moreover, when discussing the efficiency of the primary school as an instrument for teaching a basic apprenticeship, she notes that 'many obscurities remain'. Questions are easier to find than answers when it comes to areas such as the assiduousness of pupils and the length of effective schooling.[30] Given our assumption of a certain adaptability to the popular culture during the nineteenth century, its informal methods of education stand out as worthy of further exploration. So too do the influences it had on the receptiveness of children to what was taught in the schools. It is all very well showing what educational theorists and politicians were trying to achieve through the schools, but this begs the question of the extent to which they succeeded – or failed.

Our final theme, the rôle of the State in the campaign to end child labour abuse, has hardly been broached in the French context to date. The origins of the 1841 law have been thoroughly investigated, and so too have its failures.[31] Otherwise, historians have been content to portray a gallant band of 'crusaders' using the law to fight the ravages of a capitalist system deemed inherently voracious of child labour. The possibility that legislation might be counter-productive, driving the exploitation of children 'underground' and allowing small-scale units of production to flourish at the expense of large ones obeying the law, has not been

[29] Parias, *Histoire générale*, vol. 3, p. 12.   [30] *Ibid.*, p. 571.
[31] Guéneau, 'La Législation restrictive'; Touren, *La Loi de 1841*; Peter N. Stearns, *Paths to Authority* (Urbana, Ill., 1978), pp. 160–6; Lee S. Weissbach, 'Qu'on ne coupe le blé en herbe: A History of Child Labour Legislation in Nineteenth-Century France', unpublished PhD thesis, Harvard University, 1975. The latter is a very full account of the debate surrounding both the 1841 and 1874 laws on child labour.

confronted.[32] Nor has the related issue of whether the State should try to abolish or to regulate the employment of children.[33] The interaction between the forces of the labour market, which might in fact tend to exclude children from work as well as draw them in, and the pressure exerted by the State through its Child Labour Inspectors, is also open to exploration. As far as historical periods go, the 1830s and 1840s have attracted most of the attention of historians, while the fate of the 1874 law has been almost entirely neglected. Although the 1841 law on child labour was never seriously enforced, its successor of 1874 was.[34] Hence it becomes possible to discuss enforcement strategies, and to assess the impact of legislation on practice in the workshops at this later period. These are important areas of investigation, for they have policy implications for Third World countries today, as they seek to sharpen their own campaigns against the abuse of child workers.

Answers to those conundrums can only come from a study of childhood on the broadest of canvases. Rural as well as urban conditions need to be investigated, for it was in the countryside that much of the pressure to employ children was originally generated, and it was the village childhood which reformers used as a yardstick by which to judge the plight of working children in the towns. The attitudes of industrialists and working-class parents to the employment of children must be examined, as well as the efforts of Child Labour Inspectors, for the working relationship established between those on the two sides of the law was of critical importance in the latter part of the nineteenth century. The perceptions of the political and social élites on the physical and moral condition of working-class children are also of importance, as well as the underlying realities, for in the French case it was the *notables* who made the running in the reform campaign. Above all, a synthesis of the history of work and the history of education in childhood is required. In the nineteenth century the two were closely meshed, and undergoing fundamental changes. The sources are readily available for such a study: in

32 Cf., for Britain, Nardinelli, 'Child Labor', and W. H. Hutt, 'The Factory System of the Early Nineteenth Century', in F. A. Hayek (ed.), *Capitalism and the Historians* (London, 1954), pp. 160–88.

33 Cf. Guy Standing, 'State Policy and Child Labour: Accumulation versus Legitimation', *Development and Change*, 13 (1982), 613–20.

34 The fate of the 1841 law can best be explored in the local studies: see in particular, M.-M. Kahan-Rabecq, *L'Alsace économique et sociale sous le règne de Louis-Philippe* (2 vols., Paris, 1939), vol. 1, pp. 158–206; Pierrard, *La Vie ouvrière*, pp. 170–8; Yves Lequin, *Les Ouvriers de la région lyonnaise, 1848–1914* (2 vols., Lyons, 1977), vol. 2, pp. 4–9; Pierre Léon, *La Naissance de la grande industrie en Dauphiné, fin du XVIIᵉ siècle–1869* (2 vols., Paris, 1954), vol. 2, pp. 756–7; Monique Baudoin, 'Le Travail des enfants dans les manufactures de l'Isère, 1841–1870', *Le Peuple français*, 23 (1976), 31; Jean Vidalenc, *Le Département de l'Eure sous la monarchie constitutionnelle, 1814–1848* (Paris, 1952), pp. 496–8.

particular, the various enquiries into the conditions of peasant and working-class labour; the autobiographies written by men and women who experienced a childhood in the villages or popular quarters of the towns; the polemical works generated during the course of the child labour reform campaign; and the reports of Primary School and Child Labour Inspectors. Besides the documentation in the Archives Nationales, we have taken soundings from a number of local archives in the Seine-Maritime, Nord, Haut-Rhin, Vosges, Meurthe-et-Moselle, Aube, Ardèche, Drôme and Rhône departments. Inevitably too, in an expansive study such as this, we have drawn heavily on a wide range of secondary sources. The book aims to provide a general survey of its subject area, as well as original material.

This leaves us with the important question of how we define childhood. Most of the attention in the book is focussed on what the French would call the second stage of childhood. This started at the age of six or seven, the traditional 'age of discernment', when the child was ready to leave the comforting environment of the home and the family. Henceforth, he or she was considered ready to learn at school, or to move directly into providing some assistance at work. First communion was a further *rite de passage* in the Catholic childhood, usually taken at the age of twelve. Until the 1880s, it marked the end of formal education in the schools for the majority of children from humble backgrounds, and the start of a more serious 'apprenticeship' on the land or in the workshops. Inexorably, the young boy or girl was drawn further into the world of adults at this stage. Around the age of sixteen, the end of childhood was acknowledged more clearly. In rural society, young people moved from the society of children to that of youth: *la jeunesse*. In industry too sixteen was generally taken as the upper limit of childhood. Successive industrial enquiries distinguished children under this age from men and women workers, and both the 1841 and 1874 child labour laws used eight to twelve and twelve to sixteen years as their protected age categories. For young males, the age of twenty was another important turning point, since they were liable to be drafted for military service. Until they had cleared this obstacle, via the balloting procedures of the *Conseil de Révision*, they could not seriously contemplate a courtship and a settled future. *Filles mineures* also appear in our study: young women aged between sixteen and twenty-one, who were given some protection by the labour law of 1874.

Part One

The rural background

Chapter 1

The agricultural setting

Rural France in the nineteenth century was first and foremost a mosaic of regions. The landscape provided an immediate image of diversity: mountains and forests looked down on lush valleys and plains; *pays de vignoble* stood out from surrounding arable and grass lands; maritime France differed from continental France. Most importantly of all, the great open-field systems characteristic of the north and east could be distinguished from the enclosed *bocages* of the west and the irregular 'square' fields more common in the south.[1] Adolphe Blanqui, writing during the 1850s, depicted such contrasts between neighbouring *pays* in terms of oases in the desert: 'Thus, the Limagne of the Auvergne shines like a diamond at the foot of the wilderness of Cantal; the Vaucluse plain at the entry to the *terres brûlantes* of Provence; the Médoc at the threshold of the Landes; the Touraine close by the Sologne; the gardens of Annonay at the exit from the gorges of Forez.'[2]

These physical differences were matched by an equally wide variety of social structures. In much of northern France, on the vast open fields of the Ile-de-France, Picardy, the Beauce and parts of Normandy, the concentration of farms meant that a few wealthy tenant farmers and *laboureurs* held sway over a vast army of dependent agricultural labourers. Elsewhere, in the Mediterranean coastal district, the south-west, the Massif, Brittany and Flanders, society was nearer the Jacobin ideal of a 'republic of peasants'. Although the majority of farms in these areas of *microculture* were insufficient to support a family, a combination of small peasant property, rented land and *métayage* ensured a more even distribution of holdings than in the Paris basin. Then there was the contrast

[1] Marc Bloch, *French Rural History*, transl. J. Sondheimer (London, 1966), pp. 21–63; Georges Duby and Armand Wallon (eds.), *Histoire de la France rurale*, vol. 3, *Apogée et crise de la civilisation paysanne, 1789–1914* (Paris, 1976), pp. 255–77; Philippe Pinchemel, *La France* (2 vols., Paris, 1980–1), vol. 1, pp. 199–200; vol. 2, pp. 247–61.

[2] Adolphe Blanqui, 'Tableau des populations rurales de la France en 1850', *Séances et travaux de l'Académie des sciences morales et politiques*, 2nd ser., 9 (1851), 149–50.

between the societies of mountain and plain: on the one hand, the isolated and very spartan communities of the Alps, the Pyrenees, the Massif and the Vosges; on the other, the more affluent and commercially-orientated villages located on the main axes of communication. No less important were the divergences stemming from various forms of agricultural special-ization that emerged during the nineteenth century: the intensive, market-gardening type of agriculture characteristic of Flanders and Alsace; the arable farming of the great cereals belt around Paris; the cattle raising of certain districts in Normandy and the Nivernais; the sheep farming of the Midi; and the large-scale vine growing of Languedoc.[3] There was, in short, no single model of French agriculture, and rural society provided a host of settings for childhood.

What was common to all regions was the slowness of agricultural change, even when allowance is made for the element of 'dualistic' development between northern and southern France. The Agricultural Revolution, involving improved techniques of cultivation and a re-organi-zation of the land, made a very tentative start during the final years of the *ancien régime*. But it is doubtful whether progress gained any real momentum until the 1820s, or perhaps even the 1840s. Early centres of innovation were concentrated in the north and east, partly owing to their close contacts with developments in England and the Low Countries. Subsequently this most unobtrusive of revolutions spread in piecemeal fashion to the south and west. Not until the 1850s and 1860s, with improved communications encouraging the *débloquage* of the country-side, were there any signs of new methods and new attitudes among the mass of small peasant farmers. Otherwise, the traditional *polyculture* reigned supreme, as each family tried to support itself by growing its own cereals, keeping a few livestock and poultry, having a small vegetable plot and perhaps also a vine. Yields remained low, animals were of poor quality, and much of the land was left fallow.[4] Escaping from the poverty and insecurity associated with rural life in earlier centuries therefore proved a long drawn-out affair across the regions. In those caught up at an early stage by industrial and urban development, notably the Ile-de-

[3] The best introductions to rural France, summarizing a whole series of detailed local studies are: Duby and Wallon, *Histoire de la France rurale*, vol. 3, *passim*; and Fernand Braudel and Ernest Labrousse (eds.), *Histoire économique et sociale de la France*, vol. 3, *L'Avènement de l'ère industrielle, 1789-années 1880* (Paris, 1976), part 2, pp. 617–767.

[4] Jean Pautard, *Les Disparités régionales dans la croissance de l'agriculture française* (Paris, 1965), *passim*; Michel Morineau, *Les Faux-semblants d'un démarrage économique: agriculture et démographie en France au XVIIIe siècle* (Paris, 1971), *passim*; W. H. Newell, 'The Agricultural Revolution in Nineteenth-Century France', *Journal of Economic History*, 33 (1973), 677, 731; François Caron, *An Economic History of Modern France* (London, 1969), pp. 117–19; Hugh Clout, *The Land of France, 1815–1914* (London, 1983), *passim*.

France, Flanders, Artois, Picardy and Normandy, a measure of prosperity had filtered through to the villages by the early nineteenth century. But others were left behind, such as those in the centre, marooned by their mountainous terrain and poor communications. For Léonce de Lavergne, surveying the rural economy during the 1860s, the Sologne, Berri, Nivernais, Bourbonnais, Auvergne, Velay, Gévaudan, Marche, Limousin and Périgord stood out *en bloc* as the poorest regions of France.[5] The family economy of the peasants, tenaciously rooted in the southern and western parts of the country, was still exposed to its traditional scourges: spells of illness or unemployment, harvest failures, and epidemics among livestock. Moreover, if the risk of premature death during a crisis had receded since the mid-eighteenth century, a serious problem of over-population blighted village life for another hundred years or so. Seasonal migrations and the expansion of the putting-out system in industry provided some relief. But in the long run it was the new markets and new employment opportunities increasingly available in the towns during the second half of the century that paved the way for a measure of prosperity in the countryside.

Release from the sheer drudgery of much activity on the farm took even longer. The diffusion of mechanized methods in agriculture had to wait until the late nineteenth century, when the 'rural exodus' caused the labour supply to tighten. In the meantime, the peasants continued with their long, laborious days in the fields. The routine of working from dawn to dusk was only occasionally interrupted by bouts of heavy eating and drinking at the various holidays in the village calendar. The gruelling régime inherited from traditional agriculture thus continued to be felt in village society well after new and more productive methods had taken hold. Emilie Carlès could, with pardonable exaggeration, write of a last outpost of *la vieille France*, high in the Alps on the eve of the First World War: 'It was the Middle Ages almost, a country of mountain folk who knew only work, sickness and death ... Work and bread, bread and work, nothing was more important.'[6]

In these rude circumstances, the great mass of peasants and agricultural labourers could not allow their offspring to remain idle for long. Around the age of seven, following a tradition laid down over the centuries, children of both sexes began to make themselves useful around the farm. As their strength developed during their early teens, so they inserted

---

[5] Léonce de Lavergne, *Economie rurale de la France depuis 1789* (Paris, 1869), p. 62.
[6] Emilie Carlès, *Une soupe aux herbes sauvages* (Paris, 1977), p. 22. See also Olwen Hufton, *The Poor of Eighteenth-Century France, 1750–1789* (Oxford, 1974), pp. 11–24; and Weber, *Peasants into Frenchmen*, pp. 3–191.

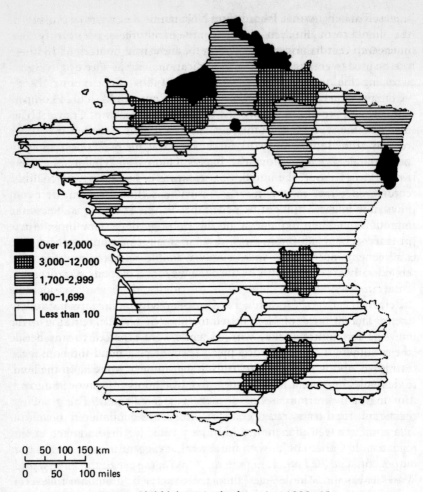

Over 12,000
3,000–12,000
1,700–2,999
100–1,699
Less than 100

0 50 100 150 km

0   50   100 miles

Map 1 Child labour in the factories, 1839–45

Source: Statistique de la France, *Industrie* (4 vols., Paris, 1847–52), vol. 4, pp. 362–7.

themselves fully into the labour force.[7] No national or regional estimate of the numbers of children working in agriculture is possible for the nineteenth century. However, data in the Industrial Enquiry of 1839–45 can be used to give an approximate indication of areas where agricultural work for children predominated. Map 1 shows that in the industrial areas of the north, north-east and Rhône corridor, agriculture had to compete with factories and domestic workshops for its child labour. Conversely, in much of the west, the south-west, the centre, the east and the alpine regions of the south-east, working the land was the main occupation for children. As *notables* from the Bresse region put it before the 1848 Enquiry on Labour, the number of 'apprentices' in agriculture could be considered equal to the number of village children who were not physically infirm.[8] It might be added that these same regions, below the famous Saint-Malo to Geneva line, were broadly speaking those where primary school education was slow to make an impact during the nineteenth century. This was *la France traditionnelle*, where the rural childhood was least affected by the dynamic forces of modern civilization. Under this system, for children as for adults, there was considerable divergence between the sexes. Parents assumed that boys would follow their fathers or their employers out into the fields, gradually picking up the ways of agriculture as they worked. Girls were expected to stay beside their mothers for a while, occupying themselves around the house, the farmyard, and where necessary during the summer months, on the land. Eventually they might be sent off to work on another farm or in a town, not least for the purpose of amassing the small *pécule* that was so important for their marriage chances. Pressure to put children to work in the countryside will therefore be traced back to three sources in this chapter: the burden of hard, manual work facing the peasant household;

[7] Ronald Hubscher, studying agriculture in the Pas-de-Calais, attempts to answer the question of when children joined the labour force by sampling the *listes nominatives* of the 1851 census. The drawback to this approach is that the gradual drift into work characteristic of the agricultural world is barely seizable through the terse entries of a census register. A ten-year-old doing casual work on a family farm was unlikely to be classified as a *cultivateur* or a *berger*, and so would go down as 'living from the work of his parents'. Hubscher's finding that, between the ages of twelve and sixteen, an increasing proportion of children was listed with an occupation should therefore be taken to indicate an availability for more serious work at this stage, rather than any sudden plunge into the active population. In a later section, using School Inspectors' reports, he makes clear his awareness that children under twelve were performing a whole range of little tasks on the land. See his *L'Agriculture et la société rurale dans le Pas-de-Calais du milieu du XIXe siècle à 1914* (Arras, 1979), pp. 168–72.

[8] AN, C 943, Pont-de-Veyle (Ain). The slow immersion of the young into agricultural work is frequently mentioned in this 'Enquête sur le travail agricole et industriel' of 1848–9. See in particular AN, C 952, Fouesnant (Finistère); AN, C 952, Plaisance (Gers); AN, C 961, Senlis (Oise); AN, C 962, Saint-Etienne-de-Baïgorry (Basses-Pyrénées). The background from the Medieval period can be traced in Ariès, *Centuries of Childhood*.

the generally low standard of living in the villages; and the need to train and prepare for adulthood.

Working the land

Work in the rural community moved with the seasons. Routines naturally varied according to the social status and regional location of each individual. Wealthy tenant farmers in, say, the Brie had little inclination to share the physical hardship of their day labourers, while big cattle raisers in the Nivernais doubtless knew more of interest rates and wholesale meat prices than of the rigours of life as a herdsman. Similarly, as Adolphe Blanqui pointed out, there was a 'capital difference' between the existence of a Breton peasant and a Champagne vine-grower, or that of a woodcutter in the Morvan and a tenant farmer in the Beauce.[9] Nonetheless, all who worked the land were tied to the cyclical rhythms of nature. The start of the agricultural year was in the autumn, when the harvest from the previous year had been stored. The peasant had first to prepare for a new round of crops, by ploughing and sowing his fields. The *araire*, the rudimentary plough which survived into the nineteenth century in much of southern France, did little more than scratch the surface of the soil, obliging the plough teams to go over the heavier soils three or four times.[10] In the Languedoc, for example: 'Ploughing finished towards the end of October. It was solitary work, five hours of silent coming and going, interspaced with onomatopoeic commands, being necessary to turn over a medium-sized field. After the vintaging, harvest and threshing festivals, winter opened on this austere note.'[11] Preparing the terraces cut into the hillsides of barren, mountainous regions like the Vivarais, Cévennes and Rouergue was even more time-consuming. Since a plough team could not hope to negotiate the narrow series of ledges, all the work had to be done by hand with a hoe, whilst additional soil and manure had to be carried up by basket.[12] Sowing began with rye, which had to be in the ground before Saint Michael's Day (29 September) if it was to resist

[9] Blanqui, 'Tableau des populations rurales', 151. See also Pierre Brunet, *Structure agraire et économie rurale des plateaux tertiaires entre la Seine et l'Oise* (Caen, 1960), *passim*; and Guy Thuillier, 'Les Transformations agricoles en Nivernais de 1815 à 1840', *Revue d'histoire économique et sociale*, 34 (1956), 426–56.

[10] Abel Poitrineau, *La Vie rurale en basse-auvergne au XVIIIe siècle, 1726–1789* (2 vols., Paris, 1965), vol. 1, p. 270; Yann Brékilien, *La Vie quotidienne des paysans bretons au XIXe siècle* (Paris, 1966), pp. 49–50; Duby and Wallon, *Histoire de la France rurale*, vol. 3, pp. 199–201.

[11] Daniel Fabre and Jacques Lacroix, *La Vie quotidienne des paysans du Languedoc au XIXe siècle* (Paris, 1973), pp. 198–9.

[12] Pierre Bozon, *La Vie rurale en Vivarais*, 2nd edn (Paris, 1963), p. 106; Roger Beteille, *Les Aveyronnais* (Poitiers, 1974), p. 28.

the early winter frosts, and continued later with winter wheat and barley. In the wine-producing regions, autumn was the season for the grape-harvest. On the slopes of Burgundy, for example, the *vendange* was generally rushed through in five or six days, with 'an explosion of work and a massive influx of labour'.[13] In the poorer regions of the centre and south, this was the season too for collecting chestnuts, eaten as a substitute for bread.

In the alpine regions, meanwhile, at the first sign of bad weather livestock was being brought down to the villages from pastures high in the mountains. Those animals that were not being sold at a local market had then to be stabled, and occasionally put out to graze whenever there was a break in the snow. With the coming of spring, the herds and flocks were re-assembled, and with much hullabaloo sent back to the *hauts pacages*. There the shepherds divided their time between moving their charges around the various meadows and making cheese.[14] In arable areas, the return of milder weather was the signal for the villagers to restart their ploughing, sowing and manuring. In northern France, oats, barley or rye could be sown as part of a three-course rotation. In the south, by contrast, the hot, dry summers ruled this out, and a biennial rotation held sway. However, olives and chestnuts provided alternative sources of food, and so too did various fruits such as pears, plums, peaches, apricots and figs. In the poorer regions of the south and west, the villagers also faced *l'écobuage*, a way of clearing land left fallow. This arduous task involved digging up the topmost layer of soil and vegetation, piling and burning the clods, and spreading the ashes back over the field.[15] Spring was the season for sowing artificial meadows of clover and lucerne, and for planting vegetables. As the Agricultural Revolution spread, so the work load required to support this diversification of crops increased. In the Rouergue, potatoes were a rarity until the 1840s, and only the better-off peasants grew vegetables such as tomatoes, haricot beans and carrots: the rest concentrated on cereals. In the north-east by contrast, *plantes sarclées* appeared everywhere at the expense of fallowing. Farmers in the Paris basin took advantage of the growing demand for meat in the capital by growing peas, vetch, lentils, clover and greens as fodder crops.[16] And in the departments of Nord, Pas-de-Calais and Somme, a thriving sugar industry emerged during the nineteenth century, supplied by local beet-

---

[13] P. de Saint-Jacob, *Les Paysans de la Bourgogne du nord au dernier siècle de l'ancien régime* (Paris, 1960), p. 288.

[14] Fabre and Lacroix, *Paysans du Languedoc*, p. 199; P. Besson, *Un Pâtre du Cantal* (Paris, 1914), pp. 61–126.

[15] Roger Beteille, *La Vie quotidienne en Rouergue avant 1914* (Paris, 1973), pp. 36–7; Brékilien, *Paysans bretons*, pp. 42–3.

[16] Beteille, *Rouergue avant 1914*, p. 38; Brunet, *Structure agraire*, p. 310.

growers. The sugar-beet was a particularly labour-intensive crop, requiring in the 1830s a small army of 20,000 labourers at harvest time.[17] Vine growing was another activity that relied on large inputs of labour during the spring and summer months. The *vigneron* was committed to a long series of tasks, including turning over the soil, clearing out weeds and pruning the vine plants.[18]

These *grands travaux* on the land came to a peak during the summer, when haymaking and the cereals harvest put intense pressure on the labour force. The rural community had to mobilize all the available hands and work them for up to sixteen hours a day, in order to gather in vast areas of hay and cereals while favourable weather lasted. Bands of migrant workers moved around the countryside at this period, taking advantage of the slight time lag between the harvests in various regions. Most of the movements were short distance, a matter of mutual aid between rural communities. But others were on a larger scale, particularly those to the great cereal-producing areas of the Paris basin and the south-east. During the early nineteenth century, for example, the Brie drew in migrants from surrounding areas, but also from the Meuse, Vosges, Côte-d'Or, Creuse, Orne, Eure and even Belgium. In the south-east, it was more a movement from mountain to plain: from the Alps and Vaucluse to the Bouches-du-Rhône, or from the Massif to the Gard.[19] The annual cycle ended with the threshing of corn. In the Mediterranean regions, teams of oxen or horses trampled it under their hooves towards the end of the summer. Further north, the flail was preferred, and the threshers waited until the autumn before starting their work.

The winter months brought some respite from the gruelling régime in the fields. Indeed, unemployment became the main concern for the village poor during this agricultural 'dead season'. During the 1830s, Abel Hugo observed that in the mountainous districts of the Auvergne, the inhabitants stayed in bed for as long as possible, taking their meals there, and only getting up to look after their livestock.[20] But in between periods of enforced inactivity, the peasant looked after his animals, cut wood, repaired ditches and, in Provence, picked olives in late December and early January. With the *veillées*, he profited from the long evenings to clear

17 Pierre Pierrard, *La Vie quotidienne dans le Nord au XIXe siècle* (Paris, 1976), pp. 126–8; Brunet, *Structure agraire*, pp. 321–3.
18 Saint-Jacob, *Paysans de la Bourgogne*, pp. 284–91; Fabre and Lacroix, *Paysans du Languedoc*, pp. 238–9.
19 Abel Chatelain, *Les Migrants temporaires en France de 1800 à 1914* (2 vols., Lille, 1976), vol. 2, pp. 155–79.
20 Abel Hugo, *France pittoresque* (2 vols., Paris, 1835), vol. 2, p. 237. See also André de Bourgoing, *Mémoire en faveur des travailleurs et des indigents de la classe agricole des communes rurales de la France* (Nevers, 1844), p. 21, cited by Guy Thuillier, *Pour une histoire du quotidien au XIXe siècle en Nivernais* (Paris, 1977), p. 206.

up numerous indoor jobs, mending tools and dressing hemp, for example. More importantly, winter was the time for industrial work, the villager readily turning his hand to a number of by-occupations. Coal mines, iron-works, brickyards, potteries and above all handloom weaving shops relied heavily on rural labour that, to a greater or lesser extent according to region, maintained its links with agriculture. In parts of, say, Normandy or the Lyonnais, some of the rural population could be tempted full time into textile production, as part of putting-out system. At the other extreme were those peasants, usually located in the more isolated parts of the south and west, who only wove occasionally for their families or for barter within a village.[21]

The peasant woman had her full share of work to do, as she shuttled back and forth between the farm and the home.[22] The central core of her activities was much the same in all parts of France, and at all times of the year, since she was responsible for the basic necessities of family life: food, clothing and child rearing. On a large farm, she could rely on female *domestiques* to shoulder some of the burden. One thinks of Mme Alphonse in the novel *Marie-Claire*, a farmer's wife who spent whole days lacemaking with her personal servant beside her.[23] Otherwise, the *maîtresse* had to rely on her own efforts, with some help from daughters and other female relatives. Martial Chaulanges came away with a most gloomy impression of the woman's predicament among Limousin share-croppers, after listening to numerous personal reminiscences: 'Mothers serving a whole household, yoked to their jobs, without leisure, without comfort and without hope, hardly sitting at the table, worn out before their time ... who can ever say enough on the devotion and sacrifice of this existence?'[24] The woman of a house was expected to rise before anyone else, to ensure that the fire was lit and that the first meal of the day was being prepared. For the rest of the time the *grande salle* of the house was very much her territory and so too was the dairy, the poultry yard and the vegetable garden.

---

[21] Braudel and Labrousse, *Histoire économique*, vol. 2, *Des derniers temps de l'âge seigneurial aux préludes de l'âge industriel, 1660–1789* (Paris, 1970), pp. 651–9; for regional examples, see Jules Sion, *Les Paysans de la Normande orientale* (Paris, 1909), pp. 175–89; Etienne Juillard, *La Vie rurale dans la plaine de Basse-Alsace* (Strasbourg, 1953), pp. 279–90; Gilbert Garrier, *Paysans du Beaujolais et du Lyonnais, 1800–1970* (2 vols., Grenoble, 1973), vol. 1, pp. 198–213; Pierrard, *La Vie quotidienne*, pp. 131–2; Carlès, *Une soupe*, p. 24.

[22] This section is indebted to Olwen Hufton, 'Women and the Family in Eighteenth-Century France', *French Historical Studies*, 9 (1975), 1–22; *idem.*, 'Women, Work and Marriage in Eighteenth-Century France', in R. B. Outhwaite (ed.), *Marriage and Society* (London, 1981), pp. 186–203; Louise A. Tilly and Joan W. Scott, *Women, Work and Family* (New York, 1978), pp. 32–3; Martine Segalen, *Love and Power in the Peasant Family: Rural France in the Nineteenth Century* (Oxford, 1983), ch. 3.

[23] Marguérite Audoux, *Marie-Claire* (Paris, 1910), p. 178.

[24] See the Preface to Martial Chaulanges, *Les Rouges Moissons* (Paris, 1975).

Some of her tasks were easily accomplished, the peasant household being unaffected by twentieth-century notions of hygiene and cleanliness. A beaten earth floor could be swept quickly, bedmaking was simple, and little was expected in the way of dusting and polishing. Other jobs were more time-consuming, particularly where young children and farm servants were numerous. Fetching water was heavy work, unless the family happened to have a private well or other source at its doorstep. Preparing food was daunting in its own way, for although much of the cooking was rudimentary, the reputation of a household at table influenced its position on the labour market. In the Pays Bigoudin of Brittany, Pierre-Jakez Hélias remembered that with low wages on offer everywhere, the quality of food was a serious consideration for farm hands: 'A farmer who did not feed his household well would have difficulty in finding *domestiques*.'[25] Gleaning wood, baking bread, hoeing vegetables, preparing pigswill and washing clothes all required an immense expenditure of energy from the female members of the household. *La lessive à la cendre*, for example, was a major undertaking on all of the family linen two or three times a year. The woman had first to soak her washing for a day or two before layering it in a washtub: the *boeri* or *bri*, if we follow the terminology of the Mâconnais. She then added herbs to perfume her linen, covered it with a coarse linen cloth (*le chari*) and sprinkled on wood ash, which served as a detergent. Next she had to *amouezi la buye*, that is to say, to pour boiling water over the tub, and collect it from a tap at the bottom for reheating. This relay, between the huge *marmite* used to heat the water at the hearth and the washtub, was maintained for the best part of a day, until the residue from the top came out *bleu clair*. On the following day, the wash would be taken to a *lavoir* or a river, for soaping, scrubbing and rinsing. Finally, the linen was spread out over bushes or heavy ropes to dry. It was the *rite féminin par excellence*, with its long sequence of dull, repetitive tasks, relieved only by the chance of sociability with other women.[26] To round off her day, at the *veillées* or at other moments of spare time, the women busied themselves with knitting and sewing for their families.

Besides domestic chores, the peasant woman was involved in agricultural and industrial work. Here the diversity of opportunities was as broad as that for the men. Where cereals were grown, which of course included areas of *polyculture* as well as more specialized regions, she worked beside her menfolk in the fields during the summer, turning grass

---

[25] Pierre-Jakez Hélias, *Le Cheval d'orgueil* (Paris, 1975), p. 382.
[26] Suzanne Tardieu, *La Vie domestique dans le mâconnais rural préindustriel* (Paris, 1964), pp. 147–51. See also Eugène Bougeatre, *La Vie rurale dans le Mantois et le Vexin au XIXe siècle* (Meulan, 1971), pp. 42–5; Pierre Charrié, *Le Folklore du Haut-Vivarais* (Paris, 1968), pp. 217–18; Hélias, *Cheval d'orgueil*, pp. 14–15; Thuillier, *Histoire du quotidien*, pp. 123–61.

with a rake during haymaking, and binding sheaves during the harvest. In the *pays de vignoble* and the sugar-beet districts she joined the rest of her family at the harvest period. In parts of Savoy, women spent the summer in the mountain pastures, taking charge of the livestock and the cheese making, while the men stayed below working the fields. And in southern France, in the Cévennes, Vivarais and lower Rhône valley, women took a prominent rôle in the cultivation of silk worms. Each May, the men collected vast quantities of mulberry leaves, whilst their wives, and daughters, having incubated the eggs, supervised the worms. In the *magnanerie*, the women separated them as they grew, changed the bedding of leaves and gathered in the cocoons.[27] On the industrial side, there were many outlets for married women in the villages who wished to work part time. They were often employed beside their husbands, handloom weaving in the Pays de Caux, for example, or sewing up goods for framework knitters in the lower Champagne, or metalworking in the Ardennes. Others worked in more specifically 'female' industries, notably the thousands of embroiderers and lacemakers concentrated in Normandy, Flanders, Lorraine and the Velay.[28]

This was the *ancien régime* in agriculture, technically primitive and labour-intensive in character, which survived well beyond 1789 in many parts of the country. The atmosphere of ceaseless activity it required in the peasant household bred an obsession with keeping all hands busy. There was no difficulty in finding various simple jobs around the farm that were suitable for children.[29] They usually began their working lives as shepherds, *la garde des bestiaux* being the task most commonly associated

---

[27] Fabre and Lacroix, *Paysans du Languedoc*, p. 183; Jean and Renée Nicolas, *La Vie quotidienne en Savoie aux XVIIᵉ et XVIIIᵉ siècles* (Paris, 1979); Bozon, *La Vie rurale en Vivarais*, pp. 130–6.

[28] See, for example, Gay Gullickson, 'The Sexual Division of Labor in Cottage Industry and Agriculture in the Pays de Caux: Auffray, 1750–1850', *French Historical Studies*, 7 (1981), 177–99; Colin Heywood, 'The Rural Hosiery Industry of the Lower Champagne Region, 1750–1850', *Textile History*, 7 (1976), 95; AN, C 945, Charleville (Ardennes).

[29] Primary sources on the working life of children in agriculture are few and far between. The administration and the official Academies took very little interest during the nineteenth century, preferring to concentrate on child labour in industry. However, some questions concerning the conditions of the young in rural as well as in urban areas were asked in the 'Enquête sur le travail agricole et industriel' of 1848–9, and in the 'Enquête Spuller' of 1882. Also, nineteenth- and twentieth-century students of folklore in France have always been concerned with various aspects of childhood, making their studies of value to the historian. Otherwise, the main sources of information are of an autobiographical nature. There is no escaping the possibility that the handful of experiences available are untypical of the period, being written by people of exceptional character. Nor can distortions from fading memories be ruled out, since most of these works were written in old age. Nonetheless, these recollections do convey a vivid impression of past childhood, and provide some indication of the variety of regional experiences.

with a rural childhood. Outside the areas of *transhumance* in the Midi, the rearing of livestock was often a small-scale, family affair. In the traditional *polyculture*, each household owned a few animals, and allowed them to graze as best they could on any local pasture land. The undemanding task of leading the animals out to the meadows, keeping an eye on them as they grazed, and bringing them back to their stables at dusk was generally given to the very old or the very young.[30] Such was the path of Tiennon in *La Vie d'un simple*, taken in the Bourbonnais during the 1830s:

It was as a shepherd on La Breure [the heath] that I began to make myself useful. The third summer after our move to Le Garibier, my sister Catherine reached the age of twelve, and so had to replace the farm servant taken on till then by my mother. She therefore abandoned her sheep for domestic tasks, and for work in the fields. Nearing the age of seven, I was to look after the flock.[31]

Other light but often time-consuming jobs which children did in order to free adults for more exacting work included minding younger brothers and sisters, picking stones from the fields, collecting dung from the roads, hoeing in the vegetable plots, and, during the summer, scaring birds and working beside the haymakers and reapers.

The age-old specialization of labour between the sexes also took root during childhood. The peasant girl slipped into the daily routines of the *fermière*, either within her own family, or as *servante* for another. Her day might begin with a long walk to the nearest town, in order to sell milk and other farm produce on the market. She would be expected to milk the cows, feed the poultry, help with the cooking, take food to the men working in the fields, fetch water from a well or spring and start the endless round of spinning. In addition, she would join in with the washing, and the making of cheese, butter and bread. The farm boy meanwhile began to bend his back to some of the heavier tasks in the fields. During his adolescence, when he had sufficient physical strength, he would learn to handle new tools, such as the spade, the plough and the flail. He would also take some responsibility for the horses and oxen, leading the plough team for his father or employer, and cleaning out the

---

[30] Arnold Van Gennep, *Manuel de folklore français contemporaine*, vol. 1, *Introduction générale et première partie: du berceau à la tombe* (Paris, 1972), p. 188; Olivier Perrin, *Galérie bretonne* (3 vols., Paris, 1835), vol. 1, p. 89; Paul Sébillot, *Coutumes populaires de la Haute-Bretagne* (Paris, 1886), pp. 61–7; Mme Charles d'Abbadie d'Arrast, *Causeries sur le pays Basque: la femme et l'enfant* (Paris, 1909), p. 140. Some children served as assistants to adult shepherds or cowherds: see, for example, Besson, *Pâtre du Cantal*, p. 81.
[31] Emile Guillaumin, *La Vie d'un simple* (Paris, 1905), p. 8.

stables.[32] In the *pays d'élevage*, where shepherding was a more onerous occupation than in areas of mixed farming, adolescent boys looked after large numbers of livestock on their own. During the 1870s, an observer in the Basque country noted that from the age of twelve shepherd boys were sent up to the mountains to live wild with their flocks during the summer months.[33]

In this way, the young took their share of the seemingly endless cycle of toil that confronted the rural population. On the family farms of the peasantry, exploited where possible without resort to outside wage labour, their contribution took the form of unpaid work for their parents. The major aim of the peasants in this sub-sector of agriculture was self-sufficiency, allowing them to avoid the uncertainties of the market. Following the Russian theorist Chayanov, this rules out any analysis of the peasant economy in terms of rents, profits and wages. Instead he proposed the labour–consumer balance: the need for the family to strike a balance between the satisfaction of its material needs and the drudgery of work.[34] But only a small minority of French peasant holdings can be considered solely within this framework. With nineteenth-century technology, 10 hectares is generally considered the minimum that was necessary in most districts to support a family. In 1882, no less than 75 per cent of agricultural holdings were found to be smaller than this, obliging their occupants to spend at least part of the year earning wages.[35] Moreover, even a farm in the range of 10 to 40 hectares, the archetypal family holding, risked being swamped by too many children of working

[32] Georges Duby and Armand Wallon (eds.), *Histoire de la France rurale*, vol. 2, *L'Age classique des paysans, 1340–1789* (Paris, 1975), pp. 279–80, 480; and *ibid.*, vol. 3, pp. 340–2; Hufton, 'Women and the Family', 3; George Lefebvre, *Les Paysans du Nord pendant la Révolution française* (Paris, 1972), pp. 277–8; Poitrineau, *Basse-auvergne*, pp. 88, 270; Angélina Bardin, *Angélina, une fille des champs* (Paris, 1956), *passim*; ·Chaulanges, *Les Rouges Moissons, passim*; Antoine Sylvère, *Toinou, le cri d'un enfant auvergnat* (Paris, 1980), *passim*.

[33] D'Abbadie d'Arrast, *Le pays Basque*, p. 158.

[34] Daniel Thorner, 'Chayanov's Concept of Peasant Economy', in A. V. Chayanov, *The Theory of the Peasant Economy* (Homewood, Ill., 1966), pp. xi–xxiii. The point is made here that the theory applies more to thinly than to densely populated areas. For an interesting application of it to the French case, see Gregor Dallas, *The Imperfect Peasant Economy: The Loire Country, 1800–1914* (Cambridge, 1982).

[35] Of the 5.7 million *exploitations* covered by the Agricultural Enquiry of 1882, over 2 million were of less than 1 hectare: tiny plots that were more gardens than farms. These were one of the various sources of support relied upon by the rural poor. A further 2.6 million were in the range of 1 to 10 hectares, concentrated largely in the 'backward' regions of the south and west. This left only 20 per cent of agricultural holdings proper, between 10 and 40 hectares, in the category of independent peasant holdings, and a mere 4 per cent that were large-scale farms, beyond the scope of family exploitation. See Ministère de l'Agriculture, *Statistique agricole de la France: Résultats généraux de l'enquête décennale de 1882* (Nancy, 1887), p. 713; and Braudel and Labrousse, *Histoire économique*, vol. 3, part 2, pp. 636–52.

age.[36] To throw further light on the background to the employment of children in the countryside, we must therefore look beyond the irksomeness of agricultural work to those forces pushing large numbers of children out onto the labour market.

Rural poverty

The custom of putting children to work at an early age was given a sharper edge by the precariousness of the peasant existence. The contribution of children to the family economy can be viewed in financial as well as in physical terms. The income which a child was capable of bringing in was small enough, but the more hard-pressed families were forced to grasp at any form of support available. The risk of sudden impoverishment was by no means confined to marginal elements in rural society. A terrifying insecurity was almost endemic to the villages in the late eighteenth and early nineteenth centuries. This was a period when the ancient problem of poverty took a new and more extensive form. Olwen Hufton estimates that in 1787 a third, and possibly a half, of the population was in poverty. By this she means that they were always vulnerable to a crisis, which could rapidly spiral them down from a precarious independence to complete indigence.[37] The most visible manifestations of distress continued to arouse concern in official circles until at least the 1840s, notably the hordes of beggars and 'vagabonds' roaming the countryside, the large outlays of relief and the outbreaks of food rioting.[38]

This swelling of the ranks of the poor, so important in determining the fate of children in rural areas, revealed the unfortunate ambiguity to economic 'progress'. The early phase of development was sufficient to keep more people alive, but it could not lift many of them beyond a very basic existence.[39] Improvements in the distribution of food from the middle of the eighteenth century onwards were the most likely cause of the

[36] See the interesting discussion in James R. Lehning, *The Peasants of Marlhes* (London, 1980), pp. 130–2. See also Hubscher, *Agriculture dans le Pas-de-Calais*, pp. 147–8, on attempts by the various socio-economic groups in rural society to adapt the number of children they had to the opportunities offered by their family patrimony. The small plots held by the *ménagers* encouraged a family strategy of one child, whilst tenant farmers had an interest in producing three or four children.

[37] Hufton, *The Poor*, pp. 11–24.

[38] Alain Corbin, *Archaisme et modernité en Limousin au XIXe siècle, 1845–80* (2 vols., Paris, 1975), vol. 1, pp. 485–519; Garrier, *Paysans du Beaujolais*, vol. 1, pp. 315–16; Gabriel Désert, 'Une société rurale au XIXe siècle: les paysans du Calvados, 1815–95', 2 vols., unpublished thesis, University of Paris I, 1971, vol. 1, pp. 321–4; Duby and Wallon, *Histoire de la France rurale*, vol. 3, pp. 66, 78–9, 145–51.

[39] Michel Morineau uses the phrase, 'The progress of misery', in contrast to economic development proper. In Lorraine and Brittany, for example, the introduction of the potato eased the effects of the old subsistence crises, but also brought a lower standard of living for the peasants. See his *Les Faux-semblants*, p. 70.

easing of the old demographic crises, which had previously taken a heavy toll on the population every few years. The result was a preliminary surge of population between 1750 and 1770, followed by another between 1816 and 1846. From a total of 18 to 20 million in 1720, the population of France rose to an estimated 25 to 27 million on the eve of the 1789 Revolution, and then on to 35.4 million by 1846.[40] This demographic increase was subdued by the standards of many other European nations, but in a country already verging on over-population during the seventeenth century, it had dire social consequences. As far as the peasants were concerned, economic growth between the mid-eighteenth and mid-nineteenth centuries was either too slow, or more likely too uneven in its impact, significantly to improve their lot.[41] What they needed was an expansion of both markets and employment opportunities in the towns. Until these new outlets appeared on a large scale, from the 1830s and more particularly the 1850s, the villagers were effectively bottled up in a series of 'closed' local economies. The pressure of numbers on resources led inexorably to land hunger, widespread indebtedness and fragmented holdings amongst the smaller peasants. Such symptoms of under-development were of course most evident in southern and western France, being well documented by historians in the cases of the Auvergne and the Limousin. But even in more affluent regions in the north and east, notably the Paris basin, Flanders and Burgundy, the general *crise agraire* had serious repercussions for the village poor.[42] This, then, was the

[40] Marcel Reinhard *et al.*, *Histoire générale de la population mondiale* (Paris, 1968), pp. 241–53, 328–32; J.-C. Toutain, *La Population de la France de 1700 à 1959* (Paris, 1963), pp. 5–33.

[41] Statistical evidence of economic growth, for all its limitations, goes back to the early nineteenth century. A recent survey of the literature by François Caron concludes: 'During the first two or three decades of the nineteenth century a rapid population growth (up 0.55 per cent per annum) was accompanied by a very slow growth in *per capita* national income (0.5 per cent).' In these circumstances, it is not surprising that the major authorities on rural society suggest that during the second half of the eighteenth century, and the first half of the nineteenth, there was no absolute 'pauperization' of subsistence farmers and agricultural labourers. However, in relative terms these groups are considered to have fallen behind landowners and capitalist farmers. To quote Ernest Labrousse: 'The crumbs of economic expansion feed badly.' See Caron, *Economic History*, pp. 10–13; Braudel and Labrousse, *Histoire économique*, vol. 2, pp. 473–97, and *idem. Histoire économique*, vol. 3, part 2, pp. 739–48; Duby, *Histoire de la France rurale*, vol. 2, pp. 418–41.

[42] Braudel and Labrousse, *Histoire économique*, vol. 2, pp. 473–97; Duby, *Histoire de la France rurale*, vol. 2, pp. 418–41. These themes run like a red thread through several local studies set in the eighteenth century, notably Lefebvre, *Les Paysans du Nord*; Saint-Jacob, *Paysans de la Bourgogne*; and Poitrineau, *Basse-auvergne*. For the turning point of the 1850s see, for example, Brunet, *Structure agraire*, pp. 391–2; André Armengaud, *Les Populations de l'Est-Acquitain au début de l'époque contemporaine* (Paris, 1961), pp. 102, 163–6; Garrier, *Paysans du Beaujolais*, vol. 1, pp. 56–7, 188–90; Désert, 'Paysans du Calvados', vol. 2, pp. 321–4.

background to the perilously low standard of living endured by a majority of peasants during the first half of the nineteenth century.

Respondents to the 1848 Enquiry noted with depressing regularity that their local populations were 'badly housed, badly fed and badly clothed'. Of these problems with the basic necessities of life, finding enough to eat was always the most pressing for the peasantry, and, incidentally, the one most critical for the welfare of the young. During the first third of the nineteenth century, with an average calorie intake estimated to have been under 2,000 per day, the French population remained vulnerable to periods of shortage and undernourishment. From the 1840s, the calorie ration gradually accelerated until it reached a 'desirable' level during the 1880s.[43] By then the villagers in all but the poorest districts were on an adequate if frugal diet. But occasional traces of the old régime lingered on. At the beginning of the twentieth century, according to Pierre-Jakez Hélias, large families in the Pays Bigoudin of Brittany continued to measure out their food sparingly, and children still squabbled over a crust of bread.[44]

The structure of the diet was equally unsatisfactory for much of the nineteenth century, with an excessive reliance on carbohydrates and fats. Bread, gruel, *crêpes*, chestnuts and potatoes were the major source of food for the peasantry, with variations according to regional tastes and conditions. At one extreme were the heavy meals of the relatively prosperous Flemish peasant: thick soups, made from bread, vegetables and colza oil seasoning, were accompanied by wheat or rye bread spread with butter, and washed down by small beer. At the other was the 'very frugal and insubstantial' food of the peasant from the Landes: bread, soup made with pepper, pimentoes and rancid fat, a gruel of maize flour, and water. In between were a multitude of refinements on the same basic themes. In the Limousin, for example, the peasant ate chestnuts, boiled potatoes, rye bread, the occasional buckwheat *crêpe*, and the inevitable soup based on cabbages, turnips and a little fat. In the Vosges, potatoes and rye bread predominated, whilst in the Basses-Pyrénées the diet revolved around maize, vegetable soup and the occasional half-litre of wine when the harvest was abundant.[45] Meat was rarely seen on the table

---

[43] J.-C. Toutain, *La Consommation alimentaire en France de 1789 à 1964* (Geneva, 1970), pp. 1979–80.

[44] Hélias, *Cheval d'orgueil*, p. 332. See also Weber, *Peasants into Frenchmen*, p. 130; and Placide Rambaud and Monique Vincienne, *Les Transformations d'une société rurale: la Maurienne, 1561–1962* (Paris, 1964), pp. 15–26. The latter work emphasizes the long-standing problem of hunger in the Savoy Alps.

[45] AD Nord, M 547/1; AN, C 956, 962 and 969; Tardieu, *Vie domestique dans le mâconnais*, pp. 96–106.

of a peasant household, since it had to rely exclusively on the products of butchering its own pig each year. Small quantities of milk, butter, cheese and eggs were occasionally consumed, but the pressing need for cash caused most dairy produce and poultry to be sold in the towns. The gargantuan feasts put away by the villagers at the regular festivals and weddings provided some relief from this monotonous fare. Vast quantities of roasts, sausages, cakes and wine or cider quickly disappeared during days of frantic celebration. But these outbursts could do no more than help the peasant resign himself to his usual meagre rations; they could not remedy the overall shortcomings in the diet.

Most importantly, the difficulty of obtaining milk, lean meat, and fresh fruit and vegetables caused deficiencies in protein, vitamins and minerals.[46] Some effort was made to cater for the special needs of children, with extra milk or wheat flour set aside for them.[47] But there were strict limits to what could be achieved. As Abel Poitrineau has stressed in the case of the plains of the Basse-Auvergne, the scarcity of milk during the eighteenth century was disastrous for the welfare of the very young and the very old alike.[48] Military conscription records in the nineteenth century would reveal the zones where poor diet bore down most heavily on the population. Variations between departments in the proportion of young men rejected for military service through failure to reach the minimum height of 5 foot 2 inches may partly be explained by genetic factors. But the tendency in the twentieth century for these disparities to disappear with rising living standards suggests that they can be taken as an indicator of poverty. The Auvergne, the Limousin, the Périgord, the southern Alps and much of Brittany emerge, somewhat predictably, as the major regions for small stature.[49] Little could be done in this sphere before the 1830s and 1840s, when transport improvements on the roads and railways gave access to a wider range of foodstuffs.

Improvements in the housing of the rural population were even slower

---

[46] See J.-J. Hémardinquer (ed.), *Pour une histoire de l'alimentation*, Cahiers des Annales, 28 (Paris, 1970); Bartolomé Bennassar and Joseph Goy, 'Consommation alimentaire, XIVᵉ–XIXᵉ siècle', *Annales ESC*, 30 (1975), 402–30; M. Aymard, 'Pour l'histoire de l'alimentation: quelques remarques de méthode', *ibid*, 431–44; Duby, *Histoire de la France rurale*, vol. 3, pp. 327–33; Corbin, *Limousin au XIXᵉ siècle*, vol. 1, pp. 53–74.

[47] Saint-Jacob, *Paysans de la Bourgogne*, p. 539, n. 2; Tardieu, *Vie domestique dans le mâconnais*, p. 98.

[48] Poitrineau, *Basse-auvergne*, pp. 105–6; and *idem.*, 'L'Alimentation en Auvergne au XVIIIᵉ siècle', in Hémardinquer, *Histoire de l'alimentation*, p. 152. See also Guy Thuillier, 'L'Alimentation en Nivernais au XIXᵉ siècle', *Annales ESC*, 20 (1965), 1175; and Bougeatre, *Mantois et Vexin*, pp. 51–6, 121. The latter reveals that even in the late nineteenth century young children risked intestinal infections from eating adult food too early: often below the age of two.

[49] J. P. Aron, P. Dumont and E. Le Roy Ladurie, *Anthropologie du conscrit français* (Paris, 1972), pp. 26–7, 86–7, 170–1, 182–3.

to materialize, there being scant concern with creature comforts for as long as the food supply remained uncertain. Well into the second half of the nineteenth century, the poor invariably had to contend with a lack of space for their families; dampness; inadequate heating, lighting and ventilation; and, in a number of regions, an ever-present fire hazard from thatched roofs.[50] Antoine Sylvère remembered one such modest farm house, taken over by his parents in the Auvergne during the 1890s: 'It looked like any other peasant cottage in the region. Animals and people, fodder and agricultural equipment sheltered in the same building, covered by a tiled or a thatched roof whose sides continued all the way down to the ground. Low doors and skylights. No windows.'[51] The absence of running water made it difficult to attempt much in the way of personal hygiene. The peasant confined himself to one complete wash and change of clothes per week, on a Sunday. For the rest of the time, he merely gave his face a quick splash of water first thing in the morning. Eugène Bougeatre reeled off a whole list of health hazards caused by poverty and isolation in the Mantois and the Vexin during the last third of the nineteenth century. These included women's skirts that were permanently edged in cow-dung, poultry given a free run of the house, flies congregating unhindered in the cooking area, stables infested with rats and mice, and dung-heaps that threatened to drain off into the houses whenever it rained.[52] Once again, children suffered disproportionately from these material deprivations. Some were marked for life when they fell into the huge open fires on the hearth;[53] others spent months each winter with coughs and running noses as they walked barefoot on cold, beaten earth floors, and huddled together in draughty corners.[54] Problems of keeping warm were aggravated by the absence of warm clothing. Piling on the heavy woollen material worn in cold weather gave some protection from the rain, and an empty sack could be used to cover the head, but sooner or later the peasant or young shepherd working in the fields was likely to be soaked to the skin. Tiennon, of *La Vie d'un simple*, retained vivid memories of working under such conditions in his early teens:

I remember one March when we were ploughing in the field containing the chestnut trees, the most distant of all our fields. There was always a strong wind from Souvigny, that is to say directly from the north, with freezing showers, sleet and some snow. These cut through my clothing, envelopping me in an icy shroud; my hands turned a purplish red, and became covered with violet spots.[55]

[50] Information drawn principally from 'Enquête sur le travail', 1848; Duby, *Histoire de la France rurale*, vol. 3, pp. 318–23.
[51] Sylvère, *Toinou*, p. 5.   [52] Bougeatre, *Mantois et Vexin*, p. 120.
[53] For an horrific account of one such accident, see Audoux, *Marie-Claire*, pp. 182–4.
[54] AN, C 962, Oloron (Basses-Pyrénées); Sylvère, *Toinou*, pp. 100–1.
[55] Guillaumin, *Vie d'un simple*, p. 54. See also Hélias, *Cheval d'orgueil*, pp. 366–7.

Such were the realities for the peasant family of poverty: *La Chienne du Monde*. The constant struggle to make ends meet ensured that from an early age children had to start earning their keep. The *crise agraire* of the eighteenth and nineteenth centuries if anything extended the traditional reliance of the poor on the work of their children, for the peasant responded to his predicament by demanding more effort all round from his family. His own plot of land would be farmed more intensively, to improve the yield of its cereal crop and to produce more vegetables. In addition, he, together with his wife, his children and any unmarried relatives living under his roof, would spend more days earning wages as agricultural labourers or domestic industrial workers. A definite shift towards income from wage labour was in fact one of the major upheavals forced on the peasantry at this period, underpinning the expansion of rural industry from the middle of the eighteenth century onwards and the increased productivity of land achieved by the Agricultural Revolution. This extra burden of work shouldered by the family made it possible for the countryside to support a larger population.[56] Demographic expansion was thus dearly bought in terms of human effort.

In the words of Emilie Carlès looking back on the full rigours of an alpine farming community:

The peasants led a very rudimentary existence. They passed the time driving themselves to draw subsistence from the soil. After the age of six, the children were obliged to participate in the primitive economy; they had no choice, they had to look after the animals, go out into the fields, and do the housework. It was the law: hard at work, grasping for material gains, as if at any moment the heavens were going to fall on their heads, the peasants lived from one end of the year to the other tied to the land.[57]

Children could earn a small wage in cash or kind by various means. There was casual work on a local farm, which at mid-century brought in 15 to 20 centimes, or the equivalent in food and clothing. When they reached their early teens, the wage normally rose to 40, 50 or 60 centimes per day, worth somewhere between a third and a half the going rate for an adult male.[58] There was wage labour for domestic industry. In the handloom weaving shops, child workers began by winding bobbins for their parents, until the time came in their early teens when they could

---

[56] Braudel and Labrousse, *Histoire économique*, vol. 2, pp. 493–4; Duby, *Histoire de la France rurale*, vol. 2, p. 439; George W. Grantham, 'Scale and Organization in French Farming, 1840–1880', in William N. Parker and Eric L. Jones (eds.), *European Peasants and their Markets* (Princeton, NJ, 1975), pp. 300–4; Hans Medick, 'The Proto-Industrial Family Economy: The Structural Function of Household and Family during the Transition from Peasant Society to Industrial Capitalism', *Social History*, 3 (1976), 291–315.

[57] Carlès, *Une soupe*, p. 21.

[58] Information drawn from the 'Enquête sur le travail', 1848.

manage their own loom.[59] Although weaving was by custom a male occupation, complemented by female handspinning, it became partially 'feminized' during the nineteenth century.[60] Mémé Santerre, for example, remembered starting her career as a handloom weaver in Flanders during the 1900s, when she was still so short that she needed special wooden blocks under her feet in order to reach the pedals. Her wages at the outset were very low: 'As far as I can remember I used to bring in two francs a week, and when my handkerchiefs were faultless, as sometimes happened, the *patron* gave me five sous as a tip . . . Later I earned up to five francs per week. I came home, and gave the money to my mother.'[61] More typically 'feminine' was needlework: lacemaking and embroidery provided such light work that they could be started around the age of five or six. Besides the established centres of the trade in the Auvergne, Normandy, Picardy and Flanders, there appeared new ones over the course of the nineteenth century in Lorraine and the Vosges. During the 1840s, it was estimated that one third of the 3,000 *dentellières* in the canton of Mirecourt (Vosges) were children, as were half of the 2,000 *brodeuses* in the canton of Réchicourt (Meurthe). In the former district, the girls under twelve averaged 15 centimes a day, which later went up to 40 or 60 centimes; in the latter, children, with no age specified, were reported to earn 50 centimes a day, and women 1 franc.[62] Beyond textiles, other handicraft trades in the countryside where convenient niches for child labour could be found included basket weaving, ropemaking, wood and metalworking. A notable example was the cutlery trade, where many small, family workshops were able to survive late into the nineteenth century. In the mountainous areas of the Auvergne, around Thiers and Ambert, the workshops were perched on the hillside, astride the fast-running streams that turned their whetting and polishing wheels. During the summer, the children of the area watched over herds of cattle up near the summits; during the winter they became wage earners, polishing incessantly beside their parents.[63]

There was also service with another household, as a *domestique de ferme*. A few started this very young: during the eighteenth century, in the bleak Sologne region, children left home from the age of seven or eight to become 'servants, shepherds, drovers or *dindeliers* with a farmer, or as

[59] Individual accounts of childhood years spent in the textile industries can be found in the 'Enquête Spuller' of 1882; see, for example, AN, C 3360[2], Rhône, and C 3370[3], Seine-Inférieure.

[60] See below, pp. 102–4.   [61] Serge Grafteaux, *Mémé Santerre* (Paris, 1975), pp. 12–14.

[62] AN, C 969 and 959.

[63] AN, F[12] 4755, Gauthier (Lyons, 15th), 12 February 1880. Henceforth, reports from the Child Labour Inspectors created by the Factory law of 1874 are cited in this form, giving the name of the Inspector, the town on which his *circonscription* was based, the number of the *circonscription* and the date of the report to the Ministry of Commerce.

apprentices with an artisan'.[64] This custom surfaces again in the evidence given to the 1848 Enquiry on Labour. The canton of Bouloire, in the Sarthe, mentioned the *patour*, a boy or a girl who started work at the age of six looking after geese, before moving on to sheep and cattle around his or her eighth year. Similarly, the canton of Grandrieu, in the Lozère explained:

As for the children, they all remain unoccupied as long as the winter lasts, that is to say for six months of the year; and those who are not necessary or useful in their own households are hired out for the other six months, earning 18 to 20 francs plus their food and lodgings; they are all employed looking after animals.[65]

Others, more numerous, waited until after their first communion to leave home. The hiring fairs held at various times of the year in the different regions helped place those without personal contacts. In the Haut-Vivarais, for example, *la feyro de la monobra* was usually held in March or April in order to bring together local *domestiques* and farmers from as far afield as the Rhône and the Dauphiné. The *servantes*, who signalled their availability for work by attaching a bouquet of flowers to their bodices, and the *valets*, recognizable by the branch of laurel worn in their hats, were taken on for a year at a time, giving them a measure of security not enjoyed by the day labourer.[66] By the time he reached the age of fifteen or sixteen, the young *valet* was likely to be earning between 20 and 80 francs a year, according to region, on top of his board and lodging. Separation from the family did not mean an evasion of all responsibility to the household budget: even with the age of majority, these absent sons and daughters maintained a flow of money and goods to their parents.[67] The gradual easing of the pressure of poverty encouraged new attitudes to the family, and the practice of boarding out declined. Nonetheless, soundings in the 1851 census registers indicate that at mid-century the practice was still common. In Lorraine, for example, in a cluster of villages bordering on the town of Lunéville, although nearly all children aged ten to fourteen were revealed to be living at home, one in seven of those aged fifteen to nineteen had been placed *chez les autres* as *domestiques* or *apprentices*.[68] Further south, in the mixed agricultural and industrial

[64] Gérard Bouchard, *Le Village immobile: Sennely-en-Sologne au XVIIIᵉ siècle* (Paris, 1972), pp. 321, 374–5. See also Georges Lefebvre, *Etudes orléanaises* (2 vols., Paris, 1962), vol. 1, p. 27.

[65] AN, C 967 and 965.   [66] Charrié, *Folklore du Haut-Vivarais*, pp. 239–40.

[67] Ronald Hubscher, 'Une contribution à la connaissance des milieux populaires ruraux au XIXᵉ siècle: le livre de compte de la famille Flahaut, 1811–1877', *Revue d'histoire économique et social*, 47 (1969), 395–6.

[68] AD Meurthe-et-Moselle, 6 M 107–8. The ten villages in the sample comprised the canton of Lunéville-Sud-Est, excluding Lunéville itself, and the communes of Marainviller and Sionviller. Their populations were employed exclusively in agriculture and the handi-

economy characteristic of certain areas of the Dauphiné, the proportions were not so very different. There in the small town of Taulignan, one in eight of children aged ten to fourteen had left home to work, as had one in six of the older group.[69]

There was, as a further alternative, the possibility of earning a little money by going out on the road for a few months. Groups of migrant workers often took a young lad along with them to run errands. Teams of *scieurs de long* from the Auvergne used him to do the cooking, and if necessary to beg food, whilst harvesters moving around the Languedoc had *lo calha* to carry clothes and run back and forth between the fields and the farm house.[70] Up in the mountains, in the Franche-Comté, the Dauphiné, the Auvergne and above all in Savoy, children were regularly recruited as climbing boys by itinerant chimney sweeps. During the autumn, the sweeps, who might be no more than fifteen or sixteen years of age themselves, moved around the villages offering 50 francs for six months of work. With food shortages a constant threat during the winter months, the poor were only too willing to hand over their offspring. The expeditions of the *petits savoyards* were mounted with a ruthless concern for profit. The children always begged their food, slept rough and dressed meanly: a cotton cap, down-at-heel shoes, sordid clothes from a charity with leather patches added to the back and knees, the whole outfit of course indelibly blackened with soot.[71] And while one child helped sweep the chimney in a house, another would try to turn a coin showing the family his marmot: 'La carita, Madame, un sou, Madame, pour y connu la marmotte.'[72]

   craft trades. The sample produced a total of 560 children aged ten to fourteen, twenty of whom were boarded out, and 505 aged fifteen to nineteen, sixty-nine of whom were in this position. The assumption is made that children hired out for the summer months would be registered with their employers, since the census was held between March and May. See Abel Chatelain, 'La Valeur des recensements de la population française au XIXe siècle', *Revue de géographie de Lyon*, 29 (1954), 273–80.

69 AD Drôme, 35 M 335. The commune of Taulignan had a population of 2,439, employed principally in agriculture, the silk industry and the usual urban artisan trades. In this case, twenty-seven of the 207 children aged ten to fourteen were working away from home, as were thirty-nine of the 222 young people aged fifteen to nineteen. In the commune of Dieulefit, also in the Drôme and with a similar type of economy, the corresponding figures were one in ten for the age group ten to fourteen, and one in seven for the age group fifteen to nineteen; AD Drôme, 35 M 115.

70 Poitrineau, *Basse-auvergne*, p. 88; Fabre and Lacroix, *Paysans du Languedoc*, p. 232.

71 AN, F^12 4830, L'Abbé Bugniot, Founder and Director of the Œuvre des petits savoyards at Chalon-sur-Saône, to the Minister of the Interior, 23 February 1862; and *idem*, *Les Petits Savoyards: ou l'exploitation de l'enfant par l'homme* (Chalon-sur-Saône, 1863); Françoise Raison-Jourde, *La Colonie auvergnate de Paris au XIXe siècle* (Paris, 1976), pp. 69, 97, 107–8.

72 Bougeatre, *Mantois et Vexin*, p. 98. See also Jean Drouillet, *Folklore du Nivernais et du Morvan* (5 vols., La Charité-sur-Loire, 1959–65), vol. 3, p. 196; and Pierre Charrié, *Le Folklore du Bas-Vivarais* (Paris, 1964), pp. 322–3.

Towards an independent household: of skills, successions and savings

Peasants were frequently accused of being indifferent to the fate of their children. The usual implication was they always put their own material interests above the welfare of their family. The death of an infant was quickly shrugged off: 'The man used to say to his wife, "But why are you crying? That child is no loss to anyone, on the contrary, there is one less mouth to feed".'[73] The survivors were put to work almost as soon as they could walk, and allegedly exploited with a bare minimum of food and clothing. In 1849 the Conseil d'Hygiène of Lapoutroie, in Alsace, thundered: 'The daughter of a peasant, once she becomes robust, is treated by her father as a real slave; her soul dries up like the bud of a young plant deprived of food, her body burns up, hardens, her hands become cracked, and she continues in this sad condition until she marries.'[74] There was no question of sending for a doctor if a wife or child was ill, unless in dire emergency: the Conseil suggested that the peasant would run all the way into Colmar to fetch a vet for his livestock, but for his family, 'he temporizes, he calculates, he fears (as he puts it) the expense'. That such a dismal assessment of family life amongst the peasantry was superficial, and increasingly anachronistic, is now beyond doubt. A hard exterior shell was a necessity amongst the village poor to protect them from the grief of repeated infant deaths. In any case, the decline in mortality, combined with the more extensive ownership of land amongst the rural population, meant that the determinants of family strategy gradually changed during the nineteenth century. A more long-term perspective eventually became possible for the majority, with the acquisition, extension and transfer of property a realistic aim.[75] This did not alter the custom of starting 'apprenticeships' in agriculture when still young. Nor did it relieve the peasant from some cruel dilemmas in his budgeting, with the need to find a balance between the viability of the family economy and the requirement to spend money on its individual members. In short, there is no reason to think that peasants were invariably callous in their rôle as parents, but equally the problems associated with launching the young into an independent existence could be formidable.[76] Many families could help their offspring by bequeathing property or teaching skills. But few could spare them a laborious childhood, in the drive to accumulate experience and savings for the future.

[73] Carlès, *Une soupe*, p. 9.   [74] AD Haut-Rhin, 5 M 2.
[75] Segalen, *Peasant Family*, pp. 8, 39.
[76] On the relationship between peasants and their children, see, for example, d'Abbadie d'Arrast, *Le Pays Basque*, p. 129; Gélis *et al.*, *Entrer dans la vie*, pp. 31–2; and Carlès, *Une soupe*, pp. 8–10.

Learning the routines of traditional agriculture was inextricably bound up
with starting work at an early age. With a primitive technology that had
barely changed over centuries, the system of farming was solidly empirical: the essential was to pass down tried and tested techniques from
generation to generation. The prominence this gave to the collective
wisdom of parents and rural community caused a 'veritable ancestor cult'
amongst the peasantry.[77] The old methods had ensured survival in the
past, and until the scientific approach of the Agricultural Revolution
emerged, there was no alternative source of authority to challenge that of
tradition. In these circumstances, there evolved a form of education which
launched the young straight into their calling without any preliminary
training. Children slowly assimilated the knowledge and skills they
needed by living and working beside experienced adults. Even comfortably-off members of the community subscribed to this educational
philosophy of 'learning by doing'. For example, the Mayor of Pettonville,
in Lorraine, informed a Parliamentary Enquiry of 1882 that he had
started his working life in agriculture at the age of ten, and added, 'The
earlier the better.'[78] During the twentieth century, the substitution of
capital for labour and the increasingly theoretical foundations of modern
agriculture made a grounding in applied science at school or college an
advantage to the farmer. But before 1914, and perhaps even before 1950,
the vocational training of the mass of the peasantry was untouched by
the influence of agricultural schools and colleges.[79] There was even
evidence of hostility to any direct encroachments by the primary schools
in this sphere. Roger Thabault found that in his village school at
Mazières-en-Gâtine the 'Practical Course in Agriculture' prepared by
the teacher during the 1890s was a failure. Sons of farmers despised the
theoretical knowledge involved, wanting to learn only by practical
experience.[80]

Acquaintance with these routines began at an early age, watching
grandparents and parents. A *cultivateur* from Saint-Maurice-sous-
Chalamon, in the Vivarais, wrote in the 1882 Enquiry:

Very small, from the age of four or five, my father and mother working together in
the fields, carried me, then seated me beside a stone; from there I watched them
work. They may have carried me even earlier, but I do not recall having paid

---

[77] Désert, 'Paysans du Calvados', vol. 1, pp. 353–4; Bercé, *Fête et révolte*, pp. 18–19.
[78] AN, C 3365.
[79] On the restricted influence of technical education in agriculture before 1914, there is
Duby, *Histoire de la France rurale*, vol. 3, pp. 418–20; and Gildea, *Education in
Provincial France*, pp. 315–20, 325–31, 353–65. See also Guenhaël Jégouzo and
Jean-Louis Brangeon, *Les Paysans et l'école* (Paris, 1976), pp. 7–13.
[80] Roger Thabault, *Education and Change in a Village Community: Mazières-en-Gâtine,
1848–1914*, transl. P. Tregear (New York, 1971), pp. 216–18.

attention to the work then. I soon began to handle the smaller agricultural tools. My children, and those of many other farmers, do the same.[81]

The peasant was the least specialized of all workers: he could at once be a farmer, shepherd, roadmender, woodcutter and industrial worker. The process of acquiring all the skills and lore of this existence was necessarily a long one, which was grafted on to the more urgent business of earning one's keep. Rather than undergo a formal apprenticeship, the farm boy or girl progressed imperceptibly through the various stages of training, always watching and imitating others. The most famous description of this gradual accumulation of experience during childhood was written by Agricol Perdiguier. In his *Mémoires d'un compagnon* he described his upbringing in a village near Avignon at the time of the First Empire. His father, a carpenter who also owned a small farm, evidently made the most of his numerous offspring. By the age of ten, proclaimed the *Mémoires*, 'I had collected horse-dung; I had hoed, and harvested grapes; I had worked with a pitch-fork and a spade; I could be a carter and a ploughman.'[82] When bad weather made it impossible to work in the fields, his father took him and his brothers into the workshop. There they were set to 'planing lengths of wood, putting nails into the angles of doorways and pine shutters, assembling groove-and-tongue joints, and making mortices'.[83]

When they reached adolescence, the young moved into a new and more critical phase in their preparation for a career. They were now forced to think in very practical terms about securing their futures, which inevitably meant looking towards marriage and the launching of a household. The ultimate aim, be it in the village or the town, was always the same: a position of independence. This was what peasant society respected above all else, not least because it proved so elusive for the majority. There was, of course, a favoured élite, who had the prospect of inheriting a viable family holding. For them, the path to maturity was relatively free of pitfalls. All they had to do was to master the various skills of agriculture, and bide their time working beside their parents. For the rest, the younger sons and daughters of the landed class, as well as the offspring of the smaller peasants, share-croppers, farm labourers and cottage workers, the years leading up to marriageable age were more hazardous. If successful they could hope for a modest stake in society. With some experience of working, a few savings, plus whatever could be negotiated from the family patrimony, there was the prospect of taking a small farm or workshop. But if they suffered any serious setbacks at this stage in their lives, they

81 AN, C 3333.
82 Agricol Perdiguier, *Mémoires d'un compagnon* (Paris, 1943), p. 13.
83 *Ibid.*, p. 16.

risked being consigned permanently to the ranks of the low-paid, the
under-employed, the dependent. Worse perhaps than the fate of struggling with a family on a small plot of land and whatever could be earned in
wages, was that of remaining on the margins of society, as a *célibataire*.
Men and women who for various reasons were unable to attract a
marriage partner were more often than not doomed to the humiliating
position of lifelong *domestique* on a farm.[84] The essential steps, then,
were to complete some kind of 'apprenticeship', to save as much money as
possible, and then to find a husband or wife who could in their turn bring
something into the marriage.[85]

The most familiar path for these adolescents was to remain on the land,
working as an agricultural labourer or farm servant. Broadly speaking,
young people living in the areas where large-scale farming predominated,
up in the north-east and along the Mediterranean coast, were likely to find
their openings as *journaliers*. Those raised in the areas of medium-sized
exploitations, above all the Massif, Brittany and Flanders, would probably reside with a family as a *domestique*.[86] An alternative, increasingly
available from the end of the *ancien régime*, was to work in rural industry.
In Normandy, for example, such was the demand for labour in the cotton
industry that there was a rush of young people into handloom weaving
during the 1820s, and the formation of a distinct class of artisans, separate
from the agricultural population.[87] The first priority for the youthful
wage earner was to build up a solid reputation in the local labour market.
The father of Pierre-Jakez Hélias started out this way on a series of farms
in the Pays Bigoudin, at the very beginning of this century:

The eldest son was first of all hired out at Kerfildro, the farm where his mother
came from. He completed his apprenticeship on the land whilst working there.
The following year he was a *domestique* at Lestrougi. Then he spent four years at
Kervinou and two years at Kergivig, where he was *grand valet*, that is to say he had
his marshal's baton. These four farms were not too distant from each other or
from Kerveillant, the birthplace. If my father changed jobs, it was not through
discontent or instability. It was to advance through the hierarchy of *domestiques*
and obtain a better wage as his reputation grew. Sometimes also it was to work for
the master who knew his business better.[88]

Farmers knew the work of all the neighbouring *valets* by keeping a close
eye on the condition of the fields and livestock left in their charge. By hard
graft, the young Pierre-Alain became renowned as a *labourer kaer*, a

---

84 The classic study remains: Pierre Bourdieu, 'Célibat et condition paysanne', *Etudes
   rurales*, 1 (1962), 32–135.
85 On the eighteenth-century background, see Hufton, *The Poor*, pp. 25–38.
86 Braudel and Labrousse, *Histoire économique*, vol. 3, part 2, pp. 658–9.
87 Sion, *Paysans de la Normandie orientale*, pp. 301–13.
88 Hélias, *Cheval d'orgeuil*, p. 23.

magnificent worker. But this was as far as he went, for he spent the rest of his years as a landless labourer. The course for a young woman could be equally limited: after a few years of work, she could have nothing more to show than a rise from the lowly position of *servante de basse-cour* to *servante de maison*, and a small stock of clothing and linen for her trousseau.[89]

Obstacles to the village poor clawing their way up the social scale were daunting. The price of land relative to wages was high: calculations for the village of Plozévet, in the same Pays Bigoudin, suggest that during the 1850s an unmarried farm labourer would have had to anticipate thirty years of saving to buy 1 hectare of land.[90] In order to secure a plot, he and his counterparts elsewhere would therefore need a career uninterrupted by prolonged illness or unemployment, and a single-minded dedication to saving. The reluctance of families with property to allow the landless to marry in to them effectively cut off one obvious short-cut to easier circumstances. Marrying below one's station in the elaborate hierarchy of property was to invite ridicule. A study of marriage partners in the Norman village of Vraiville reveals that during the nineteenth century there were two distinct networks of alliance, composed of farmers (*cultivateurs*) on the one hand, and handloom weavers on the other. The former used the institution of marriage to transfer their family property intact. They might occasionally allow an artisan or weaver to marry one of their daughters, because of an 'excess' of females, but invariably their sons married the daughters of other farmers. Amongst the handloom weavers, endogamy served a very different function, encouraging two people whose main asset was their individual skills to form a family enterprise.[91]

In so far as it is possible to generalize over a multitude of periods and regions, one might risk asserting that the last century saw a good deal of movement on both the land and the job markets, but only a limited amount of upward social mobility for the *menu peuple* of the villages. A comparison of the occupations of fathers and sons in the Beaujolais, made by Gilbert Garrier, will illustrate the point. A first sounding in three areas during the 1820s indicates a remarkable element of continuity. Amongst first-born sons, no less than three-quarters of those categorized as farmers, textile workers and artisans declared the same occupation as their fathers. Thirty years later, mobility between jobs was more in evidence. Over half of the oldest sons of *propriétaires-cultivateurs* were still following in their

---

[89] Hubscher, 'La Famille Flahaut', 383–4, 399.
[90] André Burguière, *Bretons de Plozévet* (Paris, 1975), pp. 109–10.
[91] Martine Segalen, *Le Choix du conjoint dans une commune de l'Eure* (Paris, 1972), pp. 73–124. See also Bourdieu, 'Célibat et condition paysanne', 33–58.

fathers' footsteps, but the rest, together with nearly all of their younger brothers, were becoming weavers, factory workers, *domestiques*, carriers and clerks. Moreover, two out of three of the sons of *cultivateurs non-propriétaires* had broken with their family background: a few men whose fathers had been day labourers or farm servants had managed to acquire their own land, whilst the majority had moved on to industrial and commercial jobs in the towns. This suggests some descent into the proletariat for sons of farmers, and much stability, notably for vine-growers and textile workers. There were also the first signs of social promotion within rural society, from the ranks of the wage earners. But, as was to be the case with the numerous farm hands who managed to scrape together a holding in various parts of France during the latter half of the century, these advances could prove illusory. Given that the ultimate aim in the villages was independence, and the status that went with it, many of these newly established farmers and cottage workers must have fallen far short of their ideals.[92]

Studies of social mobility in the towns point to a similar conclusion. The huge scale of the 'rural exodus', particularly during the second half of the nineteenth century, meant that the chances of rising up the social scale through migration were slim. Yet it was precisely the vision of becoming prosperously settled in a family business or a white-collar job which enticed the migrants into the towns. There were of course plenty of examples of conspicuously successful individuals within the various migrant streams. Some of the Auvergnats who came up to the Paris region during their teens to work in the scrap metal yards managed to hammer their way into their own business, with the help of relatives already established in the trade, whilst other rose from being *garçons de café* in the capital to the position of *débitant de boisson* in their own right. More typical of a mature industrial society, with its vast bureaucracies, were the sons of peasants from Provence and elsewhere who found their way into clerical work in Marseilles during the nineteenth century, or the young Lozériens who obtained secure jobs on the PLM railway in Nîmes at the beginning of the twentieth century.[93] Amongst young female migrants,

[92] Garrier, *Paysans du Beaujolais*, vol. 1, pp. 282–5; vol. 2, Table XXII. See also Burguière, *Bretons de Plozévet*, pp. 106–13.

[93] Raison-Jourde, *La Colonie auvergnate*, pp. 121–5; Louis Chevalier, *La Formation de la population parisienne du XIXe siècle* (Paris, 1950), pp. 205–13, 227–9; William H. Sewell, 'Social Mobility in a Nineteenth-Century European City: Some Findings and Implications', *Journal of Interdisciplinary History*, 7 (1976), 217–33; idem, *Structure and Mobility: The Men and Women of Marseille, 1820–70* (Cambridge, 1985), pp. 249–53; Leslie Page Moch, *Paths to the City* (Beverley Hills, 1983), pp. 171–84. See also Chatelain, *Les Migrants temporaires*, vol. 2, pp. 896–918, for the tendency of wandering artisans and hawkers to settle permanently in the towns as merchants and shopkeepers from the late nineteenth century onwards.

success usually took the form of saving enough to tempt a master craftsman or shopkeeper into marriage. In Lyons, for example, there was always some chance for a young girl coming in from the countryside, around the age of ten or twelve, to work her way up from the meanest jobs in the silk industry to marriage with a journeyman or master. Having experienced all the 'female' jobs in the Fabrique, and scraped together some savings, she made a far better partner in the workshop than the cosseted daughters of the older *canuts*. More numerous in the nineteenth century were the domestic servants who amassed a sizeable dowry, often of 1,000 francs and upwards in the cases that have come to light in Versailles at mid-century, as a basis for marriage into the urban petty bourgeoisie.[94] In Marseilles, for example, girls from a peasant background who had become domestic servants were conspicuously successful at marrying into the middle classes, driven perhaps by a restless ambition not generally found among their native counterparts. The other side of this coin was the series of snares that awaited the raw peasant youth in the towns. In Paris, according to Louis Chevalier, petty crime, madness and even suicide awaited the migrant workers who failed to settle into society.[95] Prospects for young girls cast adrift on the streets of the big cities were no less bleak. For some, the bid for independence led no further than to an early grave. Lyons fully lived up to its reputation for hostility to outsiders, taking a heavy toll on the *servantes chez les ouvriers en soie* during the eighteenth century. In the words of Maurice Garden:

It is difficult to imagine a young girl of nine or ten leaving the family farm of her own free will, to go off to the town without any welcome. Yet the registers of the Hôtel-Dieu contain indications such as the death of 'une servante de 13 ans sans condition et sans résidence', a girl of thirteen without a trade or a home in Lyons, coming to die miserably in the hospital.[96]

The underworld of criminality also awaited girls from the country, no less than boys. There was always the possibility that a new arrival from the provinces would fall prey to prostitution through the *proxénètes* who hung around the big stations, or through impatience with ill-paid work as, say, a *couturière* or domestic servant.[97]

Doubtless the majority of young migrants landed on their feet in more

[94] Maurice Garden, *Lyon et les lyonnais au XVIIIᵉ siècle* (Paris, 1975), pp. 105–20, 181; Hufton, *The Poor*, pp. 31–2: *idem*, 'Women, Work and Marriage in Eighteenth Century France', pp. 186–203; Theresa M. McBride, 'Social Mobility for the Lower Classes: Domestic Servants in France', *Journal of Social History*, 8 (1974), 63–78; *idem*, *The Domestic Revolution* (London, 1976), pp. 82–110.
[95] Louis Chevalier, *Labouring Classes and Dangerous Classes* (London, 1973), *passim*.
[96] Garden, *Lyon and les lyonnais*, pp. 95–6.
[97] Alain Corbin, *Les Filles de noce* (Paris, 1978), pp. 72–83, 109; McBride, 'Domestic Servants in France', 75.

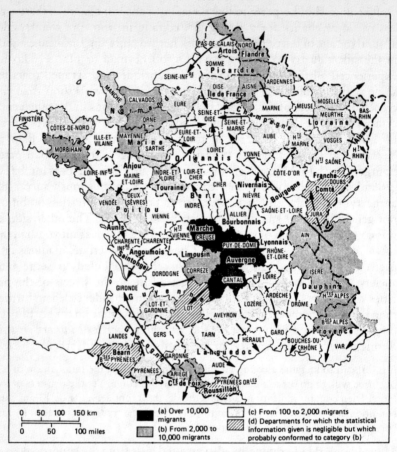

Map 2 Seasonal migrations in France in 1810

Note: this map gives an indication of the major circuits of migration along which young
people moved during the early nineteenth century.
Source: Olwen Hufton, *The Poor of Eighteenth-Century France, 1750–1789* (Oxford,
1974), p. 75.

humdrum fashion. Lacking sufficient skills or contacts for a good job in
industry or commerce, sons and daughters of the poorer peasants and
agricultural labourers were likely to move from the lower ranges of the
hierarchy in rural society to similar positions in the town. Examples of this
'horizontal mobility' during the nineteenth century are legion: herdsmen
and farmers from the Cantal moving into Paris to become water carriers,
messengers, porters and street cleaners; young men and women flocking

into Bordeaux from Aquitaine and the Pyrenees to take up unskilled work in the construction industry, the docks and domestic service; inhabitants of poverty-stricken villages in the Dauphiné, the Bugey, the Lyonnais and Savoy, following a well-trodden path to the Fabrique of Lyons, to seek employment as *tordeuses de soie, tireuses de cordes, dévideuses* and apprentice weavers; and peasants from the countryside around Toulouse melting into the working class of that city.[98] In all such cases, the first few years in town during adolescence and early adulthood were critical. This was the period when the young migrant had to put down roots, moving from the shiftless world of the lodging house, apprenticeship and the servants' quarters, to respectability through regular employment, marriage and a circle of friends in the *quartier*. Networks of kin and acquaintances from the same *pays* could help in this difficult passage. But, as in the village, an early start to the whole business of training, earning and saving was essential for those venturing out from families of limited means.[99]

Conclusion

The inheritance which the villages bequeathed to the nascent industrial society of the nineteenth century was thus one of expecting the children of the *menu peuple* to work from the earliest possible age. Around the age of five, they were permitted to move on from the close supervision of their mothers, but, for the majority of the population, childhood in the modern sense was extremely short. A couple of years in the company of others of their own age, free to wander about and play games as they chose, was all that could be expected. From then on the pressure grew to earn a living: above all, 'il fallait rapporter'.[100] A short spell in the village school was always a possibility, particularly during the winter months around the age of first communion. But, as we shall see below, in much of southern and western France, formal education in the schools barely impinged on the peasant childhood during the late eighteenth and early nineteenth centuries. Young people soon became small but far from insignificant cogs in the workings of the family economy, releasing adults from a number of

---

98 Raison-Jourde, *La Colonie auvergnate*, p. 79; Pierre Guillaume, *La Population de Bordeaux au XIXe siècle* (Paris, 1972), pp. 55–71; Maurice Garden, 'L'Attraction de Lyon à la fin de l'ancien régime', *Annales de démographie historique* (1970), 205–22; *idem, Lyon et les lyonnais*, pp. 85–120; Lequin, *Les Ouvriers de la région lyonnaise*, vol. 1, pp. 227–9, 269–71; Ronald Aminzade and Randy Hodson, 'Social Mobility in a Mid-Nineteenth Century French City', *American Sociological Review*, 47 (1982), 448–9.
99 This section is indebted to Hufton, 'Women and the Family', 1–22; Leslie Page Moch, 'Adolescence and Migration', *Social Science History*, 5 (1981), 25–51; and *idem, Paths to the City, passim.*
100 Carlès, *Une soupe*, p. 58.

simple but time-consuming tasks, and providing some contribution to the
household budget. The work of children on the land may even have
intensified during the late eighteenth and early nineteenth centuries, as a
slowly-developing economy attempted to come to terms with a formidable demographic upsurge. The ordinary peasant, poorly represented
in the political arena, inevitably bore the brunt of this struggle to match
population and resources. In the late nineteenth century, there is some
evidence that higher incomes permitted the peasant to start sparing his
wife and children some of their labours in the field.[101] Under these
circumstances, a new conception of childhood began to make an impact in
the villages. The age-old need to edge the young towards independence at
a tender age became less pressing, paving the way for a more 'extended'
childhood in the family and the school. But this is largely to anticipate, for
the employment of children in the countryside was remarkably persistent,
continuing well into the twentieth century.[102] Above all, on a small farm
or in a domestic workshop, where the separation of work from the family
characteristic of industrial society had not occurred, it was almost
impossible for children to cut themselves off from the activities surrounding them.

[101] See, for example, Grantham, 'Scale and Organization', p. 321; unfortunately there is no
statistical series available to measure the decline of child labour in agriculture.
[102] The First World War, with its systematic mobilization of adult males for the trenches,
was to draw many children temporarily back into the agricultural labour force.

Chapter 2

The nature of work for children in agrarian society

Public opinion during the nineteenth century was arguably better informed on the customs of the Red Indians in North America than on those of the peasants in its own countryside. The inhabitants of the big cities never doubted their *rêve devant les paysans*,[1] which owed more to the pastorals of classical literature than to contemporary life in the villages. Living and working conditions amongst the working classes in the towns excited a great deal of interest, from a mixture of humanitarian concern and fear of political upheaval. Those of the peasantry were largely ignored, in deference to the presumed superiority of the rural way of life.[2] And if the plight of Jacques Bonhomme was largely *terra incognita*, that of his children was even more shrouded in mist. The image proposed by the *bergeries* was a seductive one: what, on the surface, could appear more idyllic than the society of young shepherds and shepherdesses, with its innocent diversions and closeness to nature? Reality in the fields was another matter. There were advantages to being employed on the land rather than in industry. But the writings of those who experienced this childhood during the eighteenth and nineteenth centuries reveal the many hardships also.

The first stage: work as a shepherd

An investigator for Frederic Le Play could plausibly dismiss the occupations of children in a Pyrenean peasant community as 'recreations as

---

[1] The expression comes from Emile Zola, noted after an interview with the socialist leader Jules Guesde; see the Dossier Préparatoire for *La Terre* (Paris, 1980), p. 489.

[2] There were major investigations which assembled material on the condition of the peasantry, notably the 'Enquête sur le travail' of 1848, but the results were never published. The peasant lacked a Louis Villermé or an Auguste Blanqui to publicize his plight. Modern historical works have in their turn paid little attention to the employment of children on the land. See Georges Duby and Armand Wallon (eds.), *Histoire de la France rurale*, vol. 3, *Apogée et crise de la civilisation paysanne, 1789–1914* (Paris, 1976), pp. 340–2; and Crubellier, *L'Enfance et la jeunesse* pp. 118–19. For a discussion of the sources used in this chapter, see above, p. 27 n. 29.

much as work'.[3] The distinction between work and leisure activities, always difficult to make in an agrarian society, was particularly blurred in the daily existence of the young shepherds. Their jobs, appropriately enough for children who had not reached adolescence, did not require a great deal of effort. At the beginning and end of the day, when hungry, the animals in their charge were too engrossed in feeding themsleves to need much attention.[4] With a good sheep dog, the work almost took care of itself. Only in exceptional circumstances did the shepherds have to bestir themselves. When pasturing their charges near fields of crops, they had to ensure that the flock remained in the meadows, otherwise they risked embroiling their employers in acrimonious disputes with neighbouring farmers. Loubette Bellardie, working in the Limousin during the 1890s, was warned to respect the *défenses* of two wealthy neighbours known as L'Evêque and La Dame Blanche: 'The least bit of damage and they will call out the gendarmes.'[5] If for some reason the animals became scattered, it was a difficult task to re-assemble them. Tiennon of *La Vie d'un simple* recalled the exasperating business of trying to round up whole families of pigs, after they had charged off in all directions to hunt out nuts and wild fruits.[6] Above all, the children had to beware of attacks from wolves. These predators only disappeared gradually from the various regions during the nineteenth century. Fierce dogs, such as the *mostis* (mastiffs) of the Rouergue, were sometimes sent out to protect the *petits pâtres* and the flocks.[7] The young shepherd almost invariably had his courage tested at some point by an encounter with a wolf. Captain Coignet, for example, remembered that during the 1780s, when he was

---

[3] Frederick Le Play (ed.), *Les Ouvriers des deux mondes* (5 vols., Paris, 1857), vol. 1, p. 118.

[4] Martial Chaulanges, *Le Roussel* (Paris, 1972), p. 28; and *idem Les Rouges Moissons*, p. 14. Chaulanges centred his triology *La Terre des autres* on three successive generations of his ancestors in the Limousin, using a combination of family reminiscences, historical research and personal experience.

[5] Chaulanges, *Les Rouges Moissons*, pp. 23–5. See also, in two autobiographical accounts, Besson, *Pâtre du Cantal*, pp. 66–8, experiencing the same problem keeping a herd of cows away from unenclosed crops; and Ephraim Grenadou and Alain Prévost, *Grenadou: paysan français* (Paris, 1966), pp. 19–20, on having to prevent geese polluting the watering places of livestock with their feathers.

[6] Guillaumin, *Vie d'un simple*, pp. 25–6. This author also drew on the memories of old people in his village, especially those of his grandfathers, and on his own childhood experiences; the slowness of change on the land doubtless made it easy for him to understand and express the feelings of an earlier generation. See R. Mathé, *Emile Guillaumin, l'homme de la terre et l'homme de lettres* (Paris, 1966), pp. 233–41. In similar vein, Captain Coignet recalled regularly stumbling through briars in the middle of the night in order to round up his oxen for a day's work; Jean-Roch Coignet, *Les Cahiers du capitaine Coignet, 1799–1815* (Paris, 1883).

[7] Beteille, *Rouergue avant 1914*, pp. 44–5.

working in the Morvan at the age of seven, a wolf pounced on one of his sheep:

The wolf could not turn the sheep on to its back: I had time to arrive and take the sheep by its hind legs: the wolf pulled from its side, and I from mine ... But Providence came to my rescue: two enormous dogs arrived to help; they had iron collars and descended like thunder; in a moment the wolf was throttled.[8]

Such emergencies apart, the working day of a young shepherd was a relaxed affair. Valentin Jamerey-Duval, employed in the Champagne during the early eighteenth century, went as far as to say: 'As usual, I had used part of the day to sleep, and the rest to do nothing.'[9]

The children had plenty of opportunity to amuse themselves. Where several flocks were being grazed in close proximity, they could group together in order to play games and share meals. In the Auvergne, for example, when on common land high in the mountains, three or four *pâtres* could safely leave their flocks to the sheep dogs, and go off on their own to explore.[10] Alternatively, the shepherds fell back on more solitary diversions, such as wood carving, hunting or even reading. They were particularly adept at catching thrushes, larks and other small birds, and cooking them on an open fire.[11] They also communicated over long distances by curious yodelling cries which could serve as a warning if a flock was seen to be wandering into forbidden territory.[12] And if they were fortunate enough to be positioned near a road or a river, time passed quickly by as they watched the varied procession of travellers. During the 1840s, in the Limousin, Antoine Bellardie met a fair cross-section of the more mobile sections of society from his vantage point by the main road. There was the *marchand d'almanachs*, who regularly stopped off at the inn to sell thread, needles, combs and mirrors, and to bring news from the outside world. There was the performing bear and its master, and the occasional wealthy traveller in his *cabriolet*. There were the teams of

---

[8] Coignet, *Cahiers*, p. 4. See also Nicolas Restif de la Bretonne, *Monsieur Nicolas* (Paris, 1932), p. 48; Guillaumin, *Vie d'un simple*, p. 5; Chaulanges, *Le Roussel*, p. 7; Audoux, *Marie-Claire*, p. 133.

[9] Valentin Jamerey-Duval, *Mémoires* (Paris, 1981), p. 137. Falling asleep on the job, and thus neglecting a flock, was an occupational hazard; see, for example, Chaulanges, *Les Rouges Moissons*, pp. 24–5.

[10] Besson, *Pâtre du Cantal*, pp. 52–3.

[11] On the games and other activities of the young shepherds, see Van Gennep, *Manuel de folklore français*, vol. 1, pp. 188–9; Brékilien, *Paysans bretons*, pp. 153–4; Sylvère, *Toinou*, pp. 7–8; Chaulanges, *Les Rouges Moissons*, pp. 15–16; Bardin, *Angélina*, p. 95; Jules Reboul, *La Vie de Jacques Baudet, 1870–1930* (Privas, 1934), p. 55.

[12] Students of folklore have attempted to transcribe these calls, with bizarre results: take this passage from Van Gennep: 'dans une partie des Vosges dite la Bresse, les pâtres ont des cris d'appel particuliers qu'on désigne sous le nom de *iélôs*, comme: Ièlô Mi-yane, ièlô-lô-lô! (*Mi-yane* est pour *Marie-Jeanne*). En général, la vachère répond par un cri

rouleurs from the plains, whose mules and carts were announced by the
jingling of bells, the curses of the men and the crack of whips. There were
the ordinary travellers on foot, seeking directions as they went along, and
the soldiers starting or finishing their leave, who told stories of distant
campaigns and wished the shepherd a *bon numero* at his military
recruitment session. There were the young chimney sweeps from Savoy,
who described their own mountainous country and showed him their little
marmot and its tricks. There were the gypsies: dark, sinister people who
on one occasion tried to steal one of his sheep, and finally, there were the
mounted *gendarmes*, whose macabre sense of humour included threatening to arrest him and shoot his dog.[13] On the whole, therefore, the life of
the young shepherd was singularly carefree.

Yet there is a bitter sweetness to the memories of older peasants. All
enjoyed the sense of importance when first being put in charge of
livestock, and the freedom from the world of adults. At the same time, the
themes of loneliness, boredom and physical discomfort appear time after
time in their writings. Tiennon, of *La Vie d'un simple*, described a daily
routine that began before five o'clock in the morning, when he was roused
from his bed to take his flock out into the meadows. Once there, time hung
heavily on his hands: 'Sometimes fear and sadness overtook me, and I
started to cry, to cry without reason, for hours on end. A sudden rustling
in the woods, the scampering of a mouse in the grass, the unfamiliar shriek
of a bird, that was enough during these hours of anxiety to make me burst
into tears.'[14] He used to watch the shadow of an oak tree move slowly
round the gate in his field, finding it would then be eight o'clock in the
evening, and late enough to return home without fear of punishment.
Working in the depths of the countryside was always a mixed blessing.
There was the fresh air and the sun, but equally regularly there was the
rain, mist and cold wind. Children who had to work all the year round
were likely to suffer miserably from the cold and the wet during the
winter.[15] Marie-Claire, the eponymous heroine of the famous novel by
Marguerite Audoux, gave a bleak view of work at this season. Placed as a
bergère on a farm in the Sologne, she was obliged to take out her flock
during December, because the region was too poor to provide enough
fodder for all of its livestock. As well as the cold, she had to contend with
the desolate atmosphere. The mist hanging in the woods and the absolute

semblable; ... A ces chants de plein air vosgiens correspondent les *you-you-you* et les
huchements de la Savoie et de la Franche-Comté, les *bay-lèro-lèro-lèro* de l'Auvergne et
du Quercy, les *liauba, liauba* de la Suisse romande et aussi les charmants *Eho, orelo alahi
alaha iélo alaho* des vachers du Nivarnais'; *Manuel de folklore*, vol. 1, p. 189.
13 Chaulanges, *Le Roussel*, pp. 29–32.   14 Guillaumin, *Vie d'un simple*, p. 11.
15 See, for example, Chaulanges, *Le Roussel*, p. 21; Besson, *Pâtre du Cantal*, p. 126;
Reboul, *Jacques Baudet*, p. 54.

silence were oppressive for a young girl on her own: 'There were days when I felt so abandoned that I believed the world had collapsed around me, and when a crow cried out as it flew by in the grey skies, its loud, raucous voice seemed to announce the misfortunes of the world.'[16]

The second stage: working the land

Making the transition from childhood to the world of adults could be a punishing experience in rural society. Although most of the work done by young children was extremely casual, they were from time to time expected to keep pace with the gruelling routines of seasoned farm labourers. The harvest was the main period when children found themselves working beside adults. In Normandy, for example, whole families of migrants were employed on the big farms for the *grands travaux* of the summer. There they laboured at clearing thistles from the crops, removing any stones that might blunt the scythes, spreading human manure (*la gadoue*) from Paris, thinning out the sugar-beet plants, making up sheaves of corn behind the reapers, and finally harvesting the beets. These were tasks that Marie-Catherine Gardez, working the season from the age of eleven, described as 'long, tiring and monotonous'.[17] She remembered that the families, being paid at a piece-rate most of the time, could not allow any of their members to fall behind: any lapses of concentration on her part were quickly ended by gentle chidings from her father.[18] Threshing was another *corvée* for village youth. For the most part this was done in teams, the threshers being drawn up into two lines. In Brittany a strict protocol determined the arrangement of the lines. At the head would be the *maître* and his *grand valet*. The eldest son of the master would be in the second line, to the right of the *grand valet*, and next to him would be the servants living-in on the farm: the *domestiques*, the stronger *servantes*, and at the very end, the young shepherd boy. Opposite them, with the *maître*, would be the day labourers and any neighbours who were helping out. The actual threshing was of necessity strictly disciplined: first one line lifted its flails and brought them down alternatively towards the left and the right, precisely at the moment when the other line was raising its flails.[19] The fledgeling worker was trapped:

[16] Audoux, *Marie-Claire*, p. 124.
[17] Grafteaux, *Mémé Santerre*, p. 34. The author of this work was a journalist who recorded the experiences of Mémé Santerre while she was in a hospital retired and in her eighties.
[18] *Ibid.*, p. 33
[19] Brékilien, *Paysans bretons*, pp. 52–3. An excellent description of threshing can be found in Emile Zola, *The Earth*, transl. D. Parmee (Harmondsworth, 1980), pp. 276–7.

To wield the flail constantly, and with the same regular movement, in order to maintain the required harmony of the rhythms; to be unable to stop for a moment; not even to have a hand free to blow one's nose or remove a speck of dust making the neck itch: when one is still unskilled and unused to the sustained effort, is to go mad![20]

The régime tightened with adolescence. Shepherding was rarely continued for more than a few years by the young of either sex: once they reached their early teens, they began to scorn it as a childish occupation.[21] Adapting to the full rigours of labouring in the fields was no easy matter. The rural community may have existed in blissful ignorance of any rigid pattern of set working hours.[22] But, winter apart, the peasant could usually find a sufficient number of tasks to keep him occupied for a good twelve or thirteen hours a day, and when pressed, during the harvest, this could creep up to sixteen hours.[23] The villagers may also have worked at a steady pace, far removed from the hectic atmosphere of the factory. Yet there was a relentless, methodical slowness to it that tested both their stamina and their patience.[24] The long-suffering Tiennon of *La Vie d'un simple* confessed to being desperately tired after six or seven hours leading a plough team. He found the going heavy in the churned-up fields, particularly during wet weather, but always his master ploughed on imperturbably.[25] He also remembered trying desperately to move barrow

20 Guillaumin, *Vie d'un simple*, p. 56.
21 The works of Martial Chaulanges provide two examples of peasant attitudes. With adolescence, Antoine Bellardie became eager to join his friends' conversations on ploughing, digging and reaping, and to share their experience of calloused hands, developing muscles ... and girls. He was also riled by the taunts of a neighbour as he led out his flock: 'Alors, tu vas prendre un peu de bon temps? ... Mais tu as oublié ta quenouille?' His daughter Loubette in her turn became dissatisfied with shepherding at the same point: 'Pas bon signe pour une servante de rester trop longtemps bergère: il faut qu'elle ait les côtes en long ou l'esprit peu dégourdi.' See *Le Roussel*, p. 49; and *Les Rouges Moissons*, p. 38.
22 Thuillier, *Histoire du quotidien*, pp. 205–29; Edward P. Thompson, 'Time, Work-Discipline and Industrial Capitalism', *Past and Present*, 38 (1967), 42.
23 Information on working hours in agriculture was sought in the 'Enquête sur le travail', 1848; and in particular AN, C 960, Hondschoote (Nord); AN, C 964, Champlitte (Haute-Saône); AN, C 965, Ecommoy (Sarthe); AN, C 969 Corcieux (Vosges); AD Isère, 162 M1, Vif.
24 Jean Macquart embodied these peasant characteristics: 'he seemed a born farmer, with his slow, equable temperament, his love of fixed, regular tasks and his bovine placidity inherited from his mother'. Zola, *The Earth*, p. 105.
25 Guillaumin, *Vie d'un simple*, pp. 53–5. The author had experienced work as a *boiron* (*toucheur de bœuf*), although in the novel substituted his ill-tempered godfather for his grandfather; see Mathé, *Emile Guillaumin*, p. 238. His account may be compared with the key passage that opens *La Mare au diable*, where George Sand sets out to convey the 'poetic seduction' of peasant life: 'Un enfant de six à sept ans, beau comme un ange, et les épaules couvertes, sur sa blouse, d'une peau d'agneau qui le faisait ressembler au petit Saint Jean-Baptiste des peintres de la Renaissance marchait dans le sillon parallèle à la charrue et piquait le flanc des bœufs avec une gaule longue et légere, armée d'un aiguillon

loads of manure that were beyond his strength, after being goaded to prove his manhood by a *domestique*.[26] Antoine Bellardie was equally battered by his early efforts beside his father and brothers:

These were hard days. It was still dark when they had to get up and grope around to dress. When dawn began to light up the ridges, they had already carted three loads of manure to the fields. Time only to swallow a little soup, and they were off again. They ploughed during the early hours of the morning, for as long as the cows could keep going. But with a single team, only two *liées* a day were possible. And so, in the interval, they dug up the hardened edges of the fields, infested with couch-grass and fern roots. They also turned over the big hemp-field, using long wooden spades tipped with iron, clod by clod, furrow by furrow, interminably. With his back aching, his arms stiff, his knees bruised, and his hands on fire, the young lad did not want to fall behind.[27]

The Conseils de Révision for military conscription would reveal the toll this kind of heavy work took on the young, in terms of hernias, lameness, back injuries and the like.[28]

The young farm worker also had to become accustomed to the discipline of regular working. Rural society evolved its own informal methods of enforcing sustained effort from the labour force, a combination of banter and public humiliation. When the peasants were working in a group, the pace invariably settled around the average, and was maintained by constant tension between fast and slow workers. In the Haut-Vivarais, for example, a thresher who kept making mistakes was rewarded with a rabbit's foot hung on his back, and shouts of 'Au lapi! au lapi!' In the Mediterranean region, these *farces aux maladroits* often took on an overtly sexual character. The young, always a potentially weak link, could not escape this kind of attention. Again in the Haut Vivarais, if the girls fetching straw for the threshers did not move quickly enough, they were seized by the boys and had their garters removed. Similarly, at the *vendange*, teams of women and children moved through the vineyards, working to a rhythm set by their leaders. Any girl who left a bunch of grapes (a *capon*) on the vine was subject to a *caponar*: teethmarks were imprinted on her forehead, and grapes were rubbed into her face or buttocks by a young man.[29] On a family farm, or in a domestic workshop, discipline was assured on a personal basis, and was more or less

peu acéré ... Tout cela était beau de force ou de grâce: le paysage, l'homme, l'enfant, les taureaux sous le joug; et, malgré cette lutte puissante où la terre était vaincue, il y avait un sentiment de douceur et de calme profond qui planait sur toute chose.' *La Mare au diable*, pp. 19–20.

26 Guillaumin, *Vie d'un simple*, p. 57.   27 Chaulanges, *Le Roussel*, p. 52.
28 See below, p. 154.
29 Charrié, *Folklore du Haut-Vivarais*, pp. 112–15; Fabre and Lacroix, *Paysans du Languedoc*, pp. 234–9.

oppressive according to individual circumstances. Where children enjoyed an easy relationship with their parents or employers, as was the case between Marie-Catherine Gardez and her father, it was unobtrusive. But where personalities conflicted, as between Emilie Carlès and her elder sister ('the character of a pig'), it could become intolerable.[30]

Separation from the family

For children obliged to move away from home, the normal burdens of working life could be aggravated by inhospitable living conditions. The ideal was for the master to treat his servants as members of his own family.[31] In some cases, the young *domestiques* enjoyed precisely this arrangement, forming close links with members of the host family.[32] But often the children of the poor were held at arm's length by their employers. The young shepherd boys in particular existed on the margins of society. Creatures of the wild, and even of the supernatural in the eyes of the villagers, on account of the long periods they spent out in the hills, they were sometimes barely known to their masters.[33] Jean-Roche Coignet provided an early example from the eighteenth century. Having run away from home at the age of seven, he hired himself out to a couple of ageing farmers in the Morvan. He was expected to sleep rough in a barn at night, and his only contact with humanity was when food was brought out once a day:

Every evening my master came and brought my piece of bread and a two-egg omelette cooked with leeks and hempseed oil. That was my food every single day. This way of life lasted for three years. I only went to the house on Saint Martin's

---

30 Grafteaux, *Mémé Santerre, passim*; Carlès, *Une soupe*, p. 47. See also the autobiographical novel by Charles-Louis Phillippe, *Charles Blanchard* (Paris, 1913), on the difficulties experienced by a young boy from a deprived background in adapting to the atmosphere of a sabotmaker's workshop; and Louise A. Tilly, 'Linen Was their Life: Family Survival Strategies and Parent–Child Relations in Nineteenth-Century France', in Hans Medick and David Warren Sabean (eds.), *Interest and Emotion* (Cambridge, 1984), pp. 300–16, on the background to life for Marie-Catherine Gardez.

31 Louise Vincent, following in the footsteps of George Sand, was at pains to show that in the Berry masters always treated their farm servants with kindness: 'Celui qui les engage, les reçoit dans sa maison comme les enfants d'un ami, et les met au rang des membres de la famille. Le domestique peut aspirer à la main de la fille de la maison, sans manquer à aucune convenance'. *Le Berry dans l'œuvre de George Sand* (Paris, 1919), pp. 190–1.

32 See, for example, Chaulanges, *Le Roussel*, p. 92; and *Les Rouges Moissons*, pp. 20–33; Audoux, *Marie-Claire*, pp. 93–100; Besson, *Pâtre au Cantal*, p. 52.

33 The 1851 census registers for Taulignan and Dieulefît, in the Drôme, contain the occasional very bald entry for the young *bergers*. There was a twelve-year-old Victor, with no surname attached; and there was even a male aged fifteen, employed by a *propriétaire cultivateur*, with no surname or Christian name at all! AD Drôme, 35 M 115 and 335.

Day, when they did me the honour of a piece of salt pork. From there, I went back
to the straw with my clothes full of vermin.[34]

Other young farm servants were relegated to the society of their fellow
domestiques in the farmyard. From the Norman canton of Balleroy, the
local committee reported to the 1848 Enquiry on Labour that the
'unfortunate' child cowherds on the farms had to sleep in the stables close
to their charges, and survive on a meagre diet of bread and a little meat.[35]
Sleeping near the animals had its advantages during the winter, but in
summer it was stifling, and there were always the various noises to
contend with: the clanking of chains, the cataracts of urine and
excrement, prolonged scratching against the stalls, and the early morning
lowing for food.[36]

Most galling of all for those 'chez les autres' was the feeling of being an
unwelcome intruder in another household, a mere instrument of labour to
be maintained as cheaply as possible. In the words of Martial Chaulanges:

To understand the conditions of a *petit domestique* on a farm, they have to be
experienced: having no more than a bed, or more often half a bed, and a corner of
the table, rarely a measly chest for linen and a few bits of clothing; being unable,
sometimes even in the best of houses, to eat at will, or to fulfilment. When young,
the bread is cut for you; when older, you are made to feel it is being measured;
surreptitiously, a little treat is given to the daughter, or a glass of cider to the son of
the house. No question of choosing the work to be done or the tools to be used. If
someone has to go out and look after the sheep when the weather is bad, or wash
at *la serbe* when it is freezing hard enough to crack a stone, it is the servant girl who
goes. Is there a border to clear, a tough treestump to cut up? It is for the
domestique. And yet they can still tell you that you have taken a long time, that
you are spinning too coarsely, or that you are not ploughing deeply enough, and
that this evening the livestock have not had enough to eat or that they have barely
any milk.[37]

The *domestique* or *servante* was usually hired as a temporary measure, to
be dispensed with as soon as a son or daughter reached working age.[38]
Moving from farm to farm, the young servant had to adapt to the ways of
a succession of masters and mistresses. Some were easy to work beside,
others were not: they might be mean with the food, hard on themselves
and those around them, or haughty in their manner, affecting the ways of
the 'grand bourgeoisie'.[39] In short, more even than the material depri-

---

[34] Coignet, *Cahiers*, p. 5.   [35] AN, C 948.
[36] Chaulanges, *Le Roussel*, pp. 70–1.
[37] *Ibid.*, p. 132.   [38] See Lehning, *The Peasants of Marlhes*, pp. 130–4.
[39] Take the example of Angélina H., from her autobiography of the same title: a *parigote* (a
     foundling put out by the *Assistance*), she was first placed on a farm in the Sarthe at the age
     of thirteen. Her relations with the family here were agreeable, but the outbreak of War in
     1914 caused the job to disappear abruptly. Her second placing was less happy, for her

vation, which was general amongst the peasantry, the farm servant suffered from a complete and humiliating subjection to his or her employer: 'Quand on est jeune, on supporte, mais à force, on se lasse.'[40]

Village children who went out on the road also faced a difficult life, particularly the chimney sweeps. The job of the sweep was in itself hazardous, and occasionally ended in disaster. In 1884 a Factory Inspector reported the death of a *petit ramoneur* in Troyes. The boy became trapped as he descended through the narrow section of a chimney, his clothing acting as a plug. The energetic tugging of his master, which left huge abrasions across his back and shoulders, was insufficient to free him, and he suffocated.[41] Beyond that, the children risked being bullied by their employers if they failed to beg enough food and money. Some were evidently able to cope, and even thrived on the freedom of the road: the worthy Abbé Bugniot warned of 'idleness' and 'the desire to become a vagabond'.[42] But others succumbed to the rigours of their existence, and died miserably a long way from home. The *état civil* of Lunéville records the death in 1855 of a certain Eugène Rassa. The entry was notably terse: born and residing at Gy in Savoy; son of François Rassa; name and forename of mother unknown; occupation, *ramoneur*. He must have died alone, for in place of the usual relatives or friends witnessing the entry, it was officials from the hospital and the *Mairie*.[43]

Vocational training 'on the job'

Learning the ways of agriculture whilst working in the fields could be rewarding for the young farm boy or girl. This informal system capitalized on the child's desire to join the world of adults as quickly as possible, and on the close personal interest he or she could expect from a relative. If not a parent, then an uncle or aunt or a grandparent frequently took the youth in hand, helping with various tasks as they arose, and passing on the wisdom of their years. Thus Antoine Sylvère, raised in the Auvergne during the 1890s, began his working life beside his grandfather, taking on

---

mistress skimped on the food (while indulging in secret feasts with her own son), neglected her health and worked her cruelly, to the extent that public opinion forced a change in attitude. Her final move, at the age of sixteen, began promisingly, for the woman who took her on was pleasant, and fed her well. But she found herself embroiled in a marital dispute, and suffered the rancour of the husband. He begrudged her the food, with the result that she once again became undernourished, and pressed her to the limits at work, without in the least acknowledging her efforts; Bardin, *Angélina*, passim. See also the experiences of Loubette Bellardie in Chaulanges, *Les Rouges Moissons*, passim.

[40] Chaulanges, *Le Roussel*, p. 133.
[41] AN, F^{12} 4739, Delaissement (Rheims, 6th), 23 June 1885.
[42] Bugniot, *Les Petits Savoyards*, p. 37.
[43] AD Meurthe-et-Moselle, 2 E, 'Registre de décès', Lunéville, 7 October 1855.

simple tasks such as collecting pine cones and clearing weeds and always listening to the experiences of the old man.[44] Similarly, Ephraim Grenadou, born in the Beauce at the same period, gradually learned his job on the family farm, learning to plough, for example, by following the various *charrettiers* and taking over their work from time to time.[45] For the less fortunate children who were placed *en service* at an early age, the 'apprenticeship' progressed by moving from farm to farm, gleaning as much knowledge as possible from each and building up a reputation as a competent worker.[46]

In this traditional form of vocational training, children were spared the need to compete for a formal qualification, and they were hardly likely to question the relevance of their education to adult life. Nonetheless, learning to be a farmer could be a bruising, rough-and-ready affair. Some peasants made sympathetic masters, but others were hard on their charges. Tiennon, of *La Vie d'un simple*, retained bitter memories of being laughed at by the older members of his family as he tried eagerly, but unsuccessfully, to emulate their work.[47] Antoine Bellardie, of *Le Roussel*, found the early stages of working life equally hard to bear. When first placed *chez les autres*, he aroused the jealousy of other farm hands when his master, and above all the women of the family, gave him most of their attention. His comrades knew how to take their revenge:

They always chose the best tools for themselves; if there was a spade that was worn out, a mattock with a crooked handle, a verge that was hard to dig, it was for Le Roussel. Never would they help him if he fell behind in doing his part of the work. They spoke amongst themselves, but hardly ever to him.[48]

Moreover, the 'apprenticeship' was not necessarily systematic, despite its length. There was some tendency for members of a household to specialize in their functions, and this could cause problems when they came to set up on their own. Etienne Bertin ('Tiennon') suffered a near failure when he

---

[44] 'A Montsimon, je vivais une vraie vie, telle que l'aiment les enfants toujours pressés d'être des hommes. Lorsque dans les champs de pommes de terre j'enfonçais mon *fourchat* derrière la touffe d'un geste résolu, lorsque j'amenais la plante par la *chabouille* pour fracasser la motte friable sur le nez de mon sabot et disperser les tubercules propres et nets, sans une blessure, je me sentais un homme'; Sylvère, *Toinou*, p. 118; see also pp. 75–81, on other spells with his grandparents at Montsimon.

[45] Grenadou and Prévost, *Grenadou*, pp. 24–32.

[46] Crubellier, *L'Enfance et la jeunesse*, pp. 118–19.

[47] Guillaumin, *La Vie d'un simple*, p. 57. The author made it clear that he did not consider his experience unique: 'J'ai remarqué depuis que tous les débutants connaissent ces ennuis-là. Quand on commence à travailler, on a tout de suite le désir de faire aussi bien que les grands; mais on ne peut y parvenir, car on manque de force, d'adresse et d'expérience. Les autres font sonner bien haut leur superiorité, conséquence de leur âge; et l'on souffre de ne pouvoir les égaler.'

[48] Chaulanges, *Le Roussel*, p. 71.

first attempted to harvest a crop independently, because he had never learnt to sow. On the family farm, this task had always been left to his father: 'There is always the cowherd, the gardener, the sower. The cowherd never does the garden; the gardener hardly knows how to plough, or to look after livestock'.[49]

Conclusion

The custom on the land, then, was that children should be broken in gently to their working lives by the simple task of pasturing livestock or poultry. Much of their work had a casual, unhurried air to it, and their apprenticeship too proceeded at a leisurely pace, unobtrusively grafted to their daily existence on the farm. Yet for all its charms, a rural childhood could still be 'nasty, brutish and short'. There was never any hesitation in demanding heavy, disciplined work from time to time, and poverty cast its doleful shadow in the form of undernourishment, rudimentary living conditions and long hours. Children placed with other families in particular risked being exploited as all-round drudges, always treated less favourably than the sons and daughters of the house. Such abuses remained buried in the countryside during the nineteenth century. Brought up to believe in the solid, laborious virtues of Jacques Bonhomme, the ruling élites were loath to intervene in his private affairs. Child labour in agriculture was therefore never a political issue: indeed, it was hardly the stuff of a great reform campaign. Public opinion was not to be aroused until the big battalions of child workers had been formed in the factories and industrial cities of the Industrial Revolution.

[49] Guillaumin, *La Vie d'un simple*, p. 143. Sowing appears to have been a particularly sought-after skill; see Bardin, *Angélina*, p. 193.

Chapter 3

Education in rural society

Education amongst the peasantry of nineteenth-century France continued to be dominated by the Medieval notion of apprenticeship.[1] Following this approach, children were plunged headlong into the world of adults as early as possible in order to learn the 'art of living' from those around them. All of the ideas, the beliefs and the values of peasant society were transmitted in this way, as well as the manual skills needed for work. In the absence of specialized institutions, education melted imperceptibly into the normal round of activities in the village. However, as the century wore on, this informal type of education came increasingly to be supplanted by a new rival: the elementary school. A very different philosophy of education was percolating down from middle- and upper-class circles, one which required children to be sheltered from an outside world judged too dangerous and too corrupt for their sensibilities. Children were now to be taught systematically in the cloistered atmosphere of the school, before being launched on their chosen occupations.[2] The profound upheaval in customs that this extension of childhood implied was not to be achieved in the short term. The movement to school the population was spread over several centuries, starting in the case of primary education with the *petites écoles* of the reign of Louis XIV, and ending with the free, compulsory schooling of the Third Republic. The middle years of the nineteenth century, from the 1830s to the 1880s, brought a major turning point in the *scolarisation* of the rural population. Nonetheless, the impression remains that right up until the First World War, the primary school perched uneasily in the villages, as it struggled to insert itself into the mainstream of rural life. How, then, were village children educated in this hybrid

[1] We should recognize at the outset that terms such as 'education', 'socialization' and 'apprenticeship' carry twentieth-century connotations that were unknown to peasant society. Education will be taken in its broadest sense here, involving both formal and informal methods of instruction.
[2] This section relies on Ariès, *Centuries of Childhood*, *passim*.

system? What was the content of their education? And what was its relevance to the changing society of the nineteenth century?

Elementary schooling

By the age of seven, sons and daughters of the peasantry were deemed to have left the first stage of their childhood. The young boy would mark his movement away from the direct supervision of his mother by a symbolic act, *le pantalonnage* (breeching) in Brittany, a complete set of new clothing in the Landes. Henceforth, both sexes would find that their lives were increasingly embroiled in work for the family, play with other children and various activities in the local community.[3] One of the first strands in the education which the young were now ready to face could, in the nineteenth century, be elementary schooling. Unfortunately, the statistics available for the period are so unreliable that it is very difficult to determine the proportion of children who attended school. J.-C. Toutain has estimated that in 1815 approximately one fifth of those aged between five and fourteen in the population as a whole were attending school; in 1850, about a half; and in 1881, a good three-quarters.[4] However, in the present state of knowledge, this can be little more than a *jeu d'esprit*. We can say with more confidence, if less precision, that until the 1830s, only a minority of peasants attended school. The achievement of the Catholic Church under the *ancien régime* need not be dismissed out of hand, but the distribution of its *petites écoles* was always patchy. As a rule, the cities and small market towns were better served than the villages, and the network of schools denser in the north and east of France than in the south and west. In regions such as Brittany, the mountainous centre, Aquitaine and Provence, the isolation of many farms and hamlets was a major obstacle to concerted action on a school.[5]

The upheavals of the Revolutionary and Napoleonic periods were not conducive to a programme of school building, with the result that in 1829, one third of all communes still lacked a primary school.[6] The 1820s and 1830s did finally bring a new wave of school building. The *loi Guizot* of 1833 was an important influence in this campaign to bring schooling to the masses. With every commune henceforth obliged to have its own

[3] Sébillot, *Coutumes populaires*, p. 33; Van Gennep, *Manuel de folklore français*, vol. 1, pp. 166–7; Gélis *et al.*, *Entrer dans la vie*, p. 138; Hélias, *Cheval d'orgueil*, pp. 67–8.

[4] Toutain, *La Population de la France*, pp. 225–7.

[5] Allain, *L'Instruction primaire, passim*; Gontard, *L'Enseignement primaire*, pp. 17–21.

[6] Prost, *Histoire de l'enseignement*, p. 97; and Louis-Henri Parias (ed.), *Histoire générale de l'enseignement et de l'éducation en France*, vol. 3, *De la révolution à l'école républicaine* (Paris, 1981), pp. 241–4; Raymond Grew, Patrick J. Harrigan and James Whitney, 'The Availability of Schooling in Nineteenth-Century France', *Journal of Interdisciplinary History*, 14 (1983), 25–63.

primary school, municipal councils in the most recalcitrant areas were prodded into action. For several decades, though, the diffusion of schooling remained stubbornly uneven. The regional disparities inherited from the *ancien régime* continued to manifest themselves, with the west and centre particularly slow to provide additional places. Areas of small property, where there was poverty and a heavy reliance on family labour, were notorious for their low levels of attendance. During the late 1830s, a Primary School Inspector in the Touraine noted that children from this type of background worked in the fields during the summer, and in the woods during the winter, or simply stayed at home, or went begging: 'but one thing is certain: they will not be seen at school'.[7] Isolated forest areas were also noted for ignoring the school system. With so many opportunities for collecting wood, begging and poaching, the offspring of the forest-dwellers tended to run wild.[8] Cutting across these regional and social differences was the basic one of gender: primary education for girls was given a low priority both in official circles and in the peasant family. There was, for example, no legal requirement for communes to establish separate girls' schools until 1850, despite widespread hostility to 'mixed' teaching. Nonetheless, by the time primary education was made free and compulsory in 1882, nearly all children were assumed to be receiving some schooling.[9] It only remained to enforce a longer and more regular period of attendance.

Precisely how long children spent in school before the *loi Ferry* was fully enforced is equally difficult to establish. In some cases, they were packed off around the age of three or four in order to release their mothers for work in the fields.[10] The wretched infants, incapable of following the lessons, became bored with anything to do with schooling and left as soon as possible. More commonly, children waited until the age of six or seven before starting, and then spent four or five years in class.[11] Even then, attendance was sporadic. Parents had no hesitation in interrupting lessons to demand little services from their offspring. From the Pyrenees, an Inspector reported in 1843, 'One frequently sees children who go to

---

[7] F^{17} 9307, report from the Indre-et-Loire, 10 April 1840, on the years 1838–9.

[8] P. Lorain, *Tableau de l'instruction primaire en France* (Paris, 1837), p. 37.

[9] Victor Duruy, *L'Administration de l'Instruction publique, de 1863 à 1869* (Paris, n.d.), pp. 153–4; Ministère de l'Instruction publique et des Beaux-Arts, *Statistique de l'enseignement primaire*, vol. 2, *Statistique comparée de l'enseignement primaire, 1829–77* (Paris, 1880), *passim*; Prost, *Histoire de l'enseignement*, pp. 97–102.

[10] Gontard, *L'Enseignement primaire*, p. 543, and *idem.*, *Les Ecoles primaires*, p. 26.

[11] This is an informed guess, based on sampling the Primary School Inspectors' reports for the 1830s, 1840s and 1850s. For a local study which dwells on this point, see Gabriel Désert, 'Alphabétisation et scolarisation dans le Grand-Ouest au 19^c siècle', in Donald N. Baker and Patrick J. Harrigan (eds.), *The Making of Frenchmen* (Waterloo, Ontario, 1980), p. 163.

school being obliged to leave, at certain times during the day, to take food
to their parents working out in the countryside.'[12] Moreover, as is well
known, schooling for village children was largely confined to the winter.
At the first sign of good weather in February or March, they streamed out
to look after their flocks or to help with the *grands travaux*, and did not
return until October or November. This seasonal pattern had its disadvantages, being described during the 1830s as the 'real plague for
primary instruction in the countryside'.[13] It bit deeply into the time
available for teaching. During the 1840s, for example, an Inspector from
the Ain calculated that with children attending school between the age of
nine and thirteen, four winters brought an effective total of only sixteen
months in class.[14] It meant that teachers had to keep starting from scratch
with their pupils, since what was learnt at the beginning of the year was
soon forgotten during the long summer months at work. And it confined
academic studies to the period of the year when conditions were least
favourable: roads became impassable, daylight hours were short and
epidemics ran rife.[15]

If low levels of attendance undermined the capacity of the elementary
school to transform educational methods in the countryside for much of
the nineteenth century, so too did the nature of the teaching. Until the
reforms of the Guizot law began to make an impact in the 1830s and
1840s, the atmosphere in the village schools was only one step removed
from that of the traditional 'apprenticeship' in the local community. The
meagre earnings which educating the rural poor brought in obliged the
majority of *instituteurs* to seek additional sources of income. Villagers
took it for granted that their schoolmaster would double as sexton and
secretary to the Mayor, and even that he might close down his school
during the summer months to work in the fields. Besides the official lay
and religious teachers, many innkeepers, grocers, tailors, shoemakers,
handloom weavers, blacksmiths, carpenters and stonemasons did a little
teaching on the side. And in the more isolated areas, *instituteurs ambu-
lants* hired themselves out to families for a few weeks at a time during the
winter, teaching a little reading and writing on the farms. The classroom
was therefore more often than not a makeshift affair in a private house or
workshop, which was readily drawn in to the general bustle of life in the
village. Lessons were continually interrupted by the domestic life of the

12 AN, F¹⁷ 9309, report from the Pyrénées-Orientales, 31 May 1843.
13 Lorain, *Tableau de l'instruction*, p. 20. This custom was deep-rooted in rural society: as
   late as 1938, Inspectors in the Isère were still deploring absences of several weeks for
   seasonal work; Pierre Barral, *Le Département de l'Isère sous la Troisième République,
   1870–1940* (Paris, 1962), p. 291.
14 AN, F¹⁷ 9309, report of 18 October 1842.
15 Lorain, *Tableau de l'instruction*, pp. 4–6, 21–2.

teacher, by villagers wanting to register births, marriages and deaths, by customers requiring service at the counter, by work on a loom or at a bench, and by breaks to deliver finished goods.[16]

In the midst of all the hubbub, the teacher would call each child three or four times a day for a few minutes of personal instruction beside him. The 'individual' method of teaching meant that children were left to their own devices over much of the day, but it could hardly be avoided when attendance was irregular and books in short supply.[17] What it did require was a severe system of discipline, to maintain order amongst large numbers of bored children. One of the Guizot Inspectors took a particular interest in the brutality for which schoolmasters were notorious. Everywhere in his canton near Yvetôt he observed the presence of leather and wooden rods thick enough to injure a child, or at the very least to put his hands out of action for a considerable time.[18] The teacher was therefore a daunting figure for young children. The old soldier from the Napoleonic era, ending his days at Frétoy in the Morvan, was almost an archetypal teacher of the period around 1840. He was remembered sitting at the end of a long table with a rod in his hand, his 'Justice of the Peace', and a small pointed stick in the shape of a goat's horn, his *touche*. As the children read to him, he kept his dog on his knee, and huge snuff-box close at hand.[19]

All this was not to the taste of officialdom. The verdict of the School Inspectorate on the older generation of teachers was almost invariably damning, and the general run of village *instituteurs* was indeed barely equipped to fulfil the ambitions of educational reformers. The Rector of the Academy of Lyons, P. Lorain, was scathing in his summary of the position in 1833: 'The law requires the teaching in elementary schools of "morality and religion, reading, writing, elements of the French language, arithmetic, and the system of weights and measures". Consequently, the law assumes that the *instituteurs* know all of this; the law does them far too great an honour.'[20] With nothing more than a *brevet de capacité* required between 1816 and 1833, elementary school teaching was often a refuge for those who were too old, too infirm or too feeble for normal work. These characters suffered a high casualty rate from drunkenness, indolence and crass ignorance. There is no disputing the benefits that the new breed of teachers produced by the *écoles normales* would bring during the second half of the nineteenth century. Compared to their predecessors, they could teach a broader range of subjects, increase

[16] *Ibid.*, pp. 57–72; Gontard, *Les Ecoles primaires*, pp. 31–3.
[17] Gontard, *L'Enseignement primaire*, pp. 35–6.
[18] AN, F[17] * 147, report of the Inspecteur de l'Académie, canton of Fontaine-le-Dun (Seine-Inférieure), 2 November 1833.
[19] Drouillet, *Folklore du Nivernais*, vol. 1, pp. 90–1.
[20] Lorain, *Tableau de l'instruction*, p. 57.

contact time with their pupils through the 'simultaneous' method of instruction and impose more dignity on their position. Yet there was a sinister side to this 'professionalization' of teaching. Underlying much of the criticism of the old-established teachers was their failure, in the eyes of authority, to 'emancipate' children from their rural backwardness. These men (and women) were solidly implanted in their communities by bonds of family and friendship. Instead of teaching the skills and values considered appropriate by ruling circles in Paris, they responded in every way possible to the demands of the peasantry. And this meant limiting themselves to instruction in the most basic literacy, at low cost. Hence, any attempt to boost the rôle of the school in village society would have to start by prising it from the horny hands of the *prétendus-instituteurs*, *instituteurs-artisans*, *colporteurs d'instruction* and the like. Where possible, from the 1830s onwards, the older 'unofficial' teachers were deprived of their jobs, and their *écoles clandestines* driven out of business.[21]

Overlapping with the formal instruction of the elementary school was the teaching undertaken by the clergy. One of the fruits of the Catholic Counter-Reformation was a campaign by the bishops to oblige parish priests to fulfil their duties as religious teachers of the young.[22] The period spent working through the question and answer format of the catechism could still be, in the early nineteenth century, the sole experience of learning outside the popular culture for many village children. The usual practice was for the *curé* or old women, who might be members of a teaching order such as the *béates* of the Velay and Vivarais, to assemble a few children in order to prepare them for their first communion. The basics of reading were also taught in many cases, for these little groupings shaded imperceptibly into the official school system.[23] The extent of

---

21 J. Ruffet, 'La Liquidation des instituteurs-artisans', *Les Révoltes logiques*, 3 (1976), 61–76; Gontard, *Les Ecoles primaires*, pp. 26–33; François Furet and Jacques Ozouf, *Reading and Writing* (Cambridge, 1982), pp. 101–17. Useful local studies on this point include: René Boudard, 'L'Enseignement primaire clandestin dans le Département de la Creuse entre 1830 et 1880', *Mémoires de la Société des sciences naturelles et archéologiques de la Creuse*, 33 (1959), 525–35; Paul Leuilliot, *L'Alsace au début du XIXᵉ siècle* (3 vols., Paris, 1959–61), vol. 1, pp. 299–300; Jean-Philippe David, *L'Etablissement de l'enseignement primaire au XIXᵉ siècle dans le département de Maine-et-Loire, 1816–79* (Angers, 1967), pp. 59–71, 378–85.

22 Jean Delumeau, *Catholicism between Luther and Voltaire* (London, 1977), pp. 199–201.

23 Furet and Ozouf, *Reading and Writing*, pp. 102–3; Auguste Rivet, 'Aspects et problèmes de l'enseignement primaire en Haute-Loire pendant la première moitié du XIXᵉ siècle', *Actes du 88ᵉ Congrès National des Sociétés Savantes, Clermont-Ferrand, 1963* (Paris, 1964), pp. 196–8; Pierre Zind, 'L'Enseignement primaire sous la Restauration dans l'arrondissement de Saint-Etienne', *Cahiers d'histoire* (1958), 360–2. For autobiographical accounts, see Joseph Benoit, *Confessions d'un prolétaire* (Paris, 1968), p. 36; Besson,

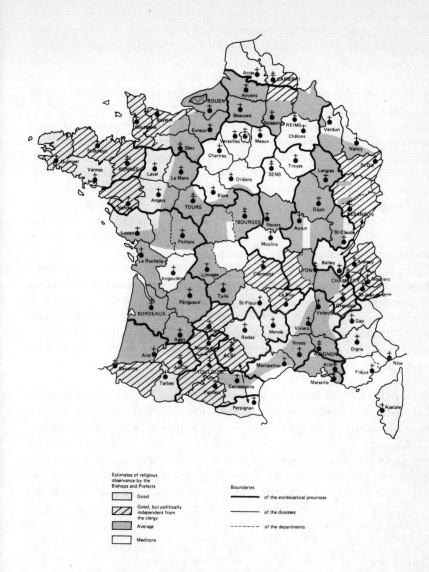

Map 3 The religious vitality of dioceses in France in 1877

Source: Jacques Gadille, *La Pensée et l'action politiques des évêques français au début de la IIIᵉ République, 1870–83* (Paris, 1967).

religious preparation varied between regions. This was because the decline of religious practice in some parts of the country was combined with a groundswell of anticlericalism. By the 1850s, the Catholic Church was clearly on the retreat in the Paris region, much of the centre, and several areas in the south. Conversely, its resurgence after the difficulties of the Revolutionary period were most in evidence in the Vendée, the north-east, Alsace-Lorraine, the Massif and a few Pyrenean districts.[24] At one extreme were dioceses like that of Rennes, in the heart of the devout Brittany, where Justices of the Peace could inform the 1848 Enquiry on Labour that they were well satisfied with the state of moral and religious teaching. Comments such as 'the clergy fulfils its mission with zeal' from Fougères-Nord, 'the only education which people are really preoccupied with' from Pleurtuit and 'very much cared for' from Pleine-Fougères were typical of this area. At the other extreme was the diocese of Orleans, where the detachment of the population from the Church was well under way by mid-century. All children continued to attend catechism classes, but instead of the two years recommended by the priests, many were allowed only five or six months by parents who gave a higher priority to acquiring literacy skills or earning money. Similar deficiencies in the religious instruction of children were noted in the diocese of Montpellier at the beginning of the nineteenth century. The major obstacles put forward in this case were parental poverty and a shortage of young, energetic priests.[25]

The modest rôle for the elementary school in rural France during the first half of the nineteenth century meant that the skills and values it sought to disseminate were slow to take a hold. As far as skills were concerned, the teaching of literacy was not entirely the preserve of the school system at this period. To save time and money, many parents took it upon themselves to teach their offspring a little reading and arithmetic. Some children learned from their friends, Valentin Jamerey-Duval, for example,

   Pâtre du Cantal, pp. 11–12; Hélias, *Cheval d'orgueil*, pp. 128–30; and Grenadou and Prévost, *Grenadou*, pp. 20–1.

24 Gabriel Le Bras, *Etudes de sociologie religieuse*, vol. 1, *Sociologie de la pratique religieuse dans les campagnes* (Paris, 1955), pp. 275–301; Yves-Marie Hilaire, 'La Pratique religieuse en France de 1815 à 1878', *L'Information historique*, 8 (1963), 57–69; Gérard Cholvy, 'Société, genres de vie et mentalités dans les campagnes françaises de 1815 à 1880', *L'Information historique* (1974), 155–66; and *idem*, 'Le Catholicisme populaire en France au XIXe siècle', in Bernard Plongeron and Robert Pannet (eds.), *Le Christianisme populaire* (Paris, 1976), pp. 199–223.

25 Michel Lagrée, *Mentalités, religion et histoire en Haute-Bretagne au XIXe siècle: le diocèse de Rennes, 1815–1848* (Paris, 1977), pp. 39–50; Christiane Marcilhacy, *Le Diocèse d'Orléans au milieu du XIXe siècle* (Paris, 1964), pp. 274–414; Gérard Cholvy, 'Religion et société au XIXe siècle: le diocèse de Montpellier', 2 vols., unpublished thesis, University of Paris I, 1972, vol. 1, pp. 490–1.

being taught to read by his fellow shepherds whilst out in the fields. Others picked up their literacy haphazardly, the grandfather of Antoine Sylvère taking ten years to do so as he followed the Mass in his book at church.[26] Conversely, it was always possible to attend school without ever acquiring any real competence in reading and writing. A Primary School Inspector in the Nord reported during the 1830s:

> I have also noticed that each year the study of the catechism absorbs three-quarters of the time that the children spend at school, with the result that the other parts of their primary instruction are almost entirely neglected, and that having been at school for several years, the pupils abandon it for ever without gaining anything more than the knowledge of how to read in a spelling book, trace a few poorly-formed characters which are dignified with the name of letters, and recite a few phrases from the catechism without understanding them.[27]

Nonetheless, the elementary schools did justifiably consider themselves the major source of access to the written culture in the countryside, and the limits to their achievement are starkly revealed by various quantitative studies of literacy.

Levels of literacy varied considerably between regions, between the sexes and between occupations. The classic schema has always been to contrast a 'literate' and an 'illiterate' France, separated by the Saint-Malo–Geneva line. On the eve of the French Revolution, the Maggiolo Enquiry found that 47 per cent of men and 27 per cent of women could sign their names on the marriage registers. But, in the words of Furet and Ozouf, 'broadly speaking, northern and north-eastern France was able to read and write by the end of the 18th century, at a time when the other France was only just embarking on the process of catching up'.[28] Map 4 shows these disparities still much in evidence at the beginning of our period. Thus in 1816–20, most of Normandy, the Paris basin, the Champagne, Lorraine, the Vosges and Franche-Comté had an overwhelmingly literate male population, whilst in great tracts of the west, centre and south, those male marriage partners able to sign their name were in a minority. Among the females, a similar pattern occurs at a lower level of literacy: in the north and east, at least half of the women were able to sign their marriage register, but elsewhere literacy had barely started to take a hold. No less important was the influence of occupation on literacy. Everywhere in the eighteenth and nineteenth centuries the peasantry, or at least its lower strata, emerge as the social group with the lowest literacy scores. Alain Corbin has made an analysis of military conscription records

---

[26] Zind, 'L'Enseignement primaire', 360–1; Jamerey-Duval, *Mémoires*, pp. 191–2; Sylvère, *Toinou*, p. 52.

[27] AN, F[17] 9371, anual report for the department of the Nord, 1837.

[28] Furet and Ozouf, *Reading and Writing*, p. 45.

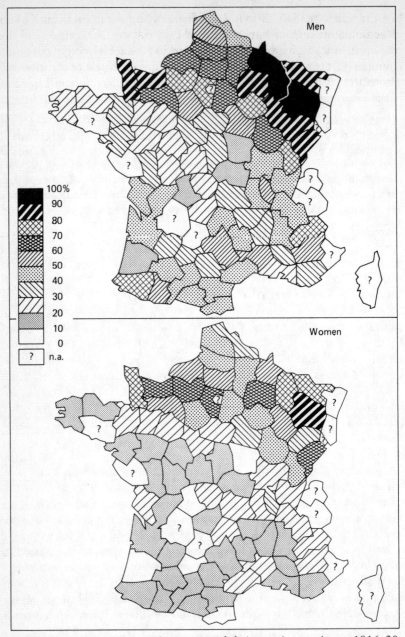

Map 4 Percentage of spouses having signed their marriage registers, 1816–20

Source: François Furet and Jacques Ozouf, *Reading and Writing* (Cambridge, 1982), p. 50.

for the years 1835–7 in two departments lying north and south of the Maggiolo line: respectively the Eure-et-Loir and the Cher. He reveals that the agricultural labourers trailed far behind a literate professional and commercial class, and failed to match the literacy levels of the industrial proletariat. In the Eure-et-Loir, farm servants, day labourers, carters, shepherds and woodcutters were between one third and one half literate. Independent farmers, a group comprising *cultivateurs, labourers, vignerons* and *jardiniers* fared better, with at least three-quarters of their number able to read and write. In the Cher, by contrast, all of the various categories in the agricultural population shared low levels of literacy. *Domestiques* and day labourers were still almost totally illiterate, and the independent farmers not so very different, being at best a quarter literate. This type of socio-occupational distribution appears again in the three departments of the Limousin region in 1848. In this case the ranks of small property owners, tenant farmers, share-croppers, day labourers and farm servants were, almost to a man, illiterate.[29] These disparities between occupations, like those between the sexes and between regions, would be much attenuated by the end of the nineteenth century. Already in the years 1871–5, 78 per cent of men and 66 per cent of women could sign their marriage registers. At the same period, the Rhône corridor and the Mediterranean south had joined the 'literate' departments north of the Saint-Malo to Geneva line, many of which were now approaching universal literacy. However, there remained a solid block of territory falling well short of this position. Taking the form of a triangle, its base ran along the Atlantic coast from Brittany to the Landes, and its apex pointed into the centre, including most of the west, the Massif and Aquitaine.[30] In these areas, literacy was presumably not yet a skill that the peasant insisted be taught to his children.[31]

Successive régimes in Paris also found it an uphill struggle to instil into the peasantry their moral and political values, despite the high priority

29 Alain Corbin, 'Pour une étude sociologique de la croissance de l'alphabétisation au XIXe siècle: l'instruction des conscrits du Cher et de l'Eure-et-Loir, 1833–83', *Revue d'histoire économique et sociale*, 153 (1975), 99–120; and *idem., Limousin au XIXe siècle*, vol. 1, pp. 330–5. See also Furet and Ozouf, *Reading and Writing*, ch. 4; *idem., Lire et écrire* (2 vols., Paris, 1977), vol. 2, *passim*; Michel Vovelle, 'Y a-t-il eu une révolution culturelle au XVIIIe siècle? A propos de l'éducation populaire en Provence', *Revue d'histoire moderne et contemporaine*, 22 (1975), 89–141; and Georges Dupeux, *Histoire sociale et politique du Loir-et-Cher, 1848–1914* (Paris, 1962), pp. 160–6.
30 Michel Fleury and Pierre Valmary, 'Les Progrès de l'instruction élémentaire de Louis XIV à Napoléon III d'après l'enquête de Louis Maggiolo, 1877–9', *Population*, 12 (1957), 71–92; Furet and Ozouf, *Reading and Writing*, pp. 5–57.
31 The study of the west by Gabriel Désert reveals that only in the 1900s did the Saint-Malo to Geneva line fade from view, with generally high levels of literacy amongst boys and girls going to school at this period tending to even out the ancient disparities between Brittany and Normandy; 'Alphabétisation et scolarisation', pp. 145–9.

invariably given to this side of education. During the eighteenth and early nineteenth centuries, elementary instruction in the countryside was left entirely in the hands of the Church, which had no hesitation in declaring its preoccupation with producing good Christians. The *monarchie censitaire* began the long process of breaking this clerical monopoly, but it continued to insist that popular education be infused with a Christian spirit. The Guizot law of 1833 proclaimed that 'moral and religious instruction should hold the front rank' at all levels of elementary schooling, in order to 'penetrate the souls of pupils with those sentiments and principles which safeguard good order and which inspire the fear and love of God'. The policy of using religious teaching in the schools to buttress the existing social order was continued under the *loi Falloux* of 1850, surviving intact until the 1880s.[32] But once again, the mediating influence of the village school had to be taken into account. During the first half of the nineteenth century, in a 'dechristianized' area, it might ignore religious instruction altogether. An Inspector in the Drôme complained on the eve of the Guizot law that 'parents were content with a little reading, writing and arithmetic, and the teachers conform to this wish', the proverbial meanness of the peasants allegedly holding sway.[33] Subsequently the missionary efforts of the teaching orders aroused resentment in some quarters. The village shoemaker who in 1882 could write 'my education was that of all those who, like myself, went to school with the *ignorantins*: that is to say insignificant', was clearly not emerging as a model Christian.[34] Nor was Antoine Sylvère during the 1890s, for he later suggested that the 'odious' school text book, the *Duties of a Christian*, drove people to anticlericalism as effectively as any Mason or free thinker.[35]

The attempt to encourage a national consciousness amongst the peasantry was equally beset with difficulties. At the outset, the administration realized the limits to what could be achieved through the schools, settling in 1833 for compulsory teaching of the French language and the metric system.[36] History and geography, subjects which were potentially fruitful channels for spreading patriotic sentiments, were usually left aside in the countryside. For example, in the canton of Privas (Ardèche), visits by the Guizot Inspector found that village schools invariably restricted themselves to teaching the catechism, the three Rs and a little grammar, whilst the two main schools in the town added geometry,

---

[32] Gontard, *L'Enseignement primaire*, pp. 6–15, 37–8; *idem.*, *Les Ecoles primaires*, pp. 4–7, 119, 233–5; Prost, *Histoire de l'enseignement*, pp. 10–11, 89; Douglas Johnson, *Guizot* (London, 1963), ch. 3; Theodore Zeldin, *France, 1848–1948* (2 vols., Oxford, 1973–7), vol. 2, ch. 4.

[33] AN, F[17] * 101, canton of Buis.   [34] AN, C 3369[1].   [35] Sylvère, *Toinou*, p. 91.

[36] R. D. Anderson, *Education in France, 1848–1870* (Oxford, 1975), p. 5.

geography and drawing.[37] The additional subjects were not made compulsory until 1867, leaving the elementary schools in much the same position in 1870 as they had been in 1833.[38] With the Third Republic, there is no doubt that the nationalist content in primary education became more prominent. The famous *Tour de la France par deux enfants*, subtitled *Devoir et patrie*, typified the new approach, with its explicit intention of spreading 'knowledge of the fatherland'.[39] Yet the testimony of people who were in the village schools at the period reveals that poor teaching sometimes produced grotesque results. Antoine Sylvère admitted that at the age of six, history and geography defied all comprehension: 'I soon knew, by correct subtraction, by how much the altitude of Chimborazo exceeded that of Mont Blanc. However, I did not know what an altitude signified.' For Pierre Besson, school was an endless sequence of dictations and sums. The only break came with geography and history. The former taught him the names of 200 waterways in France, plus all the gulfs, bays, harbours, caves, headlands, promontories, points, straits, narrows, channels, islands and islets. He could also name most of the *chefs-lieux* of the cantons, and was of course well versed on Alsace-Lorraine. Learning history involved equally prodigious feats of memory, with an emphasis on military heroes. Besson recalled being electrified on hearing of epics such as the Napoleonic campaigns, but this 'superhuman and inhuman' view of the past served to leave him disenchanted with the present.[40]

'Learning by living'

What the school system found difficult for much of the nineteenth century was to edge its way into the traditional apprenticeship within the family and the local community. The attitude of the peasant towards formal education was ambivalent. He had a good deal of respect for the world of academic learning, but at the same time he was inclined to consider it a 'useless luxury' for his own family. He might be prepared to accept some elementary instruction for his sons and daughters, but he was impatient for them to move out into the real world: witness the villager from the Pyrenees who, in 1840, insisted on withdrawing his son from school because after two weeks the boy still could not read, and had not even

---

[37] AN, F[17] * 83.　　　[38] Prost, *Histoire de l'ensignement*, p. 123.

[39] G. Bruno, *Le Tour de la France par deux enfants*, 13th edn (Paris, 1878), p. 111. See also Weber, *Peasants into Frenchmen*, pp. 332–8; and Laura S. Strumingher, *What Were Little Girls and Boys Made Of?* (Albany, 1983), *passim*.

[40] Sylvère, *Toinou*, p. 85; Besson, *Pâtre du Cantal*, pp. 27–31.

started to write.[41] The process of 'learning by living'[42] was the sole education available to some peasants, and everywhere it loomed larger than in the 'schooled society' of the twentieth century.

Watching, listening, helping: these were the ways the young acquired the skills and the knowledge necessary for everyday living.[43] For example, by watching the slow, laborious gait of the older peasants in the fields, they learned how to economize on their movements, so that they could pace themselves over a long working day.[44] By listening to the more experienced members of the community, they could pick up a mass of information on such matters as local soil conditions, times for sowing and times for harvesting, weather forecasting and the uses of various plants and animals. Above all, by helping their families or their employers they gradually mastered the skills of a rural community. Many of these skills were, it goes without saying, directly connected with agricultural or handicraft work. But there were others which would in the twentieth century be learned at school, or be handed over to specialists. Thus girls continued to learn how to bake bread, to make and mend clothes, and, most importantly, to apply *remèdes de bonne femme* to the sick and injured.[45] Boys, for their part, slowly acquired the art of *bricolage*, repairing tools, fences and household equipment wherever possible; they learned the peasants' rough-and-ready system of measurements, based on fingernails, thumbs, fists, armfuls and feet; and they became practised in complicated mental arithmetic. When Pierre-Jakez Hélias asked his grandfather how he managed to do his accounts without using pencil and paper, the old man replied: 'We have always been very poor in our family. If we had been stupid on the market, we would have died of hunger. We have therefore been condemned to using our heads to have a chance of surviving. You use yours too.'[46] The young peasant would also try his

41 AN, F[17] 9307, report of the School Inspector for the Pyrénées-Orientales, 27 December 1840. For similar attitudes in contemporary France, see M. Moscovici, 'La Personnalité de l'enfant en milieu rurale', *Etudes rurales*, 1 (1961), 65–6.

42 I owe this expression to discussion with Dr Alan Booth of Loughborough University.

43 See, for example, Lucienne Roubin, 'Savoir et art de vivre campagnard', in Jacques Beauroy, Marc Bertrand and Edward T. Gargan (eds.), *The Wolf and the Lamb: Popular Culture in France from the Old Regime to the Twentieth Century* (Saratoga, Cal., 1977), pp. 95–7; and Françoise Zonabend, *Le Mémoire longue* (Paris, 1980), pp. 116–18.

44 Hélias, *Cheval d'orgueil*, p. 307. For a more extensive 'history of movements', see Thuillier, *Histoire du quotidien*, pp. 162–82.

45 For an autobiographical account of such a rural upbringing, in the Cévennes during the 1880s and 1890s, see Raymonde Anna Rey, *Augustine Rouvière, cévénole* (Paris, 1977), pp. 11–83. Also useful are: Audoux, *Marie-Claire*, pp. 100–84; Carlès, *Une soupe*, pp. 7–76; Chaulanges, *Les Rouges Moissons*, *passim*; and Marcelle Bouteiller, *Médecine populaire d'hier et d'aujourd'hui* (Paris, 1966), *passim*.

46 Hélias, *Cheval d'orgueil*, p. 223. See also Yves Castan, *Honnêteté et relations sociales en Languedoc, 1715–80* (Paris, 1974), pp. 128–9; and Thabault, *Mazières-en-Gâtine*, p. 69.

hand at hunting and fishing. These were activities of no small significance, when a successful haul from poaching could make the difference between a nourishing meal and a half-empty belly. Dispatching small animals came easily to village children. They started young, with cruel games such as making cockchafers fly around on a piece of string until the insects dropped from exhaustion, bringing down the occasional bird with a catapult, and beating to death any moles, frogs, foxes and the like that fell into their hands.[47] Later they moved on to more serious expeditions, which might include acting as a lookout for a poacher.[48] Poil de Carotte, eponymous hero of the novel by Jules Renard, learned to shoot by accompanying his father out in the woods. He began with a series of mistakes: firing too close to a quail and reducing it to a bloody beak and a few feathers, winging a partridge, and missing a hare. But soon he was an accomplished shot, able to hit a woodcock flying fast over his head.[49]

Although training in these mundane matters was an essential part of a rural education, the peasant was not raised merely to be another beast of burden around the farm. He was heir to an elaborate popular culture, which came to life at the *veillées*, the annual festivals, and the occasional celebration such as a wedding or a royal birth. Besides bringing some respite from the daily grind of hard work and spartan food, the recreations of the peasantry lifted them above a crude, hand-to-mouth existence. Of particular importance were the myths, legends and folktales, which were passed down orally from generation to generation. These were the basis for a moral education, since they discreetly aired notions of good and evil, and the importance of human dignity.[50] In each village, a handful of individuals would build a reputation as expert storytellers. These were skilled performers, able to hold an audience for hours on end by their dramatic exposition and talent for improvization.[51] Their impact on the young at the *veillées* was considerable. In the half-light of a barn, with the whistling of the wind and the occasional screech of a night bird in the background, an old woman describing murders, shipwrecks and

[47] Information drawn from Reboul, *Jacques Baudet*, p. 55; G. Existence, 'Village', *Les Œuvres libres*, 221 (1939), 257–85; Pierre Gascar, *Le Meilleur de la vie* (Paris, 1964), pp. 46, 58–63, 210; Jules Renard, *Poil de carotte* (Paris, 1965), *passim*.

[48] Sylvère, *Toinou*, pp. 187–8.   [49] Renard, *Poil de carotte*, pp. 143–5, 148–9.

[50] See Bruno Bettelheim, *The Uses of Enchantment* (London, 1976), pp. 3–19, for the argument that some of these stories would have helped children confront deep-rooted anxieties; and Ruth Finnegan, 'Literacy versus Non-Literacy: The Great Divide?', in Robin Horton and Ruth Finnegan (eds.), *Modes of Thought* (London, 1973), p. 118. See also the interesting discussion in Robert Darnton, 'Peasants Tell Tales: The Meaning of Mother Goose', in his *The Great Cat Massacre* (Harmondsworth, 1985), pp. 17–78.

[51] Michele Simonsen, *Le Conte populaire française* (Paris, 1981), ch. 6. The best collections of French folktales are: Paul Delarue, *Le Conte populaire français* (3 vols., Paris, 1957); and the recent series of regional monographs edited by Jean Cuisenier, *Récits et contes populaires* (Paris, 1979–81).

strange, supernatural beings was not easily forgotten. At the beginning of this century Félix Chapiseau looked back to the 'légendes naïves et merveilleuses' of his boyhood in the Beauce:

Everybody listened in complete silence to these terrible stories of werewolves running across the plain, of ghosts throwing curses by the handful, of sorcerers spreading ruin and disease everywhere, of devils, covered in black fur, and always armed with long horns and menacing forks. Hair stood on end, eyes became haggard, faces looked drawn, and hearts beat faster ... When the time came to turn in, terrified children hid under their mothers' aprons on the way back to their homes. During the night, their dreams were full of hideous monsters.[52]

This art of storytelling lasted as long as the *veillée*, gradually disappearing from the countryside after 1870.[53]

Festivals in their turn helped immerse children in the popular culture. These were collective activities, involving all sections of the local community. By the early nineteenth century, their number had declined markedly from earlier levels, under the weight of ecclesiastical censure and pressing economic conditions: the 'victory of work over leisure' can be traced back as far as the second half of the seventeenth century.[54] However, the reduced calendar of *fêtes* heightened the intensity of those which survived. Each village usually celebrated its patron saint, and one or two other saint's days according to local traditions. In addition, it would observe the major cycles such as Christmas, Lent and Easter, and the agrarian festivals linked to work in the fields.[55] These latter were of particular importance to the peasant, for his was a 'cosmic christianity', counting on divine intervention in the daily struggle for existence.[56] Tiennon, of *La Vie d'un simple*, set out in forthright fashion his version of this blend of Christian and pagan beliefs. He was sceptical of the priests' teaching on Heaven and Hell, confessions and fast days:

Nonetheless, I firmly believed in the existence of a Supreme Being, who governed all, ruling the course of the seasons, and sending the sun and the rain, the frost and the hail. And since our work as farmers depends on favourable weather, I made

52 Félix Chapiseau, *Le Folk-lore de la Beauce et du Perche* (2 vols., Paris, 1902), vol. 1, p. vi. In the same vein is Martin Nadaud, *Léonard, maçon de la Creuse* (Paris, 1977), pp. 24–5.
53 Recent surveys of the *veillée* include Edward Shorter, 'The "Veillée" and the Great Transformation', in Beauroy *et al.*, *The Wolf and the Lamb*, pp. 127–40; and Weber, *Peasants into Frenchmen*, pp. 413–18.
54 Bercé, *Fête et révolte*, *passim*; Michelle Vovelle, *Les Métamorphoses de la fête en Provence de 1750 à 1820* (Paris, 1976), *passim*.
55 Crubellier, *Histoire culturelle*, p. 59.
56 Delumeau, *Catholicism*, ch. 3; Cholvy, 'Le Catholicisme populaire', 200–9; Yves-Marie Hilaire, *Une chrétienté au XIXe siècle? La vie religieuse des populations d'Arras, 1840–1914* (2 vols., Lille, 1977), vol. 1, ch. 2; and *idem*, 'Notes sur la religion populaire au XIXe siècle', in Guy Dubosq, Bernard Plongeron and Daniel Robert (eds.), *La Religion populaire* (Paris, 1979), pp. 195–7.

great efforts to please the Master of the Elements, who held a good part of our interests in his hands. For that reason, I rarely missed those ceremonies concerned with the success of the crops, and I was a faithful observer of all the little pious traditions practised in the countryside on numerous occasions.[57]

The vital ceremonies, which received different emphasis across the regions, included Palm Sunday, May Day, the Rogations and *la Saint Jean*.

The traditional rôle for the young at the *fêtes* was to purify all the households in their village. Hence they went on periodic *tournées*, collecting eggs, cakes, money and the like in return for a blessing. In Lorraine and the Champagne, the *trimouzette* (May Queen) used to go out once a year in the company of young acolytes, who would dance outside each house to a song asking for a good harvest. In Picardy, the young *pocageux* went on their rounds at Easter, whilst in the Dauphiné, bands of children expected to receive a present from each family on New Year's Eve.[58] Other activities at these holidays became increasingly associated with children during the nineteenth century, as adults or older youths began to consider them below their dignity. The *quêtes* to collect materials for the festivities became less aggressive, less extortionate, as they were handed over to the very young. Only a hint of their early character remained, as little boys recited lines such as: 'Réveille-toi, grand lourdaud, pense à la mort de tes chevaux' ('Wake up, you great lout, think on the death of your horses').[59] Similarly Carnival time in southern France lost its riotous nature when children alone disguised themselves with masks on the streets.[60] For the rest, children were able to join older members of their family in many of the entertainments which lay at the heart of these holidays, eating, drinking, singing and playing games. They also learnt to dance, either trying out steps in their own little groups, or, in areas such as Brittany, Languedoc and the Béarn, joining the *bourrées*, the *rondes* and other collective dances.[61]

When they started work, the *fêtes* took on a new significance. In most regions, Saint John the Baptist was taken as the patron saint of shepherds, so that his feast day on June the 24th was specially revered by those responsible for the flocks. A common custom was to lead the animals through the ashes left by the huge fires lit in his honour, in order to take advantage of their supposed protective powers. Some areas had more

[57] Guillaumin, *Vie d'un simple*, pp. 249–50.
[58] André Varagnac, *Civilisation traditionnelle et genres de vie* (Paris, 1948), pp. 122–3; Arnold Van Gennep, *Le Folklore du Dauphiné* (2 vols., Paris, 1932), vol. 2, pp. 393–4.
[59] Bercé, *Fête et révolte*, p. 22.
[60] See, for example, Charrié, *Folklore du Haut-Vivarais*, p. 75.
[61] Michael M. Marrus, 'Modernization and Dancing in Rural France', in Beauroy *et al.*, *The Wolf and the Lamb*, pp. 141–59; Weber, *Peasants into Frenchmen*, pp. 429–51.

specialized festivals for the young shepherds. In the mountainous heart of
Brittany, late autumn brought the *fête des petits pâtres*. After a communal
meal in the pasture lands, the children listened to a *kentel*, an edifying
song chanted by an old man of the village, which reminded them of their
duties as shepherds, and gave practical advice on how to look after the
flocks. The shepherd girls usually took as their patron a saint who had
herself been out in the fields, notably Sainte Geneviève of Paris, and later
on Joan of Arc or Bernadette of Lourdes. In the Berry their particular day
was Vendredi Blanc, the Friday falling nine days before Easter. The
bergères brought bundles of hazel sticks to be blessed: uneven in number
and of varying lengths, they were used to count sheep, and also to ward off
epidemics and wolves. Older youths, working as *garçons de ferme*, turned
to Saint Eloi, the patron saint of blacksmiths, and, by extension, of horses
and those working with these animals. In December, at the winter feast
day for the saint, horses were given bread blessed by the priest to protect
them from sickness, and in June, at *le Saint Eloi d'été*, Mass was preceded
by a spectacular blessing of the animals.[62]

The popular culture of the *veillées* and the *fêtes* was essentially an oral and
visual one, but the villagers were not entirely immune from the influence
of the printed word. The *Bibliothèque bleue* of Troyes and other
publishers of *littérature de colportage* were producing, at their peak in the
1840s, 9 million chap-books a year, with an eye very much on the rural
market. Costing only a few centimes, they were within the range of large
sections of the *menu peuple*. During the seventeenth and eighteenth
centuries, outlets were confined to the north and east of France, that is to
say in the areas where the school system had made the most impact.
During the nineteenth century, the so-called 'Gascons', hawkers from the
Pyrenees, ensured the establishment of a national market.[63] Some of the
young shepherds were able to while away the hours in the fields by reading
these little books. Early in the eighteenth century, Valentin Jamerey-Duval
claimed to know by heart all his works from the *Bibliothèque bleue*; two

---

62 Van Gennep, *Manuel de folklore*, vol 1, p. 191; Brékilien, *Paysans bretons*, pp. 201–3;
    Hilaire, *Une chrétienté*, p. 71.
63 This area has been well covered by historians. See in particular: Robert Mandrou, *De la
    culture populaire aux XVIIe et XVIIIe siècles: la bibliothèque bleue de Troyes* (Paris,
    1964); Geneviève Bollème, 'Littérature populaire de colportage au 18e siècle', in G.
    Bollème, J. Ehrard, F. Furet, D. Roche and J. Roger, *Livre et société dans la France du
    XVIIIe siècle* (2 vols., Paris, 1965), vol. 1, pp. 61–92; idem., *Les Almanachs populaires
    aux XVIIe et XVIIIe siècles* (Paris, 1969); idem., *La Bibliothèque bleue* (Paris, 1971);
    Jean-Luc Marais, 'Littérature et culture "populaires" aux XVIIe et XVIIIe siècles.
    Réponses et questions', *Annales de Bretagne et des pays de l'Ouest*, 87 (1980), 65–105;
    Jean-Jacques Darmon, *Le Colportage de librairie en France sous le Second Empire* (Paris,
    1972).

centuries later, the fictional Marie-Claire spent a winter beside her flock reading some old almanacs she had found on the farm.[64] With even the most meanly-produced publications a rarity in the peasant household, books enjoyed great prestige. They were reverently passed down within families, and were read time after time by children. The illiterate were not necessarily cut off entirely from this source of knowledge. In some families, reading aloud in the evening was a regular practice: in Brittany, for example, passages from a Breton version of the *Lives of the Saints* were a common accompaniment to mealtimes in the rural household.[65] Similarly, at a *veillée*, all that was needed was the odd peasant able to read aloud to his illiterate neighbours.

Whether the cheap literature sold in the villages tended to reflect or subvert the popular culture is open to question.[66] Certainly the *Bibliothèque bleue* drew very little of its material from the folktales that circulated amongst the peasantry, and one of its effects may well have been to boost the prestige of written over oral literature. At the same time, in no way did it convey any of the new forms of literature and scientific thought emerging in the seventeenth and eighteenth centuries, for it was firmly rooted in the Medieval cultural heritage. The pious works which figured so prominently in its repertoire were infused with an 'ancienne sensibilité religieuse', dwelling on the life, death and Passion of Jesus Christ. Moreover, its fiction drew heavily on the worlds of chivalry, enchantment and astrology.[67] After his reading in the fields with other shepherds, Valentin Jamerey-Duval was full only of 'the fantastic prowess of Richard the Fearless, Robert the Devil, Valentin and Orsin, and the four sons of Aimon', all legendary figures from the ancient *chansons de gestes*[68] In the almanacs, some shift in content may have occurred during the eighteenth century, away from predicting the future through the stars, towards stories, current affairs and empirical knowledge. However, during the nineteenth century there was a renewed stress on astrology. And from the Restoration period onwards, the whole corpus of the chap-books was increasingly swamped by short novels, which, like the earlier heroic tales, satisfied a popular taste for the melodramatic.[69] The broadsheets that

---

[64] Jamerey-Duval, *Mémoires*, p. 23; Audoux, *Marie-Claire*, p. 153.

[65] Brékilien, *Paysans bretons*, pp. 90–3; Hélias, *Cheval d'orgueil*, pp. 140–1.

[66] Roger Muchembled argues that, under the *ancien régime*, *littérature de colportage* acted as a channel for the dominant values in society. Unable to supervise village youth in the schools, the ruling groups fed them a 'sort of mass culture', which alienated them from the older popular culture, and encouraged resignation to the existing order. See his *Culture populaire*, pp. 345–59. For more nuanced views, see Mandrou, *La Bibliothèque bleue*, pp. 9–23, 149–63; and Marais, 'Littérature et cultures populaires', *passim*.

[67] Marais, 'Littérature et cultures populaires', 85–97.

[68] Jamerey-Duval, *Mémoires*, p. 192.

[69] Bollème, *Les Almanachs*, p. 39; Darmon, *Le Colportage*, pp. 158–72.

circulated in the countryside could also be seen as a reflection of the 'dreams and fears of the people', as much as the preoccupations of their masters. There was a good deal of mundane information forthcoming, with such items as the alphabet, the calendar, medical advice and model letters. But for the most part, in the words of Jean-Pierre Séguin, they preferred 'the individual to the general, the concrete to the abstract, and dream to reality'. A few heady years apart, notably the revolutionary periods of 1830 and 1848, they studiously avoided the great political debates of their day. Instead, they concentrated on anecdotal and pictur-esque accounts of supernatural interventions, strange creatures, natural disasters, notorious crimes and family quarrels.[70]

Final assessments of the 'rural cultural ghetto'[71] in which the children of the peasantry were raised have often been less than complimentary. The folklorists who flourished in the countryside after 1870 were notable for their ambivalent attitudes towards the popular culture. There was some nostalgia for a way of life that was seen to be in its death throes, or at least for those aspects of it that appealed to their conservative views on society. The peasant here emerged as something of an embodiment of all the bourgeois virtues, with his attachment to thrift, hard work and the family, not to mention his apparent predilection for festivals and games, rather than for riot and rebellion. At the same time, there was a scarcely concealed contempt for his 'primitive' customs and beliefs.[72] The upshot was to leave the peasant languishing in his parochialism, his routines and his superstitions. There was of course a grain of truth in all these observations, but little more than that.

The weight of tradition certainly bore down heavily on the villagers, being institutionalized in the passing down of knowledge from grand-parents, parents and other relatives within the family, or 'on the job'. The focus of social and cultural life was also clearly on the local community, with some broadening out towards neighbouring communes and the nearest market towns.[73] A childhood spent largely *au cul des vaches* was

---

[70] Jean Pierre Séguin, *Nouvelles à sensation: canards du XIXᵉ siècle* (Paris, 1959), *passim*.

[71] The phrase is borrowed from Vovelle, 'Education populaire', 113.

[72] For example, Félix Chapiseau, introducing his *Folk-lore de la Beauce et du Perche* in 1902, made explicit his twofold aims in writing the book. First, he wished to pass on to his sons the stories that he had heard as a child at the *veillées*. Secondly, he desired to help destroy any vestiges of these 'absurd and tenacious' ideas amongst contempories. See also Michel de Certeau, Dominique Julia and Jacques Revel, 'La Beauté de la mort: le concept de "culture populaire"', *Politique aujourd'hui* (1970), 3–23; and Jeanne Favret-Saada, *Deadly Words: Witchcraft in the Bocage* (Cambridge, 1980), pp. 227–33.

[73] General surveys in this area include Albert Dauzet, *Le Village et le paysan de France* (Paris, 1941); Claude Galarneau, 'La Mentalité paysanne en France sous l'Ancien Régime', *Revue d'histoire de l'Amérique français*, 14 (1960), 16–24; and Cholvy, 'Campagnes françaises', 155–66.

not going to do much to stimulate interests beyond the immediate surroundings; in the words of Antoine Sylvère: 'Our universe was limited to two or three leagues, which at their four cardinal points enclosed the Dore valley. We scrutinized the world with a suspicious, timid eye, observing a thousand things, most of which according to our circle did not concern us.'[74] Yet this *esprit de clocher* and attachment to routine amongst the peasantry, to adopt the usual pejorative terms, was always tempered by contacts with the outside world. Even the remotest village could expect an occasional visit from a *colporteur* or travelling artisan, who would be pressed for news of events elsewhere. On the main arteries of communication, the traffic in information would be more intense as groups of temporary migrants, soldiers and hauliers exchanged gossip with villagers along the way. There was too the possibility of a perform-ance from a mobile theatre. Deep in Provence, for example, during the First Empire, Aubin-Louis Millin noted the presence of a troupe of actors in a wretched inn at Aups, with three different plays on offer.[75] The peasants themselves travelled, either to trade at a market, or to seek work. The constant movement of young farm servants and of seasonal migrants brought a stream of information about conditions in other districts. Early in the nineteenth century, this latter influence was most in evidence in the Limousin, where the regular shuttle of stonemasons to Paris caused a few stirrings amongst the sedentary population. The capital opened the eyes of the young men to new styles of dress and to new political allegiances along class and departmental lines, some of which inevitably rubbed off on those around them.[76] As for the 'superstitiousness' of the peasantry, there is no disputing that the popular religion in rural areas was far from orthodox. To educated outsiders, it was self-evident that all the 'mad beliefs' in fantastic beings, occult forces and endless rites and taboos to stave off evil should be considered as superstitions. But the difference between religion and superstition was simply the difference between what the Church hierarchy would and would not accept, and this line moved over time.[77] By the nineteenth century, stories at the *veillées* of the devil disguising himself as a young man to carry off women, of ghosts haunting cemeteries and crossroads, of the souls of children who died before baptism taking the form of will o'the wisps or mysterious *chasses en l'air*,

[74] Sylvère, *Toinou*, p. 170.
[75] Maurice Agulhon, *The Republic in the Village* (Cambridge, 1982), p. 117.
[76] Corbin, *Limousin au XIXe siècle*, vol. 1, pp. 222–5.
[77] See Hildred Geertz, 'An Anthropology of Religion and Magic', *Journal of Interdisciplin-ary History*, 6 (1975), 71–89; Keith Thomas, 'An Anthropology of Religion and Magic II', *ibid.*, 91–109; Stuart Clark, 'French Historians and Early Modern Popular Culture', *Past and Present*, 100 (1983), 62–99. For authoritative examples of an opposing view, see Delumeau, *Catholicism*, pp. 166–72; Weber, *Peasants into French-men*, ch. 2.

were unreservedly condemned by the Church as superstitions.[78] Joining a procession round the fields with the priest during the Rogation days, as a form of intercession with God for an abundant harvest, or going to a chapel in order to invoke one of the healing saints for an illness, was considered part of a religious ceremony. But there was still some dissension within the clergy as to whether church bells should be rung during a storm, whether the shirt of a conscript could be blessed before his Conseil de Révision, or whether some of the pilgrimages to holy fountains ought to be continued.[79]

The youth group

The division of village society into successive *classes d'âge* was less in evidence during the nineteenth century than in earlier periods. The Middle Ages had seen the young, unmarried men with their own organizations, that had clearly marked them off from the world of adults on one side, and that of children on the other.[80] By the end of the *ancien régime*, these institutions had already declined in importance, some to the point of extinction. Henceforth, in place of the age categories, rural society would increasingly be permeated by the economic and social divisions of class. Seasonal migrations, and the great 'rural exodus' of the late nineteenth century, would deal further blows to the solidarity of youth. Even so, the young men of the village, those aged between sixteen and thirty or so, continued to stand as a group apart. Other members of the rural community recognized that they had particular interests, such as more time and energy for amusements than most, and a need to find a marriage partner. There was also a tacit acceptance of their traditional rôles as guardians of local morality through the institution of the *charivari*, and as moving spirits behind all festivities.[81] This framework provided by the peer group was particularly important for what might be called the character building of youth.

78 These beliefs are well documented in Besson, *Pâtre du Cantal*, pp. 14–16; Sylvère, *Toinou*, pp. 23–4; Hélias, *Cheval d'orgueil*, pp. 18–19; C. Fraysse, *Le Folklore du Baugeois* (Bauge, 1906), pp. 48–63; Chapiseau, *Folk-lore de la Beauce*, pp. 197–220, 312–49; Jacques-Marie Rougé, *Le Folklore de la Touraine* (Tours, 1931), ch. 8; Drouillet, *Folklore du Nivernais*, vol. 4, *passim*.

79 Nadine-Josette Chaline, 'La Religion populaire en Normandie au XIX⁰ siècle', in Dubosq *et al.*, *Religion populaire*, pp. 171–8; Bouteiller, *Médecine populaire*, ch. 2; Hilaire, *Une chrétienté*, ch. 2; Cholvy, 'Diocèse de Montpellier', pp. 591–8.

80 Natalie Zemon Davies, 'The Reasons of Misrule: Youth Groups and Charivaris in Sixteenth-Century France', *Past and Present*, 50 (1971), 41–75; Bercé, *Fête et révolte*, pp. 16–20.

81 See Maurice Agulhon, *Pénitents et francs-maçons dans l'ancienne Provence* (Paris, 1968), *passim*; Van Gennep, *Manuel de folklore français*, vol. 1, pp. 196–207; Bercé, *Fête et révolte*, pp. 37–52; Crubellier, *L'Enfance et jeunesse*, pp. 101–10.

Village life offered plenty of opportunities for young males to develop and display their physical prowess. Defending the honour of the village through combat, which had begun earlier in life with the *batailles enfantines*, continued through youth, receiving the quiet assent of the population at large, if not of the local authorities.[82] Vicious brawls between hostile groups of youths continually flared up at festivals, dances and weddings. Entirely typical was the fighting that occurred during the wedding of Pierre-Alain Hélias and Marie-Jeanne Le Goff at Pouldreuzic, a little before the First World War. The cause of trouble was the partiality allegedly shown by the local girls to 'outsiders' from neighbouring Plozévet. As a result, 'there were bitter words, challenges, a few individual fists flying, exchanges of those insults that can only be washed away in the first blood'.[83] Sports provided a more respectable channel for such rivalries, though they were not always so very different in character from outright warfare. Olivier Perrin noted the violence associated with *le jeu de crosse* (hurling) in Brittany during the 1830s. Lasting for up to half a day, the original game with sticks and a ball frequently descended into fights. Nonetheless, he concluded that it was all good for the young, since it taught them courage and skill.[84] Other activities at the *fêtes* tested the physical abilities of youth on a more individual basis. The young themselves organized a series of games and contests for these occasions. Athletics events included wrestling, jumping and various kinds of races. In the Mantois and Vexin, for example, there were running races, whose length depended on the age and sex of those involved, plus donkey, sack and wheelbarrow races.[85] Farcical games were also to be found everywhere in France, including climbing a greasy pole for a prize (*le mât de cocagne*), picking out a coin from soot at the bottom of a pit with one's teeth, and decapitating a live goose or other farmyard animal. The latter was known in the Haut-Vivarais as *le tir à l'oie*: 'Young men riding horses bareback used to try to cut off the head of a goose with a stave or old sabre. The goose was suspended by its feet from a rope strung across a road. To complicate the game, the competitors were sometimes blindfolded.'[86] Finally, dancing was an activity which in some regions was left largely to the young, unmarried men and women. In the Auvergne,

---

[82] For ritual battles between children surviving into the nineteenth century, see Van Gennep, *Manuel de folklore française*, vol. 1, p. 169; d'Abbadie d'Arrast, *Le Pays basque*, p. 149; Besson, *Pâtre du Cantal*, p. 17; Hélias, *Cheval d'orgueil*, pp. 302–3; Louis Pergaud, *La Guerre des boutons* (Paris, 1963), pp. 264–5.
[83] Hélias, *Cheval d'orgueil*, p. 39. In the same vein, see Chaulanges, *Le Roussel*, p. 104; and Drouillet, *Folklore du Nivernais*, vol. 1, pp. 97–9.
[84] Perrin, *Galérie bretonne*, vol. 1, p. 121.
[85] Bougeatre, *Mantois et Vexin*, pp. 241–3.
[86] Charrié, *Folklore du Haut-Vivarais*, p. 144.

Provence and above all the Pays Basque, *la jeunesse* spent a long time in advance of each festival preparing the steps for elaborate dances.

Many of these customs came to be seen as barbaric, or just plain absurd, over the course of the nineteenth century. However, the age group and its culture managed to adapt to changing circumstances. In Provence, the 'urbanized' villages and the cultural traditions of the 'domaine d'Oc' were particularly conducive to sociability amongst the young. The *chambrettes*, which sprang up during the first half of the century, could be seen as heirs to the old *abbés de jeunesse*. These were rooms in bars or private houses where young men especially used to meet to pass the time drinking, gambling and talking. They were natural breeding grounds for new political ideas, and were associated with the spread of democratic and socialist ideologies around the 1848 Revolution. There was, indeed, a certain 'politicization' of youth culture in this region, attributable to the increasing differentiation along class lines of youth groups.[87] Elsewhere in France this Mediterranean form of association did not take a hold, but there was always the possibility of meeting informally in a *cabaret* or at a weekly dance: institutions that flourished in the countryside at the end of the century.[88] Moreover, the establishment of military conscription during the 1790s created the basis for a new form of solidarity amongst young men of the same age: the *groupement des conscrits*. With the risk of seven years' military service looming over them, successive cohorts of youths tended to find common interests, together with their so-called *conscrites*. Appearance before the Conseil de Révision was accompanied by a succession feasts, processions and rituals that were intended to guarantee a *bon numero* at the lottery.[89] This event was an important staging post in the early life of a peasant. Once the hurdle of the *tirage au sort* was cleared, he was safely in the home straight towards adulthood. Upon marriage and the first child, male and female alike were considered to have moved from youth to the next stage of life. The long apprenticeship in the rural community was over.

Rural education in its social context

For most of the nineteenth century, then, the type of education prevailing in the countryside relied on informal rather than formal methods of

[87] Agulhon, *Republic in the Village*, pp. 141–4; Lucienne Roubin, *Chambrettes des provençaux* (Paris, 1970), *passim*.
[88] Bougeatre, *Mantois et Vexin*, pp. 224–7; Grenadou and Prévost, *Grenadou*, pp. 37–9; Hilaire, *Une chrétienté*, vol. 1, p. 84; Michael R. Marrus, 'Social Drinking in the Belle Epoque', *Journal of Social History*, 7 (1974), 130.
[89] See, for example, Van Gennep, *Manuel de folklore français*, vol. 1, pp. 213–15; Bougeatre, *Mantois et Vexin*, pp. 237–40; Charrié, *Folklore du Haut-Vivarais*, p. 34; Drouillet, *Folklore du Nivernais*, vol. 1, pp. 99–100.

instruction, on personal reputations established through the grapevine rather than on paper qualifications. Skills and values were acquired gradually, by participating in the work and leisure activities of adults and other young people. And if the folk wisdom of white-haired villagers was yielding ground to the *culture savante* of the schoolteachers, vocational training continued in its 'apprenticeship' form well into the twentieth century. The hesitancy in accepting a rôle for the primary schools in large areas of rural France, particularly during the first half of the century, was frequently deplored by School Inspectors. They wrote of the ignorance, indifference and thoughtlessness of parents, as well as of their poverty, in tones ranging from mild sympathy to righteous indignation. Thus in 1847 the Assistant Inspector for the Haute-Saône informed his superiors:

Most of the children who are not profiting from the benefits of instruction are deprived of it precisely by those who have the greatest interest in the matter. Guilty of the most criminal indifference, the parents, whose instruction was either non-existent or very neglected during their early years, think that the children will always have had enough, if they are given as much as them, and they act accordingly. This seems to me to be indifference beyond measure.[90]

But the Inspectorate had vested interests of their own, and the possibility remains that parental decisions were based on a 'canny comparison of costs and returns'.[91]

What concerned the peasant most about the education of his children was the extent to which it would equip them for their future jobs. Whether or not the school would have any substantial rôle to play depended on the type of work envisaged for them later in life. If the expectation was that they would have to seek employment in the towns, then there was a strong case for spending money on schooling. A few artisan groups had a chance of using skills acquired in the countryside on the urban labour market: for example, the silk weavers of southern France who moved into Lyons, or the construction workers of the Limousin and Normandy who regularly migrated to Paris. But the general run of agricultural and rural handicraft skills were redundant in the towns, leaving only the most menial jobs open to those with a traditional rustic background. Literacy skills, by contrast, could profitably be applied in a number of urban outlets. These included organizing sub-contracting work on a construction site, securing a

---

[90] AN, F^{17} 12203, report of 19 January 1847. This was a reply to the circular from the Ministry of Education, dated 14 November 1846, which began by asking the Mayor of each commune to estimate the number of children not attending school under the following headings: disability, parental indifference, distance and inadequate facilities. The Inspectors often added 'indigence'.

[91] C. A. Anderson, 'Patterns and Variability in the Distribution and Diffusion of Schooling', in C. A. Anderson and M. J. Bowman (eds.), *Education and Economic Development* (London, 1968), p. 328.

white-collar job in an office, becoming a *gendarme* or *cheminot* or starting a training as a priest or a schoolteacher.[92] Many of the arguments that erupted within peasant families over schooling hung on this issue of aspirations for the younger generation. During the early part of the century, in the Creuse, the mother and grandfather of Martin Nadaud's autobiographical character, Léonard, lined themselves up forcefully against any outlays on formal education. The mother insisted that she needed the boy to work in the fields, whilst the grandfather and several other peasants who joined in the affray insisted that learning in the schools brought nothing more than the capacity to write a few letters and to carry a book to Mass. In the words of the grandfather, 'Neither my brothers, nor you, nor I have ever learned our letters, and yet we have always had our daily bread.' However, Léonard's father worked as a stonemason in Paris during the summer months, and he intended that his son should follow in his footsteps. His desire that the boy prepare himself for life in the *chantiers* of the capital through some elementary instruction therefore won the day.[93] At the other end of the century, in the Vivarais, the same kind of debate went the other way in the fictional Baudet family, depicted by the novelist Jules Reboul. Baudet *père* revealed himself willing to make sacrifices to turn his son into a *savant*, in the hope that 'later he will find a position, where he will suffer less than us'. But the mother would have none of it, arguing, not unrealistically, that jobs where 'one walks with cane in hand' were not within the reach of their family.[94]

For those expected to remain on the land, the case for investing in formal education was less clear cut. Some sections of rural society did have a direct incentive to master literacy skills, particularly those whose trading activities involved them in writing letters, reading notices and keeping account books. Independent craftsmen in the countryside fell into this category, and so too did the big, capitalist farmers already emerging in various parts of France by the end of the *ancien régime*. In upper Normandy, for example, there were the large, wheat-growing farmers of the Vexin supplying the Parisian market, and the cattle raisers of the Bray, also locked into the trade circuits of the capital, who were by the 1780s close to 100 per cent literacy.[95] During the nineteenth century, the

---

[92] See above, pp. 44–5.

[93] Nadaud, *Léonard*, pp. 27–8. Interestingly, in 1841 the Recteur of the Academy of Limoges observed in a letter to the Minister of Education that 'the emigration, which by the way does not begin until the age of thirteen or fourteen, is less harmful than one might think for instruction. The experience soon reveals to the migrants the necessity of knowing something for success'; AN, F[17] 9308, letter of 31 December, 1841. See also Corbin, *Limousin au XIXe siècle*, vol. 1, pp. 321–35.

[94] Reboul, *Jacques Baudet*, pp. 52–3.

[95] Muriel Jeorger, 'L'Alphabétisation dans l'ancien diocèse de Rouen au XVIIe et au XVIIIe siècles', in Furet and Ozouf, *Lire et écrire*, vol. 2, pp. 101–51.

development of communications and trading opportunities in rural areas drew an increasing proportion of the peasantry into production for the market, giving further encouragement to the spread of literacy. We may recall the independent farmers of the Eure-et-Loir, three-quarters literate by the 1830s, and their counterparts in the Cher, who, although far less literate, were experiencing a faster rate of growth in their literacy scores than the agricultural labourers below them.[96] Nonetheless, for the majority of peasants, whose trading activities were of only marginal significance in the family economy, this type of pressure to send their offspring to the elementary schools could hardly have been intense.

Officialdom itself proved inconsistent on the benefits to be anticipated from education for those cultivating the land. During the 1850s, the School Inspectorate was invited to consider the influence of instruction on the wealth of the country. Most took the line that might be expected of them: the Inspector in the Nord suggested, 'In spreading enlightenment, it makes the farmer less of a slave to routine, and more qualified to understand rational procedures in agriculture'; his colleague in the *arrondissement* of Lunéville wrote along similar lines, 'It is understood that hands directed intelligently produce more than hands left to their own activities.' But not all were so convinced. Inspectors in the Aisne, for example, were inclined to think that instruction had little influence on wealth or poverty in the countryside.[97] The peasant tended to agree with this latter view, although expressing himself in more down-to-earth form. When Antoine Sylvère was shown off as a child 'able to read like a lawyer', his uncle was unimpressed: 'Why know so much? asked uncle Pierre. I have always heard it said that a man knew enough when he was capable of digging a hole big enough to bury a donkey in.'[98] Such scepticism over the returns to be expected on investment in schooling, especially beyond a very basic literacy level, was entirely rational during the nineteenth century, and well into the twentieth. Given a rudimentary level of technology in peasant agriculture, practical know-how acquired 'on the job' was more important than theoretical knowledge, and increases in output depended more on material than 'intellectual' investments. Hence expecting children to contribute through their work to the prosperity of the family holding, rather than sending them to school for an extended period, could be justified. Returning to the dispute within the Baudet family, the maternal argument for setting the boy Jacques to work

[96] Corbin, 'Conscrits du Cher et de l'Eure-et-Loir', 108.
[97] AN, F[17] 9330, 'Rapport sur l'instruction primaire dans le département du Nord', 1 May 1856; AN, F[17] 9329, 'Rapport sur l'état de l'instruction primaire, arrond. de Lunéville', 1 January 1856; AN, F[17] 9321, 'Résumé des rapports de Messieurs les Inspecteurs primaires du département de l'Aisne', 1855.
[98] Sylvère, *Toinou*, p. 52.

was outlined with admirable lucidity: 'His place is here. It is only a matter of leaving him a slightly larger plot of land, but you scarcely think of this. He will earn a few sous, and that will help us to set him up with a good position.'[99] On top of all this, the smaller peasantry had their freedom of choice effectively limited by poverty. At mid-century, officials frequently noted the difficulties faced by peasants owning or renting a small plot of land, which left them in straightened circumstances, but ruled out eligibility for free places at school for their offspring.[100] However, the main problem for this group was not so much the school pence, which could usually be absorbed, but the inability to dispense with the work of a child. To avoid the expense of hiring a farm servant or day labourer, the only way out for parents, particularly when schooling became compulsory, was to insist on a long period of work during the summer months, and to give the children various tasks before and after school.[101]

Moving on down to the agricultural labourers, and others obliged to spend much of the year working for wages, the depressing influence of poverty on schooling was even more in evidence. In principle, the labourer might be thought to have had little to lose and everything to gain from some formal education. But the precariousness of family budgets forced many children out to work with little or no time available for school. The close link between income levels and attendance at class was starkly revealed during periods of economic crisis: during the mid-1840s, for example, several School Inspectors noted the falling away in numbers at school as the price of bread rose.[102] A free place did not always help either, because the additional expense of paper, books and pens was often too much for poor families. In 1837, the Inspector in the Drôme presented a miserable picture of children from this background first languishing on the school benches for lack of materials, and then, humiliated by the taunts of *indigent* from their classmates, quickly with-

---

99 Reboul, *Jacques Baudet*, pp. 52–3. See also Jégouzo and Brangeon, *Les Paysans et l'école*, p. 9; and Lucien Bernot and René Blancard, *Nouville: un village français* (Paris, 1953), pp. 129–30. The latter work, a study of life in a Normandy village during the years 1949 to 1950, noted the contrasting attitudes of industrial workers and farmers to the school. The workers expected a great deal from education, seeing it as a way of strengthening their hand against the bosses. The farmers, on the other hand, were suspicious of it, accepting the importance of not being thought a 'donkey', but fearing that their children would become disaffected from agricultural work.

100 See, for example, AN, F^{17} 9307, School Inspector's report, Indre-et-Loire, 10 April 1840; AN, F^{17} 12203, School Inspector's report, Basses-Pyrénées, 1 March 1847.

101 For an autobiographical account, see Carlès, *Une soupe*, pp. 57–76.

102 AN, F^{17} 9311, 'Rapports des inspecteurs primaires', 1846–7. For a detailed local study on this point, there is Mary Jo Maynes, 'Work or School? Youth and the Family in the Midi in the Early Nineteenth Century', in Baker and Harrigan, *The Making of Frenchmen*, pp. 115–33.

drawing in disgust.[103] With the prospect of sending their children out on to the labour market, the poor also had to bear in mind the attitudes of employers. These were not necessarily favourable to the labourer with educational achievements behind him. Big farmers were obsessed with the notion that spreading a little learning amongst the plebs would given them ideas above their station, and hence cause them to give up manual work on the land. During the 1830s, one of the Guizot Inspectors reported that in the Gironde 'several Mayors have declared to me that the Médoc needs vine-growers and not readers; they think that a peasant who can read becomes a farmer who is disobedient, idle and argumentative'.[104] Some families were prepared to brazen it out, and, by dint of scrimping and saving, to see their offspring through elementary school, and even beyond. But the majority continued along the traditional route to a job. This involved impressing potential employers with evidence of good character, plus physical strength and co-ordination. These latter qualities were necessary for the prestigious positions of carter, blacksmith, stonemason or carpenter as opposed to the despised jobs of weaver and tailor.[105] According to Pierre-Jakez Hélias, in the Pays Bigoudin the whole population of a village measured the growth of its young, watching the little tests children put themselves through, such as pushing loaded wheelbarrows or facing up to heavy waves in the sea. Later, during adolescence, there remained a serious undertone to apparently frivolous activities. The *maîtres de ferme* judged their local youth according to a number of yardsticks, including their 'repertoire of Breton and French songs, their accomplishment in dancing the gavotte, their stength and dexterity in popular games', and also their attendance at church, and the frequency of their visits to the inn.[106] In short, the rural community had its own methods of conferring status, without recourse to the certificates of the schools and colleges.

If the major preoccupation of the peasant was preparing his children for work, the *notables* of Paris and the provinces were more interested in using education to 'civilize' the population. In the words of the Guizot administration, this meant using the school as 'an instrument of popular moralization, political stabilization, social conservatism, and economic

---

103 AD Drôme, 10 T 23, annual report for 1837.
104 Lorain, *Tableau de l'instruction*, p. 18 and n. 74. On the hostility of many rural *notables* to elementary schooling, and in particular their reluctance to channel municipal funds into it, see Gontard, *L'Enseignement primaire*, pp. 343–8, 533–8; *idem*, *Les Ecoles primaires*, pp. 38–9; Thabault, *Mazières-en-Gâtine*, pp. 55–6; Guillaumin, *Vie d'un simple*, pp. 176–7.
105 Perrin, *Galérie bretonne*, vol. 1, p. 100; Chapiseau, *Folk-lore de la Beauce*, vol. 1, p. 96.
106 Hélias, *Cheval d'orgueil*, pp. 23, 265, 303–8. See also Chaulanges, *Le Roussel*, p. 89.

progress'.[107] The 'civilization' on offer to the peasantry was a humble form, very different from that of the middle and upper classes. Until the Third Republic era, the elementary school was not seen to be a stepping-stone to further studies at the secondary and higher levels, but as a closed system, which would reinforce rather than weaken existing social divisions. As we have seen, the peasant would be instructed in basic literacy, and given a heavy dose of moral and religious education. Although in practice even this limited programme would prove difficult to achieve, the underlying aim was clear: to control and discipline, through the 'moral' force of the school system, a population rendered turbulent and ferocious by its ignorance.[108] This leads to a number of questions, including how the peasant felt about this effort to 'civilize' him, and why, before the compulsion of the *loi Ferry* in 1882, he was increasingly prepared to part with his money and the services of his children in the interests of the school. To find answers, it must be borne in mind that besides being under direct attack from external forces, the popular culture of the peasantry was crumbling from within during the nineteenth century, undermined by the creeping influence of economic and social change in the villages. As a consequence, parts of the traditional 'apprenticeship' on the land were taken over by specialized educational institutions more rapidly than the vocational training element: but not without some resistance.

The external attacks on the popular culture of the villages were formidable. From the seventeenth century onwards, the rural community found itself more and more out of step with the dynamic forces of the town, the capitalist system, the centralizing State and the post-tridentine Catholic Church.[109] The school was in the vanguard of the long campaign to conquer the hearts and minds of the peasantry, and the rôle of the *instituteur* was clearly defined: to vaunt the written over the oral culture, scientific method over custom, order and discipline over 'licentiousness'. There is no doubting the prestige of the learned culture, nor the resources at its disposal, leading ultimately to the institution of free, compulsory primary education. Yet, in much of southern and western France, it was not until the second half of the nineteenth century that the schools succeeded in gaining access to the children of the smaller peasants and agricultural labourers, and only at that late period could the teaching profession plausibly be described as 'bourgeois' in its attitudes.[110] Moreover, the countervailing forces of the rural community were far from

107 Gontard, *Les Ecoles primaires*, p. 4.
108 *Ibid.*, pp. 233–5; Prost, *Histoire et l'enseignement*, pp. 10–11; Johnson, *Guizot*, pp. 111–12; Anderson, *Education in France*, pp. 8–15.
109 Muchembled, *Culture populaire*, p. 220.
110 Cf. Crubellier, *Histoire culturelle*, p. 85, which raises the possibility of a 'bourgeois spirit' to the school even before Guizot.

exhausted. Listening to adult conversations at work or during the *veillées*, village children were exposed to a series of subversive opinions. Always 'in the air' were arguments between Bonapartists, Republicans and other political dissenters; expressions of the peasants' hatred for the rich and powerful; and the long-standing resentment of military service.[111] Antoine Sylvère went as far as to call the Pont des Feignants in Ambert his 'second school', rivalling that of the Christian Brothers. The bridge was the habitual meeting place for the outcasts of society: Le Pas Pressé, who could never reconcile himself to regular work; Le Galérien, an accomplished poacher whose fearsome nickname derived from a spell in a military prison; the Goret brothers, whose detailed knowledge of geography stemmed from a string of convictions across France for begging and vagrancy; and Le Pantomin, a labourer in the gasworks revered by the ten-year-old Toinou as 'the only master that I recognized'. In this company, Toinou and his friends picked up a very different message from that of the official school system:

This dissident circle held blasphemous views which contested the sacred rights of wealth. Ministers of religion appeared as parasites with refined tastes, delicate skins and exceedingly demanding digestive systems. According to Le Pantomin, they frequented houses where abundance reigned. The magistrature was not spared. Justice was judged. The life of the bourgeois was scrutinized.[112]

Toinou admitted his inability to resist the crushing weight of authority arrayed against such sacrilegious views, but he remembered being left with the confused feeling that 'God had an odd way of handling things in abandoning to damnation the best of men, for whom we had such admiration and affection.'[113]

Changes affecting the underlying material conditions of the peasantry had their own insidious influence on the popular culture. Values and beliefs that were appropriate to a closed community, where life was dominated by the rhythms and the poverty of traditional agriculture, could soon appear outmoded in the context of a more developed economy. Declining death rates from the middle of the eighteenth century, more roads and railways from the 1830s and 1840s, the beginnings of mechanized methods in agriculture and the growing volume of cheap printed matter flowing into the villages during the late nineteenth century all combined to undermine the old way of life. Reading and writing became useful for such purposes as keeping up with election campaigns, corresponding with distant members of the family or following national

---

[111] These are illustrated in Honoré de Balzac, *Les Paysans* (Paris, 1970), p. 105; Zola, *The Earth*, pp. 80–98; Guillaumin, *Vie d'un simple*, p. 18.
[112] Sylvère, *Toinou*, pp. 175–6.   [113] *Ibid.*, p. 176.

events in the press. The oral tradition of the *veillées* faded in the face of competition from books and newspapers. And a mechanistic view of the universe began to prevail, as man came to master rather than be at the mercy of his environment.[114] Louis Pergaud, in *La Guerre des boutons*, allowed the children of his village gang some imprint from the new age emerging before the First World War. To the suggestion that crows and owls were birds of ill omen, the leader, Lebrac, replied contemptuously that this was an 'old wives' tale', and that although such superstitions were good for people in older times, with civilization there was science to replace them.[115] Sooner or later, according to region, the peasant would welcome the village school as a source of emancipation in a changing world, even if his demands on it were usually very limited. At the same time he would lose interest in important elements of his cultural heritage, as shown by the declining interest in the *veillée* during the late nineteenth century, and the increasingly self-conscious, 'folkloric' character of the *fêtes*. However, this is not to conclude that the peasant began the century as a 'cultural and political aboriginal, like to beasts and children', and ended it 'calculating' and 'rational'.[116] Such a polarization accepts uncritically the polemics of the educational establishment of the period, and risks exaggerating the nature of the cultural transformation. *A priori*, the assertion that generations of peasants failed to surpass the mental level of children is as absurd as it is patronizing. The reasons why men acted certainly changed over the period, but there was always reasoning behind their actions.[117] As for the calculating spirit of the peasants, this was well established by the middle of the century. During the 1840s, Balzac was moved to observe, 'Self-interest has become, especially since 1789, the only motive for their ideas; for them it is never a question of knowing whether an action is legal or immoral, but of whether it is profitable.'[118]

Conclusion

When an industrial society began to emerge in France, at the turn of the nineteenth century, the long 'battle for the souls of children' was well under way.[119] But it was the towns rather than the villages which led the

114 This is a central theme of Thabault, *Mazières-en-Gâtine*, and Weber, *Peasants into Frenchmen*.
115 Pergaud, *Guerre des boutons*, pp. 252–3.
116 Weber, *Peasants into Frenchmen*, pp. 5–6, 495; Crubellier, *Histoire culturelle*, p. 85.
117 Clark, 'French Historians', 74–82.
118 Honoré de Balzac, *Les Paysans*, p. 105. See also Charles Tilly, 'Did the Cake of Custom Break?', in John M. Merriman (ed.), *Consciousness and Class Experience in Nineteenth-Century Europe* (New York, 1979), pp. 17–44.
119 See Georges Duby and Armand Wallon (eds.), *Histoire de la France rurale*, vol. 2, *L'Age classique des paysans, 1340–1789* (Paris, 1975), pp. 505–45.

way in spreading new cultural forms, based upon orthodox Catholicism, a national consciousness and the written word. The elementary school was only beginning to make its mark in the countryside at this period. Considerable material obstacles remained over much of the country, above all in the south and west, with too few schools for the dispersed population, and the poverty of many parents. Perhaps more importantly, large sections of the rural population had yet to be convinced that formal education was a worthwhile investment, holding as they did the view that 'the sun rises for the ignorant as for the learned'.[120] Meanwhile, the old informal methods of education continued to hold sway, revolving around the family, the youth group and the local community. During the course of the nineteenth century, their position would be eroded in certain important respects, but once again it was the towns that made the running with the popular culture of the artisan communities in the forefront of change.

[120] Lorain, *Tableau de l'instruction*, p. 15.

Part Two

The impact of industrialization

Chapter 4

Child labour in the industrial setting[1]

The final emergence of the capitalist system during the eighteenth and nineteenth centuries transformed the conditions of employment for children in the manufacturing sector. The critical change for children was the separation of enterprise from the family. This originated in the unprecedented scale of production and distribution required by capitalism. Obstacles to trade such as guilds and privileges were swept away by the State, and, after 1789 in particular, free competition became the order of the day. Commercial networks became increasingly elaborate, as roads, canals and eventually railways revolutionized communications, and as a merchant class grew to maturity around the great fairs and maritime ports. Industry responded to the challenge of wider markets by adopting new technologies and new forms of organization. Domestic workshops in trades as diverse as textiles, leather and metalworking first became drawn into the national and international circuits of commercial capitalism, and subsequently yielded ground in the nineteenth century to the factory system. In these circumstances, the independence of the artisan household was whittled away by mercantile and industrial interests. Sooner or later, in the majority of handicraft trades, it lost its capacity to trade in local markets, to transmit skills to its young and, most fundamentally, to own the tools of its trade. Labour, including child labour, now had to go on to the open market for work. This development aroused a good deal of comment by contemporaries, much of it overtly hostile. In 1840 Eugène Buret contrasted the rehabilitation of labour achieved by earlier generations with the theory of wages proposed by the political economists: 'Is the consequence, I ask, to sell off labour at a discount, to put it up for auction, to subject it without protection to all the caprices of competition, I was going to say to the brutal violence of industrial war, as a raw commodity?'[2] The background to the work of children in nineteenth-century industry was thus the interplay of the notorious forces of supply

[1] An early version of this chapter appeared as 'The Market for Child Labour in Nineteenth-Century France', *History*, 66 (1981), 34–49.
[2] Buret, *De la misère*, vol. 1, p. 48.

and demand, personified respectively by working-class parents and industrial employers. The evolution of these forces is the subject-matter of this chapter.

The composition of the industrial labour force

Conventional wisdom would have it that the early stages of industrialization brought something of an invasion of the shop floor by women and children. In the words of Edouard Dolléans:

Female and child labour provides a well-known manifestation of technological unemployment. The introduction of mechanization not only provoked a brutal expulsion of labour, in so far as the new machines took over tasks previously performed by several workers. It equally contributed to the replacement of adult males by female and child labour, the importance of the physical effort required for work being reduced by the machine.[3]

This view can be traced back to the social enquiries of the 1830s. Early investigators into the conditions of the urban working classes were impressed by the way steam power, mechanization and the division of labour reduced the premium on skill and physical strength, permitting the large-scale employment of what were termed 'inferior' or 'imperfect' workers.[4] A scarcity of data on the composition of the industrial labour force makes it difficult to verify this type of assertion, but a close look at the evidence available does suggest exaggeration. What emerges unequivocally, over the broad sweep of the nineteenth century, is a progressive decline in child labour.

One possible implication of the conventional view can quickly be dismissed: that the development of the industrial sector during the early nineteenth century was responsible for an increase in the proportion of women and children who worked. If it is assumed that in pre-industrial times most of them were already employed productively, then there would have been little scope for an increase in participation rates, and a consequent change in the composition of the labour force. The French census did not publish information on the distribution of the active population by age groups until 1896, but a sample taken in a number of communes from the census registers of 1851 points, if anything, to a slight

---

[3] Dolléans and Dehove, *Histoire du travail en France*, vol. 1, p. 167, cited by Maurice Bouvier-Ajam, *Histoire du travail en France depuis la Révolution* (Paris, 1969), pp. 134–5.
[4] Villermé, *Tableau de l'état*, vol. 2, p. 311; Buret, *De la misère*, vol. 2, p. 152; Joseph-Marie de Gérando, *Des progrès de l'industrie considérés dans leurs rapports avec la moralité de la classe ouvrière* (Paris, 1841), p. 53; Charles Dupin, *Du travail des enfants qu'emploient les ateliers, les usines et les manufactures* (2 parts, Paris, 1840 and 1847), part 1, p. 5.

Table 4.1 Participation rates of youth in selected communes, 1851

	Munster (Haut-Rhin)	Sotteville-lès-Rouen (Seine-Inf.)	Caudebec-lès-Elbeuf (Seine-Inf.)	Taulignan (Drôme)	Dieulefit (Drôme)	Baccarat (Meurthe)	Canton of Lunéville SE (Meurthe)
Age group 10–14							
Occupation listed	34.69	34.62	50.80	43.48	45.59	44.62	40.96
Living on parents	3.06	2.88	18.25	56.52	54.41	55.38	59.04
No information	62.25	62.50	30.95	–	–	–	–
Total	100.00	100.00	100.00	100.00	100.00	100.00	100.00
Age group 15–19							
Occupation listed	62.34	68.38	89.84	92.21	83.95	96.25	84.49
Living on parents	2.37	3.42	3.13	7.79	16.05	3.75	15.51
No information	35.29	28.20	7.03	–	–	–	–
Total	100.00	100.00	100.00	100.00	100.00	100.00	100.00

Source: census registers for 1851.

decline in employment amongst the young. A remarkably similar pattern emerges from a variety of regions and types of industrial town. As might be expected, those aged fifteen to nineteen years were, in the large majority of cases, found to be working. In the younger age group ten to fourteen, somewhere between a third and a half of the population was listed with an occupation.[5] This latter result needs careful consideration. On the one hand, it is undoubtedly an understatement, since the casual or seasonal work generally undertaken by the young barely lent itself to the neat categories of the occupational census. For example, the offspring of handloom weavers, retailers and innkeepers were expected to help out in the family enterprise, yet their work was almost impossible to label. Moreover, in some of the communes, notably Munster and Sotteville, the hard-pressed census enumerators evidently had little time for the details of child employment. On the other hand, it may well register a shift in the balance of childhood activities, away from work and towards school. Statistical evidence of rising attendance rates at primary school level during the first half of the nineteenth century does indicate, despite its wide margin of error, that formal education was biting more deeply into the working-class existence.[6] During the second half of the century, the decline in the proportion of children who worked came more clearly into focus. By 1896 the participation rate amongst the age group ten to fourteen was down to one fifth, and compulsory schooling legislation meant that nearly all of these must have been aged thirteen and fourteen.[7]

From this perspective, given a certain stability or even decline in the proportion of young women and children in the active population during the period up to 1850, the 'invasion' thesis becomes difficult to sustain. It would have to be proved either that there was a swelling of the ranks of the 'reserve army' of unemployed by adult males in particular, as they were displaced from a series of industries without compensatory employment opportunities elsewhere, or that female and juvenile workers outstripped men in the shift from agricultural employment. The former seems most unlikely, since spinning, a huge employer of female labour, was one of the first industries to be affected by technological unemployment in the late eighteenth and early nineteenth centuries. The latter cannot be ruled out entirely, since it was the young who tended to move from the villages to the towns in search of work. A survey of children under sixteen in the cotton mills of Mulhouse during the 1840s revealed that a majority had been born outside the town, notably in the smaller

5 The equivalent figure from the 1851 census in Britain was 25 per cent. This does not necessarily point to a higher participation rate in France, since our sample is biased towards small industrial towns where the census registers were exceptionally informative.

6 See above, p. 62.

7 Calculated from Toutain, *Le Population de la France*, pp. 112–21.

manufacturing centres and villages of Alsace. Thus in the *filature de coton* owned by Charles Naegely, only one in six of the 173 children listed had been born in Mulhouse or the adjacent commune of Dornach.[8] Yet even this type of evidence cannot be taken as conclusive proof that youth led the way out of agriculture and into the factories. Most of the factory children had probably come into the towns with their parents, and some may well have had an industrial background in their native communes. In any case, local studies from towns as far apart as Marseilles and Nancy, Bordeaux and Lyons suggest that newly arrived rural migrants avoided the factories, preferring jobs such as general labouring, domestic service, trading or clerical work.[9] The most that can be salvaged from the thesis, and it is an important remnant, is the conclusion that there was a growing *intensification* of work for children during the opening phase of industrialization.[10] As successive generations moved from their casual occupations in the fields to the full-time jobs on offer in the factories, the pace and regularity of effort required from them was likely to be stepped up. This would help to explain the feeling amongst early social investigators that industrial society was foisting a more prominent rôle on to the youthful element in the labour force.

Turning now directly to the share of the industrial labour force accounted for by women and children, the nineteenth century certainly brought major upheavals for various industries, even if the accepted pattern is often difficult to discern. The calico-printing industry of Alsace was one of the first to assemble large numbers of children. In 1806, to take an extreme example, seven-eighths of the 500 workers in the Gros-Davillier mill at Wesserling were found to be under the age of sixteen.[11] Yet this was a 'new' industry, organized on a large scale from its origins in the middle of the eighteenth century and so there was no question of making adult males redundant. Mechanized cotton spinning was also remarkable in the early stages for the female and above all the juvenile stamp to its labour force.[12] A rare insight into the age structure of this industry comes, once again, from Alsace, with a census of factory hands held in 1822 and 1823. The spinning mill of Heilmann Frères, located at Ribeauvillé, was a

8   AM Mulhouse, F VI Ea 3.
9   G. Friedmann (ed.), *Villes et campagnes* (Paris, 1953), pp. 159–60, 167–8; Guillaume, *Population de Bordeaux*, pp. 68–9; Lequin, *Les Ouvriers de la région lyonnaise*, vol. 1, pp. 205–71.
10 See below, ch. 5.
11 Charles Schmidt, 'Notes sur le travail des enfants dans les manufactures pendant la Révolution', *Bulletin de la Commission de recherche et de publication des documents relatifs à la vie économique de la Révolution* (1910), p. 221, n. 1.
12 See Charles Ballot, *L'Introduction de machinisme dans l'industrie française* (Lille, 1923), *passim*; Charles Schmidt, 'Les Débuts de l'industrie cotonnière en France, 1780–1806', *Revue d'histoire économique et sociale*, 7 (1914), 26–55.

typical case. By far the largest group in the mill was composed of young, unmarried women: 102 of the 260 employees were females, aged between sixteen and twenty-four years. If other adults were of minor numerical significance, the children were much in evidence, accounting for over 40 per cent of the personnel.[13] Amongst the other mills investigated there were naturally considerable variations, but generally children under the age of sixteen formed approximately one third of all workers.[14] In the case of spinning, the mechanization of the preparatory stages of production did undermine the position of certain groups of male workers. The breaking open of fibres, and the carding or combing of cotton and wool were all heavy, tiring jobs that were usually done by men. With mechanized methods, it was a simple task for a child or a young woman to feed raw cotton into the drums of a *batteur*, or to supervise a carding machine. But, as already mentioned, the principal victims of technological unemployment were female, notably the older, married women amongst the *fileuses à la main*. Tied to their homes by family responsibilities, they had little opportunity of competing for the relatively small number of jobs in the mills.[15]

Tailoring, glovemaking, ribbon weaving and the manufacture of silks were major handicraft trades whose labour forces became partially 'feminized' during the nineteenth century. But here technical progress took the form of organizational changes rather than the adoption of machinery. The case of tailoring in Paris during the first half of the century is well documented. A number of big merchant houses began to develop

[13] AD Haut-Rhin, 9 M 23; the figures were as follows:

Age group	Males	Females	Total	
8–11 years	11	16	27	(11%)
12–15 years	29	52	81	(31%)
16–25 years	21	102	123	(47%)
25 and over	25	4	29	(11%)
Total	86	174	260	(100%)

[14] For example, in the *filature* of André Koechlin, at Thann, children comprised 42 per cent of the total; in that of Bouché *neveu*, also at Thann, the figure was 35 per cent; at Guebwiller, in the mill belonging to Nicolas Schlumberger, it was 31 per cent; AD Haut-Rhin, 9 M 22–3. As might be expected, the composition of the labour force in the early British spinning mills was very similar: see, for example, Neil J. Smelser, *Social Change in the Industrial Revolution* (London, 1959), p. 188; Sidney Pollard, 'Factory Discipline in the Industrial Revolution', *Economic History Review*, 2nd ser., 16 (1963), 259–60.

[15] Joan W. Scott and Louise A. Tilly, 'Women's Work and the Family in Nineteenth Century Europe', *Comparative Studies in Society and History*, 17 (1975), 39. For the British case exclusively, with its close parallels to France, see Eric Richards, 'Women in the British Economy since about 1700: An Interpretation', *History*, 59 (1974), 335–57.

ready-made articles, to go alongside those individually measured, and in this way they put the jobs of skilled artisans under pressure. In the *confection* branches of the trade, where low cost rather than high quality was the main requirement, a handful of skilled cutters could readily service a large group of semi-skilled seamstresses.[16] A new, and ultimately scandalous twist came in the latter half of the century, with the extensive employment of orphans in the *ouvroirs* and other religious establishments. Large department stores such as the Louvre and the Belle Jardinière relied heavily on this type of labour for the manufacturing of their garments. For example, in 1886 a Factory Inspector described the organization of work in the Orphelinat du Bon Pasteur. Fifty young women and children, aged between seven and twenty-one, were expected to sew together nine dozen men's shirts each day. Those under twelve were allowed to stop working at four o'clock in the afternoon, but in typically 'sweated' conditions, the rest had to keep going during the evening until the quota was fulfilled.[17] A similar strategy was employed by the *fabricants* of Lyons. They attempted to escape their dependence on the highly-organized *canuts* of the city, by placing a growing proportion of their handlooms in the countryside. The more intricate work had to be left to the urban workers, but the villagers could be used to make up the narrow, plainer silks. By mid-century, nearly half of the 60,000 looms active in the region were to be found in rural areas. Common practice in the peasant household was for parents to continue with agricultural work, leaving the looms to their older children. The latter would in turn be assisted by their younger brothers and sisters.[18] This leaves one or two other branches of the weaving industry as rare, indeed almost unique, examples at mid-point in the century of areas where machinery allowed adult males to be displaced by women and children. In the woollen and cotton industries, as in silk, work on the handloom had traditionally been the preserve of the male, the preparatory tasks being left to wives, children and apprentices. With the coming of the power loom, this division of labour within the family could be completely transformed. During the 1840s, for example, the *patronat* of Alsace estimated that in handloom weaving, men outnumbered women in the ratio of three to one. In the mechanized sector, the position was partially reversed, with a ratio of two to one in favour of women.[19] There was

[16] Christopher H. Johnson, 'Economic Change and Artisan Discontent: The Tailors' History, 1800–1848', in Roger D. Price (ed.), *Revolution and Reaction* (London, 1975), pp. 87–114.
[17] AN, F[12] 4730, Laporte (Seine, 1st), 1886.
[18] Lequin, *Les Ouvriers de la région lyonnaise*, vol. 1, pp. 23–7, 135–6; Garrier, *Paysans du Beaujolais*, vol. 1, pp. 206–13.
[19] Kahan-Rabecq, *L'Alsace économique*, vol. 1, p. 257.

Table 4.2 *Composition of the industrial labour force, after the 1839–45 Enquiry*

Industry	Number of				Percentage of	
	Men	Women	Children (under 16)	All workers	Women and children	Children
1. Textiles						
Cotton	109,344	90,647	44,828	244,819	55.3	18.3
Wool	72,678	44,668	26,800	144,146	49.6	18.6
Linen and hemp	33,067	15,868	7,232	56,167	41.1	12.9
Silk	109,662	46,127	9,326	165,115	33.6	5.6
Mixed fibres	47,062	21,471	15,803	84,336	44.2	18.7
2. Mines, quarries	69,243	5,786	6,256	81,285	14.8	7.7
3. Basic metallurgy	63,066	3,287	6,340	72,693	13.2	8.7
4. Metalworking	41,864	4,458	6,315	52,637	20.5	12.0
5. Leather	11,751	9,320	751	21,822	46.2	3.4
6. Wood	5,150	425	262	5,837	11.8	4.5
7. Ceramics	25,187	4,222	4,089	33,498	24.8	12.2
8. Chemicals	7,547	930	606	9,083	16.9	6.7
9. Construction	26,825	2,449	2,930	32,204	16.7	9.1
10. Lighting	1,239	262	71	1,572	21.2	4.5
11. Furnishings	–	–	–	–	–	–
12. Clothing	4,147	1,945	410	6,502	36.2	6.3
13. Food	115,368	14,163	6,889	136,420	15.4	5.0
14. Transport	4,838	13	223	5,074	4.7	4.4
15. Paper, publishing	13,518	8,370	2,841	24,729	45.3	11.5
16. Luxuries	1,199	57	95	1,351	11.3	7.0
17. Miscellaneous	5,153	4,369	1,598	11,120	–	–
Totals	767,908	278,837	143,665	1,190,410	35.5	12.1

Note: the 1839–45 Enquiry does not provide a satisfactory framework for summarizing its findings, classifying industries as 'mineral', 'vegetable' or 'animal'. In order to maintain a nineteenth-century perspective on the material, we have therefore adopted the sixteen headings provided by the 1861–5 Industrial Enquiry. See T. J. Markovitch, 'L'Industrie française de 1789 à 1964 – sources et méthodes', *Histoire quantitative de l'économie française*, vol. 4 (Paris, 1965), pp. 55–7.
Source: Statistique de la France, *Industrie* (4 vols., Paris, 1847–52).

thus the possibility that the handloom weaver could find himself supplanted by his daughter.[20]

There remains the temptation to generalize on shifts within the labour force with examples drawn exclusively from textiles and garment-

[20] For comparisons with Britain, where the shift was more rapid and more disruptive for labour, see Edward P. Thompson, *The Making of the English Working Class* (Harmondsworth, 1968), pp. 297–346.

making. These were substantial industries, it must be said, employing over 50 per cent of the industrial population throughout the first half of the nineteenth century.[21] But for a proper perspective, the extent to which female and juvenile labour penetrated the industrial sector as a whole must be considered. The first overall view does not appear until the 1840s, with the Industrial Enquiry of 1839–45.[22] This has its drawbacks as a statistical source. It was hampered by widespread suspicion that the Government was using it as a cover for tax investigations. There was also confusion over its scope: in principle, it confined itself to the larger industrial enterprises, but in practice a number of *bulletins collectifs* mingled in data from dispersed industries. It does nonetheless provide a broad sample consisting of approximately half of the workers in the manufacturing sector, giving the numbers of men, women and children in each firm investigated. The results show that adult males provided 65 per cent of the total, women 23 per cent and children under sixteen 12 per cent.[23] The female and child contingents thus formed only a minority, albeit a significant one: if there were certain industries which were heavily dependent on them, there were others where their presence was barely felt.

The Enquiry shows that those industries with an exceptionally high proportion of female and juvenile labour were for the most part concerned with textile production.[24] The spinning industries were outstanding: three-quarters of the workers in linen spinning, two-thirds of those in cotton spinning, and one half of those in wool spinning were women and children. Cotton and woollen weaving, textile printing, hosiery and certain preparatory industries also recruited approximately half of their labour from these two categories. The only other industries where they formed a majority were canning and papermaking. A similar rank-order emerges if child workers are considered on their own. Again, they were of considerable numerical significance in spinning and textile printing, accounting for somewhere between one third and one quarter of the labour force in the various branches, and of some weight in weaving, providing one in six of the workforce. Otherwise, it was only in certain of the metalworking trades that they registered any sizeable proportion of the total: one fifth to one sixth. On the other side of the coin was the wide range of industries where the shift to capital-intensive forms of production did little to permit a 'dilution' of the labour force. The 1839–45 Enquiry revealed that in mining, basic metallurgy, machine-building, chemicals,

[21] Toutain, *La Population de la France*, Table 74.
[22] *Statistique de la France, Industrie* (4 vols., Paris, 1847–52).
[23] The numbers were: 767,908 men; 278,837 women; and 143,665 children.
[24] See Madeleine Guilbert, *Les Fonctions des femmes dans l'industrie* (Paris, 1966), pp. 32–41.

glassmaking, printing and grain-milling, women and child workers formed only a small minority of those employed. In other sizeable industries where mechanization was slow to make an impact during the nineteenth century, there was also very little infiltration on their part. Quarries, shipyards, tanneries, joineries and breweries were all shown to be largely adult male territory. Most important of all the masculine strongholds was the construction industry. Although largely ignored by the Enquiry, it occupied a good half million people at mid-century.[25] Women found few opportunities in this area, and younger children too were excluded from the building sites. Apprenticeships in these areas were limited to physically robust males.

In short, the influx of women and children into the workshops of nineteenth-century industry was a localized affair. In a few well-publicized areas it was sufficient to transform the whole character of the labour force: witness the fate of the older spinsters, the handloom weavers and the tailors. In the manufacturing sector as a whole it was probably only of marginal significance during the first half of the century. Even in cases such as spinning and weaving, contemporary observers tended to exaggerate the extent of change, by ignoring the considerable number of women and children occupied in these industries when they were at their artisan stage. What they had really stumbled upon were unprecedented *concentrations* of female and child labour in commercial enterprises. This was a radical departure from earlier forms of industrial organization, but it did not necessarily involve a change in the composition of the labour force.[26]

During the second half of the nineteenth century the paths of female and child labour diverged. The threat of competition from women workers continued to hover menacingly over various groups of skilled workers, as new outlets opened in such trades as metalworking, leather and printing.[27] But for children opportunities to work in industry tended to decline from the 1840s onwards. The movement was more in evidence in some industries and in some regions than others. In the Haut-Rhin, during the 1820s and again during the 1840s, children formed approximately one third of the hands in the spinning mills; by the 1860s, this proportion had fallen to one fifth. In the *imprimeries d'indiennes*, the percentage accounted for by children fell from 28 to 19 between 1839–45 and

---

25 Toutain, *La Population de la France*, Table 71.
26 As far back as 1907, Emile Levasseur noted the similarities in the percentage of women workers recorded by the Industrial Enquiries of the 1840s and 1860s. He concluded: 'One cannot therefore conclude that the proportion of women was increasing in industry, and that as a consequence women had supplanted men.', *Questions ouvrières et industrielles en France sous la Troisième République* (Paris, 1907), p. 276.
27 Guilbert, *Les Fonctions des femmes*, pp. 43–9.

1869.[28] Similarly, in the Seine-Inférieure, between the 1840s and 1870 their share of the labour force in the spinning mills fell from well over one quarter to less than one fifth, and in the *tissages de calicots*, from one fifth to one tenth.[29] By contrast, in the textile industries of Flanders, the Champagne and the Vivarais, the relative strengths of men, women and child workers remained stable at this period. A slight overall decline might be inferred from the 1861–5 Industrial Enquiry, a further partial survey of the manufacturing sector as a whole. From providing one in eight of the labour force in 1839–45, children were reduced to one in fourteen by the 1860s.[30] During the final quarter of the century, the exclusion of young children from the workshops was clearly in evidence. The Factory Inspectorate documented the dwindling numbers of those under twelve in industrial employment: the 7,800 found in 1876 had fallen to a residual 1,800 in 1884.[31] In sum, a marginal rise in the use of child labour by industry may have occurred during the first three or four decades of the nineteenth century, but from then on there was a slow, inexorable decline.

Working-class parents and the supply of child labour

Until the middle of the nineteenth century, the supply side of the market for child labour was, to say the least, open-handed. Like the peasant, the industrial proletariat normally expected its children to work. This was partly a matter of holding customary attitudes to the family and to education. Working-class parents persisted in the idea that children should be thrust out into a semi-independent existence as early as possible in life. Typically, Agricol Perdiguier remembered that during the First Empire his father, a carpenter, skimped on the schooling of his children and set them to work from an early age: 'He did not want to make us gentlemen and ladies, but vigorous workers: he did well.'[32] In time the working-class family would prolong the dependence of its children, by keeping them out of the labour force and in the schools, following the path taken by middle-class families in the eighteenth century. But this aban-

---

[28] Information drawn from AD Haut-Rhin, 9 M 22–3; *Statistique de la France, Industrie, 1847–52*, vol. 1, pp. 148–9; *idem, Industrie: résultats généraux de l'enquête effectuée dans les années 1861–5* (Nancy, 1873), pp. 562–8; AN, F^{12} 4724.

[29] *Statistique de la France, Industrie, 1847–52*, vol. 2, pp. 26–33; AD Seine-Maritime, 6 MP 5150; *Statistique de la France, Industrie, 1873*, pp. 630–3; AN, F^{12} 4724–5.

[30] *Statistique de la France, Industrie, 1873*, pp. xx–xxiv. Numbers and percentages were as follows: 1,094,046 men (64 per cent); 485,497 women (29 per cent); and 123,429 children (7 per cent).

[31] Ministère du Commerce, *Rapport sur l'application de la loi du 19 mai 1874 pendant l'année 1884* (Paris, 1885), p. 12. For vestiges of child labour in contemporary France, see Rouard, 'Enfants au travail', 9–18.

[32] Perdiguier, *Mémoires d'un compagnon*, p. 3.

donment of traditional notions of 'apprenticeship' in the outside world
was far from complete in the early twentieth century.[33]

The practice of sending children out to work was also determined by the
material condition of the working class. The household of an urban
worker, in contrast to that of an agricultural labourer, had no other
means of support apart from its wages. The detailed budget reconstruc-
tions of various social enquiries in the 1830s and 1840s revealed the
precariousness of the 'family wage economy'. Louis Villermé concluded
that many families amongst the textile workers could only remain on an
even keel in exceptionally favourable circumstances. This meant regular
employment for both husband and wife, a tight rein on the purse strings,
and a maximum of two young children. 'Suppose they have a third child, a
spell of unemployment, an illness, a poor sense of economy, an habitual or
even occasional bout of intemperance, then they will be in the greatest
difficulty.'[34] But, as he noted himself in the case of the Haut-Rhin, the
average number of legitimate births amongst the cotton workers was 4.65
between 1817 and 1834.[35] Moreover, massive lay-offs regularly followed
periods of full employment in all branches of the textile industry; poor
living and working conditions provided fertile breeding ground for
disease; and drinking sessions at the *cabaret* were an essential part of
working-class leisure.

Specific examples provided by Villermé from various occupational
groups served to reinforce this gloomy perspective. He estimated that in
Mulhouse a family of four needed an annual income of 960 francs to
support itself. The majority of workers in the local cotton industry were
unable to reach this level from their own wages alone. A spinner could
expect to earn between 600 and 900 francs a year; a handloom weaver
450 to 525 francs; a cotton printer 750 to 990 francs; and a labourer or
dyer 300 to 450 francs. A family might scrape through, or even be
comfortably off, if the wife was also earning, for she could bring in
another 225 to 330 francs. Serious problems began when the duties of
childrearing became onerous.[36] Combining motherhood and wage labour
was difficult in the towns, and so there was pressure for the wife to remain
at home, and for children to replace her in the labour force.[37] With
juvenile labour costing the family as much as it earned, Villermé reported
that the 'feeble wages' of many families 'were barely sufficient for the
indispensable needs of material life'. Much the same picture emerged from
Rouen, notably amongst the handloom weavers. In this case, Villermé

---

[33] Ariès, *Centuries of Childhood*, p. 358.
[34] Villermé, *Tableau de l'état*, vol. 2, pp. 14–15.
[35] *Ibid.*, p. 49.   [36] *Ibid.*, pp. 36–49.
[37] Tilly and Scott, *Women, Work and Family*, pp. 123–9.

estimated that the family of four needed to spend 912 francs a year on the necessities of life, yet if it was only the father and mother who were working, the total income was usually 861 francs. Unless the weaver or his wife was earning exceptionally high wages, it required one of the children to be bringing in an income to lift the family from poverty. Otherwise, at best, rent could not be paid, clothes could not be renewed or laundered and diet had to be reduced to bread and potatoes.[38]

There were sections of the working class enjoying a higher standard of living than the unfortunates in the spinning mills or weaving shops. In Nantes, for example, Guépin and Bonamy distinguished the *ouvriers aisés*, composed mainly of artisans in the building trades, from the *ouvriers pauvres* and the *ouvriers misérables*.[39] More generally, there was an élite of skilled workers in such industries as mining, metallurgy, glass-making and textile printing which could earn 3, 4 or 5 francs a day, and more. Needless to say, it was precisely these groups that tended to spend money on schooling, technical training and apprenticeships, and to delay the entry of their children into the labour force.[40] Moreover, it can hardly be coincidence that during the second half of the century, while the younger children were being gradually withdrawn from the labour force, all the available indices of real wages moved sharply and consistently upwards, after a long period of stability and even decline before the 1850s.[41] A clearer margin over subsistence for the working class in general eased the financial burden of schooling, and doubtless made legal restrictions on child labour more tolerable.[42] By the 1870s and 1880s, employers frequently claimed that children under the age of twelve were only taken on to oblige a poor family.[43] This sounds like humbug, but it was more

[38] Villermé, *Tableau de l'état*, vol. 1, pp. 144–5, 153. Further information on working-class budgets during the mid-nineteenth century can be found in the local studies, notably Kahan-Rabecq, *L'Alsace économique*, vol. 1, pp. 222–97; André Lasserre, *La Situation des ouvriers de l'industrie textile dans la région lilloise sous la Monarchie de Juillet* (Lausanne, 1952), pp. 105–27; Pierrard, *La Vie ouvrière*, pp. 198–213; Lequin, *Les Ouvriers de la région lyonnaise*, vol. 2, pp. 15–31, 45–57.

[39] A. Guépin and E. Bonamy, *Nantes au XIXe siècle* (Nantes, 1835), pp. 481–5.

[40] See below, pp. 189, 203.

[41] Fernande Braudel and Ernest Labrousse (eds.), *Histoire économique et sociale de la France*, vol. 3, *L'Avènement de l'ère industrielle, 1789–années 1880* (Paris, 1976), part 2, pp. 785–90; *ibid.*, vol. 4, *L'Ere industrielle et la société d'aujourd'hui, siècle 1880–1980* (Paris, 1979), part 1, p. 494.

[42] Jacques Rougerie notes 'une véritable révolution dans la consommation' in Paris under the Second Empire, with substantial increases in the consumption of meat, wine, eggs, poultry and cheese. At the same time, he draws attention to the limitations of real wage indices, notably their inability to take into account the influence of unemployment: 'Remarques sur l'histoire des salaires à Paris au XIXe siècle', *Le Mouvement social*, 4–6 (1968), 71–108.

[43] Reports of the Factory Inspectors: AN, F¹² 4742, Aubert (Lisieux, 8th), 28 March 1884; AN, F¹² 4752, Estelle (Nîmes, 13th), 10 January 1880; AN, F¹² 4753, Leseur (Limoges, 14th), 17 January 1887.

likely an indicator of the distance travelled since the 1830s. Most parents now felt able to give their children a few years of schooling, but there remained an underlying harsh reality. Wages in certain industries failed to keep up with the general increase. In Paris at least, textile and clothing workers, from whose families so much child labour was recruited, fared particularly badly.[44] The prolonged illness or death of a breadwinner could also still propel a family into desperate circumstances. In 1879, for example, a Factory Inspector threatened to take a silk mill owner from the Vivarais to court for employing a young girl illegally, only to be confronted outside his hotel the next morning by a tearful widow. She implored him to drop the case involving her daughter since she had five children to support.[45]

The varying pressure of poverty was not, however, the whole story. Employers also had to take into account the limited capacity of the child worker. Labour supply is partly determined by the quantity and quality of effort and skill forthcoming from those working. Under nineteenth-century conditions, children and even women usually had less strength, time and skill available for industrial work than men. Evidently, the child worker could not match the physical strength and stamina of an adult. After puberty, the same held for the average female compared to the average male.[46] In a civilization which, as Paul Leroy-Beaulieu noted during the 1870s, had barely escaped from being 'crude and little helped by the assistance of science', this drawback was by no means negligible.[47] Working hours of married women and young children could be restricted in domestic workshops by the traditional division of labour which required them to do the household chores. From the Nord, it was reported in 1848 that handloom weavers were assisted by their wives and children working approximately a third of the day, and around Tarare both Villermé and Reybaud remarked upon the large numbers of females applying themselves part time to the embroidery of muslin.[48]

As for skills, women and children had very little to offer industry. The young had not had sufficient time to develop them, and females of all ages

---

44 Rougerie, 'Salaires à Paris', p. 87. Rougerie estimates that the wage levels of the textile and clothing workers during the 1870s and 1880s were not far above those current in 1810 and 1820, the rise of the Second Empire appearing as a recuperation for losses sustained between the 1820s and 1840s.

45 AN, F[12] 4753, Estelle (Nîmes, 13th), 14 October 1879.

46 J. M. Tanner, 'Sequence, Tempo and Individual Variation in the Growth and Development of Boys and Girls Aged Twelve to Sixteen', *Daedalus*, 100 (1971), 907–30; Paul Leroy-Beaulieu, *Le Travail des femmes au XIXe siècle* (Paris, 1873), pp. 2–3.

47 Leroy-Beaulieu, *Travail des femmes*, p. 183.

48 AD Nord, M 547/1, canton of Marcoing; Villermé, *Tableau de l'état*, vol. 1, p. 185; Louis Reybaud, *Le Coton* (Paris, 1863), p. 136. See also, Grafteaux, *Mémé Santerre*, p. 13.

were hemmed in by the rigid expectations of society at large. During this period, the gaps between males and females in rates of literacy and school attendance were closing, without being eradicated: in 1837, for example, there were 1.6 million boys in the primary school system, but only 1.1 million girls. More importantly, the content of education differed for the two sexes. Official policy was to prepare girls for motherhood rather than a career. Hence an *ordonnance* of 1836 decreed that needlework should be compulsory for girls, and while boys studied the legal system of weights and measures, girls were directed towards singing and drawing.[49] A Primary School Inspector in Lille, reporting on the state of girls' schools in the city during the 1850s, mentioned in passing that 'education for girls can dispense with the mental exercises which prepare young boys for the struggles and dealings of life'. Yet even working from this premise, he concluded that the curriculum for girls was insufficiently demanding of the intellect. The *institutrices* allegedly relied on memory exercises more than the *instituteurs*, and, above all, were poorly equipped to teach arithmetic.[50]

On leaving school, options for girls were effectively limited. The canton of Le Mans noted in 1848, 'Very few girls go through an apprenticeship; nearly all of them become domestic servants or devote themselves to household chores in the parental home.'[51] Those who did wish to learn a skilled artisan trade most commonly became *couturières* or *lingères* in the clothing industry. These trades at least required a full training period of eighteen months to three years.[52] Other 'female' occupations could be learnt at a basic level in a few weeks at most, and the majority of women employed in them remained only semi-skilled at their work. Girls were set to embroidery or lacemaking beside their mothers from as early as the age of six. In the Puy-de-Dôme, it was said that a *dentellière* could start her trade after two or three lessons, and in the Vosges, that a *brodeuse* did not need a proper apprenticeship.[53]

Social convention drew some very clear lines for the sexes: a Primary School Inspector in the Vosges noted 'with sadness' two young boys learning embroidery,[54] and it was presumably unthinkable that a girl

---

49 Furet and Ozouf, *Reading and Writing*, pp. 32–4; Toutain, *La Population de la France*, pp. 225–7; Louis-Henri Parias (ed.), *Histoire générale de l'enseignement et de l'éducation en France*, vol. 3, *De la Révolution à l'école républicaine* (Paris, 1981), pp. 120–39.

50 AN, F^{17} 9318, 'Notes explicatives sur l'état de situation des écoles de filles en 1855', Lille, 15 December 1855.

51 'Enquête sur le travail', 1848: AN C 965, Sarthe.

52 *Ibid.*, AN, C 957, Outarville (Loiret); AN, C 965, Bouxviller (Bas-Rhin); AN, C 969, Courson (Yonne).

53 *Ibid.*: AN, C 962, Ambert (Puy-de-Dôme); AN, C 969, Mirecourt (Vosges).

54 AD Vosges, M 292, Mirecourt, 5 June 1857.

should set out to become, say, a mechanic or a foundryman. The reluctance of families to make the sacrifice of a long apprenticeship for a daughter was considered rational in so far as women often chose to give up full-time work when they reached marriage or motherhood. However, the married factory hand was by no means uncommon, for in desperate circumstances, a wife would always go out and earn a wage. At Guebwiller, for example, in the cotton mill owned by Ziegler, Greuter et Compagnie, forty-three married women and widows were employed in 1823 amongst a total labour force of 738. And during the 1840s, the De Canson paper mill in the Vivarais employed 148 of them amongst its total of 273 workers. Even in the domestic workshops, some wives might work long hours beside their husbands, on such tasks as handloom weaving or nailmaking.[55] The influence of custom, prejudice and vested male interest cannot, therefore, be discounted in explaining differences between the sexes in the crucial area of access to industrial skills. Either way, the result was a measure of continuity in the allocation of work rôles on the supply-side of the market. Most of the skilled trades were left to the males, women and girls being expected to orientate themselves as much towards their families as their jobs.

Employers and the demand for child labour

Our task now is to discover why, in certain industries, employers took on large numbers of youthful workers, and why, even leaving aside the influence of legal compulsion, they would eventually be prepared to part with the younger ones. The reasons put forward have been grouped under three main headings: the physical advantages of children; their cheapness; and their docility. The underlying aim will be to qualify the easy assumption that employers had a 'good bargain' with this type of labour.

The most straightforward reason given by industrialists for hiring the young was that, for certain jobs, their physique made them more suitable than adults. Some went as far as to say that a substitution of adults for children in these areas would be impossible. The number of tasks concerned was small, but they did tend to be the ones that employed large numbers of children. The best-known example is piecing, the *rattacheur* of the spinning mills being almost invariably a young boy or girl. The Mulhouse Chamber of Commerce informed the 1837 Enquiry on Child Labour, 'In the spinning mills, this task demands a delicacy in the fingers for tying threads, as well as a suppleness of the body for sliding under all

---

55 AD Haut-Rhin, 9 M 23; AD Ardèche, 14 M 10; AN, C 945, 'Enquête sur le travail', 1848, Charleville (Ardennes); Laura S. Strumingher, 'Les Canutes de Lyon, 1835–1848', *Le Mouvement social*, 105 (1978), 79–81. See below, pp. 130–1.

parts of the machinery, of which an adult would be incapable.'[56] A similar case was made in the glassworks for the *porteurs*, young boys who carried bottles from the glassblower to a furnace. In 1875 a Factory Inspector in Bordeaux observed:

A man would be unable to replace him; the child runs with his cane to the annealing furnace, and nearly always returns at the run to pick up another. His small stature and his agility permit him alone to perform this service. One can say that with its existing equipment, the glass industry cannot survive without children.[57]

It is impossible to accept all this at face value. Doubtless, in any type of economy, various jobs could always be found for which children would be particularly suited because of their small size and nimbleness. But this is very different from saying that they are essential. The employers of the nineteenth century had, of course, only experienced a society in which child work was the norm, but it is most unlikely that even they considered this to be a pressing reason for taking on the young, in private at least if not in public. One can point to the evidence of Villermé, who reported from Amiens during a crisis in the spinning industry, when all but the most skilled labour was laid off, that spinners whose machines had been stopped took over the work of the piecers. And, at a rather later date, there was the case of a glassworks in Normandy which, an Inspector noted, managed to do without children on Sunday mornings in order to conform with the law.[58] Industrialists could hardly have been unaware of these possibilities and indeed some of their statements hint at an uneasy conscience. The Chambre Consultative of Sedan (Ardennes) stated in 1837 that adults could not be employed as *rattacheurs* because they were too tall, but added rather inconsistently that the wages would have to be raised by 25 to 35 centimes per day. In similar vein, the Conseil des Prud'hommes of Bar-le-Duc (Meuse) asserted that children were more apt for certain work than adults, but also that the latter would not accept the low wages.[59] This illustrates the way the question of the physical capacities of child workers quickly shades into another: their cheapness.

A series of investigations into the wage structure of nineteenth-century France revealed that women and children dominated the ranks of the low-paid. Normally, a woman could expect to earn somewhere between a half and two-thirds the wage of a man, a child a third at the most. There was naturally considerable variation according to industry, to region and

[56] AN, F¹² 4705.
[57] AN, F¹² 4748, Jacquemart (Bordeaux, 11th), 31 December 1875.
[58] Villermé, *Tableau de l'etat*, vol. 1, p. 302; AN, F¹² 4747, Blaise (Rouen, 10th), 20 October 1887.
[59] AN, F¹² 4705.

to phases in the business cycle. But in the mid-nineteenth century the
typical pattern was for adult male wages rarely to fall below the range of
1.25 to 1.50 francs per day; for female wages only exceptionally to exceed
1.10 francs; and for those of children to be between 40 and 75 centimes.
From here it is a short step to concluding that women and children were in
some undefined way 'exploited' or 'underpaid' as a source of cheap labour
for industry.[60] This is only partly true, however, since it must be borne in
mind that low wages are generally a reflection of low productivity and
high labour costs per unit of output. Whether or not there were savings to
be made in the employment of women and children depended on the
nature of the work. Jules Simon, writing during the 1860s, suggested a
grading of tasks in industry, men doing the heavier work, but: 'In all cases
where women can do the job as well and as fast as men they are preferred.
This stems from the first economic law, one could even say the first
metaphysical law, that the force dispensed should be exactly proportional
to the result obtained.'[61] This implies that women and children were
cheap for the employer only in the sense that a small 'force dispensed'
could not expect to be paid as much as a large one.

An optimum allocation of labour resources from the point of view of
the industrialists, given the conditions prevailing on the supply-side of the
market, would therefore require that women and child workers be
assigned to the lighter, less-skilled tasks in industry, where the physical
capacity and, more importantly, the training and experience of the
average adult male, would have been under-employed. When cotton was
spun on a wheel or a jenny, the employer would find a female or child
worker more economical than a man. However, once a full-sized mule
became available, the position was reversed, since efficient operation of
this machine required considerable muscular power, and skills to which
children and most women were denied access. In between these extremes
was a variety of jobs which men, women and sometimes children could
manage, and where output depended on the amount of strength, skill and
effort put in by the individual. For example, in the Ardennes whole
families worked together in the domestic manufacture of nails and
hardware; in the cotton mills, women operated water frames and the
smaller mules beside the men; and in the silk industry, the new, youthful
contingent of female handloom weavers came to rival the established

[60] Guéneau, 'La legislation restrictive', 420; Mary Lynn McDougall, 'Working-class
Women during the Industrial Revolution, 1780–1914', in Renate Bridenthal and Claudia
Koonz (eds.), *Becoming Visible* (Boston, 1977), pp. 264–5; Patricia Branca, *Women in
Europe since 1750* (London, 1978), p. 28. Concerning children, Georges Dupeux wrote
that they 'received absurdly low wages'; *French Society, 1789–1970* (London, 1976),
p. 131.
[61] *L'Ouvrier de huit ans*, 4th edn (Paris, 1867), p. 91.

canuts of Lyons.[62] In these cases, with relatively low fixed costs and a piece-rate system of payment, labour costs remained the same for the employer, whatever the age or gender of the worker. In 1837, the Prefect of the Var noted that for the silk-weaving industry there was barely any saving for the employer in substituting teenagers for adults on the handlooms, 'given that if there is a fall in the wages, the labour is less. Wages are therefore in proportion to the work.'[63]

This suggests that industrial employers were rarely able to reduce their costs by a policy of wage discrimination: that is to say, paying women less than men, or children less than adults, for the same work.[64] Where female and child workers could be allocated tasks similar to those performed by adult males, there was usually a scale of piece-rates in operation, which made it difficult to deny them the going rate for the job. The Société Industrielle of Elbeuf, for example, was explicit in stating before a Parliamentary Enquiry of 1882 that women employed on powerloom weaving received the same piece-rates as men.[65] In a few instances, this arrangement could narrow or even eliminate differentials in earnings. A list of wages in the cotton industries of Munster for the year 1830 revealed that, amongst the spinners and handloom weavers, average female earnings in the lower ranges of skill were very close to those of the males (see Table 4.3). Similarly, in 1848 the canton of Solre-le-Château noted: 'Nails, chains, combed wool and cloth are paid by the kilogramme or *à la pièce*, and the beginner earns less because he does less, for lack of practice. Nevertheless, it is by no means rare to see apprentice combers or handloom weavers earn the same wage as the established workers.'[66] The fact that generally speaking children and even women on piece-rates had lower average earnings than the males was not necessarily a sign of wage discrimination by employers.[67] The various choices women made, or had to make, on work and family rôles tended to lower their productivity, and

---

[62] AN, C 945, 'Enquête sur le travail', 1848, Charleville (Ardennes); Simon, *L'Ouvrier de huit ans*, p. 90; Lequin, *Les Ouvriers*, vol. 1, p. 136.

[63] AN, F[12] 4705.

[64] For the theoretical background to these issues, see Alice H. Amsden (ed.), *The Economics of Women and Work* (Harmondsworth, 1980), *passim*; Gerry Rodgers and Guy Standing (eds.), 'The Economic Roles of Children: Issues for Analysis', in their *Child Work, Poverty and Underdevelopment* (Geneva, 1981), pp. 1–45; Diane Elson, 'The Differentiation of Children's Labour in the Capitalist Labour Market', *Development and Change*, 13 (1982), 479–97.

[65] AN, C 3370[3]. Interestingly, Shiela Lewenhak asserts that male negotiators for wages, fearful of competition from women workers, 'asked for the "rate for the job" for women, assured that employers would take men instead'. See her discussion in *Women and Work* (London, 1980), p. 153.

[66] AD Nord, M 547/1.

[67] See Beth Niemi and Cynthia Lloyd, 'Sex Differentials in Earnings and Unemployment Rates', *Feminist Studies*, 2 (1975), 194–201.

Table 4.3 *Wages of male and female workers in the cotton textile industries of Munster, 1830*

		Male	Female	Female as percentage of male
Spinners:	1st class	2.00 f.	1.50 f.	75
	2nd class	1.50 f.	1.25 f.	83
	3rd class	1.00 f.	1.00 f.	100
Weavers:	1st class	2.00 f.	1.25 f.	63
	2nd class	1.25 f.	1.00 f.	80
	3rd class	0.90 f.	0.80 f.	89

Note: these wages are presented in the form of average daily earnings.
Source: AD Haut-Rhin, 10 M 1, 'Renseignements sur la situation actuelle des salaires des classes ouvrières dans la ville de Munster, et sur la marche suivie par les salaires depuis 1830. Manufacture de Hartmann et fils', 19 November 1847.

hence their earning potential. Take the example of cotton spinning. In this case there is no reason to think that the women who managed to become *fileuses* were any less skilled than their male counterparts, nor that they worked shorter hours. But in so far as they were likely to be more youthful than the males, they would have had less experience in keeping their machines going. And their smaller physical capacity would have been a further disadvantage, which must at least partly explain the custom of assigning them to different types of machine. After examining the payroll of a Rouen cotton mill, Villermé distinguished the male *fileurs en fin*, with 216 or 240 spindles on their machines, from the *femmes ou jeunes gens*, with only 132 or 144 spindles. The former earned on average 660 francs a year, the latter 348 francs.[68]

The major loophole for employers was to use a pay scale graduated according to age as a way of paying a 'child's' wage for 'adult' work. Low wages for children were equitable in so far as they reflected inexperience and a lack of skill. As the Amiens Chamber of Commerce observed in 1867, 'For industrialists, the economies they make in the employment of children are often dearly paid for in terms of poor workmanship and defects in their products.'[69] But there remained the possibility of introducing an arbitrary element of qualification by age, giving artificial status to

[68] Villermé, *Tableau de l'état*, vol. 1, p. 154, n. 1.
[69] AN, F¹² 4722, letter to the Minister of Commerce, 26 June 1867. See also Joseph-Marie de Gérando, *De la bienfaisance publique* (4 vols., Paris, 1839), vol. 1, p. 258.

older workers, and allowing employers to take unfair advantage of youth.[70] This abuse was particularly in evidence amongst the small-scale workshops, where 'pseudo-apprenticeships' in low-productivity jobs were easily arranged. Children were then paid a pittance to do simple work that involved no proper training in a trade. The 'sweatshops' of the textile and clothing industries were widely suspected of such practices, though the very weight of their numbers allowed most to remain in a murky obscurity. In 1852 a *notable* from Lyons drew attention to the

distressing position of the young girls aged between twelve and twenty years who are entrusted by their parents to various workshops in the town as apprentices, *perfectionnantes* or even as workers. They are particularly to be found in those concerned with tailoring, lingerie and above all fashion, and their mistresses, whose aims are far from praiseworthy, prolong their work beyond all limits, even making the young people work whole nights, principally at the time of year when orders are pressing.[71]

The preparatory tasks in the silk industry of Lyons were also notorious for relying on a regular turnover of young girls to produce the very cheapest labour possible. According to a Factory Inspector, in the 1870s most of the *dévideuses* were still coming from outside the town, with their pay consisting of board and lodging, plus an annual lump sum for their families of 40 to 60 francs. He estimated that at the peak of activity, 7,000 young girls were involved, starting at the ages of ten to twelve.[72]

If wage discrimination was the exception rather than the rule in the manufacturing section, job discrimination, particularly against women workers, took place on a massive scale. The expectation in society at large was that in most industries, men would monopolize the jobs involving responsibility and skill, whilst women and children would be shunted off into the subordinate positions. This segmentation of the labour market tied the hands of the employer to the extent that the bargaining position of skilled males was reinforced. But it did guarantee him a large reservoir of unskilled or semi-skilled workers whose position on the market was exceptionally weak. Forced to compete for a limited range of jobs identified by custom as 'women's' or 'children's' work, they inevitably sold themselves cheap. This was the principal advantage industrial interests gained from the terms on which female and child labour was available in the nineteenth century. In the calico-printing mills of Alsace, for example, men took all the highly skilled posts as engravers and

[70] 'Wage Differentials Affecting Young Workers', *International Labour Review*, 122 (1955), 521–34.

[71] AD Rhône, 10 M, letter from M. Guilhon, member of the Société d'Agriculture, to the Prefect, 17 June 1852.

[72] AN, F[12] 4755, Gauthier (Lyons, 15th), 23 April 1878.

designers, earning 10 to 20 francs a day, and as *imprimeurs de premières mains*, earning 2.50 to 3.30 francs. At the same period, the 1830s, women had to be content with the positions of *imprimeuse de deuxième main*, which brought in 1.50 to 2.00 francs a day, or *éplucheuse* and *couturière*, which averaged around 1.20 francs a day. In the spinning mills of Normandy, the disparities were less striking. Nonetheless, the male spinners could expect to earn between 2.25 and 2.50 francs, whilst the ranks of female *veilleuses de cardes* had to be content with a miserable 60 centimes to 1 franc.[73] Equal pay for work of equal value was nowhere in sight.

Outside the factory system, the position of female workers was even more vulnerable, as a result of the social pressures that crowded so many of them into a few handicraft trades. The economist Paul Leroy-Beaulieu noted as late as the 1870s that in industries such as embroidery, lacemaking and tailoring, pay was exceptionally low because the work was physically and intellectually undemanding; because there was only limited scope for increasing productivity and earnings through mechanization; and because the bargaining power of labour was weakened by competition between full- and part-time labour.[74] As for children, the usual estimate from the *patronat* at the 1837 Enquiry was that for jobs where no great strength or skill was required, savings of a third or even a half could be made when they were used in place of an adult.[75] For the most part they continued to play their traditional rôle of mopping up small jobs around the workshops, releasing adults for more productive work. Hence rather than competing directly with adults, they complemented them or acted as assistants to them. Examples are legion, whether piecing in the spinning mills, winding and throwing shuttles in the handloom weaving shops, preparing dyestuffs in the *imprimeries d'indiennes*, opening ventilation doors in the mines, carrying bottles for glassblowers in the *verreries*, feeding rivets to boilermakers in the engineering works, threading bolts in the ironworks, folding and stacking paper in the paper mills or turning wheels for ropemakers and potters.

The relatively low wages payable to women and children gave entrepreneurs a strong incentive to adopt innovations making it possible to substitute their labour for that of adult males. Certainly there were machines that could take the strength and skill requirements out of a job, paving the way for a 'dilution' of the labour force: although higher capital costs would inevitably be incurred, these could be more than offset by

73 Villermé, *Tableau de l'état*, vol. 1, pp. 140–1.
74 Leroy-Beaulieu, *Travail des femmes*, pp. 132–9. The same point is made in: Chambre de Commerce de Paris, *Statistique de l'industrie à Paris, résultant de l'Enquête faite par la Chambre de Commerce pour les années 1847–8* (Paris, 1851), pp. 66–7.
75 AN, F^{12} 4705.

reducing labour costs through improved productivity. In 1876, a Factory Inspector posted to Rheims reported: 'Since this need for unskilled labour increases with the number of machines, and since a child of twelve to fifteen years can in an infinite number of cases do the same supervisory work as an adult, there is a hoarding of as many children as possible.'[76] The best-known example is the power loom, whose influence on the composition of the labour force in the weaving industry has already been documented. By the middle of the nineteenth century, the ranks of the handloom weavers were notable for their diversity. They included the élite *canuts* of Lyons on their Jacquard looms; the men operating the huge looms, 4 metres wide, in the woollen industry; the still relatively skilled weavers of *rouenneries* in Normandy; the part-time peasant workers of the countryside; and the village women who were left with the plainer silks, the narrower, lighter cloths, and the smaller calicoes and hand-kerchiefs. With the introduction of the power loom, this range of qualifications was narrowed, although not entirely eliminated. Certain branches of the industry, notably linen weaving, remained firmly 'mascu-line'. By contrast, cotton and woollen weaving became increasingly 'feminized', with the factory hand simply required to start up and stop a machine, to clean around it and to watch for broken threads. Other areas where the introduction of machinery brought redundancy for the male, particularly during the second half of the century, included the manufac-ture of shoes, harnesses, nails and rivets.[77] No less important than mechanization in the French case was the organizational change pushed through by merchant-manufacturers in the dispersed industries. The examples of tailoring and silk weaving revealed the strategy of moving into the medium and low quality ranges of the market, and without abandoning handtool methods, effecting an increased division of labour. The way was then open to employ cheap rural labour at the expense of the urban craftsman, to favour the semi-skilled over those with a long apprenticeship, and once again to prefer women and children to adult males.[78]

Yet the extent to which mechanization and organizational change enabled employers to displace males with low-cost female and child labour is easily exaggerated. Outside the textile industries, the shift to capital-intensive forms of production was slow to produce the light, semi-skilled work deemed suitable for women and children. To a remark-able extent, throughout the nineteenth century the work of the female

[76] AN, F^{12} 4736, Doll (Rheims, 5th), 8 November 1876.
[77] Guilbert, *Les Fonctions des femmes*, pp. 45–9.
[78] See Franklin Mendels, 'Proto-industrialization: The First Phase of the Industrialization Process', *Journal of Economic History*, 32 (1972), 241–61.

members of the industrial labour force revolved around the spindle, the loom and needle. And as far as children were concerned, a lack of maturity made them unsuitable for operating most industrial machinery. It was one thing to put a child on to a spinning jenny or a handloom, quite another to entrust one with a large machine where errors of judgement could be disastrous. Some of the accidents in which they were involved expose in macabre fashion their limitations as machine minders. In the Indre, an explosion at an ironworks in 1889 was traced back to a *mécanicien* leaving a fourteen-year-old in charge of his machine. The inexperienced youth apparently allowed the water-level in a reservoir to fall too low: the result, eight dead. And at the famous Le Creusot works it was reported, almost incredibly, that a boy of fifteen was operating a crane on a Bessemer converter in the early 1880s. In this case the youth turned the wrong wheel and poured molten steel on his workmates, one of whom was 'instantanément carbonisé par les flammes'.[79] The additional responsibility which the spread of mechanization placed on the workforce thus tended to discourage the resort to child labour.

There was another side to this coin, for eventually new technologies had the effect of driving the very young right out of the workshops. In the latter half of the nineteenth century, many of the tasks they performed were simply 'mechanized away'. By 1850, the introduction of cotton-printing machines with rollers was causing the job of *tireur* to disappear.[80] From the 1860s, there were reports of the self-actor eliminating the younger *rattacheurs* from the spinning mills.[81] In woollen textiles, chemical processes slowly made children redundant in some of the finishing trades.[82] Continuous hydraulic processes dispensed with their many services in sugar refining.[83] And in the potteries, various devices

---

[79] AN, F[12] 4734, Fache (Bourges, 3rd), 25 February 1886, and Pellet (Nevers, 3rd), 3 December 1883.

[80] The Enquiry by the Ingénieurs des Mines of 1869 revealed that in the Dollfus-Mieg mill at Dornach (Haut-Rhin), the *fabrique d'indiennes à la main* employed 110 children under twelve, and eleven aged twelve to sixteen, who together made up 46 per cent of the personnel. The *fabrique d'indiennes au rouleau*, on the other hand, employed no children under twelve, and 175 of twelve to sixteen years: 24 per cent of the personnel. The two types of printing in the Scheurer-Kott mill, at Thann, showed the same contrast. AN, F[12] 4724.

[81] AD Nord, M 613/15, letter from Dupont, Departmental Inspector, to Prefect, 6 February 1863; AD Vosges, M 277, letter from Prefect to Minister of Commerce, 16 January 1869; AD Meurthe-et-Moselle, 10 M 10, report from Garde-Mines, Marne, 1872; AN, C 3020, 'Enquête parlementaire', 1872, Richard, manufacturier à Chollet; AN, F[12] 4740, Blaise (Rouen, 7th), 20 February 1884.

[82] AD Seine-Maritime, 10 MP 1367, report on the Elbeuf cloth industry by the Departmental Inspector, 14 November 1884. The disappearance of 600–700 jobs for girls and women as *épinceteuses* is mentioned.

[83] AN, F[12] 4741, Blaise (Rouen, 7th), 4 November 1880.

took over the gruelling task of turning wheels.[84] In the 1880s, a Factory Inspector from Lyons could list as a major reason for the reduction in the number of children employed, 'The incessant perfecting of mechanisms which tend increasingly to be substituted for labour.'[85]

The formation of a disciplined factory labour force was an awkward hurdle facing the innovating entrepreneur during the nineteenth century. The sudden demand for hands following the establishment of a mill could quickly overwhelm the local labour market in rural areas, countering the advantage of cheap water power. And although the extent to which peasants and artisans were reluctant to change their work pattern is a matter of controversy, there is evidence of resistance to the machine, the factory and the discipline required by industrial concentration.[86] The resort to youthful labour provided one possible remedy for these problems, because of its docile character. The most critical period for the recruitment of factory labour was during the Revolutionary and Napoleonic Wars, when the first flourish of mechanized cotton spinning coincided with an acute shortage of manpower caused by the military campaigns. The early cotton mills therefore had little choice but to use women and children. The Prefect Scipion Mourgue, a former mill owner, informed the 1837 Enquiry, 'Under the Empire, conscription was for a long time a serious obstacle to my industry, and to get round it I installed fairly light machines throughout my mills, so that young girls could operate them.'[87]

But even children were not necessarily to be found in abundance, and more coercive measures were considered necessary. During the 1790s, Boyer-Fonfrède in Toulouse eased his shortages by arranging long-term contracts with young workers. By 1806, his so-called 'Ecole gratuite d'industrie' had recruited over 300 children for a minimum term of four years, mainly from poor families in surrounding departments.[88] More commonly, the charitable tradition of employing orphans and foundlings was given new impetus.[89] Like the English pauper apprentices, the *enfants*

---

[84] AN, F[12] 4746, Blaise (Limoges, 10th), 15 January 1878; AN, F[12] 4765, Landois (Limoges, 10th), 5 July 1880; AN, F[12] 4754, Leseur (Limoges, 14th), 17 January 1887.

[85] AN, F[12] 4755, Pellet (Lyons, 15th), 31 December 1884.

[86] See especially Michelle Perrot, 'The Three Ages of Industrial Discipline in Nineteenth-Century France', in Merriman, *Consciousness and Class Experience*, pp. 149–68; *idem*, 'Les Ouvriers et les machines en France dans la première moitié du XIXe siècle', *Recherches*, 32 (1978), 347–75. A local study with excellent material on resistance to discipline is Rolande Trempé, *Les Mineurs de Carmaux, 1848–1914* (2 vols., Paris, 1971), vol. 1, pp. 189–253.

[87] AN, F[12] 4705, Hautes-Alpes.

[88] Henri Causse, 'Un industriel toulousain au temps de la Révolution et de l'Empire: François-Bernard Boyer-Fonfrède (1767–?)', *Annales du Midi* (1957), 121–33.

[89] Hufton, *The Poor*, pp. 139–73; Schmidt, 'Notes sur le travail des enfants', 198–221; E. Soreau, 'Notes sur le travail des enfants dans l'industrie pendant la Révolution', *Revue*

assistés were employed under extremely onerous conditions. Industrialists were allowed to make them wear uniforms, to punish and reward them, to keep them until they were twenty-one and to secure their arrest if they ran away.[90] In the Year VI of the Revolution, for example, the cotton spinner Carette-Jourdain wrote to the *citoyens administrateurs* of the Somme requesting 100 children aged between ten and twelve from the Hospice Nationale at Amiens. He informed them that he already employed 200 child workers from ten to sixteen years, and that he was unable to recruit further in this locality. The administration agreed to his proposals, paying him a sum of 50 francs per child, on the understanding that he would feed, clothe and provide medical services for his charges.[91] Once the wartime crisis was over, the scale of these practices declined, as employers were keen to avoid the burdensome cost of lodging paupers. Only in isolated rural areas where labour was difficult to recruit did small pockets of *enfants assistés* persist, notably in the forest sites of many glassworks and the remote mountainous ones of the *moulinages de soie*.[92]

There remained the temptation to cloister large numbers of young females in convent-like establishments, where conditions were particularly conducive to factory discipline. The silk industry of the *midi* made extensive use of the *internat*, where adolescent girls from the age of twelve were lodged and fed at a mill, under the supervision of nuns.[93] The inevitable tendency to run these places on monastic lines suited the purposes of the industrialist all too well, the 'austere discipline' ensuring regular work habits. The first of the *internats* was founded at Jujurieux, in the Bugey, in 1835. Reporting on his visit to this mill during the 1850s, Louis Reybaud drew attention to the policy of admitting only girls and widows, that is to say those without outside ties and duties which could interfere with their work. Recruitment was confined exclusively to the mountainous areas of the Bugey, Savoy, the Auvergne and the Bresse, on

    des études historiques, 102 (1938), 159–63; Evrard, 'Le Travail des enfants', pp. 3–4; Douailler and Vermeren, 'Les Enfants du capital', pp. 8–12.

90 See the files in AN, F[15] 2458. These were far from the normal conditions for employing labour, a common enough device according to Wilbert E. Moore. He asserts that 'forced labour, in various forms and degrees, has been more common in world economic development than has free contract labour'. *Industrialization and Labor* (New York, 1965), p. 59.

91 AN, F[15] 2458.

92 AN, F[12] 4733, Linares (Orleans, 2nd), 6 February 1882, and AN, F[12] 4734, Pellet (Nevers, 3rd), 3 December 1881, in a glassworks at Souvigny (Allier); AN, F[12] 4739, Nadeau (Lille, 6th), 1882, in a *gobeleterie* at Solre-le-Château (Nord); and AN, F[12] 4759, Pellet (Nîmes, 17th), 14 January 1886, in various silk mills. Cf. Stearns, *Paths to Authority*, p. 62, 'Nowhere was there any combing of orphanages and the like as occurred occasionally in England.'

93 See Martine Benoit, 'Les Couvents ateliers au XIXᵉ siècle', *Le Peuple français*, 22 (1976), 22–6; D. Vanoli, 'Les Ouvrières enfermées: les couvents soyeux', *Les Révoltes logiques*, 2 (1976), 19–39.

the grounds that the 'female worker of the mountains is in general more resigned, more docile, less demanding than one from the plain'.[94] Reybaud estimated that in 1860 there were 40,000 girls in the south-east employed under these conditions. By 1900, the total had moved up to 100,000.[95] In some of the mills, the responsibilities of the nuns were confined to the dormitories, refectories, infirmaries and schools.[96] In others, including Jujurieux, the nuns maintained discipline in the work-shops. At the extreme were the 'charitable' establishments run entirely by the Catholic Church. In 1888, a Factory Inspector based at Grenoble distinguished between the *ouvroirs* with a genuinely charitable character, which concentrated on vocational training, and those where the commercial aspect predominated, which made a profit from the work of their inmates. Amongst the latter, he mentioned the Trappistines de Montpellier, and the Réligieuses de Recoubeau, two orders which ran their own *moulinages de soie*.[97] The perversion of religious forms for the benefit of industry was common throughout the region. During the 1880s, a Factory Inspector complained of the practice in certain mills of making the girls sing hymns and recite prayers throughout the working day, in order to avoid chatting and other distractions.[98]

This is not to say that children made an ideally submissive labour force for the industrialist. They may have been dragooned into the factories and held down to long hours at work by their machines, but they had an underlying resilience which was capable of effective resistance to the efforts of employers and overseers. Evidence on this point is admittedly hard to come by, but the occasional glimpse emerges. Sometimes a youthful stubbornness is revealed, which would have been hard to break. How else can one interpret the following description of a working day given by a fifteen-year-old girl in Lille? She informed a policeman investigating an industrial accident that she started work at 5.00 a.m. picking cotton. An hour later, she was moved to the carding room, having told an overseer that she did not like the work she was doing. But after a quarter of an hour at the hazardous task of carding, she said she felt ill at ease, so she went home to her mother ... Sent back to the mill, she resumed cotton picking, telling her companion that her mother had forbidden her to work at carding, and that if the overseer did not like it,

[94] Louis Reybaud, *Etudes sur le régime des manufacturers: condition des ouvriers en soie* (Paris, 1859), pp. 197–204. For confirmation of these points, see also Julian Turgan, *Les Grandes Usines: études industrielles en France et à l'étranger* (18 vols., Paris, 1866–89), vol. 7, pp. 209–24.

[95] Vanoli, 'Les Ouvrières enfermées', 22.

[96] AN, C 3021, 'Enquête', 1872, Montessuy et Chomer, Tisseurs (Isère).

[97] AN, F[12] 4761, Barral (Grenoble, 19th), 9 January 1888.

[98] AN, F[12] 4764, Gouttes (Saint-Etienne, 21st), 1 July 1886, and annual report for 1888.

she would leave! (Shortly afterwards, the companion was killed by a transmission shaft and the girl injured while trying to rescue her.)[99] There was also the natural effervescence and playfulness of children which the mills could not entirely suppress. Occasionally this ended in tragedy, leaving traces in the official reports. In 1850, at Saint-Pierre-les-Calais, two teenage girls had their arms broken by machinery. It emerged that they had been imprudently dancing together near a cylinder, and were caught and dragged in by their skirts. Similarly, in 1852, at Niort, a young boy came to grief during his first week in a cotton mill. He was described as 'intelligent but dissipated'. He acquired the habit of leaving his work to sit unnoticed by the overseer, on the plateau of a vertical transmission shaft, happily spinning at 45 r.p.m. (He did this once too often, and lost a leg.)[100]

The conclusion must be that in the recruitment and disciplining of workers for the factory system, children could only be a *pis aller* for employers. During the very early stages of industrialization, and subsequently in a few exceptional cases such as the silk industry, they could provide a convenient solution to pressing labour problems. But over the course of the nineteenth century, as industrialists applied themselves seriously to the techniques of management, the willingness to handle substantial concentrations of young children diminished. Once a more sophisticated attitude to labour began to emerge, with employers attempting to harness its capacities through piece-rates and other incentives, instead of relying exclusively on repressive measures, child workers came to be seen as a particularly unreliable instrument for increasing productivity.[101] At the 1837 Enquiry, a few isolated voices amongst employers' organizations revealed the beginnings of scepticism on the benefits of child labour. The Conseil des Prud'hommes of Rouen declared that juvenile labour had the awkwardness and rashness of its age, whilst the Chambre Consultative of Charleville felt that the manufacturer lost in quality what he gained in wages. There was even the conclusion from the Chambre Consultative of Privas, in the heart of the silk-producing region, that employers preferred adults, because they were 'plus attentifs et plus expéditifs'.[102] As if to prove the point, mill owners in the same area laid off all their child workers during a recession a few years later, but kept on

99 AN, F[12] 4617, police report, Lille, 15 July 1856; Pierrard, *La Vie ouvrière*, pp. 168–9.
100 AN, F[12] 4617, reports from Ingénieur des Mines, Valenciennes, 5 April 1852; and from the Prefect of the Deux-Sèvres, 2 March 1852.
101 On management, see Michelle Perrot, 'Travailler et produire: Claude-Lucien Bergery et les débuts du management en France', in *Mélanges d'histoire sociale offerts à Jean Maitron* (Paris, 1976), pp. 177–87; and Bernard Mottez, *Systèmes de salaire et politiques patronales* (Paris, 1966), *passim*.
102 AN, F[12] 4705.

their skilled adult labour.[103] In the latter part of the nineteenth century, there was a growing chorus of disillusionment with children as workers. By 1880, the Factory Inspector at Nantes was expressing a common view in noting that most industrialists were prepared to do without the under-twelves, admitting that they were only capable of mediocre quality work, and needed close supervision.[104]

Conclusion

How far do the workings of the labour market explain the persistence and eventual demise of child labour during the nineteenth century? In concert with political and ideological influences, economic forces emerge as a continuous source of both leads and lags. During the early part of the century, it was very much a case of 'all hands to the pump'. For most working-class families, the struggle to break free from the age-old scourge of poverty made a contribution in the form of paid or unpaid work from all members a necessity still. For the employers in various industries, there was a temptation to lean heavily on the labour force, with long hours, a new pace of work to match the machine and the discipline inherent in large-scale production. Women and children, who were amongst the weakest groups on the labour market, could hardly avoid taking their share of this burden. There can be little doubt that when substantial numbers of working children were concentrated in the public view for the first time, and when the various effects of labouring at a tender age were no longer buried in the family, conditions were ripe for a social reform campaign amongst the middle and upper classes.

In the maturer economy of the late nineteenth century, these pressures on the labour force began to ease. With rising incomes, families could afford greater sacrifices to secure the future welfare of their children. And with the growing substitution of capital for labour in industry, there was a basis for releasing the weakest and least-skilled members of the active population from their toils. This is not to suggest that industrial capitalism should be seen as mellowing into a purely benign influence on child workers. As we shall see, although some industrialists anticipated and provoked the stipulations of child labour legislation, others bitterly

---

[103] AD Ardèche, 15 M 4, Weights and Measures Inspector of Largentière to Prefect, 5 September 1849. Much the same policy was adopted during the crisis of the 1880s; see AN, F^{12} 4761, Barral (Grenoble, 19th), 4 October 1886.

[104] AN, F^{12} 4745, Durassier (Nantes, 9th), 23 November 1880. See also AN, F^{12} 4722, replies to the 1867 Enquiry from the Chambers of Commerce of Mulhouse and Amiens; and AN, F^{12} 4734, Villenaut (Nevers, 3rd), 30 December 1876; AN, F^{12} 4743, Aubert (Lisieux, 8th), 31 December 1879; AN, F^{12} 4744, Jaraczewski (Amiens, 9th), 22 January 1886; AN, F^{12} 4752, Estelle (Nîmes, 13th), 31 January 1878.

resisted all attempts by the State to impose a new pattern of childhood. And there remains open the question of the exact impact of industrialization and urbanization on the lives of working-class children.

Chapter 5

Working conditions for children in industry

The issue of whether the plight of child workers improved or deteriorated with industrial development was hotly disputed in the nineteenth century. The general drift of opinion has always been that their work became more onerous, with the long, gruelling hours of the early textile mills firmly implanted in the popular view of the Industrial Revolution. The oft-quoted passage from Villermé, describing conditions in the cotton and woollen industries of Alsace during the 1830s, has set the tone for much subsequent discussion:

They remain on their feet for sixteen or seventeen hours a day, at least thirteen in an enclosed space, without changing either their place or their position. This is no longer work, or a task, it is torture; and it is imposed on children of six to eight, badly fed, badly clothed, and obliged to cover, at five in the morning, the long distance which separates them from the workshops, and which finally exhausts them in the evening when they return home.[1]

Although no enemy of the factory system in general, Villermé concluded that excessive working hours were one of its major drawbacks, which could only be changed by administrative decree or by law.[2] The industrialists, for their part, took a more optimistic view. Without necessarily denying that life for the proletariat in the towns was becoming increasingly miserable, they argued from the 1830s onwards that the extension of the factories was the most likely source of benefits for employer and employee alike. In particular, they felt, the growing use of machinery in industry would reduce the physical burden of work, and in the long run bring a shorter working day.[3] The key questions, then, concerned the ways in which industrial development affected the age at which children

[1] Villermé, _Tableau de l'état_, vol. 1, p. 91. [2] _Ibid._, p. 355.
[3] See, for example, AN, F^{12} 4705, Lille Chamber of Commerce, 1837; AD Nord, M 613/5, letter from the Lille Conseil des Prud'hommes to Minister of Commerce, 14 September 1840; AN, F^{12} 4722, depositions from the Lille Chamber of Commerce and Sedan Chambre Consultative, 1867.

started on the shop floor, their working hours and the intensity of effort expected from them.

Elements of continuity

During the 1820s and 1830s, when these aspects of working-class life were first brought to light, children in the towns were still drifting slowly into work in much the same way as previous generations on the farms and in the domestic workshops. The dismal backdrop of poverty for much of the urban population forced children into a precocious independence. Generally speaking, industry was less able to provide jobs for the very young than agriculture. What the towns could offer in compensation was a range of casual occupations that would bring in a few sous. The *gamins* of Paris, for example, had a quick eye for the little services required by those with money in their pockets. The commercial sector provided jobs as messengers, delivery boys and street traders. The rich could be tapped for the odd coin by opening carriage doors, lowering steps or hiring out umbrellas and opera glasses; the public at large by street singing, acrobatics and travelling circuses. These apparently anarchic *petites industries nomades* were in reality highly organized with a hierarchy of older youths supervising and training the young, clearly defined territories and strict punishments for those breaking the rules.[4] For children who suddenly found themselves on their own, deserted by their parents, say, or thrown out by an employer, this kind of activity could be the only way of keeping body and soul together. At the age of ten, Norbert Truquin ended up on the streets of Rheims, following the death of his master in the woolcombing industry. He and another *gamin*, whose mother had died and whose father was unemployed, survived by scavenging vegetables from the market, selling the pins and nails they picked out of streams for 5 centimes a pound, scraping mercury from public urinals for a pharmacist and running errands when a fair came to town. They also joined a small *bande* of vagrants, and for a short time took up another common occupation amongst urban youth: petty theft.[5]

A few branches of industry were prepared to take on young children. The 1837 Enquiry on Child Labour found that they could be hired from the age of five or six in the textile industries of Mulhouse, Roubaix, Rouen, Cholet, Lyons and Vienne. The small workshops of the handloom

---

[4] Alain Cottereau, 'Méconnue, la vie des enfants d'ouvriers au XIXᵉ siècle', *Autrement*, 10 (1977), 117–20. See also Martine Untrau, 'J'avais dix ans, j'habitais le 20ᵉ, c'était 1900...', *ibid.*, 105–16.

[5] Norbert Truquin, *Mémoires et aventures d'un prolétaire à travers la révolution* (Paris, 1977), pp. 25–6; Alain Faure, 'Enfance ouvrière, enfance coupable', *Les Révoltes logiques*, 13 (1981), 13–35.

weaving industry were the commonest source of employment for these *petiots*, using them to wind bobbins or, in the silk industry, to assist the weavers. This trickle of recruits gradually increased with the older age groups. Minimum ages of seven, eight or nine were frequently reported to the Enquiry, but even in the textile industries it was not uncommon for children to wait until ten or twelve before starting work. From the woollen industry of the Champagne region, for example, the Rheims Chamber of Commerce noted: 'There are indeed a few young children in our workshops, called *ploqueurs*, from the age of seven or eight, but their number is infinitely small, and nearly all the others are aged nine to thirteen.'[6] Some indication of the capacity of various factory-based industries to make use of child labour comes from the 1822–3 census in Alsace. The *imprimeries d'indiennes* were conspicuous for their willingness to assemble large concentrations of young children. In the two mills owned by Gros-Davillier-Roman and Company at Wesserling and Husson, children under twelve heavily outnumbered those aged twelve to fifteen.[7] In the spinning mills, by contrast, there was more of a tendency to delay entry, for here it was the older age group that predominated. In the Heilmann mill at Ribeauvillé, for example, there were twenty-seven children aged eight to eleven, compared with eighty-one aged twelve to fifteen.[8] Paper, glass, mining and metalworking were further areas where young children under the age of twelve could readily be accommodated. If, during the second half of the century, technical and organizational conditions discouraged the resort to the very youngest age groups, this did not prevent some fierce rearguard actions to hold them in their jobs. Spinning and glassmaking were two industries which were notable for their reluctance to yield up their under-twelves during the 1870s and 1880s.[9] Other industries were able to remain aloof from such controversies, since their customary starting ages were much later. Quite typically, the age of sixteen or seventeen was mentioned for beginning an apprenticeship in the metallurgical industries of the Vosges at mid-century.[10]

The working hours of children employed in industry were also close to those established by custom on the land. The notion of a fixed working day fits uneasily into a 'pre-industrial' context, especially where child workers were concerned, but according to the 1848 Enquiry on Labour

---

6 AN, F[12] 4705, Conseils des Prud'hommes of Mulhouse, Rouen, Cholet and Lyons, Chambre Consultative of Roubaix, Rheims Chamber of Commerce. See also AN, F[12] 4706, 'Rapport du Bureau des Manufactures sur les réponses à la circulaire du 31 juillet, 1837'.

7 AD Haut-Rhin, 9 M 22; the mill at Wesserling had forty-six children under twelve, and twenty-five aged between twelve and sixteen; at Husson, the respective figures were twenty-six and twenty.

8 AD Haut-Rhin, 9 M 23.   9 See below, pp. 313–18.

10 AN, C 969, canton of Monthureux-sur-Saône.

the peasant attempted to fill the daylight hours with a twelve- to
thirteen-hour day.[11] This was precisely the norm in most factories, where
children almost invariably worked the same hours as adults. Ironworks,
paper mills, glassworks, construction sites and even textile mills in
certain regions were specifically mentioned during the 1830s and 1840s as
working a twelve-hour day. At the same period, the spinning mills of the
cotton and woollen industries imposed a *travail effectif* of thirteen and a
half hours, fully deserving their evil reputation for stretching the working
day. This, let it be emphasized, meant starting work at five o'clock in the
morning and continuing through until eight at night, with one and a half
or two hours off for meal breaks. On top of this, when orders were
pressing, the mill owners had no compunction about working their
employees into the night. This could mean keeping their machinery going
until 10.00 p.m, or not stopping at the end of the week until Sunday
morning. Some capitalists went a step further, and attempted to compensate for the high fixed costs on their investments in plant and machinery by
imposing a two-shift system of work. This was clearly an innovation
brought in by the nineteenth century, found particularly in the foundries,
paper mills and textile factories. The Rouen Chamber of Commerce
mentioned to the 1837 Enquiry that a few of the water-powered spinning
mills in its locality ran continuously for twenty-four hours a day, stopping
only to change over labour. The night shift started at eight o'clock in
summer and ten o'clock in winter: adults and children alike then worked
until five in the morning.[12] However, the consensus at the Enquiry was
that night work for children was the exception rather than the rule.

The régime in the smaller workshops was little different. The main body
of skilled artisans, such as carpenters, locksmiths, shoemakers and
blacksmiths, usually worked for twelve hours a day. But where a trade fell
into the hands of commercial capitalism, there was pressure to exceed this
limit. Obliged to compete on the national or international market with a
minimum of protection from their own associations, the labour force
found the traditional constraints on working hours being swept away.
Villermé repeatedly observed that hours in the domestic workshops of the
textile industry were longer than those in the factories. Both in Alsace and
Lyons he noted that the handloom weavers worked for up to fifteen hours
a day during their peak season, starting at daybreak and not giving up
until ten or eleven o'clock at night.[13] Some child workers were inevitably
drawn into this frenetic daily routine. Norbert Truquin was one such
victim, employed in the woolcombing trade of Rheims from the age of

---

[11] See above, pp. 22–7.   [12] AN, F¹² 4705.
[13] Villermé, *Tableau de l'état*, vol. 1, pp. 23, 366; vol. 2, p. 85. See also AN, F¹² 4705,
Conseil des Prud'hommes of Lyons, 1837.

seven. The *peigneurs de laine* were a group who found themselves struggling at mid-century with overcrowding in their trade and the beginnings of competition from mechanization.[14] The desperately long hours they were forced to work brought the young Truquin one long round of misery. He rose at three every morning, to prepare for a working day that lasted from 4.00 a.m. to 10.00 p.m. The combination of these extended hours, the heavy atmosphere of the workshop and the effort of pulling impurities from the wool with his teeth rendered him almost insensible:

During the first days, I set myself to it willingly, I tried to do well; but soon sleep was so uppermost that I slept on my feet; this however was not through any failure on my part to employ all my energy to keep going; I used to take the air outside to stay awake, but as soon as I came back in I fell asleep once more; I used to go out several times to overcome my apathy, but in vain; it was too much for me ... In vain I bit my hands, and banged my head against the wall to resist the desire for sleep; nothing worked.[15]

Improved productivity combined with pressure from the labour movement brought some relief from these punishing hours during the latter half of the century. The Second Empire period saw movement towards a ten-hour day, particularly in the big urban centres such as Paris and Marseilles.[16] Factory Inspectors' reports during the 1870s and 1880s frequently mentioned the ten or eleven hours of *travail effectif* put in by children in most industries. However, they also emphasized that the spinning mills and weaving sheds continued to work an exceptionally long day, with twelve hours being the norm. Women and young girls were, absurdly enough by the standards of the time, the workers most likely to have to exceed average hours. The girls employed in the *moulinages de soie* of the Ardèche and neighbouring departments were one especially vulnerable section of the labour force. Most were aged between ten and their mid-twenties, and with the mills usually sited in isolated mountain valleys, a high proportion lodged in dormitories during the week. Their labour was therefore all too easily abused. During the 1860s, and again during the 1870s, various observers revealed that the 'ancient usage' of working from 4.30 in the morning until 7.00 at night was being maintained.[17] The *modistes*, *couturières*, *fleuristes* and *brodeuses* of the Paris 'sweatshops' were another group whose bargaining power was

---

[14] See A. Audiganne, *Les Populations ouvrières et les industries de la France* (2 vols., Paris, 1860), vol. 1, pp. 119–22.
[15] Truquin, *Mémoires*, p. 21.
[16] Georges Duveau, *La Vie ouvrière en France sous le Second Empire* (Paris, 1946), p. 239.
[17] AD Ardèche, 15 M 3–4, reports of Vérificateurs des Poids et Mesures, and l'Ingénieur des Mines; AN, F[12] 4752, Estelle (Nîmes 13 [th]), 22 December 1876 and 22 January 1881.

insufficient to resist sudden demands for massive overtime. Girls who refused to go on into a fifteen-, sixteen- or even eighteen-hour day were, according to a Factory Inspector, immediately fired.[18] As for expecting night work from child workers, traces of this practice persisted in the odd industry with a 'continuous process' such as paper and glassmaking. The *verriers, la viande à feu* as they grimly called themselves, preferred where possible to avoid working in the heat of the day. In the early twentieth century Léon and Maurice Bonneff wrote an impassioned account of a visit during the middle of the night to a glassworks situated in the suburbs of Paris:

The furnaces were working flat out; the gaping mouths of their openings threw a scarlet glimmer onto the walls, which silhouetted the shadows of the glassworkers. Half-naked men, their bodies steaming, the sweat running from all their limbs, withdrew balls of fire from the crucible, and took them off on their rods: the hall was full of moving stars. The torrid breath of the openings threw us back stifled, towards the doors; around us, threading their way between the *cueilleurs* and the *souffleurs*, children were running silently and quickly. They carried pieces of glassware, cooled rods, buckets of water heavier than themselves. We stopped one as he went by. He was wearing short breeches which stopped at the knee; a head-band framed his flushed cheeks; black circles under his eyes betrayed his fatigue; the face was sunken and dried up: the face of an old man.[19]

The boy admitted to being nine years of age, well below the minimum age of thirteen required by law, and it was asserted that he often worked over the normal ten-hour day. This type of industry apart, however, night work for children was more a feature of the early rather than the later phases of industrialization.

Time, work-discipline

Where the new industrial society of the nineteenth century brought sweeping changes for child workers was in the continuity of effort required. The seasonal rhythm of work characteristic of agriculture and the rural handicraft trades was much attenuated in the industrial workshops of the towns. The influence of the weather was not entirely absent, however. Any industry using water power was vulnerable to stoppages when streams froze over or ran dry. The cotton-spinning industry of the Vosges, many of whose mills were situated on tiny streams up in the mountains, was notoriously vulnerable to interruptions brought on by summer drought.[20] The calico-printing industry was also exposed to

18 AN, F¹² 4730, Laporte (Seine, 1ˢᵗ), n.d. (1889).
19 Léon and Maurice Bonneff, *La Vie tragique des travailleurs* (Paris, 1908), p. 70.
20 AN, C 969, cantons of Corcieux, Monthureux, Raon-l'Etape, Senones (Vosges); Robert Lévy, *Histoire économique de l'industrie cotonnière en Alsace* (Paris, 1912), p. 116.

fluctuations in activity over the seasons. During the eighteenth and early nineteenth centuries, bleaching and drying operations were hampered by rain and frost: around 1780, the Oberkampf works had a long 'dead season' running from November to March, when the working day fell from its normal twelve-hour minimum to less than nine hours.[21] Moreover, as a fashion industry, its production ebbed and flowed according to seasonal demand. The Mulhouse *indienneur* Daniel Schlumberger asserted in 1845 that he had to increase the hours of his child workers between mid-February and mid-April, and again between early September and mid-October, in order to cope with peaks in the market.[22] Other industries where activity moved with the seasons included tailoring, hatmaking, sugar refining and construction. Nonetheless, the six months of relative freedom from work granted to rural children was replaced in the towns by more regular employment throughout the year. Metallurgy, spinning, weaving, papermaking, china and tanning were all industries which employed substantial amounts of child labour, and which were specifically mentioned in the 1848 Enquiry as attempting to work without interruption twelve months a year.[23]

More decisively, the daily and weekly schedule of work changed with the coming of the factory and the 'sweatshops'. The peasant and the artisan had some scope for deciding the pace of their work, taking up and dropping tasks as they saw fit, or alternating periods of half-hearted work with frantic bursts of effort immediately before a deadline.[24] Young children must have benefited more than most from this approach to work, given the range of minor jobs left to them. Once employed in the factories, they faced the whole disciplinary network of employers, foremen and rule books.[25] Regular attendance in the workshop was the first requirement of the new régime. Old habits of taking days off, especially *le saint lundi*, and of wandering in and out of the workshop at will, were no longer tolerated. Looking ahead a little to evidence from the 1870s, a report from a Factory Inspector in Troyes isolated the essential difference when discussing the local hosiery industry. Attempting to explain the lack of education

[21] Serge Chassagne, Y. Dewerpe and Y. Gaulupeau, 'Les Ouvriers de la manufacture de toiles imprimées d'Oberkampf à Jouy-en-Josas, 1760–1815', *Le Mouvement social*, 97 (1976), 56–7; see also Lévy, *L'Industrie cotonnière en Alsace*, pp. 96–7.

[22] AD Haut-Rhin, 10 M 5, letter to the Prefect, 30 April 1845.

[23] See the replies to Question 13 in the 'Enquête sur le travail', 1848, AN, C 943–69.

[24] Edward P. Thompson, 'Time, Work-Discipline and Industrial Capitalism', 56–97.

[25] See Perrot, 'The Three Ages of Industrial Discipline', *passim*; Alberto Melucci, 'Action patronale, pouvoir, organisation. Règlements d'usine et contrôl de la main-d'oeuvre au XIXe siècle', *Le Mouvement social*, 97 (1976), 139–59. There is also the general thesis on the disciplining of society in the late eighteenth and early nineteenth centuries, put forward by Michel Foucault. It is surely overdrawn, but its discussion of new modes of discipline in military, judicial, industrial and educational establishments is pertinent to our theme: *Discipline and Punish* (Harmondsworth, 1977).

amongst the young in the town, the Inspector referred to the habits of
'indiscipline and drunkenness' amongst the framework knitters:

Contrary to the generally expressed opinion, that work in the family is far more of
a moralizing influence, or at least far less of a demoralizing influence, than work in
a big establishment, I have had the sad experience in Troyes of the disorder to
which the first type of work can produce ... In areas where large factories are
located, the workers absorb from their childhood habits of order and discipline:
the bell rings at six in the morning, and everyone must appear without the slightest
delay. Nobody leaves the workshops until the bell rings again at midday or seven
o'clock in the evening. There is no question of going out for a stroll or a drink
during the day: the worker who tried it would be fired immediately ... In Troyes,
by contrast, in all the courtyards, in all the houses, there are numerous small
workshops of three or four workers at most, without an employer or a foreman to
supervise them. In addition, wages are high, so that it is enough to work for four
days a week to earn a living. Hence under the most futile pretext, because it is hot,
because a funeral or wedding procession is passing by in the street, or because the
comrades opposite offer *une politesse*, the workers leave their frames in the middle
of the day, and once the first glass is emptied, they cannot stop.[26]

Doubtless life in an artisan workshop was rarely as free-and-easy as this
might suggest, for only a highly paid minority could afford much in the
way of time off for drinking.[27] All the same, children on the farms and in
the handicraft trades never had to endure the rigid framework surrounding the working day in the factory. The 'sweating' of a trade also had the
effect of undermining the autonomy of the labour force. Low wages and a
considerable 'reserve army' of unemployed made girls in the clothing
industry extremely vulnerable to the constant, harassing attention of a
maîtresse. The silk reelers of Lyons were in a similarly weak position. In
1866, the plight of ten-year-old Marie Péchard, an *apprentie dévideuse*,
was drawn to the attention of the legal authorities in the city. The
Procureur informed the Prefect that the girl suffered from an *ophtalmie
scrofuleuse* which had twice put her in hospital, and which was being
considerably aggravated by the conditions of her work. His investigations
revealed that she was employed by a certain Dame Bernard, together with
two girls aged fourteen and another of thirteen:

From their depositions, collected separately and carefully checked, it emerges that
the children were subjected to sixteen hours of work per day. They started
between five and six in the morning, and did not stop until ten or eleven o'clock at
night. They were only allowed meal times as rest periods, and their sole recreations
consisted of sweeping and tidying the workshop after dinner at two o'clock.[28]

26 AN, F¹² 4736, Doll (Rheims, 5ᵗʰ), 22 September 1875.
27 See Duveau, *La Vie ouvrière*, pp. 243–8.
28 AN, F¹² 4722, letter from Procureur Impérial to Prefect, 16 April 1866.

This type of abuse proved extremely difficult to stamp out, since there were literally hundreds of small workshops involved. In the 1880s and 1890s there was still the occasional court case concerning young girls driven when orders were pressing to fourteen or fifteen hours of *travail effectif*, presumably under the same relentless régime.[29]

The second requirement of the new industrial régime was a consistent level of effort over the working day. The discipline inherent in any large-scale organization of work was not unknown to farm children, but it was an experience confined to certain times of the year. In sharp contrast to the young shepherds, the factory children were constantly watched over by adults, whose interest was to prevent any lapses of concentration, any talking or playing with friends, or any unscheduled breaks. The price of high productivity and high-quality work in the early factories was this elaborate system of surveillance. The main risk for child workers was that the means of enforcing these rules would descend into brutality. Their small size made them especially vulnerable to rough handling by overseers and other adult workers. Industrialists were sensitive on this issue. They had no qualms about reporting the employment of seven-year-olds in the mills, or the fifteen hours spent at work, but they could hardly expect public opinion to accept the physical intimidation of children. Predictably, employers' organizations replying to the 1837 Enquiry stated firmly that the ill-treatment of children was rare, and that occasional outbursts by their employees were immediately punished. Some preferred to stress instead the system of fines which was the generally approved response to minor infringements on the shop floor.[30]

But there were a few cracks in this defensive cover. The Conseil des Prud'hommes of Sainte-Marie-aux-Mines wrote enigmatically that children were treated 'severely' but not badly; the Conseil in Rheims regretted the abuses of strength which continued to occur, despite a tightening of procedures over the previous decade; that of Vienne went as far as to assert: 'The workers who direct the children can only do so with blows, but there are no acts of inhumanity.' Other sources of information were scarcely more reassuring. Villermé, for example, conceded that the large majority of industrialists would not tolerate the corporal punishment of their child workers. Yet he noted that 'many overseers and ordinary workers confessed to me that they beat them [the children], and even

---

[29] AD Rhône, 10 M, *procès-verbaux* against Mme Rangot, 22 October 1888, and Mme Monreynaud, 22 May 1891; see below, p. 310.

[30] For example, AN, F^{12} 4705, Chambre de Commerce and Conseil des Prud'hommes of Orleans (Loiret), and Chambre de Commerce of Strasbourg (Bas-Rhin). According to one estimate from the 1840s, each child worker in a particular spinning mill lost on average one day of pay per month in fines; AD Vosges, M 284, letter from Gérard to Sub-Prefect of Saint Dié, 9 November 1846.

maintained that the use of this method was very often necessary'.[31] He and others could not refrain from recounting much unsavoury hearsay on this point. A footnote of his mentioned that certain establishments in Normandy employed the *nerf de boeuf* as a working tool on the machines. The Comte de Tascher referred to this fearsome instrument in the Parliamentary debates of 1840, and in addition claimed to know of a *patron* who intimidated his apprentices with a red-hot iron.[32] More concrete evidence occasionally came to the surface, suggesting a less dramatic but more plausible picture. For example, in 1846 an unsigned letter to the Prefect of the Vosges from workers in a spinning mill complained of various abuses by their Director, M. Mercier. One of these was that he regularly chastised his younger employees, in order to goad them on during their long working day. Subsequent enquiries revealed this allegation to be true. Mercier had a reputation for treating all of his workers sternly, and he 'sometimes in effect gave the children a kick in the backside or a slap when he found them talking to their friends or neglecting their work'.[33] Another letter, in this case from a group of *fillettes* employed on silk spinning in the Ardèche, made a similar charge during the 1880s. The girls asserted that they were being abused by their overseers, and although the local Factory Inspector hinted at a certain amount of exaggeration, he concluded that their complaint was essentially justified.[34] In short, although a well-run enterprise could minimize the cuffings and beatings of children, it remained a widespread abuse in large- as in small-scale workshops.[35] A measure of ill-temper on the part of employers, overseers and parents was after all only to be expected

31 Villermé, *Tableau de l'état*, vol. 2, pp. 115–16.
32 The historiography of the *nerf de boeuf* is interesting. The major source is Villermé, but he was quoting a newspaper article in the *Industriel de la Champagne* of 2 October 1835. The authority for the statement was always dubious: 'Le fait, ajoute M. le rédacteur, m'a été affirmé à Paris par plusieurs fabricans, et par des femmes de fabricans, qui frémissaient en le racontant.' Villermé concluded on a cautious note: 'Je rapporte ce fait, mais je ne le regarde que comme une rare exception.' However, such a haunting image could not be allowed to rest in obscurity, and no account of child labour in the factories has been considered complete without some reference to this gruesome implement. See Villermé, *Tableau de l'état*, vol. 2, p. 116, n. 2; Emile Levasseur, *Histoire des classes ouvrières et de l'industrie en France de 1789 à 1870*, 2nd edn (2 vols., Paris, 1904), vol. 2, p. 125, n. 2; Touren, *La Loi de 1841*, p. 14; Evrard, 'Le Travail des enfants', 9; Georges Dupeux, *French Society, 1789–1970* (London, 1976), p. 131.
33 AD Vosges, M 284, anonymous letter to Prefect, from Celles, 20 October 1846; letter from Gérard to Sub-Prefect of Saint Dié, 8 November 1846.
34 AN, F12 4761, Barral (Grenoble, 19th), 12 January 1890.
35 For an extreme case of ill-treatment of a child in a domestic workshop, there is the testimony of Norbert Truquin. The boy was regularly hit with the back of a hand on his nose, whipped with a rope, and assaulted with a broom, in a manner it would be difficult to imagine possible in a factory: *Mémoires*, p. 21; see Clark Nardinelli, 'Corporal Punishment and Children's Wages in Nineteenth-Century Britain', *Explorations in Economic History*, 19 (1982), 283–95.

under nineteenth-century conditions. All had to contend with the fatigue of long working hours, tight deadlines for fulfilling orders and earnings that could be jeopardized when children made mistakes.

If the disciplinary system of the workshops did not invariably depend on physical violence, it could hardly avoid a hierarchy of managers and foremen, together with a whole series of rules and regulations. Some of the latter were directed towards ensuring the safety of the labour force, insisting, for example, that machinery be cleaned only when it was switched off, and that moving transmission belts be left alone. But the overriding aim was to maximize the productivity of labour.[36] To this end, besides articles banning drinking, swearing, smoking, writing on the walls and movement between workshops, there were usually sanctions for a lack of application, poor-quality workmanship and damage to the machines. With the background of a State firmly committed to *laissez-faire* principles, and a labour movement which was only beginning to find its feet, the early factory masters had few constraints on their power in the workplace. They were therefore able to take an aggressive stance in the drawing up of their *règlements d'atelier*, and in the wielding of their authority. How then did children react to this apparently oppressive system?

The material on which to base an answer is perilously thin, given that so few industrial workers from the nineteenth century wrote autobiographies. But there is a hint of a diversity of experience: between rural and urban workers, those in small and those in large workshops, not to mention the individual influence of particular employers and foremen. Some children undoubtedly found factory work hard going. A *tourneur mécanicien*, representing the engineering workers of Nancy at the 1882 Parliamentary Enquiry, left the impression that he had been thrown into a bear garden. He had started work at the age of eleven in a forge, and, perhaps significantly, would have had no relations in the works, his father being a gardener. His first job was operating a water-driven hammer, and he suffered bitterly from the brutal attention of the *forgerons*: 'The smallest fault led to a beating, always bad examples before one's eyes.'[37] The experience of Gaston Lucas, in a small workshop in Poitiers, had much in common with this. Starting his apprenticeship as a locksmith at the age of fourteen, he too had to face the impatience of adults around the forge. In this case it was mainly his *patron*: 'He laid about your head with

[36] Melucci argues that the pressure to increase the pace of work effectively undermined any safety regulations in the early factories. The evidence of accident reports, which frequently showed children injured while cleaning moving machinery, would seem to bear this out. See Melucci, 'Action patronale', 147; and below, pp. 176–7.

[37] AN, C 3364, Chambre Syndicale des Ouvriers Mécaniciens de Nancy (Meurthe-et-Moselle).

blows from his cap at the slightest false manoeuvre. But if you overheated his iron, or made him miss a weld, he was unable to control himself. He would have hurled his hammer into your face. For him, iron was sacred.'[38] At least in this case the young apprentice respected the competence of his master, and felt he was learning a worthwhile trade.

Other reminiscences of the factory were more favourable than those of the unfortunate *tourneur*. The *Mémoires* of Norbert Truquin mentioned a brief spell in a woollen-spinning mill at Amiens during the 1840s. He resented the repression of all political discussion during working hours. But, sorely bruised by his experience of woolcombing in Rheims, he did find the factory more tolerable than the domestic workshop. In the mill he was 'amongst society', and he considered the *contre-maîtres* more concerned with the quality than the quantity of work. When they were not around, 'we told stories, or discussed plays in the theatre, some jokers improvised a pulpit and amused themselves preaching; time passed cheerfully'.[39] Augustine Rouvière too stressed the sociability of factory work, on the strength of her years in a *filature de soie* during the 1890s. Brought up in a rural area of the Cévennes, she followed the custom of replacing her mother in the mill immediately after her first communion. By her own account, she stands as something of a living advertisement for paternalism in industry. She saw herself as part of a community, closely attached to the spinner and his family. This employer in his turn knew all the girls by name, and was considered a *bon patron*. Her recollections of the working day were:

Today I think that we were happier in our *filature* than in those large, anonymous factories, surrounded by the noise of all those heavy machines, without anyone to share our sorrows and our joys. We young people used to sing, especially hymns, Protestants as well as Catholics. At work we were all sisters. We were allowed to talk, to gossip, to discuss our weekends. The essential thing was to keep working. From neighbour to neighbour, how many confidences were covered by the noise of the reeling machines![40]

Hymn singing and non-stop work could hardly have been to everyone's taste. But, as an Ingénieur des Mines had observed in 1873, the girls rarely complained, since they preferred industrial work to the alternative of domestic service. The latter was more remunerative and provided better material conditions, but the mills allowed the girls the liberty of one day a week off work between Saturday and Sunday night.[41]

All this might be taken to suggest that children willingly accepted and adapted to the work schedules of the capitalist régime. Such was not

---

[38] Adelaide Blasquez, *Gaston Lucas, serrurier* (Paris, 1976), p. 44.
[39] Truquin, *Mémoires*, pp. 50–1.
[40] Rey, *Augustine Rouvière*, p. 47.   [41] AN, F[12] 4726, report of 12 November 1873.

always the case. During the late nineteenth century, in the textile industry above all, they showed signs of militancy. For example, in 1876 a Factory Inspector came across a threatened general strike amongst children aged twelve to fifteen in the weaving industry of Flers. The strikers were demanding shorter hours and better pay, and at the time of his visit they had already stopped a weaving shed with three hundred adults and forty-five children.[42] More generally, the piecers of the spinning mills were particularly prominent, affected as they were by an increased pace of work, and the tendency for new technology to make them redundant. The vast majority of these efforts ended in humiliating failure, scorned by employers and adult workers alike.[43] Nonetheless, they do indicate a degree of solidarity amongst child workers which, against all the odds, could be translated into action. René Michaud gave an account of one such action on the eve of the First World War. Although trivial enough in itself, it does provide evidence of resentment towards a domineering employer, leading to collective resistance. The context was a small, family enterprise in Paris manufacturing cardboard boxes, and employing twenty workers, none of whom was over eighteen. The root cause of the strike was the *patronne*, who occupied a post near the door and continually shouted at any one moving about or pausing. When she attempted to impose the usual fine equivalent to half-an-hour's work for a late return from lunch of one minute, a group of five waited outside for the full thirty minutes. The next time they tried this, they found themselves locked out, and so they stayed away for the whole afternoon. The result was a victory for the young rebels, since the next day everything returned to normal. Michaud was emphatic that he preferred the atmosphere of the large workshop to this *bagne familiale*. Moving to a shoe factory employing fifty people, he found that he was no longer shouted at for being a few minutes late, and that he was able to organize his own work. He also preferred the foreman to a small employer: 'Here, under the orders of men, I felt myself a man and a full-fledged worker.'[44]

    In conclusion, the organization of work in the factories had the disadvantage of an impersonal, indeed instrumental, relationship between employers, foremen and child workers. The extensive hierarchy and regulations necessary for the functioning of any large, bureaucratic organization, and the aim of maximizing productivity and profits when little attention had to be paid to the welfare of the labour force, combined to create an exceptionally harsh environment in the early factories. In its

[42] AN, F[12] 4742, Aubert (Lisieux, 8th), 28 May 1876.
[43] Michelle Perrot, *Les Ouvriers en grève* (2 vols., Paris, 1974), vol. 1, pp. 313–18.
[44] René Michaud, *J'avais vingt ans: un jeune ouvrier au début du siècle* (Paris, 1967), pp. 51–65.

most degenerate forms, it could involve the bullying of juvenile labour by ill-tempered employers and foremen, and abnormally long working hours. But there was always the possibility of mitigating circumstances, with a humane management, work beside a relative, and comradeship with other young people. Contrasted to this form of production was the small workshop, with its informality and the personal bonds between master and *campagnon* or apprentice. Marie-Catherine Gardez, for example, passed a tranquil childhood in the company of her parents and sisters, much of it handloom weaving in the family cellar.[45] If this scale of production had great potential for creating a very suitable environment for child workers, it could in exceptional circumstances deteriorate into the worst possible forms of exploitation. A child who was unfortunate enough to be placed with a vicious or exceptionally acquisitive employer under these circumstances risked constant physical and mental abuse of a kind which it would have been impossible to inflict in the more public conditions of the factory. Norbert Truquin, who might be described as the French equivalent of the famous Robert Blincoe, was able to leave eloquent testimony to the ravages of the domestic workshop.

Work on the machines

Finally, the factory system in particular required work with machinery. As in Britain, many contemporary observers found it difficult to come to terms with the technology of the Industrial Revolution.[46] There was awe and wonder at the prospects of increased productivity held out by mechanized methods. Yet there was also concern over their impact on the welfare of labour. Eugène Buret proclaimed boldly in 1840: 'The history of the progress of the cotton industry is the history of the progress of misery; with each of the miraculous discoveries applied to spinning or weaving, the labouring classes have descended one step down the ladder of misery.'[47] Charles Dupin was equally ambivalent in his attitude to the machine, despite his experience of teaching in the Conservatoire des Arts et Métiers. During the 1840s, when reporting to the Chamber of Peers on proposals for child labour legislation, he emphasized the 'great physical conquest over the forces of inorganic nature achieved in the eighteenth century'. On the one hand, he argued, it provided man with an auxiliary for his work, increasing 'manufacturing power' and easing the burden on

---

[45] Grafteaux, *Mémé Santerre, passim.* See also Benoit, *Confessions d'un prolétaire*, p. 69, on the silk weavers' shops; and Emile Zola, *L'Assommoir* (New York, 1962), *passim*, for the easy-going atmosphere of the laundry shop run by Gervaise Coupeau.

[46] British reactions are extensively investigated in Maxine Berg, *The Machinery Question and the Making of Political Economy, 1815–1848* (Cambridge, 1980).

[47] Buret, *De la misère*, vol. 2, p. 153.

the labour force. On the other, it required a longer and more intensive effort: 'The workers become in some ways accessories, more or less sacrificed to huge impulsive forces harnessed from inanimate nature.'[48] Women and children being amongst the first groups of workers to experience the very mixed blessings of mechanization, close attention was paid to their predicament by both opponents and defenders of the factory system.

The lightening of the physical burden on children in industry was a protracted affair. Some of the developments in the artisan trades were, from this point of view, regressive, for they weighed heavily on the younger members of the labour force. The most pathetic 'victims' were probably the *tireurs* and *tireuses* of the silk-weaving industry: children who pulled the pattern-making cards of the *canuts* in Lyons. Their working day involved a continual bending and stretching, which Villermé considered beyond their physical capacity. By the 1830s, when he made his observations, the Jacquard loom was making the *tireurs* redundant. But on the broader looms, used for making shawls, children were still employed as *lanceurs*, throwing a shuttle for up to fifteen hours a day.[49] And then there were the children in the coal mines. By the middle of the nineteenth century, the adoption of the steam engine and other technical advances had transformed the whole scale of operations in the industry. In the larger pits, upwards of two or three hundred children under the age of sixteen were assembled to assist the miners. Underground work for women and girls was the exception rather than the rule during the last century: generally they were employed at the pit-head in the sorting of coal and loading of waggons.[50] Boys under ten were forbidden by a decree of 1813 from going down the mines, and although this was not always respected, the very young usually started work on the surface. Only around the age of twelve were they considered strong enough for the rigours of the pit itself. There they helped with the ventilation system, opening and closing the *portes d'aerage*, and working fans. They also assisted the *boiseurs* or *raccomodeurs*, who were responsible for shoring up the galleries with timber. Their major activity, however, was the transporting of coal from the depths of the mine, where the faceworkers had hacked it from the seams, to the lift shaft. The youngest undertook the

---

48 Dupin, *Du travail des enfants*, part 1, p. xxiv; part 2, pp. 4–5.
49 Villermé, *Tableau de l'état*, vol. 1, pp. 366, 442. See also AN, F^{12} 4705, Conseil des Prud'hommes of Lyons, 1837, for the last vestiges of the *lanceurs*, Reybaud, *Condition des ouvriers en soie*, p. 160, and AN, F^{12} 4831, letter from Conseil des Prud'hommes of Lyons to Minister of Agriculture, 14 February 1867.
50 In 1886 a Factory Inspector in the Nord mentioned that females did go underground in certain pits near the frontier, following the Belgian practice; AN, F^{12} 4743, Delattre (Lille, 8th), 15 January 1886.

first stage, shifting coal from the face to the main galleries. Until the 1840s, this was extremely laborious work, with the children hitched to tubs that had to be dragged along on wooden skates. With the installation of railway lines and wheeled waggons, the burden was reduced.[51] Even so, loading and pushing these *waggonets* deep underground was an arduous task; in the words of Emile Zola:

It was certainly not an easy road. From the coal face to the incline was about sixty metres, and the rippers had not yet widened the tunnel, which was a mere pipe with a very uneven roof, bulging at every moment. At some points a loaded tub would only just go through and the haulage man had to flatten himself and push kneeling down so as not to smash his head. What was more, the timbers were already giving and snapping and long, pale rents appeared as they gave in the middle, like crutches too weak for the job. You had to be careful not to scrape your skin off on this splintered wood, and as you crawled on your belly under the slowly sinking roof, which could snap oak props as thick as a man's thigh, you felt a haunting fear that suddenly you would hear your own spine crack.[52]

The rest of these *hercheurs* or *rouleurs* worked on the larger, horse-drawn waggons in the main galleries. They were responsible for leading the horses, operating the braking systems, loading the cages at the bottom of the pit-shaft, and laying down new track.[53]

A new set of problems came at the end of the century, with the introduction of pedal-operated sewing machines. These were extensively used in lingerie, tailoring, glovemaking and corsetry, being operated by girls or women called *mécaniciennes*. The Factory Inspectorate concluded that where there was an alternation of hand and machine stitching, as was usual in these trades, there were no ill effects. But in the manufacturing of shoes, where the *piqueuses de bottines* were likely to be on their machine all day, the job risked becoming intolerable. Particular attention was drawn to an American machine, widely used in the workshops, that could manage 300 stitches per minute. An Inspector calculated that with each depression of the pedal producing five stitches, the girl had to move her feet once every second, which was equivalent to 3,600 movements per

51 AD Nord, M 611/6, Conseil des Prud'hommes of Valenciennes, 'Rapport sur le travail des enfants', 1842; Trempé, *Mineurs de Carmaux*, vol. 1, p. 114.

52 Emile Zola, *Germinal*, transl. L. W. Tancock (Harmondsworth, 1954), p. 53. For similar descriptions in quarries and phosphate mines, see the Factory Inspectors' reports in AN, F[12] 4736 and 4739, Delaissemont (Rheims, 5th and 6th), 8 May 1880 and 1887; and AN, F[12] 4745, Delattre (Nantes, 9th), April 1885.

53 This section relies on AN, C 3018, Compagnie Houillière de Carvin and Houillières de Courrières (Pas-de-Calais), 1872; AN, C 3019, Compagnie des Charbonnages d'Anzin (Nord), 1872; AN, F[12] 4739, Nadeau (Lille, 6th), 1879 and 1884; AN, F[12] 4744, Jaraczewski (Amiens, 9th), 14 January 1888; Trempé, *Mineurs de Carmaux*, vol. 1, pp. 114–15; and Lequin, *Les Ouvriers de la région lyonnaise*, vol. 1, pp. 124–5.

hour, or nearly 40,000 over the normal eleven-hour day.[54] René Michaud, a young male who worked with a similar machine making cardboard boxes, remembered:

The stapling machines were treacherous, especially those for the corners: we had to produce five hundred boxes an hour, two thousand kicks on the pedal, and so two thousand times, a little forefinger came near the moving head of the machine, which, responding to the action of the pedal, punched in the staple.[55]

An error of judgement was therefore like to result in injury, as Michaud found to his cost, having the top of a finger half crushed.

Power-driven machinery would eventually eliminate human beings, and children especially, as 'prime movers' in most of industry. Factory owners liked to argue that their juvenile employees worked only intermittently, and so were not tired out by their jobs. La Motte Bossuet, one of the most important cotton spinners in the Nord, insisted that the *bacleurs* (bobbin boys) in his mill had only three hours of *travail effectif* per day, since they spent most of their time sitting in front of the machines, taking messages for the spinners, attending school or sweeping up. In these circumstances, he questioned whether mere attendance at the mill could be counted as work.[56] In similar vein, the silk throwers of the Vivarais claimed that at any given time in their mills, up to one third of the girls would be found resting, as they waited for a worthwhile number of threads to break on their winding machinery.[57] But this was at best a partial view. Other observers were struck by the mental as well as the physical fatigue brought on by work in the mills. The *rattacheur* of the spinning industry in particular had to remain alert for the full working day, waiting to rush forward and mend any one of up to 500 threads. All the while he or she had to be careful to avoid fast-moving belts, transmission shafts and gearings. And to make matters worse, there was the constant whirring and crashing of the machinery; the heavy, dusty atmosphere of the workshops; and the piercing shout of the spinners and foremen.[58] As for the silk-throwing industry, the Inspector of Weights and Measures at Largentière gave short shrift to the pleadings of the mill owners:

The brief and unlimited rests inherent in the work of children in the *fabriques* are as necessary to these young workers as the feeble breaks taken by workers in the fields or by those employed in other industries. Their youthful age and their sustained attention require that rests of two or three minutes refresh them from

54 AN, F¹² 4730, Laporte (Seine, 1ˢᵗ), 1888.   55 Michaud, *Un jeune ouvrier*, p. 57.
56 AD Nord, M 613/1, letter to Prefect, 9 January 1853.
57 AD Ardèche, 14 M 4, letter from Louis Blanchon to Prefect, 27 August 1852.
58 For example, AD Seine-Maritime, 10 MP 1363, letter from Beaufour (Departmental Inspector) to Prefect, 16 July 1867; AN, F¹² 4747, Blaise (Rouen, 10ᵗʰ), 10 July 1887.

time to time, and allow them to accomplish a task, which only appears light in the eyes of a *patron* who has not been a worker himself.[59]

Not all factory children were pushed so hard. The *tireurs* of the calico-printing works were a notable example of a group who enjoyed relatively short hours and relatively light work.[60] The conclusion remains that with the machine there was a relentless enervating pace to the work that was unknown to children occupied in the fields or the handicraft trades.

Conclusion

The common view that the 'fixed working hours, mandatory work assignations, steady pace of work, and presumed monotonous tasks' of the factory milieu invariably clash with the cultural background of workers is open to challenge.[61] The contrast between agricultural and industrial working conditions is often exaggerated, and the factory system could encompass a whole range of authorities. In France, there was the occasional example of out-and-out philanthropy, such as that provided by the Duc de Liancourt in the late eighteenth century. There was the enlightened self-interest characteristic of the Alsace *patronat*, and the stern, Catholic paternalism found among many employers in Lille. And then there were the lower depths of the vicious, backstreet workshops, found in the big cities of Paris and Lyons. Nonetheless, as far as child workers were concerned, the weight of evidence does point to the early stages of industrialization producing 'increasing misery' in nineteenth-century France. To be more specific, there was a definite intensification of work for that substantial group of children employed in the factories and the workshops of commercial capitalism. The age of starting work may not have changed much, nor the hours of labour put in each day, but a more relentless application to the tasks at hand was required. From the 1840s and 1850s onwards, there was some lightening of the burden, as working hours shortened, and as management practices became less crude. However, there was always the possibility that the speeding up of machinery and carefully calculated bonus systems would at least partially offset the decline in physical brutality or petty regulations. There was also the continuing problem of the 'sweatshops', which were so important in

---

59 AD Ardèche, 15 M 4, letter from Teyssier to Prefect, 16 July 1859.
60 AD Haut-Rhin, 10 M 4, report of Paul George and F. T. Herrgott, Docteur en médecine (cantons of Cernay, Massevaux, Delle and Belfort), 14 June 1842; Villermé, *Tableau de l'état*, vol. 1, p. 437.
61 Herbert Blumer, 'Early Industrialization and the Laboring Class', *Sociological Quarterly*, 1 (1960), 7. This article appears to be based on twentieth-century experience in Latin America.

major French industries such as silk and clothesmaking. The overall impression remains that if, in the long run, industrialization brought some improvements in the working conditions of children, things had to get worse before they got better.

••

Chapter 6

A physical decline in the race?

From discussing changes in the working conditions of children, it was but a short step to looking at the impact of industrial employment on their physical and intellectual welfare. The issue was raised in 1828 by Jean-Jacques Bourcart, during the course of a famous speech to the Société Industrielle de Mulhouse. He proposed that juvenile labour in the spinning mills be given legal protection, on the grounds that:

The industry of our country has developed in an extraordinary manner, but if on the one side it has eased the misery of the working class by providing work, it has not contributed, or at least has barely contributed, to their moral and physical improvement ... It is noticeable that children employed for too long in the workshops have feeble bodies and feeble health, and that, not having time to look after their education, they cannot develop morally.[1]

Such forthright criticism of the new industrial system was not to the taste of the majority of employers, threatening as it did one of their most cherished liberties: that of running their enterprises unhindered by the intervention of the State. There followed a long and emotive propaganda war between reformers and apologists for the unfettered expansion of the industrial sector. This chapter confines itself to the first part of the debate, concerning the physical state of children employed in industry. Here we must follow contemporaries and cast our net widely, for the direct effect on health of conditions in the workshops was only part of the story. The various occupations also had an indirect effect, through the way of life associated with them. Due emphasis will therefore be given to the housing, the diet and the overall urban environment experienced by different groups of child workers. As a preliminary, the chapter investigates ways of measuring the impact of industrialization and urbanization

---

[1] 'Proposition sur la nécessité de fixer l'âge et de réduire les heures du travail des ouvriers des filatures', *Bulletin de la Société Industrielle de Mulhouse*, 1 (1828), 325.

on the health of the child population during the first half of the nineteenth century.

Measuring the damage: military recruitment figures

The assumption amongst reformers was that children in urban working-class families were physically inferior to the offspring of peasant and middle-class households. It followed that, in the short term at least, the expansion of the industrial sector could only cause a partial 'bastard-ization of the race'. There was no shortage of observers perceiving a contrast between the wretched youth of the industrial centres, and their more robust peers in the villages or the bourgeois *quartiers* of the towns. In 1827 Jean Gerspach dwelt on the morbid, downcast air of the factory children in Thann, suggesting that they lacked the gaiety which came naturally to others of their age.[2] A few years later, a Factory Inspector in this same district of Alsace was struck by the differences between the ragged children of the town and the healthier constitutions of young people out in the adjacent valley.[3] Villermé too was disturbed by the spectacle of child labour in the textile industries:

Everywhere pale, enervated, slow in their movements, tranquil in their games, they offer an exterior of misery, suffering and despondency, which contrasts with the ruddy complexions, the well-fleshed look, the liveliness and the numerous signs of vigorous health which one notices amongst children of all ages, as one moves from a manufacturing area to an agricultural canton.[4]

But however valuable these testimonies to the plight of working-class children might have been, reformers were aware that their case would be buttressed most effectively by the provision of statistical evidence of deteriorating health. This was the period, during the 1820s and 1830s, when numerical methods were starting to be applied to problems of public health, with the expectation that they would give scientific proof to various hypotheses.[5]

[2] Jean Gerspach, *Considérations sur l'influence des filatures de coton et des tissages sur la santé des ouvriers* (Paris, 1827), p. 18.

[3] AD Haut-Rhin, 10 M 4, 'Inspection des fabriques, cantons de Thann et de Saint-Amarin', 2 May 1842.

[4] Louis R. Villermé, *Discours sur la durée trop longue du travail des enfants dans beaucoup de manufactures* (Paris, 1837), pp. 60–1.

[5] For the background on the 'statistics movement', see Erwin H. Ackerknecht, 'Hygiene in France, 1815–1848', *Bulletin of the History of Medicine*, 22 (1948), 117–55; Anne Elizabeth La Berge, 'Public Health in France and the French Public Health Movement, 1815–1848', unpublished thesis, University of Tennessee, 1974, pp. 37–71; Bernard-Pierre Lecuyer, 'Médecins et observateurs sociaux: les Annales d'hygiène publique et de médecine légale, 1820–1850', in François Bédarida *et al.*, *Pour une histoire de la statistique* vol. 1, *Contributions* (Paris, 1977), pp. 445–75; William Coleman, *Death is a Social Disease* (Madison, Wisc., 1982), pp. 124–48.

One of the most obvious sources of statistical material was the Ministry of War, for its recruitment records could be used to compare the condition of military conscripts aged twenty in industrial and agricultural areas.[6] Villermé was particularly adept at marshalling this data, his figures on the poor showing of the manufacturing centre of the Haut-Rhin in comparison to neighbouring departments being quoted frequently in reformist literature. He calculated that over the five-year period 1824 to 1828, 12.70 per cent of young men were classified as medically unfit for military service in the Haut-Rhin, compared to 7.80 per cent in the Bas-Rhin, 8.77 per cent in the Meurthe and 4.07 per cent in the Doubs. He also revealed that in Amiens, to assemble 100 men fit for service, it required 193 conscripts from the well-off classes, but 343 from the poor.[7] Modern historians have also taken an interest in military recruitment statistics, notably in a recent study covering the whole of France, department by department, during the years 1819 to 1826.[8] Comparing the two sets of findings, it is now clear that Villermé gave a distorted impression, by selecting a limited number of examples highly favourable to his argument.

[6] Military recruitment operated according to the following procedure between 1818 and 1872. At the beginning of each year, all young men who had reached the age of twenty were required to register at their local Mairie. This provided the annual 'class' of conscripts. A few months later these men assembled at the *chef-lieu* of their canton for the *tirage au sort*: a drawing of lots to give every individual a number. After that, the *conscrits* faced the Conseil de Révision for a final selection process. The Conseil worked its way through the class list, in ascending numerical order, examining the men to determine whether or not they could be accepted for military service. Sons of widows, those responsible for orphans and a few other categories were able to gain exemptions, as well as those found to be physically unsuitable. The Conseil continued to examine men until it had fulfilled its quota for the contingent, which incidentally explains why the conscripts were eager to draw a high number at the *tirage*: *un bon numero*. The contingent was composed of men fit for service, plus a number of others given a dispensation as regular soldiers, official schoolteachers, theological students and so forth. The summary of these operations in the Nord, for 1819, was therefore recorded in a number of columns which included: the total in the age group, the 'force de la classe' (9,295); the number of men examined (2,705); the various exemptions, including those for 'infirmities, deformities or lack of height' (837); the number declared 'good for service' (796); and the total of the contingent (1,153). These departmental totals were the product of figures for each canton. For an account of these procedures, and the surrounding folklore, see Michel Bozon, *Les Conscrits* (Paris, 1981).

[7] Villermé, *Tableau de l'état*, vol. 2, p. 245. A further important work in this field by Villermé was the 'Mémoire sur la taille de l'homme en France', *Annales d'hygiène publique et de médecine légale*, 1 (1829), 351–95; however this was not used in connection with child labour reform. See also Gerspach, *Santé des ouvriers*, p. 18; Adolphe d'Angeville, *Essai sur la statistique de la population française* (Bourg, 1836), pp. 38–49, 322–33; *Le Moniteur*, 16 June 1839; Buret, *De la misère*, p. 360; Dupin, *Du travail des enfants*, part 1, pp. 55–6; Dr Thouvenin, 'De l'influence que l'industrie exerce sur la santé des populations dans les grands centres manufacturiers', *Annales d'hygiène publique et de médecine légale*, 36 (1846), part 1, 16; Reybaud, *Le Coton*, pp. 102–3.

[8] Aron *et al.*, *Conscrit français*. This work includes a critique of the source, discussing the likelihood of different standards obtaining between Conseils de Révision, attributable to medical and administrative incompetence, abuses of power and fraud: pp. 203–16.

At the same time, there is plenty of evidence available in the military archives to support his contention that industrial and urban development were taking a heavy toll on the health of working-class children.

At first sight, the case made from the recruitment statistics by critics of the modern industrial system appears decidedly weak. The manufacturing departments were far from conspicuous in their struggles to form a military contingent. In most difficulty, over the period 1819 to 1826, were three solidly agricultural departments, the Corrèze, the Allier and the Hautes-Pyrénées, all being obliged to reject approximately half of the men they examined. Some industrial centres were certainly revealed in an unfavourable light. The Aube, the Seine-Inférieure, the Vosges and the Marne were all in the lowest quartile of departments. But in the top quartile were the Nord, the Haut-Rhin and the Seine.[9] More damagingly perhaps, departments in the economically developed north and east of France tended to have a higher proportion of so-called tall men (over 5 foot 7 inches) than those in the relatively backward south and west, and a correspondingly lower proportion of small-statured men (under 5 foot 4 inches). In so far as height can be taken as an indicator of environmental rather than genetic factors,[10] this would point to the commonsense conclusion that economic development favoured the physical condition of a population. However, reality was not so simple, for the harsh side-effects of early stages of industrialization were also hinted at in the military records. Departments with high percentages of exemptions for *faiblesse de constitution* were heavily, though not exclusively, concentrated in the north-east. Similarly, the incidence of scrofula[11] and chest diseases

[9] In 1840, Charles Dupin asserted that the ten most agricultural departments in the country produced 4,029 medical exemptions for every 10,000 men capable of serving in the army, whilst in the ten most industrial departments the equivalent figure was 9,930: *Du travail des enfants*, part 1, p. xlvii. This 'deep and powerful wound' is not apparent in the 1820s if one follows the statistical procedures of Emmanuel Le Roy Ladurie and his team. Their figures show that in the ten *least* agricultural departments an average (mean) of 41.02 per cent of the men examined were rejected on medical grounds, compared to 40.67 per cent in the ten *most* agricultural departments; Aron *et al.*, *Conscrit français*, pp. 124–5, 172–3. Close examination of the records for 1837–9 by Lee S. Weissbach reveals that Dupin had to choose his examples carefully to illustrate his argument. At this period the Seine-Inférieure and the Nord had a higher percentage of medical exemptions than the national average, but the Haut-Rhin and the Seine a lower percentage. See his 'Qu'on ne coupe le blé en herbe', pp. 93–4.

[10] On this point, see the discussion in Emmanuel Le Roy Ladurie, N. Bernageau and Y. Pasquet, 'Le Conscrit et l'ordinateur. Perspectives de recherche sur les archives militaires du XIXᵉ siècle français', *Studi Storici*, 10 (1969), 291–2.

[11] 'Scrofula' was the term still used during the first half of the nineteenth century for tuberculosis, particularly that affecting other parts of the body than the chest.

was high in much of the north and east – though conspicuously low in Normandy.[12]

A similar pattern of light and shade for the manufacturing areas is discernible when one moves from the broad canvas of France in its entirety to a more intensive study of a sample of five departments in the northern part of the country. These were examined at the level of the canton, over the same years 1819 to 1826.[13] They included the most notorious centres for child labour in industry – the Haut-Rhin, the Nord and the Seine-Inférieure – and, to provide a certain contrast, the Meurthe and the Aube. To begin with, the results for the Conseils de Révision in the cantons with the highest and lowest proportions of men employed in agriculture were compared.[14] Once again, the conclusions of Villermé were only partially confirmed. The height of the conscripts was taken as the main indicator of their physical condition, since this gave a far larger sample than any of the numerous causes for medical exemption. Comparing the two sets of averages in Table 6.1, one finds that the more industrial and commercial cantons of the Nord and the Seine-Inférieure had a significantly less favourable distribution of stature than the more agricultural cantons. However, in the Meurthe, the position was reversed, and in the Haut-Rhin and the Aube, the two profiles were almost identical.[15]

12 For an extended commentary on the significance of these figures, see Jean-Paul Aron, 'Essai d'histoire anthropologique', in Aron *et al.*, *Conscrit français*, pp. 193–262.

13 A national view of the conscript population based on the canton level is to be found in M. Demonet, P. Dumond and E. Le Roy Ladurie, 'Anthropologie de la jeunesse masculine en France au niveau d'une cartographie cantonale, 1819–30', *Annales ESC*, 31 (1976), 700–6.

14 A major drawback of the *comptes sommaires* as a historical source is their lack of detail on the industrial population. A few trades of potential use to the army, such as wood and metalworking, were classified apart, but most industrial and commercial occupations were grouped together in one 'catch-all' column. We have therefore used the agricultural population (*laboureurs, charretiers* and *employés aux travaux de la campagne*) as the most precise indicator available of the occupational structure of a canton. It might be added that using the 'other occupations' column to distinguish 'agricultural' from 'industrial and commercial' cantons does not usually alter the rank order significantly. Arranging all twenty-nine cantons of the Haut-Rhin according to the two criteria produces a Spearman's Rank Correlation Coefficient of 0.88 (significant to the 1 per cent level).

15 These conclusions are confirmed by the more demanding Spearman's Rank Correlation Coefficient. All of the cantons in the five departments were ranked according to the percentage of men employed in agriculture, and the percentage of short men (under 5 foot 4 inches). In the Haut-Rhin and the Aube, there was no significant correlation between the two sets of rankings. In the Nord and the Seine-Inférieure there was a negative correlation (i.e. a high ranking in the proportion of men employed in agriculture was associated with a low ranking in the proportion of short men), albeit a weak one, with coefficients of −0.393 and −0.324 respectively (significant to the 1 per cent and 5 per cent levels). By contrast, in the Meurthe there was a positive correlation, with a coefficient of 0.47 (significant to the 5 per cent level). Correlating the rankings according to agricultural employment and tall men produced the same pattern in reverse. The Haut-Rhin and the Aube had no significant result, the Nord and the Seine-Inférieure had

This suggests that there was no single 'model' for the conscript population of the manufacturing areas, but a variety of patterns according to individual circumstances. In the Seine-Inférieure, textile centres such as Rouen, Elbeuf, Yvetôt and Fécamp, and commercial areas such as Dieppe and Le Havre, had more than their fair share of undersized men, and relatively few men of large stature. By contrast, in the Meurthe the more traditional societies of Nancy and Lunéville, based on administrative, commercial and artisanal activities, could muster proportionately more tall men than neighbouring agricultural areas, and suffered fewer 'dwarfs'. In between these extremes stood the Aube and the Haut-Rhin, both of them expanding manufacturing centres. In the Haut-Rhin, military records identified Mulhouse, Thann, Saint-Amarin, Sainte-Marie-aux-Mines, Colmar, Guebwiller and Giromagny as the least agricultural cantons in the department. These were indeed major centres for the spinning, handloom weaving or printing of cotton. This did not prevent them from having the most marginal differences in the distribution of stature from the cantons at the opposite, agricultural pole.

The records of conscripts considered 'fit for service' in these cantons, as opposed to those 'exempt through infirmity, deformity or lack of height' also showed marked divergences between regions. The industrial and commercial centres of the Nord and the Seine-Inférieure once again fared relatively poorly.[16] So too did those in the Meurthe, contradicting the earlier evidence. In these three departments, the conventional view that agricultural cantons were experiencing much less difficulty in assembling a military contingent than industrial ones was confirmed. But against this must be set the cases of the Haut-Rhin and the Aube. There the proportions accepted and rejected in the two sets of cantons were close,

---

a weak but statistically significant positive correlation and the Meurthe a negative correlation.

[16] During the 1840s, Charles Dupin went through a similar exercise to our own, concluding that in the Nord, the Seine-Inférieure and the Eure the proportion of conscripts rejected in industrial cantons was twice as high as in agricultural ones. Our findings support the general drift of his argument, though it is interesting to note that his method of expressing the figures magnifies the difference between the cantons. Applying our data for the period 1819–26 to his selection of cantons in the Nord produces very different orders of magnitude according to the method followed. Following the Dupin procedure, the calculation would be that for every 1,000 men classified as fit for service, 1,470 were rejected on medical grounds in the industrial cantons, compared to 841 in the agricultural cantons. The method employed by Le Roy Ladurie and his colleagues would show these same industrial cantons rejecting 40 per cent of the conscripts examined, the agricultural cantons 32 per cent. This means that the former approach places the industrial cantons 75 per cent over the agricultural ones in the proportion of men physically unfit for service, the latter method only 25 per cent over. See Dupin, *Du travail des enfants*, part 2, pp. 55–6.

Table 6.1 *A comparison of stature and fitness for military service amongst military conscripts in the cantons with the highest and lowest proportions of men employed in agriculture: five departments, 1819–26*

Department	Stature				Exemptions		
	No. of men measured	Percentage of tall men	Percentage of men of medium height	Percentage of short men	No. of men examined	Percentage fit for service	Percentage medically exempt
Haut-Rhin							
Ind. and comm. cantons	965	38.46	35.97	25.57	2,445	34.27	38.90
Agricultural cantons	800	40.50	35.50	24.00	1,941	36.42	36.48
Nord							
Ind. and comm. cantons	2,170	40.69	36.45	22.86	5,336	28.82	38.76
Agricultural cantons	1,812	48.95	35.65	15.40	4,485	35.72	35.99
Seine-Inférieure							
Ind. and comm. cantons	2,093	42.28	37.22	20.50	8,842	24.43	47.26
Agricultural cantons	1,189	49.37	34.06	16.57	3,862	31.05	47.13
Meurthe							
Ind. and comm. cantons	833	45.02	36.13	18.85	3,050	19.15	48.75
Agricultural cantons	717	37.52	38.49	23.99	2,458	25.47	51.91
Aube							
Ind. and comm. cantons	641	38.38	34.32	27.30	2,232	27.87	49.06
Agricultural cantons	363	34.16	35.54	30.30	1,213	29.68	48.23

Sources: AN, F⁹ 159; AN, F⁹ 218; AN, F⁹ 228; AN, F⁹ 240ᴬ; AN, F⁹ 248, 'Comptes numériques et sommaires sur les jeunes gens, classes de 1819 à 1826'.

Notes:

(a) The percentages of tall, medium and short men for each set of cantons add up to 100.00; the percentages of those fit for service and medically exempt do not, since figures for non-medical exemptions are not included.

(b) Tall men were over 1.706 metres in height, short men under 1.625 metres. Grounds for what we have labelled a 'medical' exemption came under the general headings of physical disabilities, deformities and failure to reach the minimum height requirement of 1m. 570 cm. (*c.* 5 feet 2 inches).

(c) Cantons with the lowest and highest percentages of conscripts employed in agriculture were as follows (figures in brackets give the average percentage):

Haut-Rhin: Mulhouse, Thann, St-Amarin, Ste-Marie-aux-Mines, Colmar, Guebwiller, Giromagny (27.41); Lapoutroie, Hirsingen, Fontaine, Wintzenheim, Landser, Ensisheim, Dannemarie (62.18).

Nord: Lille-Centre, Lille-Sud-Est, Lille-Sud-Ouest, Lille-Nord-Est, Clary, Roubaix, Dunkerque-Ouest, Dunkerque-Est, Solesmes, Carnières (10.74); Hondschoote, Wormhoudt, Pont-a-Marcq, Bourbourg, Cassel, Orchies, Seclin, St-Armand, Steenvorde, Quesnoy (56.87).

Seine-Inférieure: Rouen, Dieppe, Le Havre, Elbeuf, Valmont, Maromme, St-Valéry, Yvetôt, Fécamp, Doudeville (8.57); Envermeu, Bellencombre, Duclair, Clères, Buchy, Longueville, Argueil, Londinières, Aumale, Neufchâtel (36.66).

Meurthe: Nancy-Ouest, Nancy-Est, Nancy-Nord, Lunéville-Nord, Lunéville-Sud-Est (25.97); Toul-Nord, Haroué, Toul-Sud, Domèvre, Vézelise (55.20).

Aube: Troyes, Romilly, Aix-en-Othe, Méry, Arcis (29.52); Mussy, Essoyes, Piney, Soulaines, Chaource (70.95).

Table 6.2 *A comparison of stature and fitness for military service amongst military conscripts in selected urban cantons and the rest of their departments, 1819–26*

Department	Stature				Exemptions		
	No. of men measured	Percentage of tall men	Percentage of men of medium height	Percentage of short men	No. of men examined	Percentage fit for service	Percentage medically exempt
Haut-Rhin							
Mulhouse	203	51.23	29.55	19.22	425	44.71	33.18
Rest of department	3,550	39.94	37.02	23.04	8,722	35.16	36.12
Nord							
Lille (5 cantons)	1,027	40.99	34.47	24.54	2,666	24.53	41.04
Rest of department	10,052	48.45	34.65	16.90	23,857	35.35	35.10
Seine-Inférieure							
Rouen	650	41.23	37.38	21.39	3,626	19.42	50.72
Rest of department	6,221	45.06	35.07	19.87	21,556	29.25	46.94
Meurthe							
Nancy (3 cantons)	532	44.17	37.03	18.80	2,100	17.05	50.24
Rest of department	3,876	45.02	34.88	20.10	13,311	24.30	48.21
Aube							
Troyes (3 cantons)	311	37.94	35.69	26.37	1,168	25.43	50.26
Rest of department	1,717	38.50	34.36	27.14	5,588	30.30	48.71

Sources: as Table 6.1

with minor differences of only one or two percentage points.[17] Achille Penot therefore had some justification for asserting that the spinning

[17] Here we might note that the Spearman's Rank test produced a slightly different picture to the comparison of extreme cases amongst the cantons. Continuing the procedure used in n. 15, the list of agricultural rankings was compared, first with a ranking according to the percentage of men found fit for service, and secondly to one for the percentage of men gaining a medical exemption. In the Haut-Rhin and the Aube there was no significant correlation – but neither was there in the Nord. In the Seine-Inférieure there was a positive correlation between agricultural employment and fitness for service, as Villermé would have predicted (the coefficient was 0.40, which was significant to the 1 per cent level). However, the 'reverse' correlation, between agricultural employment and medical exemptions, did not materialize. Only in the Meurthe did this latter appear, and then it was a positive correlation (of 0.432, significant to the 5 per cent level), with high agricultural rankings associated with a high ranking on the medical exemptions scale.

workers of Alsace were not the poor, stunted creatures, incapable of defending their native soil, that hostile observers often depicted.[18]

Pursuing this approach further, by comparing results in a number of cantons dominated by a big city with those in the rest of their department, produced more ambiguities (Table 6.2). The five cantons of Lille spawned an exceptionally large crop of undersized men in the Nord, and was correspondingly deprived of tall men. But to balance this, the canton of Mulhouse was remarkably well served with tall men when compared to the rest of the Haut-Rhin. Otherwise, the distribution of stature was close in the urban cantons and their surrounding hinterland.[19] Where the conscript population of the urban cantons did appear more consistently unhealthy was in the formation of a military contingent. Four of the five in our sample had higher percentages rejected on medical grounds than the rest of their departments, and, above all, substantially lower proportions considered fit for service. Mulhouse provided the exception to the rule, with a significantly better recruitment record than its department.[20]

The notion that variations in the military recruitment statistics of the departments, or even of the cantons within a department, will provide unequivocal evidence of child labour in industry acting as a depressing influence on the physical condition of the population proves unfounded. There is a strong hint that this might have been the case, particularly in the figures from the Nord and the Seine-Inférieure, reinforcing the generally baleful influence of the big cities. But, bearing in mind the results from Mulhouse, no sweeping condemnation of the expanding industrial centres is possible on this basis. To put it another way, if the young men of the manufacturing districts were often revealed to be in poor physical condition, so too were many of the villagers. What the *comptes sommaires* of the Conseils de Révision for the 1820s reveal most clearly is the generally low standard of health of the conscript population as a whole. A sad list of afflictions, including such now-unfamiliar scourges as goitres, scabies, leprosy and scrofula (tuberculosis), led to approximately 40 per cent of young men being classified as unfit for military service. But this need not be the last word on the matter, for the method of making comparisons between areas has its drawbacks. The departments and the

[18] Achille Penot, *Statistique générale du département du Haut-Rhin* (Mulhouse, 1831), pp. 317–18.
[19] The chi-square test was applied to the data in Table 6.2, in order to determine whether the differences observed in the distribution of stature between the urban cantons and the rest of their departments were statistically significant. In the cases of Lille and Mulhouse they were, to the 1 per cent level. In the other three towns they were not, meaning that the differences observed could have arisen by chance.
[20] Here the chi-square test shows that differences in the recruitment records of the towns and their departments were all statistically highly significant, to the 0.1 per cent level (1 per cent in the case of Troyes).

cantons were administrative units, which aggregated population of different occupations, levels of income and types of rural and urban commune. Hence the overall figures on stature or medical exemptions could mask considerable disparities between the constituent groups of the population.

To circumvent this problem, one needs to follow up the approach taken by Villermé in Amiens, and examine the individual conscript dossiers. The most comprehensive study of this kind concerns the recruitment operations for the year 1868. At this later period, a sample drawn from southern and western France by Professor Le Roy Ladurie and his colleagues reveals agricultural labourers to be the most disadvantaged socio-occupational group in society. No less than 29 per cent of their number were found to be under 5 foot 3 inches in height, compared to 20 per cent of farmers, 18.3 per cent of industrial workers, 16.6 per cent of artisans and 12.7 per cent of those from a commercial or upper middle-class background. The sample was also used to show that educated men, able to read and write, were in better physical shape than the illiterate: only 14.5 per cent of the former were of small stature, compared to 26.1 per cent of the latter. A more restricted sample for the same period in Paris points to a similar pattern, with the hierarchy of occupations accurately mirrored in the heights of the conscripts. Guy Soudjian used the percentage of conscripts able to afford a *remplacement* (substitute for his military service) as an indicator of wealth.

He found that this correlated very closely with the average heights of the various occupations, although it might be noted that the disparities were not large. At the top of the list he placed professional men, with 60 per cent *remplacés* and an average height of 168.5 centimetres (approximately 5 foot 6 inches). He then moved through the other occupational groups in descending order of wealth and esteem, including students and sons of *rentiers* (167.7 cm.), agriculturalists (167.3 cm.), chemical and dye workers (166.8 cm.), textile and clothing workers (166.5 cm.), metal workers (166.3 cm.), construction and leather workers (166 cm.) and, at the bottom of the scale, day labourers: hardly any of this latter group could afford a substitute, and their average height was 165.7 centimetres (approximately 5 foot 5 inches).[21] Two conclusions present themselves at this point. First, Villermé and several other writers during the first half of the nineteenth century were entirely justified in linking low-paid jobs with

[21] Le Roy Ladurie *et al.*, 'Le Conscrit et l'ordinateur', *passim*; Guy Soudjian, 'Quelques réflexions sur les statures des jeunes Parisiens sous le Second Empire', *Ethnologie française* (1979), 69–84. See also Levasseur, *Histoire des classes ouvrières*, vol. 1, pp. 729–31; Corbin, *Limousin au XIXᵉ siècle*, vol. 1, pp. 101–5; Lequin, *Les Ouvriers de la région lyonnaise*, vol. 2, pp. 2–4, Tables 42–9; Phillipe Wolff (ed.), *Histoire de Toulouse* (Toulouse, 1974), pp. 449–50.

ill-health. Their essential point, that the physical condition of the urban working class was giving cause for concern, was therefore sustainable through an examination of military recruitment records. Secondly, though, they could be accused of exaggerating the differences between industrial and agricultural populations, by failing to take into account regional variations and the difficult circumstances of the village poor.[22]

Measuring the damage: child mortality rates

If large numbers of twenty-year-old males left detailed evidence of their physical fitness in the archives of the Ministry of War, other, less fortunate, young people left their mark for posterity in the death registers. This latter source of data was used extensively by members of the public health movement, on the implicit assumption that the death rates of a population could give some insight into the physical condition of the living. Certainly the registers of the *état civil* had the advantage over military recruitment records of not being confined to the male sex and to one narrow age group. Early 'statisticians' in this field were particularly concerned to demonstrate that the poor were more likely to experience a premature death than the rich.[23] Once this was accepted, it was reasonable to assert that the abuse of child labour in industry was putting working-class lives in jeopardy. Charles Dupin, addressing the Chamber of Deputies in 1840, referred to young workers perishing as victims of an 'excess of barbarity' in the mills. Later in the century, during the 1860s, Jules Simon wrote of the 'exceptional mortality' amongst children in the big manufacturing centres, the result of a lack of care, long working hours from the age of eight onwards and, in some cases also, of 'precocious vices'.[24] However, a careful examination of the 'hygienist' literature shows that the statistical evidence gave only limited support to this line of argument.

First, the work of the statisticians showed disparities in the death rates between various social and occupational groups to be greatest during the early years of life, rather than during the years when children were likely to be employed in industry. To take two pioneering examples, both Achille Penot and Louis Villermé used the death registers of Mulhouse to

---

22 This is not to ignore certain contradictions in the literature, notably those concerning the extent of the disparities between agricultural and industrial populations. These may partly be attributable to the less precise definitions in terms of occupation and income or wealth commonly used in rural areas, and partly to changes occurring over the period 1819–69.

23 See Edmonde Vedrenne-Villeneuve, 'L'Inégalité sociale devant la mort dans la première moitié du XIXe siècle', *Population*, 16 (1961), 665–98.

24 Dupin, *Du travail des enfants*, part 1, p. xxxiv; Simon, *L'Ouvrier de huit ans*, pp. 120–1.

demonstrate the heavy mortality endured by the new working class. Penot estimated that between 1812 and 1827, children in the town had a one in two chance at birth of reaching the age of ten, whereas in France as a whole the equivalent age was twenty-one. Amongst older age groups, the differences were less acute: at five years the 'probable life' was forty-five years in Mulhouse and fifty in France. Villermé for his part investigated the distribution of mortality amongst various occupations within the town. His figures indicated that between 1823 and 1835 the 'approximate probable life' of the newly born child of a manufacturer was twenty-eight years, compared to the one and a half years for the child of a handloom weaver, and the one and a quarter years for the child of an ordinary spinning worker. This was such a massive divergence that it was barely credible, and Villermé went no further than to conclude that 'mortality is considerably higher for certain occupations or social conditions than for certain others, principally in the first year of life'. From the age of ten onwards, he added, the differences between the classes were less marked.[25] Secondly, Villermé was at pains to emphasize that occupation was only an indirect or mediated influence on health, operating through the general environment of food, clothing, housing, working hours and morality.[26] This did not stop him campaigning for a law to regulate child labour, but it remains a useful reminder that the workshop was merely one of several nefarious influences in the working-class existence. Thirdly, the limitations to early statistical techniques cannot be ignored. In his study of Mulhouse, Villermé adopted the method of comparing mortality in a given age group with the total number of deaths. This, as he was well aware, was of dubious value, being made necessary by the lack of information available on the age structure of the population. Even today, with statistical techniques better understood, there is no denying that problems of methodology and of sources make investigations into nine-teenth-century urban and occupational mortality tantalizingly difficult. On the one hand, there is the prospect of finding a dramatic illustration of the 'physical aggressiveness' of industrialization and urbanization.[27] On the other, there is the daunting task of using data from a 'proto-statistical' age to try to pin down an elusive reality.

Higher rates of mortality amongst children in the towns compared to those in the countryside would give some indication that the employment of children in industry was a destructive influence on health, if only in an

[25] Villermé, *Tableau de l'état*, vol. 2, pp. 256–7, 279; Vedrenne-Villeneuve, 'L'Inégalité sociale', 670–1, 680–3.
[26] Villermé, *Tableau de l'état*, vol. 2, p. 258.
[27] This phrase is borrowed from Lequin, *Les Ouvriers de la région lyonnaise*, vol. 2, p. 9.

indirect manner. The evidence we have assembled on child mortality rates in a selection of towns during the mid-1850s goes some way towards showing this to have been the case.[28] Unfortunately it cannot be claimed that even these age-specific rates are anything more than a broad indication of relative levels of mortality in town and country. The figures for the age group one to four are particularly unreliable, since many young children born in the towns did not appear in either the urban death registers or the urban census lists. Some were overlooked during the quinquennial censuses. Others were sent out to wet-nurses or homes for foundlings in the countryside, where the odds were that they would soon end up in the village death registers. On balance, our figures probably underestimate urban mortality for the under-fives. This would therefore tend to corroborate the finding of Villermé and Penot that it was among the very young that the towns most deserved their grisly reputation as 'tombs of the race'. Etienne Van de Walle and Samuel Preston, in their recent study of female mortality during the nineteenth century, have emphasized that it was this same age group one to four that suffered exceptionally high rates in Paris, when compared to the rest of France.[29] Our own uncorrected figures from the Statistique de la France for the department of the Seine point in the same direction. Similarly, in Nancy, Roubaix and Mulhouse at least, the excess mortality of the urban populations compared to the rest of the departments was greatest at this stage of childhood.

In subsequent age groups, the general falling away in mortality rates to a minimum in the life cycle around the age of thirteen was apparent in town and country alike. With adolescence, a new complication comes to the fore: the mobility of the population. Ideally, one would wish to measure the mortality of individuals who had always lived in the same urban environment. But migrants create what Dr Jean-Noël Biraben has called 'un facteur de perturbation', which even in the twentieth century is difficult to eliminate.[30] In our samples of the age group fifteen to nineteen, for example, a substantial proportion were not natives of the town in which they died: approximately one third in Caudebec-lès-Elbeuf, a half in Nancy and Roubaix and an overwhelming three-quarters in Mulhouse.

---

28 The 1850s were selected for study since the 1851 census was the first to publish data on the age structure of the population. This decade is still close to the initial period of debate in the child labour reform campaign, between say 1826 and 1841.

29 'Mortalité de l'enfance au XIXᵉ siècle à Paris et dans le département de la Seine', *Population*, 29 (1974), 102. On interpreting statistics for this age group, see also Guillaume, *Population de Bordeaux*, pp. 133–7; Chevalier, *Labouring Classes*, pp. 327–9; and A. Bideau, G. Brunet and R. Desbos, 'Variations locales de la mortalité des enfants: l'exemple de la Châtellénie de Saint-Trivier-en-Dombes, 1730–1869', *Annales de démographie historique* (1978), 7–29.

30 'Quelques aspects de la mortalité en milieu urbain', *Population*, 30 (1975), 510–11.

Table 6.3 *A comparison of child mortality rates in selected towns and their departments, 1853–5*

Town (department)	Population in 1851	Age group			
		1–4 ‰	5–9 ‰	10–14 ‰	15–19 ‰
Bordeaux (Gironde)	130,927	–	10.0 (1.75)	7.4 (1.37)	11.8 (2.27)
Nancy (Meurthe)	45,129	55.2 (1.74)	16.8 (1.27)	11.8 (1.44)	14.7 (1.46)
Roubaix (Nord)	34,698	68.1 (1.34)	11.4 (0.90)	7.1 (0.99)	10.0 (1.14)
Mulhouse (Haut-Rhin)	29,574	67.4 (1.34)	13.4 (1.05)	8.6 (1.09)	8.3 (0.85)
Caudebec (Seine-Inf.)	7,292	44.2 (0.98)	9.8 (0.92)	5.8 (0.85)	5.6 (0.72)
Seine (France)	1.4 m.	100.0 (2.65)	18.4 (1.86)	8.6 (1.28)	15.5 (1.89)
France	35.8 m.	39.7	10.2	6.7	8.6

Note: figures in brackets show the divergence between the town and rest of its department, the latter standardized at 1.00. A number greater than 1.00 therefore indicates that the town had a higher mortality rate than the surrounding area.
Sources: population of each group calculated from the censuses of 1851 and 1856. Deaths in the towns extracted from the communal death registers, 1853–5. Figures for Bordeaux calculated from Pierre Guillaume, *La Population de Bordeaux au XIXe siècle* (Paris, 1972), Table LXXV, p. 279, concerning 1853 only.

There is no way of determining how long these individuals had lived in the town, nor of calculating their particular mortality rates. What one can emphasize in relation to adolescent mortality is the divergence between the big, old-established cities of Paris, Bordeaux and Nancy on the one side, and the new manufacturing centres of Roubaix, Mulhouse and Caudebec on the other.

Contemporaries had no difficulty in recognizing that Paris 'paid a heavier tribute' to death than other towns. Officials from the Statistique de la France calculated the 'number of people living for each death' in various categories of population. For those aged fifteen to nineteen, the figures in 1853 were seventy-one in the department of the Seine, ninety-nine in the rest of the urban population of France, and one hundred and seventeen in the villages.[31] Our own figures indicate that the mortality rate in the metropolis was almost twice the national average for this group. Bordeaux and Nancy also appear to carry a substantial burden of mortality for those in their teens, relative to the equivalent population in

[31] Statistique de la France, *Mouvement de la population en 1851, 1852 et 1853* (Strasbourg, 1857).

Table 6.4 *Child mortality in selected towns, 1853–5: male and female rates compared*

Area	Gender	Age group			
		1–4 ‰	5–9 ‰	10–14 ‰	15–19 ‰
Bordeaux	Male	–	9.4	4.6	12.2
	Female	–	10.6	10.3	11.4
Nancy	Male	57.9	15.0	9.9	11.9
	Female	52.7	18.6	13.6	17.6
Roubaix	Male	84.5	10.2	5.9	8.7
	Female	51.9	12.5	8.2	11.3
Mulhouse	Male	62.1	13.2	8.8	8.5
	Female	73.4	13.7	8.4	8.3
Caudebec	Male	38.9	8.5	3.0	4.2
	Female	49.5	11.0	8.4	7.0
Seine	Male	101.7	17.7	7.4	15.5
	Female	98.3	19.0	9.7	15.5
France	Male	40.1	10.0	6.2	8.1
	Female	39.4	10.4	7.3	9.0

Sources: as Table 6.3

their departments. By contrast, the three mill towns emerge in a more favourable light. Size, and the availability of land for housing in these newly expanding towns, may have been an influence here. Yet it is worth spelling out that in the age groups ten to fourteen and fifteen to nineteen, when the direct influence of industrial labour on mortality rates might be expected to surface most clearly, all of these towns were very close to the level prevailing in the rest of their departments.

The influence of gender on the mortality rates of young people of working age in the towns is also of interest. There was some tendency for the rates in our sample to be higher for females than males, as can be seen in Table 6.4. However, when the comparison is made with the corresponding rates for the rest of the department, the urban influence is sometimes diminished, since there was also an excess female mortality in the hinterland. Standardizing the male and female rates for the departments at 1.00, the excess (or deficit) in the urban mortality rates emerges as follows for the age group fifteen to nineteen:

	Male	Female
Bordeaux	2.65	1.93
Nancy	1.37	1.53
Roubaix	1.18	1.11
Mulhouse	0.81	0.90
Caudebec	0.62	0.80

In Bordeaux, the excess mortality of young males stands out clearly. Although the young females of the town had a considerably higher death rate than their counterparts in the small towns and villages of the Gironde, the rate for the males appears even more serious. This may well reflect the effects of heavy manual work on a section of the population, on top of other pernicious urban influences, for Bordeaux was a town with limited opportunities for women's work. Smaller divergences of some significance are also manifest in Nancy and Caudebec-lès-Elbeuf, although the latter may simply be a symptom of the small sample available. In Nancy, however, the figures suggest that conditions in the 'feminized' embroidery trade for which the town was famous should be looked at closely.

There remains the possibility that juvenile employment in industry and the associated urban way of life had debilitating effects on the population which affected death rates at later, more vulnerable, stages of life. A surge in the death rates of the urban population between the ages of twenty and thirty has often been commented upon by demographers. The official view in the 1850s was that the twenties were the 'age of passion'; and during the 1890s, Emile Levasseur referred to the 'contrary excesses of work and pleasure' at this stage of life. More recently, in the 1970s, Pierre Guillaume has taken a less censorious line in his demographic history of Bordeaux. He discovered that tuberculosis was responsible for half of the deaths in the age group twenty to twenty-nine during the 1850s. His conclusion was that 'this upsurge can therefore be explained by entry into the active population, and by living and working conditions: the uprooting from the family, which often involved a deterioration in housing and living conditions, and the promiscuity of the workshop'. By 1883, it might be added, this phenomenon was difficult to perceive, and by 1913 it had disappeared entirely.[32] Generally, though, it becomes increasingly difficult with the older age groups to argue plausibly that excess urban

---

[32] *Ibid.*; Emile Levasseur, *La Population française* (3 vols., Paris, 1889–92), vol. 2, p. 401; Guillaume, *Population de Bordeaux*, p. 136.

mortality can be attributed to the effects of child labour, let alone to measure the impact.

Statistics on occupational mortality should, in principle, give a clearer insight into the plight of child labour. Most importantly, they can avoid all the problems encountered with correlations between areas, for it must be admitted that the apparently 'normal' death rates amongst adolescents in, say, Roubaix could partly reflect a very healthy urban bourgeoisie compensating for a weakened proletariat. In practice, such statistics are almost impossible to assemble for the youthful section of the population. The major obstacle is the casual approach to the registration of children's occupations in the census. This was particularly evident in the big cities, where the census enumerators were presumably too hard-pressed to pay much attention to the jobs of the younger members of a family.[33] Yet it was precisely in this type of commune that there was a chance of assembling a sufficiently large sample of deaths to compare with the occupational census. Attempts to measure the disparities in mortality between various occupations therefore had to be abandoned, even for the 1850s, when the occupational census was exceptionally informative on juvenile occupations.[34] What could be gleaned from demographic sources for this decade was some indication of the related phenomenon of mortality according to the occupation of fathers. Table 6.5 presents an estimate of the death rates for children in various socio-economic categories in the town of Mulhouse between 1851 and 1855. The sources are still not entirely suitable for this type of exercise: one in six of the age group fifteen to nineteen was found to be living with another household as an apprentice, lodger or domestic servant, meaning that the census registers could give no information on the occupation of their parents. Fortunately the younger age group of ten to fourteen did not suffer from this drawback, its entries on parental occupations being almost complete. Both cohorts reveal children from comfortably-off backgrounds having significantly lower chances of a premature death than the rest of the population. The sons and daughters of *patrons* and white-collar workers formed a small élite in Mulhouse, but their presence in the death registers was even more privileged.[35] Amongst the *classes populaires*, the pattern was less consistent. In the older age group, the wage earners (*les ouvriers*)

---

33   The *listes nominatives* of 1851 for Roubaix and Nancy are a case in point. Those for Lille and Rouen had disappeared entirely.

34   For the paucity of studies concering occupational mortality in nineteenth-century France, see Bernard-Pierre Lecuyer, 'Les Maladies professionnelles dans les Annales d'hygiène publique et de médecine légale', *Le Mouvement social*, 124 (1983), 45–69; Alain Cottereau, 'L'Usure du travail: interrogations et refoulements', *ibid.*, 3–9.

35   The relatively small size of the sample made it impossible to provide separate estimates of the death rate for the two sexes.

Table 6.5 *Child mortality in Mulhouse according to the socio-economic status of fathers, 1851–5*

Socio-economic status of fathers	Number of deaths	Total population in 1851	Death rate ‰ p.a.
Age group 15–19			
Employers and white collar	6	256	5
Wage earners	71	923	15
Independent	37	436	17
Dead or missing	28	564	10
No information	5	462	–
Total	147	2,641	11
Age group 10–14			
Employers and white collar	13	358	7
Wage earners	63	1,242	10
Independent	28	413	14
Dead or missing	33	256	26
No information	1	40	–
Total	138	2,309	12

Sources: AD Haut-Rhin, 5 E 337, death registers, commune of Mulhouse, 1851–5; and AD Haut-Rhin, 6 M 110–11, census registers, commune of Mulhouse, 1851.

and the independent artisans and tradesmen appear at a severe disadvantage, though presumably the lack of information for many entries in the census has the effect of exaggerating the disparities. In the younger age group, perhaps more dependent on parental support, it was the orphans, the illegitimate and the abandoned who stood out as the most vulnerable section of juvenile society. Interestingly, children of wage earners emerged slightly below the average death rate in this sample.

In retrospect, it is difficult to avoid the conclusion that statistics bandied about during the first half of the nineteenth century were responsible for the creation of a number of myths. One was that the Conseils de Révision of the military establishment witnessed lines of hale and hearty lads from the villages towering over feeble specimens of humanity typical of the factory system. Another was that the industrial workshops were sacrificing a generation of child 'martyrs' in the unremitting struggle for profits.

That these images existed more in the minds of contemporaries than in the world at large does not make them unimportant. The fact is they were potent weapons in the campaign to curb the excesses of child labour. As has been pointed out recently, Villermé and his colleagues in the public health movement were mainly interested in using statistics for the purposes of publicity, and it was not crucial for them if their work would not stand up to rigorous examination. Their public was not well versed in statistical method, but it could be won over by the simple exposition of a few figures.[36] This is not to accuse the early 'hygienists' of cynicism, but merely to emphasize that they were not disinterested parties in the presentation of evidence. A more detached view would suggest that the statistics available for the period will not allow any confident assertion that the onward march of industrial progress was 'bastardizing' the race. What does come more into focus is the wretched physical condition of the majority of children from the labouring classes of town and country alike. The urban members of this great tide of poor may have attracted most attention from reformers, but they are best seen in the context of a whole nation teetering on the brink of over-population up until the middle of the nineteenth century. The manufacturing interest therefore had some grounds for feeling hard done by. Poverty on the land was making its mark on the physical condition of the population as surely as poverty in the towns, and the die was cast for many slum children long before they entered industrial employment. At the same time, the statistics provided plenty of ammunition for those determined to improve the lot of juveniles working in industry. There were no grounds for complacency when cohorts of working-class children were being decimated in their early years, were still trailing behind bourgeois levels of mortality during their adolescence, and in black spots such as Lille or Rouen were hard put to form a military contingent. Pondering the extent to which child labour had an impact on health may in practice turn out to be a *question mal posée*, given the problem of untangling the relative weight of the various influences at work. Villermé was not unaware of this problem, for he wrote:

I do not seek to establish whether the poor succumb most readily to their lack of nourishment; to the poor quality of their food; to their excessive work; to the bad air; to illness brought on by their trades, humidity, unhealthy lodgings, squalor or overcrowding; to the anxiety of being unable to raise a family; or even to the intemperate habits common amongst them.[37]

---

[36] Coleman, *Death is a Social Disease*, pp. 125–36.
[37] Louis R. Villermé, 'Mémoire sur la mortalité en France dans la classe aisée et dans la classe indigente', *Mémoires de l'Académie Royale de Médecine*, 1 (1828), 80.

It is indeed only in this broad perspective that the plight of children in the industrial centres can be understood.

Living conditions in the towns

For young children who had survived the early traumas of childbirth, infant diseases and perhaps also wet-nursing in the countryside, the urban environment was scarcely welcoming.[38] Some of the major ports and industrial centres were poorly located from the point of view of health. Rouen, Bordeaux and Lyons suffered from the influence of nearby marshland, while Lille had to contend with a damp low-lying site, high annual average rainfall and an intricate network of almost stagnant canals.[39] More importantly, the towns proved ill-prepared for the rising tide of migrants that surged in over the course of the nineteenth century. Some efforts were made to adapt existing amenties to new circumstances, but for much of the period the tendency was to adorn the streets with fine public buildings rather than to grapple with the underlying problems of public hygiene.[40] In Toulouse, for example, the population more than doubled between 1815 and 1914, yet until the Second Empire the municipal authorities were content with the eighteenth-century pro-gramme of building bridges and laying out squares. The heart of the old city was left intact, a squalid maze of narrow, stinking streets. Sewers were few and far between, and with many of the inhabitants continuing the peasant custom of raising poultry, goats or pigs in their houses, the roads were regularly piled high with various forms of excrement. Lille was no better served by its local administration. Before 1870 wells and bore-holes were the sole sources of drinking water, and all risked pollution from canals, leaking cesspools or industrial waste. Sewage disposal was a matter of allowing small traders, the *bernatiers,* to purchase the contents of household cesspools, which they emptied into their carts and resold to neighbouring farmers. Street cleaning was also left to private enterprise, producing a further procession of foul-smelling carts which spilled some

[38] For extensive discussion of these aspects of infancy, see Gélis *et al., Entrer dans la vie;* George D. Sussman, 'The Wet-Nursing Business in Nineteenth-Century France', *French Historical Studies,* 9 (1975), 304–28; and Anne Martin-Fugier, 'La Fin des nourrices', *Le Mouvement social,* 105 (1978), 11–32.

[39] Michel Mollat (ed.), *Histoire de Rouen* (Privat, 1979), p. 318; Louis Desgraves and Georges Dupeux (eds.), *Bordeaux au XIXe siècle* (Bordeaux, 1969), pp. 13–19; André Latreille (ed.), *Histoire de Lyon et du lyonnais* (Toulouse, 1975), p. 318; Monique Dineur and Charles Dugrand, 'Le Choléra à Lille', in Louis Chevalier (ed.), *Le Choléra: la première épidémie du XIXe siècle* (La Roche-sur-Yon, 1958), pp. 49–50; Pierrard, *La Vie ouvrière,* pp. 49–50.

[40] Georges Duby (ed.), *Histoire de la France urbaine,* vol. 3, *La Ville classique* (Paris, 1981), pp. 570–93; and *ibid.,* vol. 4, *La Ville de l'âge industriel: le cycle haussmanien* (Paris, 1983), pp. 313–25.

of their contents on the roads, and dumped the rest in *dépôts* bordering on the town.[41] Not until the 1860s were there any signs of a general movement in the towns and cities to pipe in drinking water for the *classes populaires*, and to put the sewerage system on a proper footing.[42] Well into the nineteenth century, therefore, the towns provided an exceptionally favourable environment for water- and food-borne diseases. Children were the main victims of these maladies, with typhoid and above all diarrhoea carrying off many to an early grave, and leaving others physically vulnerable to illness later in life. The backward state of public amenities will go a long way towards explaining the excess mortality of the towns amongst infants and the very youngest children.[43]

The risk of infection for children was heightened by overcrowded living quarters. Housing conditions in the towns may well have deteriorated steadily throughout the nineteenth century, a consequence of relying on market forces to accommodate the swelling numbers of low-income families.[44] With space at a premium in the centre of the cities, the inevitable outcome of this policy was a massive density of population in the poorer areas. In Toulon at mid-century the municipal council estimated that an average of thirty to forty persons was living in each house in the central parts of the town, compared to an average of ten to twelve in the well-off districts.[45] A number of employers, with one eye on the mastery of their labour force, set up *cités ouvrières*: special schemes to

[41] Wolff, *Histoire de Toulouse*, pp. 445–60; Pierrard, *La Vie ouvrière*, pp. 50–5, 107–41. See also Lion Murard and Patrick Zylberman (eds.), *Le Petit Travailleur infatigable*, special issue of *Recherches*, 25 (1976), 32–45; Charlene Marie Leonard, *Lyon Transformed* (Berkeley, 1961), pp. 85–93; Latreille, *Histoire de Lyon*, pp. 317–20, 391; Maurice Agulhon, *Une ville ouvrière au temps du socialisme utopique: Toulon de 1815 à 1851* (Paris, 1970), pp. 39–41, 50–60; Corbin, *Limousin au XIXe siècle*, vol. 1, pp. 81–8; Chevalier, *Labouring Classes*, pp. 200–14; Mollat, *Histoire de Rouen*, pp. 308–19.

[42] See J.-P. Goubert, 'Eaux publiques et démographie historique dans la France urbaine: le cas de Rennes', *Annales de démographie historique* (1975), 116.

[43] Samuel H. Preston and Etienne Van de Walle, 'Urban French Mortality in the Nineteenth Century', *Population Studies*, 32 (1978), 275–97. For an up-to-date account of British parallels, see F. B. Smith, *The People's Health* (London, 1979), pp. 136–94.

[44] There is no shortage of general surveys of working-class housing in the nineteenth century. See in particular Duby, *Histoire de la France urbaine*, vol. 4, pp. 314–19; the special issue of *Annales de démographie historique* (1975), on 'Démographie historique et environnement'; and Gabriel Désert, 'Aperçus sur l'industrie française du bâtiment au XIXe siècle', in J.-P. Bardet, P. Chaunu, G. Désert, P. Gouhier and H. Neveux, *Le Bâtiment*, vol. 1, *Maisons rurales et urbaines dans la France traditionelle* (Paris, 1971), pp. 35–120.

[45] Agulhon, *Une ville ouvrière*, p. 57. These densities continued through the nineteenth century. To take an individual case, during the 1880s a wool spinner informed a Parliamentary Enquiry that he, his wife and three children lived in two rooms measuring 12 square metres each, and that the house contained sixteen rooms and forty-three people; AN, C 3370³, Saint-Aubin (Seine-Inférieure). See also Chevalier, *Labouring Classes, passim*.

provide cheap, subsidized housing for the working classes, such as those at Le Creusot and Mulhouse. But these private initiatives, begun in the 1830s, failed to gain momentum. The limited resources available to the general run of wage earners created too tight a margin for their finances. Calculations made by philanthropic societies revealed that even with cheap credit and limited profits, a very basic type of working-class housing was only within reach of the 'aristocracy' of labour.[46] Intervention by local authorities in the housing market proved equally ineffective. A Law on Insanitary Dwellings of 1850 permitted municipal councils to establish Commissions which could make investigations and recommend action. But these rarely produced concrete results. The main drift of municipal activity in the middle of the nineteenth century, and beyond, was to improve the street system, and certainly not to channel funds into the construction of working-class houses. In these circumstances, the housing stock was never adequate to cope with the successive waves of migrants. All that the market could come up with for the *classes populaires* was a drab series of one- and two-roomed houses and apartments, with primitive sanitation and insufficient living space.

The gravity of the housing problem varied between towns. During the 1840s, the doctors Villermé and Thouvenin agreed that pressure was greatest in the old-established centres. Workers in Roubaix and Tourcoing were therefore better housed than their counterparts in Lille; those in Elbeuf, Louviers and Darnétal more favoured than those in Rouen; and the Vosgiens of Saint-Dié, Senones, Schirmeck and Remiremont had the advantage over Alsacians in Mulhouse and Sainte-Marie-aux-Mines.[47] Thouvenin, for example, was impressed by the groupings of little houses in Roubaix, the *forts*,[48] but considered Lille 'placed by degradation at the bottom of the social scale'. *Notables* who ventured into the slums of the big cities wrote as if they had descended into some strange and repulsive underworld: dark, sinuous streets; walls suppurating with damp; an evil-looking mud on the cobbles; powerful smells wafting from doors and windows; and hordes of pale, sickly-looking children assaulted their senses from all sides. As they moved into the dwellings, more 'hideous things' awaited them. At mid-century, Victor Hugo described four children left alone in a cellar in Lille: 'The oldest rocking the smallest as it cries – she is six years old, but looks more like four – damp floor – puddles

[46] Lequin, *Les Ouvriers de la région lyonnaise*, vol. 2, pp. 17–18.
[47] Villermé, *Tableau de l'état, passim*; Dr Thouvenin, 'De l'influence que l'industrie exerce sur la santé des populations dans les grands centres manufacturiers', *Annales d'hygiène publique et de médecine légale*, 36 (1846), part 2, 277–96.
[48] These are discussed in Martine le Blan, 'Notes sur une étape dans la genèse d'un espace industriel: la construction des "forts" roubaisiens dans la première moitié du XIXe siècle', *Revue de Nord*, 63 (1981), 67–72.

of water between the tiles.' Most of these infamous *caves* were in the process of being closed up at this point, but accommodation above ground was not necessarily much better. Families had to put up with damp, draughty rooms; filthy bedding that was shared by individuals of both sexes and all ages; and the constant stench of cooking, unwashed bodies and nearby latrines.[49] To the south, in the silk-weaving towns of the Lyonnais, the problem was more one of workers existing in apartments that served as workshops, kitchens and dormitories.[50] Sleeping quarters for the young apprentices who lodged with the *canuts* were a persistent scandal, which Factory Inspectors were still confronting at the end of the century. Thus in 1878 the Inspector Gauthier called a meeting with the Prefect of the Rhône and the President of the municipal council in Lyons to discuss the poor health of the girls amongst them. This he attributed in part to the custom of making apprentices sleep in small closets in the workshops, which lacked ventilation and encouraged epidemics.[51]

Doctors living and working in the new industrial towns were acutely aware of the links between slum housing and ill-health. In 1849, for example, the Commission d'Hygiène Publique of Munster observed: 'It is particularly in the working class, where children are abandoned, deprived of maternal care, denied the necessary cleanliness, and surrounded by poor hygienic conditions, that they are consumed by scrofula, rickets and various eruptive diseases.'[52] Elsewhere, on the principle that 'man is a poison for man', tuberculosis, typhoid fever and anaemia were also laid at the door of squalid housing.[53] Modern medical opinion would have some reservations on these assessments, but the rôle of the towns in providing an environment conducive to contagious diseases is not in dispute. Damp and dirt were, as we have seen, as common in the villages as in the town, and evidently they took their own toll.[54] But what made the urban slums

---

[49] Notes by Victor Hugo cited in Pierre Pierrard, 'Habitat ouvrier et démographie à Lille au XIXᵉ siècle', *Annales de démographie historique* (1975), 39. See also Adolphe Blanqui, *Des classes ouvrières en France pendant l'année 1848* (Paris, 1849), pp. 69–72.

[50] Lequin, *Les Ouvriers de la région lyonnaise*, vol. 2, p. 17.

[51] AN, F¹² 4755, Gauthier (Lyons, 15ᵗʰ), annual report, 18 December 1878. Inspectors in Paris noted the same practice, accepted by the apprentices as a custom of their corporations. In 1886 the Inspector for the Seine drew attention to the plight of the apprentice pastry-cooks. In one establishment, he found two young lads sharing a bed in a cabinet which had a surface area of 4 square metres, and a height of 2 metres. In another, the apprentices were expected to sleep in a closet over an oven, in a small, windowless room adjoining the shop. Their filthy sheets were inhabited by a 'legion of cockroaches' and other insects attracted by the warmth; AN, F¹² 4730.

[52] AD Haut-Rhin, 5 M 2, 'Extrait du registre des procès-verbaux de la Commission d'hygiène publique et de salubrité du canton de Munster', 11 August 1849.

[53] AD Vosges, M 287, letter written by A. Chevreuse, *médecin*, 23 February 1878.

[54] See above, p. 34.

especially dangerous for the health of young people was the constant exposure to so many people in a confined space.[55] Congestion was thus a key element in the *condition ouvrière*. It allowed diseases such as diphtheria, scarlet fever, measles, smallpox and various chest ailments to flourish, and blight the existence of the juvenile population.[56]

Deficiencies in the diet of working-class children made their impact on health by lowering resistance to disease. Here urban families were recognized to be in a less precarious position than their rural counterparts, with more variety in the food they were able to afford. Bread remained the mainstay of their diet throughout the nineteenth century, accompanying the endless succession of daily soups, but meat and wine were also consumed regularly. Moreover, in contrast to housing, the long-term movement during the nineteenth century was clearly one of improvement. The 1840s witnessed the last serious crisis in the supply of bread, and, from the 1880s, the residual tremors in the cereals' market disappeared. In the second half of the century, too, milk, sugar, fruit and fresh vegetables came increasingly within reach of working-class budgets, starting the shift away from the traditional reliance on starch-based foods.[57] All this would help to explain the substantial numbers of tall youths in the middle and upper reaches of urban society, and the secular tendency for child mortality rates to decline.

However, this optimistic perspective must be qualified in a number of ways. To begin with, the food situation of the urban population may have deteriorated between the end of the *ancien régime* and the construction of a railway network under the Second Empire. In the case of Paris at least, it has been argued that during the 1780s food consumption was more than adequate to keep the population healthy, but that subsequent revolutionary upheaval and mass immigration disrupted the old equilibrium, leaving the inhabitants vulnerable to tuberculosis and cholera epidemics.[58] Secondly, recurrent economic crises wreaked havoc with family budgets. This was very obviously the case around 1817, and the period 1853 to

---

[55] See Biraben, 'La Mortalité en milieu urbain', 510. For historical assessments, see the articles by J.-P. Bardet, Adeline Daumard and Pierre Pierrard in *Annales de démographie historique* (1975).

[56] Statistics on the causes of death amongst children only became available at the end of the nineteenth century. See Guillaume, *Population de Bordeaux*, p. 141; Preston and Van de Walle, 'Urban French Mortality', 284; Duby, *Histoire de la France urbaine*, vol. 4, p. 279.

[57] For an informative general survey, see Fernand Braudel and Ernest Labrousse (eds.), *Histoire économique et sociale de la France*, vol. 4, *L'Ere industrielle et la société d'aujourd'hui siècle 1880–1980* (Paris, 1979), part 1, pp. 496–9. See also above, pp. 32–3.

[58] Robert Philippe, 'Une Opération pilote: l'étude du ravitaillement de Paris au temps de Lavoisier', in Hémardinquer, *Histoire de l'alimentation*, pp. 60–7.

1856. But even later in the century, spells of unemployment and sharp rises in the cost of foodstuffs were a constant hazard for the working class, requiring drastic measures of retrenchment. The only way out was a hasty descent into the lower depths of the housing market, and a return to the most basic kind of food: 'bread, always bread, and more bread'.[59] Finally, there was the disparity between poor and not-so-poor to be considered, the former existing at a level uncomfortably close to that of the smaller peasants and agricultural labourers.

Some of the more highly paid industrial workers and their families enjoyed a relatively generous food ration. The master silk weavers of Lyons were better fed than most workers in France, and skilled labour in 'virile' industries, such as metallurgy and glassmaking, also had a reputation for eating well. But below this élite, the mass of textile workers and the unskilled labour of the towns suffered from the nutritional inadequacies of their diet. This was partly a matter of an unhealthy balance to the food intake. In Mulhouse and other manufacturing towns in Alsace, meals for the spinners and handloom weavers during the 1830s were based on potatoes, thin soup, a little milk and butter, some poor-quality noodles and bread. Meat and wine were only consumed twice a month, on pay days. In the textile centres of Normandy, an industrialist reckoned that at the same period a six-year-old child normally existed on a pound of bread a day, a small portion of butter or cheese, potatoes and a clear soup. Likewise in Lille, Villermé set out a daily fare for the poor consisting of potatoes, a few vegetables, thin soups, a little butter, cheese, milk or *charcuterie*. Only one of these foods was normally eaten with bread, and water was the sole drink within the household.[60] Such diets, however monotonous, were adequate for the nourishment of an adult. But from the point of view of child development, they contained too many starchy and fatty foods, particularly in the heavy soups often given to settle the young, and not enough dairy products and fruit. A lack of calcium and vitamins would account for the prevalence amongst working-class children of deficiency diseases such as rickets and scrofula, and go some way to explaining their susceptibility to gastroenteritis and infections of the chest and throat. A further drawback to the popular diet was the poor quality of much of the produce that had to be eaten. In Lille, for example, municipal authorities under the July Monarchy and the Second Empire fought a protracted and only partly successful campaign against the sharp practices

[59] *Ibid.*, p. 63. On the 'hypermobility' of those on modest income, see J.-P. Bardet, 'Pour conclure: historique et environnement', *Annales de démographie historique* (1975), 76.
[60] Villermé, *Tableau de l'état*, vol. 1, p. 102. Extensive investigations of working-class diets can be found in many local studies, including Pierrard, *La Vie ouvrière*, pp. 203–13; idem, *La Vie quotidienne*, pp. 65–79; Lequin, *Les Ouvriers de la région lyonnaise*, vol. 2, pp. 32–9; and Corbin, *Limousin au XIXe siècle*, vol. 1, pp. 65–74.

of farmers and tradesmen. The proletariat, forced to rely on the dregs of the food market, risked finding its bread adulterated with potato starch or copper sulphate, its meat and fish gone bad, its milk watered and its fruit either unripe or rotting.[61] Once again, whereas for adults the stomach disorders and intestinal diseases that resulted were debilitating, for young children they could prove fatal.

Child labour and health

By the time they reached the workshop, the children of working-class families were already likely to have been weakened in running the gauntlet of the urban slum. From this unpromising start, they had to launch themselves on to the long years of working life which sooner or later would wear down their health. To begin with, they faced a process of selection on the labour market. As on the land, some trades were more prestigious than others, and so were able to cream off the strongest children available. Basic metallurgy in particular had a reputation for waiting until boys had reached their teens before hiring them, and for taking only those with a solid, muscular physique.[62] Textiles stood at the opposite pole, though within its numerous branches, the woollen industry was frequently observed to employ children who were on average two or three years older than those in cotton, and power-loom weaving was seen to rely less on young children than spinning or calico printing.[63] This preliminary screening would eventually be reflected in statistics on disease or mortality by occupation, as some industrialists were quick to point out. Dorestan-Guilbert, a manufacturer from the Seine-et-Oise, stressed before a Parliamentary Enquiry of 1872 that military recruitment operations needed to be interpreted with this in mind. He noted, with some exaggeration: 'There is one thing which people do not take into account for industry: it is that we have to make do with the few young people whose infirmities or defective constitutions rule out employment with their parents elsewhere.'[64] Once their working life was under way, children faced a number of health hazards on the shop floor, which were combined in varying proportions by different industries. For the purpose of analysis, these will be divided into three categories. First, there was the threat to various organs from a noxious working atmosphere; secondly, the

---

[61] Lasserre, *La Situation des ouvriers*, pp. 143–4; Pierrard, *La Vie ouvrière*, pp. 204–11.
[62] See, for example, AN, F^{12} 4739, Nadeau (Lille, 6th), annual report for 1877.
[63] Villermé, *Tableau de l'état*, vol. 1, p. 440; Thouvenin, 'De l'influence', part 1, 27; AN, F^{12} 4705, Conseil des Prud'hommes de Bolbec, 23 October 1837; AN, F^{12} 4742, Aubert (Lisieux, 8th), 1 October 1875.
[64] AN, C 3020.

risk of injury from an industrial accident; and thirdly, the insidious wearing down of the constitution through long hours of manual labour.

Most of the unhealthy working environments noted by the medical profession were created by the textile industries. In the early mills, people, machines and raw materials were sealed together in seemingly disastrous proximity. The first impression made on outsiders as they walked into these establishments was the stifling atmosphere, a powerful combination of high temperatures, humidity, fibrous dust, droplets of oil and noxious gases. Jean Gerspach was one of the first doctors to publicize these conditions, on the basis of his experience in the cotton mills of Alsace. He described the typical *filature* of the 1820s as being hot and humid, with a minimum temperature of 25 degrees centigrade and windows that were kept permanently shut. The smells of human bodies and oil from the machinery hung heavily in the air, together with clouds of cotton dust. This latter, he observed, was particularly thick in the areas where young girls worked preparing the raw cotton for spinning. Twenty years later, in 1846, Thouvenin made a more systematic examination of working conditions in the textile industries, to intervene in what had become a widespread debate over their influence on health. His tone was less critical than that of his predecessor, which may in part reflect a change of circumstances. Where fine cotton yarn was being spun, he recorded temperatures of 20 to 25 degrees but for coarse yarns the temperature was only 15 to 16 degrees. And although the windows remained closed, he asserted the air was constantly renewed by the opening of doors, the movement of the machines and the openings for drive-shafts. However, he did concede that 'Dust and cotton duvet fly about continually in all the workshops, and are breathed in by the workers.' Outside the cotton industry, he was most disturbed by the environment in silk spinning. Again it was the preparatory processes that he considered most danger-ous, with their concentration of dust in closed workshops. Woollen and linen textiles he found less unhealthy than cotton, though the combing and sorting of flax produced a further dust hazard, and the extreme humidity required for linen spinning obliged the female workers to stand all day on a wet floor.[65]

Such polluted atmospheres bore down heavily on the textile workers, young and old alike, providing 'hot house' conditions for contagious diseases, and attacking the lungs with particular severity. Contemporary medical opinion linked a whole list of maladies to employment in the mills. Villermé emphasized two diseases: pulmonary tuberculosis, *la phtisie cotonneuse*, which allegedly struck women and children working

[65] Gerspach, *Santé des ouvriers*, pp. 7–8; Thouvenin, 'De l'influence', part 1, *passim*.

Table 6.6 *Cause of death amongst the juvenile population (aged ten to nineteen) of Mulhouse, 1853–5*

Cause of death	Total in sample		Employed in mills	
	Number	%	Number	%
Cholera	55	29.89	9	20.00
Typhoid fever	48	26.09	14	31.11
Pulmonary TB	37	20.11	15	33.33
Other	44	23.91	7	15.56
Total	184	100.00	45	100.00

Source: AD Haut-Rhin, 5 E 337, death registers of Mulhouse, 1853–5.

in the preparatory stages of cotton spinning with special virulence, and scrofula: 'We know how common this scourge is, marking children and young people with its swellings, its scars, its infirmities, its hideous deformities, especially in certain places at the heart of the big towns.' The Commission d'Hygiène Publique of Guebwiller, in the Haut-Rhin, came to the same conclusion at mid-century. The working class of this cotton town suffered the 'sad privilege' of being most prone to tuberculosis, and more commonly, to scrofula. Eye inflammations caused by dust were also common, though the Commission noted that, exceptionally for a manufacturing town, typhoid fever was rare. Thouvenin ranged more widely, blaming dust in the silk mills for catarrh, chronic eye infections, arthritis, pneumonia and tuberculosis.[66] Some indication of the incidence of tuberculosis amongst the juvenile population in a cotton town comes, by chance, from Mulhouse in the period 1853 to 1855. During this period the cause of death was pencilled in by an unknown hand on the *registres de décès.* The usual difficulties with nineteenth-century diagnoses arise when analysing the data: nonetheless, three killer diseases stand out amongst the age group ten to nineteen years (Table 6.6). Cholera topped the list, with an outbreak in 1854 accounting for fifty-five of the 184 deaths covered.[67] This epidemic was of course most exceptional, which leaves

[66] Villermé, *Tableau de l'état,* vol. 2, pp. 211–12, 243–4; AD Haut-Rhin, 5 M 2, 'Extrait du registre des délibérations de la Commission d'hygiène publique et de salubrité du canton de Guebwiller', 6 August 1849; Thouvenin, 'De l'influence, part 1, 37. For a recent account of industrial diseases in Victorian Britain, see Anthony S. Wohl, *Endangered Lives* (London, 1983), ch. 10.

[67] Cholera was a disease that usually spared children and struck down the old rather than the young. However, its impact on the adolescent population in Mulhouse was clearly far from negligible. Studies of the epidemic in Paris and Lille reveal that it was the poor rather than the rich who died, factory workers and unskilled labour rather than industrialists

typhoid fever as the most important 'normal' cause of death, with forty-eight cases. Both of these maladies are usually contracted through contaminated water or food, and so cannot be linked directly to occupation. However, the statistics do show a relationship between employment in the cotton mills of the town and the third major cause of death: *tubercule pulmonaire* or *phtisie pulmonaire*. In the total population of the sample, tuberculosis was responsible for one in five of the deaths; in the group which could be identified as working in the spinning mills, calico-printing works, or power-loom weaving shed, the proportion was one in three.[68]

The novelty of conditions in the factories meant that the first social enquiries of the 1820s concentrated their attention on *la grande industrie*. However, reformers could hardly fail to notice the problems faced by the labour force in the smaller workshops. There was soon plenty of evidence to show that children living and working beside their parents in the handicraft trades could suffer from an environment every bit as harsh as those found in the mills. Doing industrial work in the home more often than not had the effect of aggravating already squalid living conditions. Silk ribbon weaving was one of the exceptions, in that it demanded a clean workshop.[69] Lacemaking and embroidery also had some advantage during the summer months, for being mobile they could be taken out into the fresh air. But in winter, like the handloom weavers, the *dentellières* and *brodeuses* were frequently criticized for crowding themselves into miserable hovels in order to share heating, lighting and company. During the 1860s the Sub-Prefect of Mirecourt visited one such workshop in the Vosges:

In a low, smokey room, with bare walls, marbled here and there by the greenish traces of permanent dampness, with an oppressively high temperature, maintained by an iron stove, whose heat was also used to cook food for the family, which spread an evil, sickly smell, could be distinguished, through the uncertain glimmer flickering across the place, five or six young girls, grouped around a lamp, which barely gave them any light, and which gave off a thick, fetid smell. These were the lacemakers. Their pale, thin faces, their dull expressions, their red, watery eyes, were all indicators of the fatigue which overwhelmed them, and of the poor food on which they exist.[70]

---

and professional men. See Chevalier, *Le Choléra*; Monique et Charles Engrand, 'Epidémie et paupérisme: le choléra à Lille en 1832', in Marcel Gillet (ed.), *L'Homme, la vie et la mort dans le Nord au 19e siècle* (Lille, 1972), pp. 43–63; Patrice Bourdelais and Jean-Yves Raulot, 'La Marche du choléra en France: 1832 et 1854', *Annales ESC*, 33 (1978), 125–42.

68 The results are significant to the 5 per cent level. It goes without saying that a small sample drawn from one town will not provide very convincing evidence, but in the absence of statistics on the cause of death until the 1880s, such early data is very precious.

69 Lequin, *Les Ouvriers de la région lyonnaise*, vol. 2, p. 17.

70 AD Vosges, M 292, 'Copie d'un rapport de M. le Sous-Préfet de Mirecourt à M. le Préfet des Vosges', 3 November 1864.

In the woolcombing shops, as Norbert Truquin found to his cost, whole families were condemned to spend all day breathing the nauseous fumes from charcoal stoves. Handloom weavers had to keep their rooms cool and humid, to prevent the sizing of their yarns drying too quickly. Rag-pickers in the big cities lived with the filthy cast-offs from the society around them.[71] And then there were the trades that created a dust problem. The cutlery trade was one such, with its wheels for polishing and sharpening. Towards the end of the century, children of both sexes in the Auvergne were still putting in long hours in the vitiated atmosphere associated with this work. The result, according to a Factory Inspector, was a series of small statures, curved spines, tuberculosis in various parts of the body and a general weakening of the constitution.[72] The manufacture of mother-of-pearl buttons in the Vosges was another. A well-meaning if eccentric doctor in the region blamed colds and bronchitis amongst the labour force on the dust they breathed in at work. His recommendation, apparently not well received, was that the men should grow their moustaches to retain the fine particles, and that children should put on artificial ones made of lint.[73]

The vulnerability of children to industrial accidents was not a major issue for reformers during the 1830s and 1840s. However, it was eventually realized that the list of weak chests, anaemic complexions, stunted growths and so forth commonly attributed to the factory system would have to be rounded off with the mutilated limbs of accident victims. In December 1851 the Ministry of Commerce launched an official enquiry on the subject, to which twenty-four Prefects responded. One of its findings, not surprisingly, was that children were particularly at risk, on account of their weakness and inexperience.[74] The Prefect of the Nord reported that in 1853, of eighty-one injured workers treated in the Saint-Sauveur hospital, thirty-five were under fifteen years of age, and fifty-seven under twenty.[75] Attacks on children by 'monsters with arms of iron and teeth of steel' were particularly common in the spinning mills,

---

71 Truquin, *Mémoires*, pp. 50–1; Thouvenin, 'De l'influence', part 1, 39; Raison-Jourde, *La Colonie auvergnate*, pp. 108–9.
72 AN, F[12] 4755, Gauthier (Lyons, 15th), 12 February 1880.
73 AD Vosges, M 287, A. Chevreuse, 23 February 1878.
74 The point had already been made during an early investigation into industrial accidents at Troyes: Lhoste, Gréau and Pigeotte, 'Rapport fait au conseil de salubrité établi près de l'administration municipale de la ville de Troyes sur les accidents auxquels sont exposés les ouvriers employés dans les filatures de laine et de coton', *Annales d'hygiène publique et de médecine légale*, 12 (1834), 10.
75 AN, F[12] 4617, 'Note résumant l'état de la question sur les accidents dans les manufactures', 26 September 1854.

with their encumbered space and uncovered gearings, though they were far from having a monopoly.[76]

Many children came to grief after entanglements with drive shafts, belts and flywheels. These seized their victims by the hair or clothing, and dashed them to pieces on surrounding surfaces. Often the noise of machinery, and the distance between an accident and the source of power, caused an agonisingly long gap between the first screams of pain and the stopping of a machine. A *procès-verbal* against Filipo Hollebecq, a spinner in Tourcoing, revealed the gruesome details of one such incident. The victim was a piecer, who was seen to be lying injured with his right arm completely detached from his shoulder, one of his thighs broken, and his entire head and body covered with lacerations. Eye witnesses told of how he had been holding the two ends of a belt which his brother was trying to mend when, for some unknown reason, it had wrapped him around a fast-moving transmission shaft. Fifteen or so revolutions had hammered his body against the ceiling, a steam pipe and a block of wood, with ultimately fatal results.[77] Another serious type of accident occurred when children were crushed by heavy machinery. The 1851–2 Enquiry brought to light cases of legs broken by papermaking machines, and two boys of fifteen decapitated by a steam hammer in an ironworks.[78] Most lethal, however, was the self-actor of the spinning mills. François Hilby, a thirteen-year-old *bobineur* from Kayserberg, became a typical casualty when he failed to scramble from under a machine quickly enough. The local Commissaire de Police wrote in his report:

Hilby's corpse was stretched out on the floor in a small pool of blood. A froth tinged with blood covered his mouth, and a jagged wound at least eight centimetres in length bled freely below his ear. Probing this area, the interior of the cranium was quickly penetrated. As to the manner in which this lesion was produced, the irregularity of the incision, the caving in of the skull and the torn-off ear all indicate the action of a powerful shearing or compressing force. It is enough to see a self-acting machine, with the part known as the 'chariot' moving into the immobile frame, to understand that a human head caught between the two would be crushed, and that death would follow instantly.[79]

Finally, there were the fingers, hands and arms caught in the metal teeth and gearings of various machines. Children were particularly exposed to

---

[76] The quotation is from Jules Perin, *Le Travail des enfants employés dans les manufactures* (Paris, 1869), p. 16. The section that follows adapts to child labour the classification proposed in AD Haut-Rhin, 10 M 10, report on accidents by Dr Durvell, of Guebwiller, 18 January 1852.

[77] AD Nord, M 614/7.

[78] AN, F[12] 4617, reports from the Prefects of the Haut-Rhin and the Moselle.

[79] AD Haut-Rhin, 10 M 10, letter from Commissioner of Police, Kayserberg, to Prefect, 27 April 1868.

the injuries that followed from this type of mishap, because they were often expected to clean these parts whilst they were still moving. It was sometimes noted that Saturday, the day reserved for cleaning, was an ill-fated day for children.[80]

The influence of manual labour on the health of children was, and still is, a contentious issue.[81] Villermé argued passionately that the 'agony' of long hours of unremitting toil was the principal ruin of children's health.[82] But if there was convincing evidence to show that the small frame of a child could easily be overtaxed on the shop floor, it was equally clear that a moderate amount of work could have beneficial effects on health. Besides bringing in some income to offset the debilitating effects of poverty, it could help develop the physique better than the likely alternative of an aimless, idle existence.[83] Much depended on the nature of work in the various trades. One or two enjoyed a benign reputation. The forges and foundries of basic metallurgy were generally thought to encourage a rude health amongst their juvenile employees. During the 1870s, for example, the Conseil d'Hygiène of Montluçon, in the Allier, was prepared to admit a 'travail de gymnastique' in the ironworks, which developed the bodies and fortified the health of children.[84] Glassworks were sometimes put in the same category, though many observers considered the tasks they demanded of children disastrous for health.[85] Amongst the textile industries, calico printing was singled out as the branch least harmful to child welfare, on account of its relatively short working hours.[86]

At the opposite extreme were those industries which required either too much or too little effort for the development of an immature body. Amongst the former, the silk industry of the Lyons region stood out as a major culprit. Years of pulling cords as a *tireur* during childhood gave the *canut* a characteristic limp, which, according to Villermé, made him

---

[80] Studies of industrial accidents include Lhoste *et al.*, 'Rapport fait au conseil de salubrité', 5–25; 'Accidents occasionnés par les appareils mécaniques dans les ateliers industriels', *Annales d'hygiène publique et de médecine légale*, 43 (1850), 261–89, a report compiled by a Special Commission in Lille; Pierrard, *La Vie ouvrière*, pp. 150–61; Duveau, *La Vie ouvrière*, pp. 276–80.

[81] See Rodgers and Standing, *Child Work*, pp. 32–3.

[82] Villermé, *Tableau de l'état*, vol. 2, p. 91.

[83] See, for example, de Gérando, *De la bienfaisance publique*, vol. 1, pp. 246–7.

[84] AN, C 3023.

[85] In the Rhône, for example, compare the favourable comments on the glassmaking industry in AD Rhône, 10 M, letter from Ingénieur des Mines de Saint-Etienne to Prefect, 27 June 1842; and letter from the Mayor of Givors to the Prefect, 10 December 1843; with the view of the glass workers, who described their own condition as 'Puny physique, having started work too early'; AN C 3369, Deposition of the *verriers et tailleurs de cristaux*, Lyons, 1882.

[86] Villermé, *Tableau de l'état*, *passim*; AN, F^{12} 4705, Conseil des Prud'hommes of Bolbec, 1837; AN, F^{12} 4722, Rouen Chamber of Commerce, 1867.

readily identifiable on the streets.[87] If the *tireurs* were disappearing by the 1830s, other heavy jobs continued late into the century. These included reeling, delivering heavy packages and rolling on woven material at the far end of the handlooms, all of which could cause hernias or deformities of the limbs. In 1872, according to the Ingénieur des Mines of the Loire:

In Saint-Etienne and the surrounding area there are many small reeling shops employing young girls. Their work is more laborious than that in the factories powered by water wheels, because they are obliged to stand turning their wheels with their feet all day long. These workshops are dispersed amongst families employing at most five to seven workers each.[88]

The women who ran these establishments were notorious for bringing in large numbers of young girls from the countryside, and taking advantage of their isolation to impose impossibly long working hours. As the poor 'human machines' became completely worn out, so the *maîtresses* replaced them with newcomers. In 1850 *Le Progrès* of Lyons found evidence of these abuses in the death registers of the *hôpital*, with 400–500 deaths per year amongst these girls from exhaustion and chest diseases.[89] Allegations of overworking young children were also made against parents in the domestic workshops of the cotton industry. In Normandy, for example, they were accused of producing generations of feeble workers.[90] Handloom weaving was held responsible for various maladies affecting adolescents by local observers. The combination of a permanently crouched position at the loom and a continual movement of the limbs was said to cause chest illnesses, problems with the veins and curvature of the spine.[91] Metalworking, too, was a substantial handicraft trade still open, in the 1840s, to the charge of moulding the bodies of its child workers. In the Ardennes, boys and girls alike started a life of constant hammering around the age of nine or ten. As a result, the nailmakers usually had one shoulder higher than the other, walked with a pronounced limp and had their fingers deformed to the extent that they could not pick up a coin from a table.[92]

The alternative of gaining no exercise at all from work was equally destructive of young people's health, or so the cruel fate of many

87 Villermé, *Tableau de l'état*, vol. 2, pp. 242–3.   88 AN, F[12] 4726.
89 *Le Progrès*, 2 April 1870. See also AN, F[12] 4705, Conseil des Prud'hommes of Lyons, 1837 and AN, F[12] 4722, E. Pariset, 'Travail des enfants dans les manufactures. Rapport à la Chambre de Commerce de Lyon', 15 June 1867.
90 AD Seine-Maritime, 10 MP 1362, Conseil d'Arrondissement of Yvetôt, 1852. The Conseil asserted that children aged five or six were spending all day reeling in poor hygienic conditions, and so grew up to be *peu robustes*.
91 Charles Noiret, *Mémoires d'un ouvrier rouennais* (Rouen, 1837), p. 124. See also AD Rhône, 10 M, letter from Departmental Inspector, Chépié, to Delattre, 20 October 1880.
92 AN, C 945, canton of Charleville (Ardennes).

lacemakers and embroiderers suggests. The child *brodeuses* of the Vosges started work at five in the morning, and during the winter might continue through until eleven o'clock at night. With their eyes continually on the grey material in front of them, they spent the whole time tracing out delicate arabesques, stars, fruits and flowers for their genteel clientèle. Such long hours of close work, cooped up in a foul atmosphere and supported by the most meagre food ration, put a heavy strain on their eyesight, and left them vulnerable to tuberculosis, asthma, scrofula and bone deformities.[93] Girls in other 'female' trades, notably the *couturières*, *lingères*, *modistes*, *confectionneuses* and *fleuristes* of Paris and the big provincial cities, risked the same intolerable combination of long hours and delicate, precise work.[94]

In the mechanized industries, tasks given to children were rarely exacting enough to pose a direct threat to health. The problem was more one of wearing down a feeble body with long hours of enervating labour in front of a machine. The scandal of excessive working hours for young children was what outraged Villermé more than anything else during his visits to the textile centres in the 1830s. The sixteen or seventeen hours they spent on their feet in the cotton and woollen textile industries was, he argued, a punishing régime which needed to be compared to the twelve-hour day put in by convict labour.[95] Some of the industrialists replying to the 1837 Enquiry on Child Labour were of the same opinion. The Conseil des Prud'hommes of Rouen thought the fifteen-hour day in the spinning mills too long for all workers, but for children in particular, especially as many of them lived 2 or 3 kilometres away from their place of work. Their colleagues in Bolbec also condemned cotton spinning as pernicious for health, through the excessive hours spent in an unwholesome atmosphere. The Chambre Consultative of Louviers was concerned with the effects of night work on children, and sent in a medical report to support its case. Dr Picard, of the *hospice* in Louviers, blamed the pale, sickly generation of *jeunes vieillards* on premature night work, combined with insufficient and poorly-prepared food. More specifically, he linked scrofula and various digestive disorders with nights worked before the age of twelve.[96] During the 1870s, further complaints over long hours and night work for children were made by a number of industrialists, notably in relation to cotton spinning and silk throwing.[97] Interestingly, in the Ardèche a local doctor made the link between pulmonary tuberculosis and what might be called

[93] AD Vosges, M 292, letters from Sub-Prefect of Mirecourt to Prefect, 27 July 1855, and 3 November 1864. See also AN, C 962, canton of Arlanc (Puy-de-Dôme).
[94] AN, F¹² 4731-2, reports of Factory Inspectors (Seine, 1ˢᵗ), 1874–92; P. Leroy-Beaulieu, *L'Etat moderne et ses fonctions*, 2nd edn (Paris, 1891), pp. 329–30.
[95] Villermé, *Tableau de l'état*, vol. 2, p. 89.   [96] AN, F¹² 4705.
[97] These can be found in the Parliamentary Enquiry of 1872–5, AN, C 3018–23.

l'usure au travail. Besides the possibility of contagion in the silk mills, he suggested that the high incidence of tuberculosis amongst young female silk workers could be attributed to poor food, a lack of fresh air and laborious work for which the girls were insufficiently developed.[98] This was a plausible case, for the risk of infection in a crowded workshop was considerably heightened when the individual constitution was rendered vulnerable by poverty and an exhausting work load.[99]

Employers prepared to admit in public that their enterprises could undermine the health of children were always in a minority. How then did the majority defend themselves against the barrage of criticism from reformers? To begin with, at the 1837 Enquiry, they were prepared to meet it head-on. The Conseil des Prud'hommes of Sedan saw no evidence in its researches of children being worked beyond their limits; the Chambre Consultative of Privas considered the exercise required in the silk mills to be harmless; the Lille Chamber of Commerce described work in the spinning and weaving industries as 'the best gymnastics to give them to favour their physical development'. Most expansive of all was Scipion Mourgue, Prefect of the Hautes-Alpes and a former cotton spinner of twenty-five years standing. At the 1837 Enquiry he warned against the dangers of a 'false sensitivity', which took unnecessary pity on the condition of children in the factories. He claimed never to have met a piecer who could not take a thirteen-hour day. His employees had started work at five in the morning, and ended at eight o'clock at night, with two hours off for breaks in between: 'The child therefore enjoyed the time so necessary to recuperate with a long night of sleep, and returned with pleasure to his work the next day, fresh, lively and in good form.'[100] This type of assertion we might note, boded ill for the enforcement of child labour legislation.

A more sophisticated approach was to suggest that time was on the side of the factory system. Left to itself, so the argument went, the onward march of industrial progress would bring less arduous labour and a safer workplace. In 1840 the Conseil des Prud'hommes of Lille decided to launch a counter-offensive against its 'accusateurs mal informés'. The Counsel admitted that conditions in the early mills had been grim, with children having their limbs deformed and their bodies worn out by their efforts on hand-operated machines. However, since that time a revolution

---

98 AD Ardèche, 15 M 3, report by Doctor Bouzol, Le Cheylard, n.d.
99 See Alain Cottereau, 'La Tuberculose: maladie urbaine ou maladie de l'usure au travail?', *Sociologie du travail*, 20 (1978), 192–224; and *idem*, 'L'Usure au travail: interrogations et refoulements', *Le Mouvement social*, 124 (1983), 3–9.
100 AN, F[12] 4705; AD Nord, M 613/5, letter from Lille Chamber of Commerce to Ministry of Commerce, 27 April 1840.

favouring the health of the labour force was alleged to have taken place. The introduction of steam power allowed the workers to conserve their energy, and the construction of bigger buildings provided a superior working environment: 'We had to build palaces for an industry more brilliant and more rich in machinery.'[101] Later in the century, at the 1867 Enquiry on Child Labour, the Chambre Consultative of Sedan reiterated this line. They contrasted conditions in the 1840s, when children worked a full fourteen- or fifteen-hour day, with those current in the 1860s. A twelve-hour day, and clean, well-ventilated workshops meant better hygiene and less physical effort than in the past. At the same Enquiry, the Mulhouse Chamber of Commerce stressed that nearly everywhere factories fulfilled the conditions of hygiene that could be expected of them, and that 'the spinning mills, which have given rise to so many exaggerated recriminations, are today distinguished more than ever by the good layout of clean, spacious, well-ventilated premises'.[102] There was some justification for these claims. The adoption of power-driven machinery in the textile industries gradually eliminated the extremes of effort required in some of the small workshops, even if it substituted problems of its own for child labour. Moreover, over the course of the nineteenth century, a number of innovations improved the working environment of the mills: the shift from water to steam power helped reduce dampness; the installation of ventilators did something to clear dust from the atmosphere; and various security measures were taken to cover the moving parts of machinery. Yet even in the latter part of the nineteenth century, there was little room for self-satisfaction. As far back as 1826 Dupont in Lille had noted the differences between large, purpose-built spinning mills, and older ones housed in unsuitable buildings.[103] This dichotomy would continue throughout the century: on the one hand, a limited number of 'model' establishments that were spaciously laid out, and equipped with best-practice technology for heating and ventilation; on the other, a mass of smaller mills and domestic workshops that were often unhealthy, makeshift affairs.[104] The all-conquering hygienic 'palace' for industry remained a utopian dream.

Conclusion

In conclusion, although a wholesale deterioration in the physical condition of the working class during the first half of the nineteenth century

[101] *Ibid.*, letter to Minister of Commerce, 14 September 1840.   [102] AN, F¹² 4722.

[103] J. B. Dupont, *Mémoire sur les moyens d'améliorer la santé des ouvriers à Lille* (Paris, 1826), p. 37.

[104] For a comprehensive account of the structure of the textile industries at mid-century, and the impact of the 'cotton famine' during the 1860s, see Claude Fohlen, *L'Industrie textile au temps du Second Empire* (Paris, 1956).

remains difficult to prove, there is plenty of evidence to support Jean-Jacques Bourcart in his contention that the development of industry was doing little or nothing to encourage an improvement. The early period of industrialization saw an unfortunate coincidence of a number of morbid influences on health: a food supply that could barely cope with the rising population; an urban infrastructure bursting at the seams from new patterns of settlement; factories which crammed machinery, drive-shafts and raw materials into any available space; and a gruelling work régime limited only by the last tolerance of the human frame. The second half of the nineteenth century would bring some improvement in all of these spheres, as well as the gradual elimination of child labour from the workshops. In the interim, working-class children were prominent as victims of the new industrial society. It was the very young who were killed off in large numbers by rudimentary water and sewerage facilities; it was children whose growth was stunted by an inadequate diet; and it was child workers who suffered most from infectious conditions, sleep deprivation and an arduous work routine in the mills.

Chapter 7

A moral and intellectual decline?

The allegation that industrial development was undermining the physical condition of the population was worrying enough for *notables* during the mid-nineteenth century, not least because it implied a threat to the military strength of the country. The possibility that there was also a moral and intellectual decline under way was if anything more disturbing. In their minds, moral corruption and the politics of their opponents were inextricably linked. The great fear was that a deterioration in the general education of the *classes populaires* would prepare the ground for some kind of social and political revolution. Time and again reformers of various political hues argued that industrial society was prising away working-class children from established institutions, such as the family, the Church, the school and the apprenticeship system, only to thrust them into the unsavoury atmosphere of the factory and the slum. Deprived of 'wise counsels', the *gamins* of the city were exposed to all manner of debauchery and political extremism – or so the argument ran. Sorting out fact from fantasy in all this is not easy. Accusations of declining moral standards amongst the young are far from specific to the 1830s and 1840s. Nonetheless, it is possible to discern a number of changes, if not an overall decline, affecting the various strands of the popular education in the towns during the early nineteenth century.

The rôle of the working-class family

The main focus of attention for social thinkers concerned with the moral welfare of working-class children was the degradation of family life in the industrial towns. Attitudes to industrial capitalism might vary considerably, from the barely-concealed hostility of Catholic authors such as the Vicomte Alban de Villeneuve-Bargemont or the Baron Joseph-Marie de Gérando, to the qualified approval of a Villermé or an Adolphe Blanqui. But all could agree that the factory and the city were subverting the solid domestic virtues associated with peasant farming and the handicraft trades. Writing in the 1830s, Villeneuve-Bargemont thought it best for children to go into agricultural employment when they left school, it being his impression that the sexes did not mix when working the land, and that debauchery was less widespread in the countryside than in the towns. He was prepared to concede in principle that machinery and big capital could bring wealth and civilization to society, but in practice he saw the so-called 'English system' producing only a physical and moral weakening of the young. Bundled into the factory at the earliest possible age, the working-class youth was soon corrupted by the experience of profligacy, drunkenness, and disorder, which would make him in his turn the head of a miserable, demoralized family. De Gérando took a similar theme, linking the growing depravity of the working class with the progress of industry. For him the separation of women and children from husbands and fathers made the factory a constant source of temptation into vice. Both of these authors pinned their hopes for the future on a return to the traditional Catholic values, demanding a proper moral and religious education for the proletariat, and a programme of patronage and charity from the well-off 'gens de bien'.[1]

Other observers were more wholehearted in their support for industrial society, but this did not prevent them from pinpointing its baneful influence on family life. There was some inclination, notable in the writing of Thouvenin, to throw the responsibility for failure on to the working class itself, accusing parents of drunkenness and debauchery. Villermé in the 1840s, and Audiganne in the 1860s, both accused a section of the proletariat in Alsace of providing such a poor upbringing that children were driven away from home into a 'precocious independence'. Respectable opinion viewed the rootless population of the lodging houses with a jaundiced eye, and it was particularly alarmed at the idea of the young being plunged into this dangerous milieu.[2] For the most part, though, reformers concentrated their fire on the disruptive influence of the factory system. Its characteristic mingling of large numbers of workers, young and old, male and female, was held responsible for a whole series of scandals: mothers lured from their place in the home; children exposed to the sordid conversations of adults; young girls seduced by their employers and foremen; and prostitution by women factory operatives during the

[1] Villeneuve-Bargemont, *Economie politique chrétienne*, passim; idem, *Discours prononcé à la Chambre des Députés* (Metz, 1841); de Gérando, *Des progrès de l'industrie*, pp. 5–6, 53–6, 130. See also the useful survey by Katherine A. Lynch: 'The Problem of Child Labor Reform and the Working-Class Family in France during the July Monarchy', in *Proceedings of the Western Society for French History*, 5 (1977), 228–36.

[2] Dr Thouvenin, 'De l'influence que l'industrie exerce sur la santé des populations dans les grands centres manufacturiers', *Annales d'hygiène publique et de médecine légale*, 37 (1847), part 3, 83–111; Villermé, *Tableau de l'état*, vol. 1, p. 35; Audiganne, *Les Populations ouvrières*, vol. 1, p. 179.

Table 7.1 *Residence patterns of children in selected communes, 1851*

	With parents	With other kin	In lodgings	In service	Total number in sample
			Percentage living:		
Age group 10–14					
Haut-Rhin					
Mulhouse	98	1	–	1	117
Thann	98	2	–	–	117
Munster	99	1	–	–	98
Seine-Inférieure					
Sotteville-lès-Rouen	98	2	–	–	102
Caudebec-lès-Elbeuf	91	8	–	1	128
Drôme					
Taulignan	87	3	3	7	69
Dieulefit	87	3	1	9	71
Meurthe					
Baccarat	94	2	1	3	65
Rural sample	95	3	–	2	417
Age group 15–19					
Haut-Rhin					
Mulhouse	82	5	2	11	104
Thann	88	2	6	4	104
Munster	87	3	5	5	85
Seine-Inférieure					
Sotteville-lès-Rouen	92	3	–	5	117
Caudebec-lès-Elbeuf	88	5	2	5	128
Drôme					
Taulignan	73	10	8	9	79
Dieulefit	82	4	5	9	78
Meurthe					
Baccarat	83	5	9	3	80
Rural sample	83	3	2	12	372

Note: the rural sample from the Meurthe concerns ten communes from the canton of Lunéville south-east.
Sources: 1851 census, *listes nominatives.*

'fifth quarter' of the day. The overall impression was that the miseries of life in the factory and the slum caused the typical worker to spend little time with his family, to be indifferent to the company his children kept, and so to neglect his duties concerning their education, be it moral, religious or intellectual.[3]

How far, then, did industrial and urban development tear asunder the working-class family, in both the physical and emotional senses, and deprive children of the parental guidance they needed? One obsession amongst reformers and industrialists that can quickly be dismissed as insignificant concerns the practice of young people leaving home early for some kind of bohemian existence in the *garnies*. An examination of residence patterns in a variety of industrial towns at mid-century shows the vast majority of children and adolescents to be living at home with their parents (Table 7.1).[4] Children under fourteen were almost unknown in lodgings, the silk-throwing industry of southern France providing an exception with its provision of dormitories for young girls during the week. There was also the occasional example of a child living with an older brother or sister, and a small number of very young domestic servants residing with their employers. In the age group fifteen to nineteen, there were rather more cases of young people living away from their parents either as domestic servants, lodgers or co-residents with kin. The proportions varied slightly according to local conditions, with some differences between the sexes also evident. In big towns, the examples of Mulhouse and Sotteville (on the outskirts of Rouen) suggest that more young females than males were living away from home, because of the outlets for domestic service. In smaller industrial towns, such as Thann, Munster and Baccarat, it was more likely to be young males who made the move, as they became live-in apprentices or lodgers.[5]

[3] These themes run like a red thread through Villermé, *Tableau de l'état*; Buret, *De la misère*; Blanqui, *Des classes ouvrières*; Reybaud, *Le Coton* and *Conditions des ouvriers en soie*.

[4] Table 7.1 may be compared with Table 7.11 in Michael Anderson, 'Household Structure and the Industrial Revolution: Mid-Nineteenth-Century Preston in Comparative Perspective', in Peter Laslett and Richard Wall (eds.), *Household and Family in Past Time* (Cambridge, 1972), p. 234. Our results are similar, except that the rural sample from Lorraine does not differ from the urban samples in the way that the one from rural Lancashire does.

[5] The percentages for those aged fifteen to nineteen living with their parents were as follows:

	Male	Female
Mulhouse	89	78
Thann	87	90
Munster	81	92
Sotteville	96	90
Caudebec	88	88
Taulignan	77	71
Dieulefit	79	85
Baccarat	71	93
Rural sample	74	92

Nonetheless, these categories remained a small proportion of the total, the inevitable move away from parents barely starting at this stage of life. The fact was that few working-class adolescents could afford the luxury of an independent existence. The price of setting up on one's own included the loss of important services given freely by the mother to members of her own family, as well as higher payments on food and rent.[6] If anything, therefore, the industrializing society of the nineteenth century was causing parents and children to live together under the same roof. The reason for this was the decline in the *ancien régime* practice of sending children out to other families as apprentices or servants. Even in the Lorraine villages the impact of new economic and social forces on the family could be seen. The large numbers of embroiderers (male as well as female) living with their parents in 1851 was an example of 'proto-industrialization' encouraging parents to keep their offspring at home for a longer period than had hitherto been customary.[7]

Reformers were on firmer ground when they asserted that the factory system was weakening family links at work, though they surely exaggerated the extent of change. From the 1830s onwards, they were always keen to contrast the free-for-all of the factory with the stern exercise of paternal authority in the domestic workshops. In 1859 Louis Reybaud enthused over the advantages for morality which the small-scale organization of the silk-weaving industry created, with 'the daughter remaining under the supervision of the mother, the young wife under the supervision of the husband'.[8] But there was a tendency to forget that children watching over the flocks in the fields saw very little of their parents, not to mention the custom amongst the poor of sending their offspring 'chez les autres'. When in 1837 industrialists were first asked to estimate the proportion of children belonging to parents in their workshops, they presented a highly variegated picture. Their representatives in Lille, Saint-Quentin, Bar-le-Duc and Vienne dismissed family ties as unimportant, whilst their counterparts in Mulhouse, Roubaix, Bolbec, Evreux, Besançon and Chalabre considered them the norm. Estimates of the proportions involved varied from one fifteenth to three-quarters, with the Bureau des Manufactures concluding that one third was the most

---

[6] Louise A. Tilly, 'Individual Lives and Family Strategies in the French Proletariat', *Journal of Family History*, 4 (1979), 148; Michael Anderson, *Family Structure in Nineteenth Century Lancashire* (Cambridge, 1971), p. 53.

[7] For British parallels see Michael Anderson, *Approaches to the History of the Western Family, 1500–1914* (London, 1980), pp. 26, 79; Richard Wall, 'The Age at Leaving Home', *Journal of Family History*, 3 (1978), 181–202; David Levine, 'Industrialization and the Proletarian Family in England', *Past and Present*, 107 (1985), 168–203.

[8] Reybaud, *Conditions des ouvriers en soie*, p. 18.

common response.[9] Such conflicting views do not inspire great confidence, but the quantitative evidence provided by factory and population censuses confirms the overall impression of diversity.

The survey of textile mills undertaken in Alsace during the years 1822 and 1823 gives an early hint of the rôle of family links amongst the industrial labour force.[10] It appears from a 'family reconstitution' exercise that only a minority of children were employed in the same establishment as their fathers.[11] For example, in the integrated spinning, weaving and printing works owned by Gros, Davillier, Roman et Compagnie at Wesserling, the proportion was one third; in a similar mill run by the same firm at Huseren it was nearer to a quarter; and in the cotton-spinning mill of Heilmann Frères at Ribeauvillé, it stood at one tenth. Given that a printer or a spinner could only anticipate having children of a suitable age to be a *tireur* or *rattacheur* for a limited number of years in his working life, this would be consistent with some inclination to recruit within the family. The low figure for the mill at Ribeauvillé can be accounted for by the predominantly female and youthful character of the spinners. However, this limited opportunity for fathers to work beside their children did not necessarily leave the rest of the juvenile labour force cast adrift in an alien environment. In the three mills already mentioned, and in the woollen mill run by Martin Thyss at Buhl, a good 40 per cent of the under-sixteens had older brothers or sisters present. With everyone 'cousin to someone else' in these mill towns, the shop floor was crisscrossed by a tight-knit web of relationships between members of the same nuclear family, other kin and neighbours. Such contacts secured a job in the first place, since workers were responsible for hiring their own child assistants, and ensured a measure of security and protection for the young.[12]

The occupational census can be used to give a further perspective on the influence that fathers could exercise over their children at work. Once again, there is evidence of an effort by working-class families to place sons, and, where possible, daughters, in the same trade as their fathers.

---

[9] AN, F[12] 4705–6. See also W. M. Reddy, *The Rise of Market Culture* (Cambridge, 1984), pp. 172–3.

[10] AD Haut-Rhin, 9 M 22–3.

[11] Families were reconstituted using surnames, the grouping together of individuals with the same name, place of birth and place of residence. An element of guesswork inevitably creeps in with this type of exercise, and so, to avoid any spurious accuracy, we have given the broadest indications of the proportions involved, rather than percentages.

[12] One can hardly fail to mention the extensive debate amongst historians of the British Industrial Revolution over the changing rôle of the family in the factory. The main protagonist is Neil J. Smelser, with his famous *Social Change in the Industrial Revolution*. Our conclusions, however, come closer to those of his critics: M. M. Edwards and R. Lloyd-Jones, 'N. J. Smelser and the Cotton Family: A Reassessment', in N. B. Harte and K. G. Ponting (eds.), *Textile History and Economic History* (Manchester, 1973), pp. 304–19; and Michael Anderson, 'Sociological History and the Working-Class Family: Smelser Revisited', *Social History*, 3 (1976), 317–34.

Workers in highly-paid skilled jobs were especially inclined to try to secure the succession for their offspring. This was revealed at mid-century in Baccarat, a town dominated by its famous *cristallerie*. Almost all of the sons of the *tailleurs de cristal* and *verriers* were listed as apprentice glassworkers. This nepotism did not prevent a substantial inflow of new blood from outside the labour 'aristocracy'. Over half of the apprentices were the sons of *journaliers*, that is to say casual labourers for the glassworks and for local farmers.[13] A similar pattern emerges in the mill towns of the cotton and woollen industries. In the small Alsacian town of Munster, spinners, calico printers and those listed simply as 'factory workers' invariably had their sons and daughters follow them into the mills. Yet they could not provide nearly enough child labour to satisfy the voracious appetite of the textile industries. That contingent was outweighed by the offspring of casual labourers, handloom weavers, artisans in the construction and handicraft trades and the occasional peasant or vine-grower. The result was that in 1851 only a third of children pursued the same occupation as their fathers, though over half could probably count on a brother or sister at work.[14] In Normandy, in the cotton town of Sotteville, sons and daughters of spinners became *rattacheurs*, *dévideuses* and *veilleuses des cardes* in the mills, although it was noticeable that those over the age of sixteen tended to be weavers, seamstresses, cobblers or construction workers. Handloom weaving was also a trade that remained firmly fixed in the family, as might be expected. However, overall the proportion of sons and daughters following in their fathers' footsteps was only a little above one third: both the mills and the weaving shops had also to recruit amongst artisan and unskilled labouring families.[15] Very different was the position in silk throwing, another heavy employer of juvenile labour. Throughout southern France, this particular branch of the textile industry effectively separated parents from their daughters. Sons in this area were expected to follow their fathers into agriculture, leaving industrial work in the silk mills to the daughters. These young girls had little chance of support from an adult relative at their place of work. In Dieulefit, for example, a third of the girls under sixteen were likely to have a sister beside them, but another half were probably without a close relative.[16]

Mothers, it might be added from this analysis of census registers, were not usually to be found working outside the home. Some young mothers were forced by poverty to pursue factory work after their children had been born, and so too were many widows at a later stage in the family

---

[13] AD Meurthe-et-Moselle, 6 M 103, census of 1851.   [14] AD Haut-Rhin, 6 M 112.
[15] AD Seine-Maritime, 6 M 108.   [16] AD Drôme, 35 M 115.

cycle. But otherwise married women were the exception rather than the rule in the factories. Most working mothers chose jobs that could be carried on in the home, often helped by the fact that their children were earning. Many complemented the work of their husbands, setting up handlooms or stocking frames, weaving, knitting, checking finished woollen cloth for imperfections, sewing hosiery goods, serving in cafés or restaurants, or helping to run a shop. Others took on their own trades, usually clothesmaking, embroidery or lacemaking. Thus in Sotteville-lès-Rouen the 1851 census listed the odd *fileuse* or *bobineuse* from the cotton mills amongst the mothers of young families. But far more common were *trameuses* and *tisseuses* from the handloom weaving shops; *couturières*, *modistes*, *repasseuses*, *dentellières* and *ravaudeuses* from the clothing trades; wives assisting husbands from the retailing sector, including butchers, bakers, grocers, fruiterers, innkeepers, haberdashers and junk dealers; and finally *journalières* (casual labourers) from the very bottom of the labour market.

The framework for family life was therefore pressed in various directions by the onset of industrialization, but overall it was certainly not destroyed. This still leaves open the question of whether circumstances in working-class areas permitted any warmth and substance to the relationship between parents and children. Critics of the industrial system argued that long hours of monotonous work in the factories, combined with a daily struggle to make ends meet, were reducing the urban proletariat to the most basic material existence. Certainly, living and working conditions in the towns visited by Villermé, Blanqui and others during the 1830s and 1840s were barely compatible with the cosy intimacy in the home idealized by the middle classes. Young children could not expect to see much of fathers who put in a ninety-hour week on the shop floor, and who spent much of their leisure time drinking with friends in the *cabaret*. Working-class mothers for their part suffered constant harassment from the burdens of overcrowded living quarters, frequent childbirths and housework for a large family. Children were therefore frequently sent out to play in the streets, where they milled around endlessly in small gangs, the *vagabonds* so distrusted by 'respectable' opinion. Once they started work, young people had to compress much of their family life into Sundays, with leisurely meals and *promenades* beside the bourgeoisie on the main streets and in the parks. Even this traditional day of rest was far from sacrosanct in the world of industry. During periods of peak demand, mill owners expected their labour force to work through Saturday nights. And on Sunday mornings, custom was for the youngest workers to tidy up the workshops and clean machinery.[17] A certain distancing of parents from their children was thus inherent in early industrial society, with such heavy demands for time to be spent outside the immediate family. This was not so very different from relationships in the peasant families, though the growing separation of work from home and the absence of the winter *veillées* served to aggravate the position in the towns. Yet there remains the danger of sliding into an absurd *misérabiliste* position, depicting a new generation of working-class youth as completely demoralized by its material conditions.

Working-class leaders like Charles Noiret or Claude-Anthimé Corbon were indignant that their fellow workers should be written off so easily as immoral and outside 'society'.[18] The distorting influence of middle-class ideology on perceptions of immoral behaviour amongst the *classes populaires* cannot be discounted. Some of these misunderstandings between the classes were superficial. Villermé, for example, could not resist the occasional puritanical attack on the self-indulgence of young people. In Saint-Quentin, he criticized the girls for 'their taste for dressing up, their love of luxury'. In Lyons, it was the silk workers' habit of wearing bourgeois-style clothes that drew his fire. And, most tellingly, in Mulhouse he noted 'quite a large number of young girls and women whose interest in fashion, coquettish behaviour and facial expressions betray unchaste morals'. But in this latter case the evidence of promiscuity was based entirely on hearsay, leading one to suspect that the *débauches pernicieuses* of the female cotton printers were largely a figment of the author's imagination.[19]

More fundamental were differences in approach to organised religion. From early in the nineteenth century, the Catholic Church came to associate the progress of industry with a decline in religious observance. In the words of a priest from the Tarn, as he welcomed his bishop during a pastoral visit:

Alas! We at Labastide have a workshop. The labouring population, of all ages and both sexes, is numerous here. It is among this group that virtue has terrible assaults to withstand, when she does not succumb. And it is the workers who loose off

---

[17] The best accounts of this existence in the historical literature concern the Second Empire period, in particular Duveau, *La Vie ouvrière*, pp. 419–33; and Pierrard, *La Vie ouvrière*, *passim*.
[18] François-André Isambert, *Christianisme et classe ouvrière* (Paris, 1961), p. 212.
[19] Villermé, *Tableau de l'état*, vol. 1, pp. 32, 122, 363.

flights of irony, malevolence and clumny against religion, its holy practices and sometimes its ministers.[20]

Recent historical research has shown that this growing disillusionment of the proletariat with the Church was by no means uniform across the regions. Flanders, the Pays de Caux and the north-eastern part of the diocese of Le Puy could be cited as areas which have survived through to the present as bastions of the Christian faith despite substantial industrial populations. In the Nord, for example, the textile workers of Roubaix-Tourcoing and the Lys valley were conspicuously *pratiquants* in the nineteenth century, and so too were the coal miners of the region. In southern France, the woollen towns of Lodève, Mazamet, Castres, Bédarieux and Millau provided a further oasis of Christianity, partly because of a long-standing rivalry between Catholics and Protestants, partly because of a close relationship between the labour force and the surrounding countryside. As with the peasantry, these regional variations were complemented by a basic division between the sexes: working-class women were far slower to desert the churches than their menfolk. Nonetheless, by mid-century the clergy were coming to accept that the popular classes in most urban and manufacturing centres would have little contact with organized religion. The new 'barbarians' of the workshops and the slums were found to be either indifferent, or downright hostile.[21]

For the social thinkers of the 1830s and 1840s, whether staunch Catholics or liberal reformers, the moralizing role of the Church amongst the labouring classes was of prime importance. The implication in their writing was that as the working class distanced itself from the Church, so it wilfully chose to cut loose from conventional morality. But this was to ignore the political dimension to religious affairs. A Catholic hierarchy that aligned itself with the powerful rather than the oppressed, with the rich rather than the poor, was itself largely responsible for driving away its working-class congregations.[22] In Rouen, local *notables* made cynical use

[20] Jean Faury, *Cléricalisme et anticléricalisme dans le Tarn, 1848–1900* (Toulouse, 1980), p. 259.
[21] Le Bras, *Etudes de sociologie religieuse*, vol. 1, pp. 281–301; Fernand Boulard, *Premiers Itinéraires en sociologie religieuse* (Paris, 1954), pp. 41–64; Monique Vincienne and Hélène Courtois, 'Notes sur la situation religieuse de la France en 1848', *Archives de sociologie des religions*, 6 (1958), 112–14; Gérard Cholvy and Yves-Marie Hilaire, *Histoire religieuse de la France contemporaine, 1800–80* (Toulouse, 1985), ch. 8.
[22] See Paul Droulers, *Action pastorale et problèmes sociaux sous la Monarchie de Juillet chez Mgr d'Astros, archevêque de Toulouse, censeur de Lamennais* (Paris, 1954), pp. 1–6; Isambert, *Christianisme et classe ouvrière, passim*; Jean Bruhat, 'Anticléricalisme et mouvement ouvrier en France avant 1914', in F. Bédarida and J. Maitron (eds.), *Christianisme et monde ouvrier* (Paris, 1975), pp. 79–115; François Lebrun (ed.), *Histoire des catholiques en France* (Toulouse, 1980), pp. 349–55.

of the Church during the 1830s as a *bon gendarme* for a society threatened by working-class agitation. There was the unsavoury spectacle of 'Voltairian' members of the Conseil Général voting subsidies for the archbishopric, the seminaries and religious schools, and of the Church compromising with a régime that it had all too obviously despised in 1830. Inevitably, Charles Noiret lumped in the Church with his class enemies, the *patrons*, and this type of polarization could only increase under the influence of republican and socialist ideologies. The Nord witnessed the same failure of the Catholic Church to come to grips with the new world of the industrial proletariat. The clergy continued to dream of returning to old social hierarchies, and so remained firmly in the camp of the *notables*.[23] The growing disaffection of the French proletariat with the Catholic Church can therefore be understood without any suggestion of a lapse into immorality or an abnegation of responsibility for the moral education of children.

Most important of all, two contrasting attitudes to childhood lay behind many of the allegations of immorality in the reformist literature. Like the peasants, the urban working class persisted during the nineteenth century with the traditional notion of 'apprenticeship', launching its offspring into the hurly-burly of the streets, the workshops and the *cabaret*, to learn by first-hand experience. For the middle classes, recently won over to the view that children should be educated in a sheltered environment, this was anathema.[24] A series of *bêtes noires* emerged in their discourse: the idle vagabond of the street gangs, the revolutionary *gamin*, the promiscuous factory girl, and the drink-sodden youth of the bars. Thus Eugène Buret asserted that vagrancy amongst children was the nursery of theft: 'Once a young worker has succeeded in living one day outside the workshop, once vagabondage, the petty trading of the streets has procured him one day's existence, his morality and his future are finished.' Adolphe Blanqui warned that in the big cities of Paris and Lyons, young people in the workshops were an easy prey to 'all subversives of the social order'. Louis Villermé was disturbd by the *libertinage* and *moeurs peu chastes* of the young in the Alsacian textile mills, not to mention the turbulent scenes in the bars of Saint-Quentin:

Loud conversations, bursts of laughter, raucous singing, shouting, the clink of glasses, the banging of fists on tables, all maintain a continual, deafening noise. Most of the talk revolves around pleasure and debauchery; nothing of any

---

[23] Nadine-Josette Chaline (ed.), *Le Diocèse de Rouen-Le Hâvre* (Paris, 1976), pp. 249–52, 257–60; Pierrard, *La Vie ouvrière*, pp. 362–83; Yves-Marie Hilaire, 'Les Ouvriers de la région du Nord devant l'église catholique, XIXᵉ–XXᵉ siècles', *Cahiers du Mouvement social*, 1 (1975), 223–43.

[24] See above, pp. 3, 61.

seriousness crops up. I have been afflicted by the sight of young people under fifteen or seventeen in the midst of all this.[25]

Doubtless there was a regular crop of casualties in the harsh process of 'learning by living', such as the young lad drawn into crime by older youths, or the working girl pressured into illicit sex by a foreman abusing his power. But the *notables* might be accused of exaggerating these problems, and of failing to see the strengths of the system. There was the early independence of working-class youths compared to the 'infantiliz-ation' of young people in bourgeois households. There was the strong solidarity of the *bande* and the working-class community, as against the individualism preached to the offspring of the middle classes. There was too the popular culture of the towns with its own songs, games and festivals, which educated men barely deigned to notice.[26]

In conclusion, it is not difficult to show that early commentators laboured under a number of misapprehensions concerning the family life of the working class. Contrary to their assertions, the new industrial society was not snatching a rising generation of adolescents from the bosom of the family, nor was it inherently hostile to family ties on the shop floor. The depiction of proletarian communities riddled with drunkenness, promiscuity and indifference to the upbringing of children remains uncon-vincing, however many times it may have been reiterated. In the last resort, it is impossible to make such sweeping generalizations on the personal qualities of such a vast number of people. Nonetheless, as in the controversy over the physical condition of working-class youth, what mattered for subsequent political events was the fact that the reformers were convinced that many parents were either unwilling or unable to fulfil their duties towards their children. It was on this basis that they launched their campaign for State intervention in the factories, and it was by predicting the direst consequences for society at large that they made their impact, such as it was, on public opinion. There was enough truth in their allegations to force the attention of those in power. In the case of the family, the effects of industrial concentration and unrestricted compe-tition were far from negligible. The increasing scale of migrations from country to town, the minimal leisure time granted to the labour force in the textile mills and the workshops of the 'sweated' trades, the unwelcom-

---

[25] Buret, *De la misère*, vol. 2, p. 4; Blanqui, *Des classes ouvrières*, p. 154; Villermé, *Tableau de l'état*, vol. 1, pp. 31–2, 124.

[26] See, for example, Robert M. Isherwood, 'Entertainment in the Parisian Fairs of the Eighteenth Century', *Journal of Modern History*, 53 (1981), 24–48; Patricia Hilden, *Working Women and Socialist Politics in France, 1880–1914: A Regional Study* (Oxford, 1986), pp. 51–64; Georges Duby (ed.), *Histoire de la France urbaine*, vol. 4, *La Ville de l'âge industriel: le cycle haussmanien* (Paris, 1983), ch. 5.

ing conditions of the overcrowded tenements compared to the attractions of the *cabaret*, all served to obstruct the development of family bonds. Critics of the nascent industrial society of the mid-nineteenth century therefore did have sound humanitarian reasons for demanding reform. There was also the all-important political dimension. The persistence of traditional 'apprenticeships' in the towns meant that young people were being exposed to the turbulent atmosphere of the workshop and the bar: two places correctly identified by bourgeois opinion as breeding grounds for attitudes and ideologies that were subversive to the prevailing order.

A crisis in the apprenticeship system

A number of contemporary observers also accused industrial society of debasing the old-established apprenticeship system of the towns. Eugène Buret was one such critic, who noted that as industrial work became more mechanical, so the demands made on the training and intelligence of the labour force were reduced. He foresaw the increasing division of labour in the industrial sector producing a new class of *automates*, prone to revolutionary activity or at the very least to excessive drinking in the *cabarets*, and in desperate need of a solid moral education to allow them to use their liberty.[27] The eighteenth and nineteenth centuries did indeed witness a series of shocks for traditional methods of vocational training in the workshops. But the question remains of the overall seriousness of the so-called *crise d'apprentissage*.

Under the *ancien régime*, the *corporations* (guilds) had supervised the vocational training of the young, laying down various rules to ensure that the trades were taught 'completely and satisfactorily'. A minimum age was specified, usually around twelve, on the assumption that very young children could not be taught properly. Written contracts were required between parents and masters and the latter were limited to taking one or two apprentices at a time. All of the 'rudiments and secrets' of a trade had to be passed on to the newcomer, certain guarantees being required from the master to prove that he was equal to his task. Parents were expected to make some kind of payment to the master, varying according to the length of the apprenticeship, as a way of indemnifying him for the burdens of instruction, although in the final months the apprentice was customarily paid a wage. Finally, the young apprentice had to live with his master, and be treated as one of the family. This allowed him to absorb the whole ambience of his trade, and, as nineteenth-century commentators liked to point out, to benefit from the moral influence of the craftsman. Such were the general principles: but by 1789, practice in the workshops was

27 Buret, *De la misère*, vol. 1, pp. 304–9; vol. 2, pp. 152–8.

somewhat different, causing a cloud to form over the whole institution. Abuses included allowing the sons and sons-in-law of masters to undergo a shorter period of training than 'outsiders', and sales by the monarchy of *titres de maîtrise* to those who could afford them. In 1791, the entire corporate edifice fell to the *décret d'Allarde*, leaving apprenticeship schemes to the forces of supply and demand.[28]

Freeing apprenticeship from the semi-official control of the corporations did not prevent many established customs and practices continuing more or less intact into the nineteenth century. Some groups of workers were still able to maintain a firm grip on entry into their trades, accepting only the sons of existing craftsmen. A long line of complaints from seemingly helpless entrepreneurs ensued, notably in the paper, glass and metallurgical industries. At the beginning of the century, a paper manufacturer from the Puy-de-Dôme bemoaned the fact that all apprentices, except those with at least three generations in the industry behind them, were proscribed, unless they made a payment of 150 francs to the workers.[29] In similar vein, *notables* from the canton of Trélon, in the Nord, fulminated against the *privilège de race* of the glassblowers. They alleged before the 1848 Enquiry on Labour that the enforcement of family successions held the factory owners in subjection, and obstructed progress in industry.[30] Also, the majority of entrants into the artisan trades continued to undergo a formal apprenticeship, that is to say an extended period in the workshops devoted to on-the-job vocational training. Carpenters, masons, sawyers, tailors, locksmiths, coachmakers, coopers, tanners and *couturières*, to name but a few, usually started out this way, with some form of agreement between parents and masters over conditions.[31] A detailed investigation into the nature of apprenticeship in Paris during the 1840s, undertaken by the Chamber of Commerce, revealed a great diversity of conditions. A total of 18,116 cases were investigated. The majority were based on a verbal agreement, though a little under a quarter had written contracts. Three years was the commonest length stipulated, though two and four years were also common. A whole range of permutations emerged for idemnifying the master, as the following figures for the main categories will show:

2,367   fed, lodged and laundry   no payment

28 J. P. Guinot, *Formation professionnelle et travailleurs qualifiés depuis 1789* (Paris, 1946), pp. 26–35, 43–4.

29 AN, F¹² 2369, 'Mémoire concernant les abus que les ouvriers papetiers exercent dans les manufactures, par Serve fils', 1806. In 1848, the canton of Thiers (also in the Puy-de-Dôme) informed the Enquiry on Labour that parents of apprentices from outside the trade paid an indemnity of 60 francs to workers in the *fabriques*.

30 AD Nord, M 547/1.

31 Information from the 1848 Enquiry on Labour, and the Spuller Enquiry of 1882.

1,564	fed and lodged	lump sum paid
4,832	fed and lodged	no payment
2,010	neither fed nor lodged	lump sum paid
4,706	neither fed nor lodged	no payment

The Chamber concluded that there were two forms of apprenticeship in the capital. On the one hand, where the apprentice set out to learn a difficult trade, requiring a long period of training, he was obliged to compensate his master by payment of his board and lodging, or, later on, by more productive work. On the other hand, where an easy trade was involved, the novice could render immediate service. His position was then close to that of a young worker, except that he received no wages, his work being remunerated by some contribution to his upkeep, and by the advantage of being able to pick up his trade through watching others.[32]

No less importantly, the survival of the *compagnonnages* meant that the custom of tramping round the country to perfect a trade was maintained. The *compagnonnages* were associations of journeymen, and unlike the parallel corporations of masters, they had had no legal recognition under the *ancien régime*. The Allarde law therefore made no difference to their status, and although the Revolutionary and Imperial régimes made life difficult for them, the Restoration saw a healthy resurgence of activity. Most of their members were young, aged between eighteen and twenty-five, and employed as stonemasons, joiners, carpenters, locksmiths, tanners, dyers, ropemakers, basketworkers, hatmakers, or other such trades inherited from the Medieval period. Promoting both the technical and the moral education of entrants into this skilled élite of labour was one of the central aims of the various *devoirs*. After completing an apprenticeship, the *compagnons* were expected to go on a Tour de France, working in a succession of towns to learn the manufacturing procedures particular to each province. Equipped with his stave, his flask and his bag for tools and clothing (*la malle au quat' nœuds*), the young lad took to the road for an odyssey that would last several years. At each of the towns he came to, he was placed in a workshop by a *rouleur*, to take care of the technical side of his training. He might also attend evening classes run by a fellow *compagnon*, the *école de trait*, to learn a very practical version of geometry and technical drawing. At the same time, he gradually acquired the moral values of his craft through living *chez la Mère*. Lodging, or at least taking meals with the Mother of his *devoir*, he was obliged to obey rules against bad language, brawling within the

---

[32] Chambre de Commerce de Paris, *Statistique de l'industrie à Paris*, pp. 56–9.

house, excessive drunkenness and disorderly dress.[33] Agricol Perdiguier confessed to a fascination with the exceptional severity of the régime amongst the *gavots* in Avignon: 'No familiar greetings, no ridiculous expressions: but something grand, sublime, fraternal. All this attracted me, won me over, I was already half a *gavot*.'[34] Such was the position until the middle of the nineteenth century. At that point, it must be admitted, the movement found itself increasingly out of touch with the industrial working classes. Its arcane rites and traditions of exclusiveness began to lose their appeal in a world where rationalism and class-consciousness were the order of the day. Without ever disappearing, the *compagnonnages* steadily retreated to the margins of the labour movement.

These elements of continuity with the past could not mask the serious problems confronting apprenticeship under the *laissez-faire* system. The focus of discontent was the agreement between masters and the parents of apprentices, it proving difficult to balance the interests of the two parties. For the master, there was the risk of a contract broken prematurely, and inadequate compensation for the costs of training an inexperienced worker. As early as the Year V of the Revolution, the Directory was seeking ways to end this abuse. The preamble to draft legislation in this area noted, 'The bad faith with which many individuals carry out their apprenticeship contracts is another kind of disorder harmful to industry: every day apprentices run away from the workshops where they learnt their trade without putting in the time they undertook to give in return for the effort and care required for their instruction.'[35] For the parents, there was the fear of a child being left with servile or repetitive tasks which would not provide an adequate knowledge of the trade. The increasing division of labour evident over the course of the nineteenth century, even in the small-scale workshops, could only aggravate this concern. Anthimé Corbon, the most prominent critic of the state of vocational training during the 1850s, warned that a stream of half-trained workers was issuing forth from the *ateliers*, talking the jargon of their trade, but lacking a firm grip on the essential skills. He gave as an example the predicament of the numerous adolescents of both sexes employed in the production of fancy goods: the famous *articles de Paris*. Although commonly known as apprentices, they would in his view, have been better described as *enfants de peine*. His conclusion was pessimistic. 'What means are there, I beg of you, to force the master to safeguard the morality and the intelligence of

33 Emile Martin Saint-Léon, *Le Compagnonnage* (Paris, 1901); Emile Coornaert, *Les Compagnonnages en France* (Paris, 1966); Luc Benoist, *Le Compagnonnage et les métiers* (Paris, 1966); Sewell, *Work and Revolution in France*.
34 Perdiguier, *Mémoires d'un compagnon*, pp. 101–2.
35 AN, F¹² 2366, 'Projet de Message au Conseil des 500, Vendémaire, an 5'.

an apprentice, and to initiate him into the secrets of his trade with tact, kindness and zeal?' Corbon admitted that he had no answers.[36]

The gradual dismantling of the traditional apprenticeship system from the eighteenth century onwards meant that the coming of the factories, with their informal and often cursory training procedures, merely added impetus to an established trend. The term 'apprentice' was generally held to be inappropriate for the condition of children employed in the mechanized industries. Child workers were invariably paid a wage soon after they entered a factory, and there was no obligation on the part of the employer to provide them with anything more than a job during working hours. In the textile mills, children sacrificed a month or two at most as they picked up the simple job of piecing or reeling.[37] In the coal mines of the Loire, boys of eleven or twelve spent their first four months underground accompanying an experienced miner, learning how to sense danger and cope with the gruelling physical side of their work.[38] And in the paper mills, a short period of training was all that was necessary in the first instance. During the 1880s, an *employé à la manufacture de papier* looked back on his summary introduction to the trade as a youth: 'A foreman showed me what I had to do. In a few days I could do the job.' The eleven-year-old Jeanne Bouvier was even more dismissive of her initial training in a silk mill. At the end of her first day at work, when asked by her mother whether she found the job difficult, she replied

Oh! It is as easy as anything. You go like this to find the end, and then when you have found it you have to add it to the one wound on to the *roquet* [large bobbin]; you make a knot like this . . . (I showed her the movements). Then you must round off the *tavelle* with ligaments so that the *flotte* [hank] can be reeled without breaking the yarn.[39]

However, it is misleading to suggest that this was the sum total of vocational training in *la grande industrie*. The factories needed skilled as well as semi-skilled labour, meaning that there were in effect two grades of labour in industry, destined to follow divergent paths as the years went by. At the lower level were the workers whose instruction on the shop floor would go no further than a quick initiation into simple repetitive tasks. They were often from the poorest backgrounds, having been pushed out

---

[36] Anthimé Corbon, *De l'enseignement professionnel* (Paris, 1859), pp. 9–37. See also AN, F[12] 4830, Conseil Général des Manufactures, session of 12 January 1842, discussing the state of apprenticeship in France, and the need for legislative intervention; and Guinot, *Formation professionnelle*, pp. 71, 102–4. For English parallels, see Charles More, *Skill and the English Working Class, 1870–1914* (London, 1980), ch. 3.

[37] Numerous references to these practices can be found in the 1837 Enquiry into Child Labour, and the 1848 Enquiry on Labour.

[38] AN, C 956.

[39] AN, C 3370[4], Neuville-les-Dieppe; Jeanne Bouvier, *Mes mémoires* (Paris, 1983), p. 57.

into a series of casual jobs from an early age. Deprived of any real skills, such unfortunates were condemned to a life of insecure, low-paid work, providing the numerous *journaliers* and *manœuvres* of the urban labour market.[40] Above them were the young people whose talents, or more likely family connections, would allow them to proceed further. In order to produce their skilled grades of labour, the factories followed a régime akin to that of the family farms and workshops. Children were made to work their way up through a series of tasks beside an adult, until imperceptibly they mastered their trade. After a few years, the *rattacheurs* of the cotton mills could become spinners; the *goujats* of the ironworks, *forgerons*, and in the most elaborate hierarchy of all, the aspiring glassblower had to be successively a *chauffeur de cannes*, *porteur à l'arche*, *chauffeur de paraisons*, *tendeur de pontils* and *grand gamin*, before at the age of about twenty, he could be a *second souffleur*.[41] The career of one Martin Milleck followed just such a path in the spinning industry, mapped out for posterity by his *livret*. In 1854, at the age of fifteen, the document shows him leaving his village in lower Alsace to join his father, who was already working in Mulhouse. His first four months in the town were spent as an apprentice reeler at the Linch mill. Subsequently he was employed for two and a half years by Charles Naegely, starting as a *bobineur* and ending as a *rattacheur*, and for a further year by Dollfus-Mieg, still as a piecer. A short spell between March 1858 and February 1859 saw him promoted from piecer to spinner at the Dollfus mill, at which stage he would have been aged nineteen or twenty. Three more employers appear on his *livret*, the last entry in 1863 describing Milleck as a *conducteur de self-acting*.[42]

For many employers, talk of a crisis of apprenticeship must have appeared absurd. The informal procedures that came to the fore in the nineteenth century would, from their perspective, have been a welcome sign of flexibility in a previously rigid system. Breaking the stranglehold of the *corporations* meant that thousands of jobs were made available to rural workers, willing and able to meet the rising demand for low- and medium-quality goods. The 1848 Enquiry on Labour revealed that children in the villages and small towns commonly learnt their skills from their parents, without undergoing any formal apprenticeship.[43] Sur-

---

40 AN, F¹² 4705, Conseil des Prud'hommes of Strasbourg, 1837; AN, F¹² 4731, Commission of Inspection, Seine, 6th *arrondissement*, 1881.
41 AN, F¹² 4727, 'Rapport sur le travail dans les verreries', 1874. A similar but less elaborate hierarchy was given in the same year by the Syndicat des Verreries à Bouteilles. On 'following-up' in England, see More, *Skill*, ch. 6.
42 AD Haut-Rhin, 10 M 1.
43 The same point was also made in the Spuller Enquiry of 1882 and in the replies from the Prefects to a Ministerial Circular of 1853 on apprenticeship, AN, F¹² 4830.

rounded by the materials and tools of a trade from their earliest years, the offspring of, say, handloom weavers or hatters could pick up their technical know-how relatively painlessly. Similarly, in the factories, children were considered to be learning on-the-job. The practice of employing child labour was sometimes justified in terms of the need to start learning a difficult trade when still young. In 1840, for example, the director of the *cristallerie* at Baccarat asserted that 'the apprenticeship must be started early, to avoid the risk of never acquiring the degree of dexterity which makes the skilled workers'.[44] There was also a common assumption that the labour force needed to be broken in as quickly as possible to the discipline of work. The Mulhouse Chamber of Commerce was unctuous in proclaiming this positive rôle for child labour: 'One cannot conceal the fact that employment in the factory is a benefit for young workers, by inspiring at an early age the habits of work and order, whilst at the same time providing relief for their families and encouraging the growth of the population.'[45]

Such considerations were cold comfort for groups of skilled workers whose livelihoods were threatened by the relentless advance of mechanization and the division of labour. Not all trades were affected with equal intensity, but everywhere there was the veiled threat that technical progress might cause fully apprenticed craftsmen to be made redundant. In some cases, the writing was on the wall in the eighteenth century. The handloom weavers of the cities, to take the most numerous group affected, first had to contend with competition from cheap rural labour, before succumbing gradually over the course of the nineteenth century to the power loom and its semi-skilled operatives. Other trades appeared more sheltered, yet could not in the long run escape some decline in status and security. Printing workers found some of their work being taken over by less-skilled female labour during the second half of the nineteenth century, whilst the renowned cabinetmakers of the capital were undermined by increasing specialization. During the 1870s, the Conseil des Prud'hommes of Paris concluded that a decline in the number of 'good' workers was under way, on account of deficiencies in the system of vocational training:

But it is above all in the small workshops that apprentices are numerous, because it

---

44 AD Meurthe-et-Moselle, 10 M 27, 'Notice soumise au Conseil Général de la Meurthe par un de ses membres, sur le projet de loi relatif au travail des enfants dans les manufactures', 1840. See also AN, F[12] 4705, Chambre Consultative of Charleville, 10 September 1837; and AD Nord, M 611/8, letter to Prefect from Commission of Inspection in Lille, 5 February 1844.

45 AN, F[12] 4705. Information also from AN, F[12] 4830, report from Chambre de Commerce of Le Havre, 22 January 1849; and from Chambre Consultative des Arts et Manufactures of Saint-Dié, 12 August 1849.

is there that they can be profitable for the *patron*. He supervises their work himself, and it is certainly not in constantly doing the same thing that one can become a worker. Can an *ébéniste* be trained as an apprentice, placed in one of those firms in the *faubourgs*, which using machine tools to simplify and accelerate the work, only manufacture night-tables in a certain fashion or tables for sewing machines? Can one produce a chairmaker from the child whose only work consists of assembling the various parts of a chair which arrive already made up from the provinces or from abroad, and which have to be dismantled for transport purposes? The child given this work will, at the end of a very short time, be as capable as the best worker of rendering useful services to his employer, but he will certainly not be more skilful at the end of his apprenticeship than he was after six months.[46]

From their perspective, the *crise d'apprentissage* was very much a reality.[47] Moreover, even those without a vested interest could, with good reason, be disturbed by the direction industrial society was taking vocational training. Once again, there was a dilemma from the trade-off observable between increased productivity and the maintenance of the dignity of labour. The machine operative of the factory system might well help create unprecedented wealth for society, some of which would trickle down to him, but the costs in human terms were considerable. The spectacle of a whole class trained only to do jobs that were at once highly specialized and routinely mechanical was indeed far from reassuring.

Schools and the 'moralization' of the working class

The institution destined to fill the moral and intellectual void allegedly opening up in the lives of working-class children was the elementary school. For those who considered that the proletarian family was incapable of fulfilling the demands made on it, and that the traditional apprenticeship had outlived its usefulness, the school system offered a ready substitute.[48] The demands to be made on the intellect of children from the labouring classes would in truth be limited, with a syllabus that went little beyond the basics of literacy and numeracy. The elementary schools were to concentrate on the task of instilling moral and religious values into their pupils. The great fear amongst the *notables* was that the schools would produce 'a sort of half-learning, vague, incomplete and sterile', to quote Adolphe Blanqui on the education of the workers in

---

[46] AN, F[12] 4831, report of 20 February 1877. See also Lee Weissbach, 'Artisanal Responses to Artistic Decline: The Cabinetmakers of Paris in the Era of Industrialization', *Journal of Social History*, 16 (1982), 67–81.

[47] See Guinot, *Formation professionnelle*, *passim*.

[48] For similar moves across the Channel, see Richard Johnson, 'Educational Policy and Social Control in Early Victorian England', *Past and Present*, 49 (1970), 96–119.

Lyons.[49] What they were interested in, as has been demonstrated many times over, was the maintenance of existing social and political inequalities, so that until the 1880s at the earliest, the system of primary education was to be geared to encouraging 'order and economy' amongst the working class.[50]

There were signs that this campaign might be more successful in the towns than in the countryside. A number of Primary School Inspectors noted that industrial and commercial activities stimulated an interest in formal education that was largely absent in agricultural areas. During the 1840s, for example, the Rector of the Academy at Poitiers drew attention to differences between maritime and agricultural districts in the Charente-Inférieure. In the latter, education was not seen as an essential condition for improving the existence of a family, with the result that village schools were deserted during much of the year. In the maritime districts, by contrast, the trading and manufacturing activities of the population gave an incentive to acquire a basic education. Children therefore spent a longer period at school than in outlying areas, and attended during the summer as well as the winter.[51] Certain occupational groups in urban society, whose work required a measure of theoretical knowledge, were indeed renowned for their efforts to educate their children in the schools. Stonemasons, carpenters, joiners, locksmiths, and 'similar trades' were singled out under this heading in 1837 by the Lille Chamber of Commerce.[52] The atmosphere in urban areas was also recognized to be more favourable to education than that in the villages. In 1855, the School Inspector for the Aube remarked:

As a matter of fact, children in the towns are initiated at an early stage to all the ideas circulating around them, and participate in the intellectual movements which can be felt in the big centres of population. Knowing infinitely more than children in the countryside, they are better prepared for the instruction given in the schools.[53]

The political temperature tended to be higher in the cities than elsewhere, and working-class children could hardly avoid some contact with the ferment of ideas that was particularly evident around 1830 and 1848. New cultural forms were also likely to be pioneered in urban areas, some

---

49 Blanqui, *Des classes ouvrières*, p. 153.
50 Thouvenin, 'De l'influence', part 3, 95. On the bid to 'civilize' the population and create a disciplined labour force through formal education, see in particular: M. J. Bowman and C. A. Anderson, 'Human Capital and Economic Modernization in Historical Perspective', in F. C. Lane (ed.), *Fourth International Conference of Economic History, Bloomington, 1968* (Paris, 1973), p. 261; Prost, *Histoire de l'enseignement*, pp. 10–11; Gontard, *L'Enseignement primaire*, pp. 452–5; idem, *Les Ecoles primaires*, pp. 233–5; Johnson, *Guizot*, ch. 3.
51 AN, F[17] 9310.   52 AN, F[12] 4705.   53 AN, F[17] 9322, report of 30 April 1856.

of which were aimed largely at a plebeian market. There were for example the puppet shows mounted by members of the working class in bars or cellars. Lyons was the birthplace of the most famous of these, Guignol, which was the French equivalent to Punch and Judy. By the 1830s, this had reached its classic form in the *café-théatres*. The theatre was always placed at the end of a long cellar. Groups of workers sat around drinking and smoking, listening to a sharp dialogue that reflected the daily affairs of the city. Special sessions were laid on for children in the afternoons.[54] And then there were the broadsheets hawked in the streets of the big cities. Their *forte* were stories about notorious crimes, disasters, military campaigns, exotic beasts, and the like. The material was presented in anecdotal form with the stress on personal experiences to make them acceptable to the *menu peuple*. Although reticent about political issues, the *canards* must have aroused some interest in a wider world, and heightened interest in the written word.[55]

The density of population characteristic of the towns brought a further advantage in the form of easy access to schools for children. More specifically, it allowed large numbers of pupils to be assembled, which was deemed essential for the workings of the two most innovative teaching institutions of the early nineteenth century: the Lancastrian and the Christian Brothers schools. During the opening years of the Restoration, it was the *écoles mutuelles* which occupied the limelight. Their monitorial system, which trained some of the best pupils in a school to teach the other children, was well suited to a period when there were 'great needs and limited resources'.[56] The manufacturing areas of France produced a flurry of initiatives along these lines. In Alsace, Protestant manufacturers from Mulhouse took the lead, forming a Commission for Mutual Teaching in 1818. Three years later there were fifty-three Lancastrian schools in the region, including classes patronised by Japy at Beaucourt, Hartmann in the Munster valley and Gros and Romain at Wesserling.[57] Flanders had its first *école mutuelle* in 1816, when the Anzin Mining Company brought in the young Benjamin Appert from Paris to teach the children of its employees. Over the following years, with the active support of the Prefect, other monitorial schools sprang up in Condé-sur-l'Escaut, Saint-Amand, Valenciennes, Douai and

---

[54] Paul Fournel, *L'Histoire véritable de guignol* (Paris, 1981). See also A. Desrousseaux, *Mœurs populaires de la Flandre française* (2 vols., Lille, 1889), vol. 1, pp. 167–70.

[55] Jean-Pierre Séguin, *Nouvelles à sensation: canards du XIXᵉ siècle* (Paris, 1959), *passim*.

[56] Prost, *Histoire de l'enseignement*, p. 117. It might be noted that the French borrowed the description 'mutual method' from Bell, but in practice applied the monitorial system associated with Lancaster.

[57] Leuilliot, *L'Alsace au début du XIXᵉ siècle*, vol. 3, pp. 297–309; Raymond Oberlé, *L'Enseignement à Mulhouse de 1798 à 1870* (Paris, 1961), pp. 28–32.

Lille.[58] After this promising start, which produced a total of 1,500 schools across the country by 1821, the Lancastrian movement rapidly lost ground to its bitter rival, the Christian Brothers. The 'mutual method' had become too closely associated for its own good with the political campaigns of the Liberals. In the hostile climate of the period of Ultra reaction, after 1820, it proved vulnerable to accusations of indiscipline, rote-learning, inadequately trained monitors and, above all, superficial moral and religious education.[59] The 'simultaneous method' of the Frères, in which the entire class was treated as a unit for teaching, took over as the preferred replacement for the old individual method.[60] The Brothers made rapid strides forward, starting the Restoration with 52 schools and 17,000 pupils, and ending with 380 schools and 87,000 pupils. Although viewed with distaste by liberal municipal councillors, their policy of providing only free places helped make them popular with the urban poor. Towns where Guizot's Inspectors singled out Christian Brothers schools for the high quality of their teaching included Lyons, Rheims, Troyes, Abbeville and Sainte-Marie-aux-Mines.[61]

Such encouraging developments in the towns could not alter the prevailing feeling in official circles that the bid to 'civilize' the labouring classes would have to overcome powerful forces of inertia, or even outright hostility. As the School Inspectorate service became established on a proper footing during the 1830s and 1840s, a welter of evidence began to accumulate from various regions to support the contention from reformers that the expansion of the industrial sector was directly responsible for low levels of school attendance. From the Haut-Rhin, there came the stark assertion that 'the numerous factories which bring honour and prosperity to the department are also fatal to the progress of primary education'. From the Aisne, the Inspector wrote, 'Barely can the children turn a spindle when they are attached to a wheel or harnessed to a machine, and then it is goodbye to the school.' And from the Oise, the theme recurred with the observation that in the industrial cantons

58 Pierre Pierrard, 'L'Enseignement primaire à Lille sous la Restauration', *Revue du Nord*, 217 (1973), 127–31.
59 Raymond Tronchot, 'L'Enseignement mutuel en France de 1815 à 1833', unpublished thesis, University of Paris I, 1972, *passim*; Gontard, *L'Enseignement primaire*, pp. 314–27, 372–80.
60 Local studies with accounts of a conflict between Lancastrian and Christian Brothers schools, in addition to those on Alsace and Flanders, include Henri Contamine, *Metz et la Moselle de 1814 à 1870* (2 vols., Nancy, 1932), vol. 2, pp. 184–97; Vidalenc, *Le Département de l'Eure*, pp. 576–83; Zind, 'L'Enseignement primaire', 370–2; David, *L'Etablissement de l'enseignement*, pp. 83–131.
61 AN, F¹⁷ * 142, Rhône; AN, F¹⁷ * 125, Marne; AN, F¹⁷ * 86, Aube; AN, F¹⁷ * 141, Haut-Rhin. See also Gontard, *L'Enseignement primaire*, pp. 381–6; and Anne Querrien, 'Travaux élémentaires sur l'école primaire', *Recherches*, 23 (1976), 5–189.

children were put to work as soon as they could earn a few sous, leaving little or no time for their schooling.[62] Some statistical evidence also survives to confirm the allegations of reformers. A survey of child workers in the textile mills of Mulhouse, undertaken in 1843, revealed numerous examples of derisory periods at school, lasting only a few weeks, or even a few days. At the Charles Naegely mill, one third of the 173 children had spent a maximum of three months in school and a further third between four months and a year. Some of the remainder, it might be added, claimed extended periods in class of six, eight or even ten years.[63] A hint of similar schooling patterns comes from Rouen during the Second Empire period. At the Ecole Bachelet, located in the Rue du Vert Buisson, exactly half of a sample of 167 children who registered between 1854 and 1866 spent a year or less in class. This was not necessarily the sum total of their schooling, for some may have attended other schools. But the differences between the various occupational backgrounds of the children are suggestive. Only one quarter of a group whose fathers were *employés* (clerks) were limited to a year at school, compared to approxiately half of those from artisan and shopkeeping families, and almost two-thirds of those whose origins lay in the textile industries or unskilled jobs.[64]

Of the various hurdles that had to be crossed in industrial areas, the first was the purely material one of creating enough school places for working-class children. This required a commitment of public funds to provide the free schooling on which families with low incomes depended. Town councils were slow to respond to a challenge which, with only one in four children estimated to be attending school in 1813, was a formidable one.[65] In effect, they had to leap forward from the *ancien régime* tradition of helping out a restricted number of pauper children to the new ambition of subsidising mass schooling. The Town Council of Lille, for example, allocated a paltry 1,500 francs in subsidies to its teachers in 1818, plus another 1,000 francs to support a charity school run by the Filles de Sainte-Thérèse. These sums produced approximately 300 places, in a town that reputedly harboured an indigent population of 30,000.[66] The position in smaller communes was not necessarily any better. In 1833, the Guizot Inspector in Dieulefit (Drôme) noted that there were only 30 free

62 AN, F¹⁷ 9307, Haut-Rhin, 25 August 1839; AN, F¹⁷ 9308, Aisne, 1 January 1842; AN, F¹⁷ 9307, Oise, *arrondissement* of Clermont, 17 October 1840.
63 AM Mulhouse, F VI Ea 3, 'Travail des enfants', 1843.
64 AD Seine-Maritime, 144 TP 2, 'Registre d'inscription, Ecole Bachelet', 1853–70. The register gave the following information on each boy: name, date of birth, parents' occupation, vaccination record, date of registration at the beginning of the school year and (in some cases) date of leaving. The school career of all boys whose names began with 'L' was investigated.
65 Furet and Ozouf, *Reading and Writing*, p. 103.
66 Pierrard, 'Lille sous la Restauration', 123.

places in the schools for a population of 12,000. These, it transpired, were provided out of charity by the teacher, there being no money available for this purpose from the public purse.[67] The recipients of free places were not always from the proletariat, and doubtless there was much string-pulling around the town halls. During the 1820s, to take a case in point, an *instituteur* in Roubaix sent the Mayor a list of his ten *élèves gratuites*. One of these was the nephew of a curate, another was the son of 'your former head servant', and four were the 'sons of clerks'. This left only the offspring of a spinner, a cook, a ditcher and an innkeeper as the obvious candidates for assistance.[68] A steady inflow of migrants from the country-side aggravated the problem in the more expansive manufacturing centres. Achille Penot calculated that in Mulhouse the ratio of school children to population declined from 1:26 to 1:45 between 1819 and 1827.[69]

A second task involved refashioning the teaching profession so that it could fulfil its mission amongst the working class. No simple solution could be anticipated here, since different religious denominations and political groupings would inevitably jostle for control of education. Throughout the nineteenth century, the schools were a focus for struggles between Catholics and Protestants, and, more importantly, between the Church and the State. The ruling élites of the period were thus divided on the direction which primary education should take, the conflict between Lancastrian and Christian Brothers schools being merely an opening salvo in the *lutte scolaire*. Nonetheless, there was a good deal of common ground amongst the opposing factions, notably in the conviction that the labouring population needed more elementary schooling. The Catholic Villeneuve-Bargemont was to be heard in 1837 demanding special courses on technical drawing, mechanics and geometry, to supplement the religious education and elementary instruction provided by the schools. At the same time, Eugène Buret complained that children in manufacturing areas were only being taught basic literacy, to the neglect of their moral education. The *instituteurs*, he added, were not up to their job.[70]

The first systematic enquiry into the quality of primary school teaching was launched by Guizot in 1833. This revealed the urban *instituteurs* in a generally more favourable light than their rural counterparts, but there was no shortage of criticisms. Most of the brickbats were reserved for the weaker masters in the private school sector. Some of the private schools were reputable establishments, able to charge a petty bourgeois clientèle

---

[67] AN, F[17] * 101.
[68] AM Roubaix, R I a 2 letter from the Chevalier de Préville to Mayor, 17 December 1827.
[69] Figures cited in Oberlé, *L'Enseignement à Mulhouse*, p. 36.
[70] Villeneuve-Bargemont, *Economie politique chrétienne*, p. 440; Buret, *De la misère*, vol. 2, p. 4.

as much as 10 francs a month for their services. But others had a miserable, down-at-heel air about them, and, being unable to exact more than a franc or two per month from a handful of pupils, barely provided a living for their owners. In Rouen, the Inspector visited twenty-one private schools, with anything between nine and sixty pupils on their rolls. All were listed as using the old 'individual method' of teaching, and as providing only very elementary teaching. The syllabus varied according to the fees charged: 1.75 francs secured the three Rs; 2.50 francs added the catechism and grammar; and 6 francs brought in spelling, geography and history. The teachers were compared unfavourably with their rivals in the monitorial and Christian Brothers schools, being assessed as merely 'quite good', 'limited in their education', or occasionally even 'ignorant'.[71] In Lyons, the picture was similar. A third of the twenty-nine private schools covered by the enquiry still used the 'individual method', and if most of the teaching was described as satisfactory, some of it was condemned as very poor.[72] In Troyes, the Inspector brought out the contrasts between the private schools more clearly. Of the seven establishments he visited, three were rated very highly, one was satisfactory and three were written off as 'feeble'. The teacher in one of these latter was said to be discouraged by dwindling numbers of pupils in his school; the second made little impact despite his zeal and aptitude; and the third was depicted losing his temper and hitting children in class.[73] The 1833 Enquiry praised most of the *écoles mutuelles* and Christian Brothers schools in the industrial towns for the excellence of their teaching and discipline. Their contribution in handling large numbers of pupils, with or without the aid of municipal subsidies, was recognized. However, the monitorial schools in particular were not beyond criticism from the Guizot Inspectors. Two of the four *écoles mutuelles* in Rouen were written off as 'feeble', and only one of the four in Troyes was considered successful, teaching in the others being variously described as 'satisfactory', 'feeble' and 'detestable'. There were, in short, plenty of good teachers in the towns, but there remained a hard core who fell far short of the standards expected by the academic hierarchy.

A third problem to be faced, and one which caused much handwringing in bourgeois circles, was the weakness of demand for elementary schooling in working-class areas. This was partly a matter of low-paid families finding it difficult to afford the costs of primary education. An official from Normandy observed during the 1840s that a worker who earned 1.25 francs a day could hardly be expected to

---

[71] AN, F^{17} * 147.　　　[72] AN, F^{17} * 142.　　　[73] AN, F^{17} * 86.

support a family and pay school fees.[74] Free places would go some way towards providing a solution. Yet the fact remained that for a poor family, the major burden of formal education was not the outlay on school pence, but the loss of income from a potential member of the labour force.[75] Employers and School Inspectors were well aware that it was above all the better-off workers in the artisan trades who sent their children to school. They also noted that attendance in class invariably fell away during an industrial recession. An Inspector in the Champagne region noted at mid-century, 'the worker from the countryside and the towns understands the advantages of education. But when he is in need, poverty represses his instincts to plan for the future and his paternal ambition, and he falls back into thoughtlessness.'[76] This was not the whole story, however. Material hardship was only one of several forces keeping children out of the schools: cultural attitudes must also be brought into play. There was a common assumption amongst outside observers that working-class parents were ignorant, greedy and indifferent to the benefits of education.[77] Such sweeping judgements are difficult to accept. Many individual cases deserving these criticisms may well have existed, but it is unlikely that a whole class of people can be condemned so roundly. More plausible is the contention that decisions were taken, more or less consciously, on the basis of a hard-headed appraisal of the costs and benefits of education.[78] Once again, a divergence between official and popular conceptions of education can be discerned. Working-class parents, it goes without saying, did not set out to have their children 'civilized' in the interests of social stability: they may even have resisted such efforts. What they were interested in was securing an education that would prepare their offspring for life in the popular quarters of the town. Like the peasants, their attitudes were down-to-earth, prosaic even, with the emphasis on skills and knowledge that would have a practical application.

[74] AD Seine-Maritime, 10 MP 1362, report by Weights and Measures Inspector, *arrondissement* of Yvetôt, 20 November 1847.

[75] See Mark Blaug, *An Introduction to the Economics of Education* (London, 1970), pp. 47–9. Simple arithmetic will show that a child earning 30 to 50 centimes a day would bring in far more than the 4 or 5 francs a month charged by many private schools.

[76] AN, F^{17} 9322, reports of 30 April 1856. Information drawn also from: AN, F^{12} 4705, Lille Chamber of Commerce, 29 September 1837; AD Nord, M 611/8, letter from spinners in Lille to Prefect, 5 February 1844; AN, F^{17} 9307, report of School Inspector, Seine-Inférieure, for 1839–40; AN, F^{17} 9312, report of School Inspector, Rhône, 25 January 1848.

[77] Villeneuve-Bargemont, *Economie politique chrétienne*, p. 440; Lorain, *Tableau de l'instruction*, p. 31; AN, F^{12} 4705, submissions from the Prefect of the Haut-Rhin, Conseil des Prud'hommes of Rheims, Avignon Chamber of Commerce and Chambre Consultative of Sommières.

[78] Anderson, 'Patterns and Variability', in Anderson and Bowman, *Education and Economic Development*, pp. 328–9.

This approach did not require a long period on the school benches. Significantly, teachers who provided a very basic instruction in the three Rs and the catechism were often well respected in their local community, even when the *inspecteurs primaires* disapproved of their activities. One of the monitorial schools in Troyes was run by an ex-soldier, who had spent eleven years as a prisoner-of-war in England. The Guizot Inspector had little good to say of him, reporting that he was lacking in capacity and deficient in his teaching methods. All the same, he had 1,100 pupils in his school, and the Inspector had to concede that he was 'liked and esteemed' by the population.[79] There was presumably some recognition that the ability to read and write was an asset in urban society, with its increasing resort to the printed word and written forms of communication. There may have been the vision of a better future for the younger generation. There was too the long-standing concern to prepare children for their first communion by means of the catechism. Girls in particular were sent to school to prepare for a 'good first communion', as part of their preparation for motherhood. Indeed, the religious teaching orders were far more in favour with parents for their daughters than their sons. In 1850, 45 per cent of girls in the primary schools were taught by the *congrégations*, compared to only 15 per cent of boys.[80]

To balance these aspirations, there loomed the realities of the labour market. The number of jobs that required primary education as a formal qualification were few and far between in early industrial society, the bureaucracy for industry, commerce and the administration still being relatively small.[81] The Heilmann spinning mill at Ribeauvillé, to take an example from the 1820s, employed 46 men, 106 women and 108 children. Out of this total of 260 personnel, only 5 clerical and supervisory staff needed to be literate to hold their positions. A further 11 mechanics, locksmiths and joiners would have benefited from elementary instruction as a basis for their technical training. The rest, machine minders of various grades, could do their work without being literate let alone versed in the arts of grammar, history and geography.[82] Looking

79 AN, F[17] * 86.
80 These and related issues are discussed in Jacques Ozouf, 'Le Peuple et l'école: note sur la demande populaire d'instruction en France au XIXe siècle', in *Mélanges d'histoire sociale offerts à Jean Maitron* (Paris, 1976), pp. 167–76; and Furet and Ozouf, *Reading and Writing*, pp. 126–30. British parallels can be seen most clearly in Thomas W. Laqueur, 'Working-Class Demand and the Growth of English Elementary Education, 1750–1850', in Lawrence Stone (ed.), *Schooling and Society* (Baltimore, 1976), pp. 192–205.
81 This case has been well aired in the British literature by Michael Sanderson: 'Social Change and Elementary Education in Industrial Lancashire, 1780–1840', *Northern History*, 3 (1968), 131–54; see also his 'Literacy and Social Mobility in the Industrial Revolution in England', *Past and Present*, 56 (1972), 75–103.
82 AD Haut-Rhin, 9 M 23.

ahead to 1866, when a national perspective first becomes possible, the census indicated that there were nearly 3 million *ouvriers* employed in the industrial sector, but only 116,000 engineers, managers and clerks.[83] Again, girls were more affected than boys by this type of consideration. Since most of them were destined for lowly manual occupations within the textile industries, the clothesmaking trades and domestic service, parents could see little incentive to invest in their education. As already mentioned, the prevailing assumption among parents and educationalists alike was that females should be prepared for a rôle in the home rather than in the wider world.

A combination of necessity and calculation, then, does much to explain why so many industrial workers skimped on the schooling of their children. Literacy statistics bear witness to the limited imprint of the elementary schools on the industrial proletariat. During the 1830s, according to a sample of military conscripts taken by Alain Corbin, 41.1 per cent of industrial workers in the Cher were able to read at least, which was comfortably above the scores registered by independent farmers and agricultural labourers, but below the 50.1 per cent achieved by the artisans. In the Nord, more obviously in the mainstream of economic development, Robert Gildea further emphasizes the divide separating workers from small- and large-scale industry. His sample of military conscripts from the 1850s has wood workers, cobblers, tailors and farriers with literacy levels of 80 per cent and over, compared to the 42.7 per cent recorded by textile workers, and the 36.6 per cent of the miners.[84]

On the other side of the coin, the practical aspects of vocational training and work experience for the young were anything but neglected by the industrial proletariat. Bending to popular demand, there were occasional examples of schools combining manual work with elementary instruction. This was most in evidence in the lacemaking areas of the east. During the 1830s an Inspector in the Vosges noted with satisfaction that an *institutrice* had divided her class into two so that she could teach one group whilst the other concentrated on its needlework. By the 1840s and 1850s, the situation had clearly got out of hand, with many girls' schools coming to resemble *ouvroirs*: the workshops run by convents to help young people develop their craft skills. One outraged Inspector reported that parents were sending their children to school on the express condition that they did not learn to read and write, so that they would not be

---

[83] Statistique de la France, *Population, résultats généraux du dénombrement de 1866* (Paris, 1869), pp. 20–1.
[84] Corbin, 'Conscrits du Cher et de l'Eure-et-Loire', 118; Gildea, *Education in Provincial France*, p. 230. See also Furet and Ozouf, *Reading and Writing*, ch. 5.

disturbed from their lacemaking. Schools were having to remain open from 4.30 in the morning until 8.00 o'clock in the evening, and, having cleared out some of their equipment to make way for the lacemaking pillows, they found themselves saddled with the constant rattling of wooden pegs.[85] More commonly, parents expected children to learn their skills and gain experience on the shop floor. The rapid launch into the labour market that this entailed could easily be interpreted in an unfavourable light. In 1856 a School Inspector for the Aube wrote:

One of the areas where one particularly notices the effects of this indifference [towards religion] on the young people in the schools is Romilly-sur-Seine, a manufacturing town, almost entirely devoted to industry, whose working population seems only to be interested in two things: work and pleasure. There, the children are generally dissipated, turbulent, impolite, unconcerned about education and moral issues, passionately interested in games and recreations, and already initiated into bad habits above their age, when not prematurely corrupted.[86]

Such a jaundiced observer was perhaps not one to understand the motivation of families engaged in a dispersed, somewhat 'dishonourable' industry like hosiery, the speciality of Romilly during the nineteenth century. No hint is given that a lack of employment outlets for educated men and women in a small industrial town might help to explain the reluctance to send children to school. Nor is there any recognition that there would be a strong incentive to buckle down early to the business of learning to be a framework knitter. Similar considerations apply to child labour in the factories: years spent in the workshops at this stage in life could be seen as a form of investment for the future. In 1875 a Factory Inspector in Rouen commented on the resistance by parents to compulsory schooling for children aged thirteen and fourteen who lacked a primary education certificate. The new measure, he observed: 'is particularly hard on the working population when these children have acquired through five or six years of industrial experience special knowledge and a manual dexterity which makes them valuable workers and which assures them relatively high wages'.[87] There is no reason to suspect that parents in the earlier part of the century would have thought any differently.

---

[85] AN, F[17] * 159, Vosges, 1833; AD Vosges, M 292, dossier on lacemaking in the schools during the 1850s; AN, F[17] 9335, report on girls' primary schools, *arrondissement* of Mirecourt, Vosges, 1 January 1857. See also Furet and Ozouf, *Reading and Writing*, pp. 108–9.

[86] AN, F[17] 9322.   [87] AN, F[12] 4742, Aubert (Lisieux, 8th), 30 July 1875.

Conclusion

To suggest that two or three generations of working-class children were cast into some kind of cultural limbo, with no worthwhile stimulus to their moral and intellectual development, is to go beyond the bounds of credibility. There were, for a start, too many dimensions to the popular education for any wholesale decline to take place over the course of the nineteenth century. Family life as it had been known to peasants and craftsmen may well have been transformed by the growing separation of work from the home in the manufacturing sector. Contact between the young and the priesthood was much reduced by the loss of authority by the Catholic Church in most working-class areas. And the Medieval-style apprenticeship of the *corporations* eventually succumbed to the pressure of new technologies and the *laissez-faire* system. But working to offset these changes were various new institutions: the elementary schools; the broadsheets and chap-books of the publishing industry; the popular theatres; and the labour movement, with its message that working-class people should study and think for themselves. A stress on decline also insults the memory of a whole class of people, depicted as being crushed by their circumstances. In reality, men, women and children from the *classes populaires* were engaged in a long process of struggle to adapt to changing circumstances. Some were more successful at promoting the interests of their children than others. Artisans and other skilled workers were often able to resist assaults on apprenticeship and *compagnonnage* traditions, and to take advantage of opportunities in the school system. For the industrial proletariat proper, the early years were more difficult. However, free school places and catechism classes offered some chance of a little formal instruction, and connections on the shop floor were a means of obtaining a rudimentary training and work experience. What we are left with is the early period of industrialization, brutal and uncontrolled in its effects, which was conspicuous for the obstacles it raised to popular education. During the second quarter of the nineteenth century a clutch of disruptive influences came clearly into focus. These included industrial development that allowed young children to earn wages all the year round; a long working day which pre-empted time required for social and cultural activities; and the swamping of school facilities by unprecedented waves of migrants. The clearest indicator of this phenomenon is provided by a study of literacy in the Nord. François Furet and Jacques Ozouf have shown a succession of cantons falling behind in the rank order of literacy as the first stages of industrialization swept over

over them.[88] Such information was not available to Jean-Jacques Bourcart and his fellow campaigners for factory reform, but it lends support to the contention that the growth of industry and the towns had not contributed, or at least had barely contributed, to the moral development of the working class.

[88] 'Literacy and Industrialization: The Case of the Département du Nord in France', *Journal of European Economic History*, 5 (1976), 5–44. We might note that the article does not claim to have proof of an absolute decline in average literacy levels for any canton, because it is obliged to use different sources of data at the early periods. However, it does consider such a fall likely in five cantons between the periods 1750–90 and 1826–7.

Part Three

The State intervenes

Chapter 8

1841: an experiment in social legislation

Child labour first became an issue in the political arena during the 1820s and 1830s. As we have seen, evidence that the youngest and most vulnerable members of the labour force were suffering from abuses on the shop floor began to accumulate in the writings of social investigators. Mechanization and heightened competition in industry were held responsible for the imposition of excessively long hours and a gruelling pace of work on large numbers of women and children. The effects of the new régime were widely canvassed. Reformers wrote passionately of child 'martyrs' in the mills, disastrous military recruitment figures in the industrial cantons, a new breed of 'barbarians' emerging in the slums, and so forth. The case did not by any means go unchallenged. Time and again, we have noted employers indignantly asserting that the allegations of a physical and intellectual decline were exaggerated. We have also come across their emphasis on the positive achievements of the factory system, with the argument that it was bringing improved working conditions and more disciplined attitudes amongst the labour force. Nonetheless, there was something of a consensus on the misery of many working-class children in the manufacturing areas. The first task of the reformers was to convince those in power that State intervention was the appropriate response.

The ground prepared: a changing climate of opinion

The immediate stimulus to action on factory legislation was provided by men like Jean-Jacques Bourcart and Louis Villermé, with their revelation of abuses of child labour on the shop floor. By the 1830s, French industry had surmounted the upheavals of the Revolutionary and Napoleonic era, and, sheltering behind a protectionist barrier, had benefited from two decades of relative tranquility.[1] The scale of manufacturing, and the

---

[1] It might be noted at this point that France did not attempt an equivalent to the British Health and Morals of Apprentices Act of 1802. This was not for lack of abuses in the

attendant problems affecting the labour force, had by this stage reached substantial proportions. However, although the material conditions appeared ripe for a reform campaign it remains to ask why public opinion became sufficiently receptive for it to be successful. Why, in other words, did abuses which had existed for many years suddenly become 'intolerable'? For an answer, we must turn to the changing ideas and attitudes of the period: debates on childhood and the rôle of the State in economic and social affairs were crucial in providing a favourable climate of opinion for the 1841 law.[2]

A surge of interest in the first of these areas, childhood, can be traced back to the *ancien régime* period. According to the classic thesis of Philippe Ariès, the discovery of childhood occurred relatively late in Western civilization. Medieval society, he concluded, tended in practice to blur the distinction between adults and children, by launching the young headlong into the world at large around the age of seven. A first dent in this indifference to childhood occurred during the sixteenth century, when mothers began to indulge themselves more freely in 'coddling' their infants. More significantly for Ariès, during the seventeenth and eighteenth centuries, a small band of moralists and teachers achieved some success amongst the aristocracy and the upper middle classes in imposing the concept of an extended childhood. The dominant classes became aware of the particular nature of childhood, with its innocence and weakness. The 'essential event' for Ariès was the increasing rôle for the schools, which isolated children from the corrupt world of adults, and imposed their disciplined, rational approach to childrearing. This change of attitude was paralleled by a reorganization of the family, the emphasis shifting from preserving the lineage to tightening the sentimental bonds uniting parents and children. The growing desire for privacy in the home

employment of *enfants assistés* in the cotton mills during the opening phase of development. French entrepreneurs were as adept as their British counterparts in twisting the charitable tradition of providing work for orphaned and abandoned children to their own commercial uses. However, the precarious state of the French textile industry at this period was not likely to encourage legislative intervention. The first generation of textile mills was decimated during the French Revolution, and the second flourished only in the hothouse conditions of the Continental System, suffering heavily during the economic crises that marred the final years of the Napoleonic régime. One might add that the 1802 Act is usually considered an off-shoot of the Elizabethan Poor Law, an institution that had no parallel in *ancien régime* France.

2 See the debate in the British literature between MacDonagh and his critics, especially: Oliver MacDonagh, 'The Nineteenth-Century Revolution in Government: A Reappraisal', in P. Stansky (ed.), *The Victorian Revolution* (New York, 1973), pp. 5–25; Jennifer Hart, 'Nineteenth-Century Social Reform: A Tory Interpretation of History', *Past and Present*, 31 (1965), 39–61; H. Parris, *Constitutional Bureaucracy* (London, 1969), pp. 267–70.

helped turn the family in on itself, paving the way for its 'modern', child-centred form.[3]

The work of Ariès has not been without its critics. They have pointed to the difficulty of finding sources that can throw light on the feelings of parents for their offspring, and hence to the vagueness evident throughout *Centuries of Childhood* on the timing of change in various regions and social groups. They have noted flaws in the logic of his arguments. For example, it is paradoxical, to say the least, for Ariès to suggest that an increased awareness of the needs of children has produced the disciplined régime in the schools, when he barely conceals his preference for the 'gay indifference' of the Medieval apprenticeship system. They have also disputed some of his findings on empirical grounds. Investigations into diaries, autobiographies and folklore studies have led to the counter-view that parents in *ancien régime* France were far from being indifferent to the fate of their children, even if their conception of childhood was different from that current in the twentieth century. Moreover, the existence during Medieval times of *la jeunesse*, an institution whose last vestiges we have already noted in nineteenth-century rural society, indicates some recognition of an intermediary stage between childhood and full adult status.[4] What remains is an acceptance by many historians that the seventeenth and eighteenth centuries saw unprecedented discussion of various problems associated with childhood. A twin-pronged attack was mounted on traditional child-rearing practices, which anticipated the major themes we have encountered in the nineteenth century.

In the first place, the beginnings of demography during the late seventeenth and early eighteenth centuries revealed appallingly high levels of infant and child mortality. Politicians as well as doctors became drawn into discussion of this issue, for this was a period when the strength of a nation was still measured in terms of its manpower. The neglect of young children, particularly by foundling hospitals and mercenary wet-nurses,

---

[3] Ariès, *Centuries of Childhood*, *passim*. It should be noted that this translation is an abridged version of the French original, which also leaves out all of the illustrations; cf. *L'Enfant et la vie familiale sous l'Ancien Régime* (Paris, 1973).

[4] Jean-Louis Flandrin, 'Enfance et société', *Annales ESC*, 19 (1964), 322–9; Georges Snyders, *La Pédagogie en France au XVIIe et XVIIIe siècles* (Paris, 1965), pp. 8–11; David Hunt, *Parents and Children in History* (New York, 1972), pp. 32–50; Lloyd B. de Mause (ed.), *The History of Childhood* (London, 1974), pp. 5–6; Françoise Loux, *Le Jeune Enfant et son corps dans la médecine traditionelle* (Paris, 1978), *passim*; Peter Fuller, 'Uncovering Childhood', in Martin Hoyles (ed.), *Changing Childhood* (London, 1979), pp. 71–108; Adrian Wilson, 'The Infancy of the History of Childhood: An Appraisal of Philippe Ariès', *History and Theory*, 19 (1980), 132–53; Michael Anderson, *Approaches to the History of the Western Family* (London, 1980), pp. 39–64. Ariès himself has confronted some of these criticisms in his 'Préface à la nouvelle édition': *L'Enfant*, pp. i–xx. A useful work in the British literature is Linda A. Pollock, *Forgotten Children* (Cambridge, 1983), *passim*.

came to be denounced as a national evil. In the second place, the religious upheavals of the Reformation and Counter-Reformation left in their wake a widespread feeling that private and public morality were in decline. Moralists criticized the selfishness of wealthy parents in the big cities who sacrificed the interests of their children for their own pleasures, and thus compromised the future vigour of the national élite. The outcome of these concerns was an intense period of theorizing on childhood during the eighteenth century. Manuals advising parents on how to raise their children began to appear, of which the famous *Emile* by Jean-Jacques Rousseau was only one among many. Their message was that parents should take a closer interest in the development of their children, instead of leaving such matters to servants. Mothers were encouraged to breast-feed their children, to play games with them and to abandon swaddling. The revolutionary nature of these proposals was far from being matched by practice in society at large. At the beginning of the nineteenth century, the 'modern' family and long periods of schooling were still confined to a narrow élite. Reforms to help abandoned children or infants sent out to nurse were also slow to make an impact.[5] Yet new ideals were definitely in the air by this period, and important precedents had been set. The eighteenth-century example of taking steps to preserve the lives of young children was already in the background when reformers confronted the new threats to health brought by industrial development. Moreover, the 'bourgeois' model of family life, leaving 'the child in the school, the wife in the home and the man in the workshop',[6] was influential in shaping élite attitudes to factory legislation.[7]

The debate influencing reformers in the realm of political economy began with publication of Adam Smith's *Wealth of Nations* in 1776. Smith and his disciples built up a powerful current of opinion in favour of *laissez-*

---

[5] Information in this section drawn from: Shelby T. McCloy, *The Humanitarian Movement in Eighteenth-Century France* (Frankfurt, 1957); Roger Mercier, *L'Enfant dans la société du XVIIIe siècle* (Dakar, 1961); Snyders, *La Pédagogie en France, passim*; Jacques Donzelot, *The Policing of Families*, transl. R. Hurey (London, 1980), ch. 2; Gélis *et al.*, *Entrer dans la vie, passim*; Jean-Louis Flandrin, 'L'Attitude à l'égard du petit enfant et les conduites sexuelles dans la civilisation occidentale', *Annales de démographie historique*, (1971), 143–210; *idem, Families in Former Times: Kinship, Household and Sexuality* (Cambridge, 1979), ch. 3; John Somerville, *The Rise and Fall of Childhood* (Beverly Hills, Cal., 1982), ch. 12.

[6] AN, F¹² 4718, Conseil Général of the Aisne, 1871, quoted in a letter from Prefect of Aisne to Minister of Commerce, 18 January 1872.

[7] See Philippe Meyer, *L'Enfant et la raison d'Etat* (Paris, 1977), pp. 9–27; Priscilla Robertson, 'Home as Nest: Middle Class Childhood in Nineteenth-Century Europe', in de Mause, *History of Childhood*, pp. 407–31; and Anna Davin, 'Child Labour, the Working-Class Family, and Domestic Ideology in 19th Century Britain', *Development and Change*, 13 (1982), 633–52.

faire, which was influential in France as well as in Britain. This created a hostile climate for social legislation, and so it was only when a counter-current in favour of State intervention made some headway that child labour reformers had some chance of achieving their aims. The emphasis throughout the *Wealth of Nations* was on the advantage to be gained from competitive markets and economic individualism. Assuming a beneficial character to economic institutions, Smith was distrustful of government intervention in the economy. Whether he took this free market approach to the extreme of ruling out all Government initiatives in social affairs is doubtful. What is clear is that his followers tended to narrow the focus of their subject to the issue of growth, leaving them open to the charge of indifference to questions of social justice. Nowhere was this more the case than in France. The first writer to popularize the ideas of Adam Smith on the Continent was Jean-Baptiste Say. The original edition of his *Traité d'économie politique*, published in 1803, was a great success, and further editions appeared in 1817, 1819 and 1826. In his hands, economics became a purely theoretical and descriptive science, untainted by moral and political considerations. This approach had the advantage of intellectual rigour, but it brought with it a certain frigidity. Say died in 1832, without ever wavering from his hostility to laws which claimed to improve the condition of working men. The succeeding generation of liberal economists in France have sometimes been labelled 'optimists'. They assumed that all shortcomings in the economy were attributable to restrictions on liberty. It followed that the remedy for these defects would be a greater and more perfect liberty.[8] These men were on hand during the 1830s and 1840s to apply their principles to the issue of child labour. Charles Dunoyer used the forum of the Academy of Moral and Political Science to air his doubts on the value of factory legislation. He disputed the right of the State to protect minors whose interests were being neglected by parents and tutors. However incompetent the tutors, he argued, the law confided in them the persons and most precious goods of children, including their labour. He conceded that exceptionally bad cases could be pursued in law, but he saw many 'dangers and inconveniences' in setting general limits to the hours worked by children. He feared that it would prove the thin end of the wedge. If the work of children could be limited, then it was logical to follow suit with women, feeble or infirm adults, and finally

---

[8] Information drawn from Donald Winch, 'The Emergence of Economics as Science', in Carlo M. Cipolla (ed.), *The Fontana Economic History of Europe*, vol. 3, *The Industrial Revolution* (London, 1973), pp. 507–47; Charles Gide and Charles Rist, *A History of Economic Doctrines* (London, 1915), pp. 106–18, 324–6; Robert Goetz-Girey, *Croissance et progrès à l'origine des sociétés industrielles* (Paris, 1966), pp. 144–8.

the whole of the working class: the law of the maximum lurked around the corner![9]

Had such views prevailed, as they surely did in France during the first third of the nineteenth century, the most flagrant abuse of child labour would not have been considered an affair of State. In the event, they aroused considerably opposition, not surprising in a country with a long *étatiste* tradition. The opening salvo was fired by Simonde de Sismondi. Sismondi was a Swiss-born economist who started his professional life as a fervent admirer of Adam Smith. Personal experience of economic crises and hardship amongst factory workers caused him to rethink his ideas, leading in 1819 to the *Nouveaux principes d'économie politique*. Sismondi rejected the abstract method favoured by Ricardo and Say, proclaiming that political economy should be a moral science, resting on experience, history and observation. He was also critical of the exclusive interest in the creation of wealth characteristic of orthodox classical economics, countering that distribution was as important as production. This led him to take a less optimistic view of economic growth than his opponents, with the assertion, for example, that machinery could cause unemployment and wage reductions for some workers. He expressed concern that unlimited competition was pressuring entrepreneurs to economize on men as well as materials, leaving women and children to shoulder the burden of production. In a famous passage, much quoted by reformers, he attacked the common assumption that the employment of children boosted national prosperity:

If the children did not work at all, their fathers would have to earn enough to support them, until their strength developed. Without this, the children would die young, and labour would soon cease. But since children have been earning a part of their living, it has been possible to reduce the wages of the fathers. Their activity has not produced an improvement in the incomes of the poor. All that has occurred is an increase in the amount of work performed but it has been paid the same amount as before. Alternatively, a fall in the daily wage rate is possible, leaving the total payment to labour unchanged. The nation has therefore not profited from the children of the poor being deprived of the only good fortune in their lives: enjoyment of the age when the body and the mind develop in happiness and freedom.[10]

Sismondi went on to challenge the Smithian assumption that there existed a natural identity of individual and general interests, thereby undermining the very basis of *laissez-faire*. Although considered a better critic than

[9] 'Discussion entre MM. Blanqui, Passy, Dunoyer, De Beaumont, Franck et Mignet sur ce qu'il faut entendre par l'organisation du travail et sur les effets de la loi qui règle le travail des enfants dans les manufactures', *Séances et travaux de l'Académie des Sciences Morales et Politiques*, 8 (1845), 197–8.

[10] J. C. L. Simonde de Sismondi, *Nouveaux principes d'économie politique* (2 vols., Paris, 1819), vol. 1, p. 353.

reformer, he was one of the first thinkers in France to advocate factory legislation and a positive rôle for the Government in directing the economy.[11]

This type of humanitarian reaction against the 'stern implacabilty' of liberal political economy continued into the July Monarchy period. The social thinker who adhered most closely to the ideas of Sismondi was Eugène Buret. His prize-winning essay for the Academy of Moral and Political Science concerning the poverty of the labouring classes was vehement in its rejection of contemporary economic orthodoxies. It castigated the classical school for studiously ignoring the poverty that went hand in hand with wealth in advanced civilization. Buret also rejected the emphasis on liberty and competition, considering the theories of his opponents to be based on a transitory régime of 'conquest and anarchy' in industry. He concluded that the limits of wealth and opulence were near to being reached, and, on the assumption that man only obtains a little good at the price of great evil, he envisaged the period of sacrifice and misery being near to an end. A new social order would then be possible in which the poor emancipated themselves through work rather than charity.[12] The work of Villeneuve-Bargemont also bore the imprint of Sismondi, and in his case the principles were more closely applied to the campaign for factory legislation. Villeneuve-Bargemont viewed political economy as one of the less welcome imports from England, accusing it of breaking the ancient alliance of labour and Christian virtue. The materialism of this 'new religion' was shown to be ruinous for the working class. Anticipating the critique of 'consumerism' under industrial capitalism that would later be made by Marxists, he wrote:

Systematic efforts are made, at the price of the morality of the workers, to stimulate new tasks and habits which were previously unknown, and which could only be satisfied with the advance of general prosperity; yet at the same time, by a cruel contradiction, there is the desire that they be forced to work for the lowest possible wages.

On this basis, he pleaded before the Chamber of Deputies for limitation of working hours for adults as well as children, and for the emphasis to be given to the religious teaching of the young.[13] To some extent, this kind of

---

[11] See Gide and Rist, *Economic Doctrines*, pp. 170–98; and Maxime Leroy, *Histoire des idées sociales en France*, vol. 2, *De Babeuf à Tocqueville*, (Paris, 1962), pp. 300–23.

[12] Buret, *De la misère, passim*; and Hilde Rigaudias-Weiss, *Les Enquêtes ouvrières en France entre 1830 et 1848* (Paris, 1936), *passim*.

[13] Villeneuve-Bargemont, *Discours*, pp. 1–17; and *idem, Economie politique chrétienne, passim*. His work is extensively discussed in Goetz-Girey, *Croissance et progrès*, pp. 245–77. A similar perspective, inspired by Catholicism, emerges in P. M.-S. Bigot de Morogues, *Recherches des causes de la richesse et de la misère des peuples civilisés* (Paris, 1834); and de Gérando, *De la bienfaisance publique*: and *idem, Des Progrès de*

thinking was absorbed by mainstream liberal economists. Adolphe Blanqui was one such, who began by assuming that there was no possible conflict between the growth of production and the harmonization of different classes in society. Experience of the economic crisis of the late 1830s caused him to rediscover the ideas of Sismondi, and to become aware of the poverty that accompanied wealth. Although remaining orthodox on the general issue of Government intervention in the economy, he went further than his colleague Dunoyer in accepting the responsibility of the State for the 'tutelage of childhood', and so was able to support legislation on child labour.[14]

The reform campaign, 1827–41

With these underlying movements opening the way for a reform campaign, it remained for the principal actors to step forward.[15] The first pressure group to make any impact was the Société Industrielle de Mulhouse. Under the inspiration of Jean-Jacques Bourcart, it held a number of debates on the issue of child labour during the late 1820s. The original proposal, that the hours of all workers be limited by law, proved too strong for a special committee of the society. Even a watered-down alternative, calling for a twelve-hour working day for children, aroused spirited opposition in the plenary sessions. Rendered cautious by economic recession and the political upheavals that would bring down the Restoration, the Society shelved the proposals indefinitely in 1829. However, the efforts of the more reform-minded members soon bore fruit. Following up his primary education law of 1833, François Guizot sent the Society a special questionnaire on child labour in industry. This time the membership was more decisive, using the opportunity to demand a minimum starting age of eight, a ban on night work for children under twelve, and a literacy test for industrial employment. They also pressed for graduated working hours according to age, though they added as a rider that 'the simple presence of children in the workshops, however

l'industrie. Certain parallels might be discerned here with the combination of evangelical Christianity and High Toryism that motivated British factory reformers such as Michael Sadler, Richard Oastler and Lord Ashley. See Cecil Driver, *Tory Radical: The Life of Richard Oastler* (Oxford, 1946); and J. T. Ward, *The Factory Movement, 1830–55* (London, 1962).

14 'Discussion entre MM. Blanqui, Passy', 189, 199–200; Blanqui, *Des classes ouvrières*, pp. 5–17; Francis Demier, 'Adolphe Blanqui: un économiste libéral face à la Révolution industrielle, 1794–1854', unpublished thesis, University of Paris X, Nanterre, 1981, pp. 1–3, 622–5. For discussion of the stance of British liberal economists in the nineteenth century, see Ward, *Factory Movement*, p. 413.

15 This section is indebted to Touren, *La Loi de 1841*; Guéneau, 'La Législation restrictive'; and Weissbach 'Qu'on ne coupe le blé en herbe'.

prolonged it might be, is without inconvenience, and is even a benefit for them, as for their parents who can keep them by their side'.[16] The Académie des Sciences Morales et Politiques helped the reform campaign to keep up its momentum during the mid-1830s, launching Louis Villermé on his celebrated tour of the textile manufacturing areas. In 1837 he announced some of the preliminary results of his researches, with his *Discours sur la durée trop longue du travail des enfants dans beaucoup de manufactures*. Without making specific proposals, Villermé stressed the need for a law to regulate working conditions for children, and to encourage their primary instruction.[17]

At this point, the Government bowed to the weight of petitions from Mulhouse and the Académie. With a marked lack of enthusiasm, the Minister of Commerce, Martin du Nord, consulted the Prefects, Chambers of Commerce, Conseils des Prud'hommes and Chambres Consultatives des Arts et Métiers on the conditions of child labour and on the advisability of legislation. The results showed the manufacturing lobby to be divided in its outlook. Industrialists in Mulhouse, Strasbourg, Rouen, Troyes, Lyons and Villefranche were conspicuous in their condemnation of existing practices, and their forthright demands for a law. By contrast, representatives from Lille, Valenciennes, Saint-Quentin, Nancy, Yvetôt, Evreux, Cholet, Orleans, Rheims, Bar-le-Duc and Vienne were either hostile to the principle of State intervention, or prepared to accept only the weakest possible measures. A third group, drawn mainly from the less-developed regions of the south and west, failed to reply. The overall impression left by the 1837 Enquiry was of lukewarm interest in change. Most employers' organizations were willing to see a minimum starting age of eight or nine, a ban on night work for juveniles and some provision for schooling. But, ominously, there was no consensus on the key issue of limits to working hours. Some organizations in Mulhouse, Lyons and Troyes wanted working hours to be graded according to age or the type of job. Others, notably in Rouen, wanted a twelve-hour day for men, women and children alike. This left a majority sceptical of the whole exercise, which they envisaged being fraught with difficulties. The Lille Chamber of Commerce was prepared to recognize the philanthropic intentions of the Société Industrielle in Mulhouse, and the utility of parts of the English law, but it warned the Government to procede with 'extreme circumspection' when interfering with the liberties of industry. Restricting the working hours of children would be difficult, it predicted, especially in the case of the piecers employed by the spinning industry. The *rattacheurs*

[16] AD Haut-Rhin, 10 M 4, reply to questionnaire from the Recteur de l'Académie de Strasbourg, 6 March 1837.
[17] Villermé, *Discours*, p. 68.

would either have to work the same hours as adults, or two children would have to be employed instead of one, with the attendant risk of labour shortages. Combining primary education with factory work was also considered impractical, and the only solution put forward by the *lillois* was less than generous: putting back the minimum working age to nine, so that children could first complete their studies. Other employers' organizations gave dark hints that factory legislation might handicap French industry on foreign markets, and deprive working-class families of much-needed income from their children: 'More important than the fatigue of the workshop is the need to eat', thundered the Bretons of Morbihan.[18] The Government under Molé appeared willing to let matters drift. Any decisive action risked stirring up a hornet's nest, with influential industrialists from the Nord implacably opposed to State intervention. Moreover, in sharp contrast to the British experience during the 1830s, there was little pressure from below to stir Ministers.[19] The labour movement was still reeling from the repression initiated in 1834, and took no interest in the issue at this stage. Public opinion was equally lethargic: there was no Dickens around to stir the imagination with lurid tales from a French Coketown.[20]

Only the vigorous efforts of a few, isolated individuals during the late 1830s prevented the campaign from sinking in this sea of indifference. The ever-persistent Société Industrielle de Mulhouse once again petitioned the legislature for action. The banker Delessert raised the issue with the Minister of Commerce in the Chamber of Deputies. Daniel Legrand, a philanthropic industrialist from the Vosges, published a number of letters on the subject to influential figures in public life. In the Academy, Villermé presented his final report on the condition of the textile workers, with its recommendation of legal measures. There was even the occasional intervention from the Roman Catholic hierarchy: the Archbishop of Rouen, for example, took a stand in his Lenten message of 1838.[21]

When child labour reform came to be debated in the legislature, during

---

18 AN, F^{12} 4705. See also André Tudesq, 'Comment le grand patronat considère le travail des enfants en 1840', *Huitième colloque d'histoire sur l'artisanat et l'apprentissage* (Aix-en-Provence, 1964), pp. 25–37.

19 See Ward, *Factory Movement, passim*, and R. G. Kirby and A. E. Musson, *The Voice of the People: John Doherty, 1798–1854, Trade Unionist, Radical and Factory Reformer* (Manchester, 1975), ch. 10.

20 See J. Calvet, *L'Enfant dans la littérature française* (2 vols., Paris, 1930), vol. 1, *passim*; and Claude Salleron, 'La Littérature au XIXe siècle et la famille', in R. Prigent (ed.), *Renouveau des idées sur la famille* (Paris, 1954), pp. 67–71.

21 The passive attitude to child labour reform adopted by the vast majority of Roman Catholic priests may be contrasted with the vigorous campaigning efforts of many Anglican (but not Catholic) clergy in the north of England during the 1830s and 1840s; see Ward, *Factory Movement*, pp. 423–6.

the summer of 1839, there was at last the promise of action, though most of the contributers were as concerned to praise the efforts of manufacturers as to condemn the abuse of child workers. Billaudel, reporting to the Chamber of Deputies, lingered on the difficult nature of the question:

On the one hand, sympathy for suffering and unfortunate creatures, the desire to give prompt aid with energetic measures; on the other, the liberty of commerce and industry, respect for paternal authority, respect for misfortune itself: for who would dare to advise taking from a father and a mother, burdened with a large family, the help that they can receive from the hands of their children.

Pursuing this careful balance, he mentioned the benefits of industrial development, which allowed the 'most numerous and most impoverished classes to procure for themselves a multitude of goods hitherto unknown'. At the same time, the concentration of labour was responsible for certain 'drawbacks', which were easy to foresee, but difficult to avoid. Members of the Government who took part in the discussion were no less equivocal. In the Chamber of Peers, the Minister of Finance began by admitting that there was no more haunting spectacle than that of the factory children, but he ended up stressing the dangers to industry from Government intervention. Assuming that any reduction in the working hours of children would inevitably limit the hours of adult operatives, the Minister envisaged two equally unpalatable alternatives. One possibility was that wages would fall in the same proportion as hours, which would allow industrial prices to remain stable, but would depress the total quantity of goods produced. The other was for the wages paid to children to rise, as a means of attracting more of them into industry, but the consequence here was an increase in prices, and a fall in consumption. Cunin-Gridaine, the new Minister of Commerce and a former manufacturer from Sedan, was more forthright: he informed the Deputies that abuses of child labour existed, but only as exceptions to the rule. He found the principle of legislative intervention difficult to accept, given the substantial variations in conditions between regions and between industries.[22] In January 1840 he therefore proposed a bill which merely authorized the Conseils Généraux and the departments to draw up regulations as and when they saw fit. The Minister and his scheme were soon overtaken by events in the Chambers.

A committee set up by the Peers to study the bill concluded that the situation in France demanded more forceful measures.[23] Debate in the

[22] *Le Moniteur*, 1 and 16 June 1839.
[23] The members of the Committee were: the Comte de Tascher, a representative of the Society for the Encouragement of Primary Instruction; Victor Cousin, philosopher and future Minister of Public Instruction; Pellegrino Rossi, economist; the Marquis de Louvois; and de Gasparin. Its President was the Baron Joseph-Marie de Gérando, whose books on poverty we have already cited, and its secretary, the Baron Charles Dupin.

Chamber tended to follow its lead, under the powerful advocacy of
Charles Dupin.[24] He explained:

What do we want from a law? To establish protective conditions for children
which can in no case be infringed. What do we grant to the government? The
power to protect the children even further, the option of reducing even the length
of work which we lay down, if for some industries it is judged overwhelming and
pernicious.

This position attracted some fire from its flanks. Gay-Lussac, representing
the manufacturing interest, was hostile to State intervention, depicting it
as the 'start of Saint-Simonism or Phalansterism'. He denied the public
character of a factory: 'it is a sanctuary which should be as sacred as the
paternal household, and which can only be violated under extraordinary
circumstances, for social interests'. On this basis, he asserted that the State
should restrict itself to exhortations, appealing to the generous sentiments
of employers. At the other extreme, there was the occasional assault on
the whole system of industrial capitalism. The Comte de Montalembert
reflected a traditional Catholic view in asserting that to introduce a
factory into a rural area was to introduce a source of disorder, immorality
and misfortune. The majority of Peers took a middle course, voting a
series of modest reforms. These included a minimum starting age of eight
in industry, graduated working hours according to age and a ban on night
work. However, the Peers obviously paid heed to the liberal strictures of
Victor Cousin, newly appointed as Minister of Public Instruction, and
rejected compulsory schooling for child workers.[25]

A further enquiry among the Conseils Généraux in July of 1840
allowed the Minister of Commerce an appraisal of the three projects, put
forward in turn by the Government, the Peers and the Deputies. The
replies showed the *notables* of the manufacturing areas to be moving

[24] Charles Dupin played a rôle akin to that of Lord Ashley in Britain. Born in 1784, his
father was a Deputy in 1791, and a member of the Corps Législatif between the Year VIII
and 1804. After studying at the Ecole Polytechnique, Dupin joined the Corps de Génie
Maritime, and helped organize the French fleet during the Napoleonic Wars. This
promising career with the Navy was terminated during the Restoration, when his liberal
sympathies aroused the suspicions of the new régime. He therefore concentrated
exclusively on his scientific and statistical researches, teaching at the Conservatoire des
Arts et Métiers in 1826 and 1827. During the latter year he was elected a Deputy for
Castres (Tarn) and he subsequently joined the 221 Deputies who helped overthrow the
Polignac administration. Under the July Monarchy, he lost his seat in the Chamber for a
while, but was made a Councillor of State and became identified with the conservative
forces in the régime. A new electoral success in 1834 allowed him to become Minister for
the Navy: but he only lasted for three days in office! He was elevated to the Chamber of
Peers in 1837. See his entry in A. Robert, E. Bourloton and G. Cougny, *Dictionnaire des
parlementaires français* (4 vols., Paris, 1891).

[25] *Le Moniteur*, 6, 10 and 11 March 1840. The bill was passed by a majority of ninety-one
to thirty-five votes.

steadily towards accepting the idea of reform.[26] This cut the ground from under the feet of opposition in the Chamber of Deputies. During the debates of December 1840, representatives from Lille, Rouen and Elbeuf attempted a rearguard action in the name of the 'liberty of work'. They claimed that the proposed law would drive children from the large to the small workshops, and lead inexorably to a regulation of adult labour. The one major concession they did manage to secure was the abandonment of a salaried Inspectorate in the final draft of the law: this controversial issue would be left at the discretion of the Government. Final voting in the Chambers occurred during the following February: the Peers cast 185 votes for the bill, 50 against; the Deputies, 104 for and 2 against. On 22 March 1841, the *loi sur le travail des enfants* was officially promulgated.

The law was to apply, on the one hand, to all factories and workshops using machinery or a 'continuous fire', on the other, to all firms with twenty or more workers concentrated in a workshop. Children under eight years of age were banned from working in these types of industrial plant. From eight to twelve years, they were permitted to work for eight hours, divided by a rest period; from twelve to sixteen years, the limit was raised to twelve hours, again divided by rest periods. Night work was completely forbidden for children under thirteen, and for those aged thirteen to sixteen it could only be authorized in exceptional circumstances. Attendance at school was, in the event, made compulsory for all working children under the age of twelve, following intensive lobbying by Charles Dupin. Young people over the age of twelve who possessed a certificate stating that they had received primary instruction could be exempt from any further schooling. An Inspectorate was to supervise the execution of the law, and a scale of fines was drawn up: a maximum 15 francs for each offence, with a cumulative total not exceeding 200 francs in the first instance; and 16 to 100 francs, with a total not exceeding 500 francs for persistent offenders. Finally, the Government was allowed at its discretion to draw up *règlements d'administration publique*, which could extend the law to other types of workshop, raise the minimum working age in specific industries and exclude children from dangerous occupations or unsuitable workshops. More generally, it was empowered 'to ensure good morals and public decency on the shop floor, to oversee the primary instruction and religious teaching of the children, to prevent all harsh treatment and abusive punishments of them and to enforce the conditions of salubrity and security necessary for their life and health'.

This piece of legislation was heavily indebted to the example of earlier

26 AN, F[12] 4705.

British and Prussian laws. The leader in the field was Britain, with a series of Acts that stretched back to 1802. During the 1830s the Bureau des Manufactures in Paris collected a comprehensive dossier of material on the British experience for the Ministry of Commerce. It included translations into French of reports by the Inspectors Horner, Howell, Rickards and Saunders, and an assortment of statistics, law reports and models of registers. Members of the French legislature frequently referred to the British experience during their debates on factory reform. Opponents of a law were keen to stress the difficulties experienced in enforcing the 1833 Act: the impression they liked to give was that it had become a dead letter. However, the reformer François Delessert proved better informed on British affairs. He was able to cite evidence from the reports of Stuart and Horner illustrating the offensive mounted by the Inspectorate after 1836, and the moves afoot to strengthen the 1833 Act with new legislation.[27] By this period, the question of child labour was being studied across Europe. In 1840, the Minister of Commerce invited Hippolyte Carnot to visit Switzerland and Germany in order to study official measures in these countries.[28] Carnot quickly published his report which concentrated on legislation in Prussia and various small German states. French observers did not necessarily accept that their neighbours provided appropriate models for their own conditions. Jean-Jacques Bourcart crossed the Channel in 1838 to see for himself how British legislation worked. He approved of the 1825 law, but concluded that its successor of 1833 went too far with its limit of nine hours of work per day for children under eighteen, and its system of salaried Factory Inspectors. The economist Rossi was even more dismissive of foreign experience. His speech to the Chamber of Peers in 1840 rejected Prussian and Austrian examples, on the grounds that these countries were not constitutional monarchies. He saw little more value in the British experience, since the system of public administration was very different from that of France. Nonetheless, in limiting hours according to age categories, and in combining primary schooling with industrial work, the French law was following a well-trodden path by 1841.[29]

27 *Le Moniteur*, 16 June 1839.
28 Hippolyte was the son of Lazare Carnot, a member of the Committee of Public Safety during the Revolution and a leading innovator in the field of education. He followed in his father's footsteps, becoming President of the Society for Elementary Education during the 1840s and eventually, under the Second Republic, Minister of Public Instruction.
29 AN, F¹² 4704, 'Préparation de la loi de 1841'; Hippolyte Carnot, *Lettre à Monsieur le Ministre de l'Agriculture et du Commerce sur la législation qui règle, dans quelques états de l'Allemagne, les conditions du travail des jeunes ouvriers* (Paris, 1840); Jean-Jacques Bourcart, *Du travail des jeunes ouvriers dans les manufactures, usines ou ateliers* (Paris, 1840), pp. 1–15; *Le Moniteur*, 6 March 1840.

Conclusion: the motives of the reformers

The derivative nature of the 1841 law does not alter the fact that it was the first example of social legislation in France: never before had the State intervened in the relationship between employer and employee. It was imposed from above, on a largely unwilling and indifferent labour force, by a diverse group of industrialists, professional men and politicians. This was in stark contrast to the British experience, where child labour reform, in conjunction with other causes such as the Ten-Hour Day, Poor Law reform, tariff protection and Chartism, created a huge groundswell of working-class militancy. The fear of revolution and shorter working hours for adults lurked in the background during the French debate, but there was no direct pressure from the labour movement for a law. During the 1830s and 1840s the labouring classes in France were poorly organized, nowhere more so than in the big factory towns such as Lille and Rouen. The *avant-garde* of the movement continued to be more oriented towards republicanism and utopian forms of socialism than towards reformist legislation: the problems of *la grande industrie* were as yet barely impinging on its outlook.[30] *L'Atelier*, the first working-class newspaper in France, was in fact hostile to the 1841 law, dismissing it as a mere palliative from a bourgeois state.[31] During the run-up to the law, the Government restricted its consultations to a narrow circle of *notables*. The 1837 Enquiry on Child Labour was a private affair, consisting of written reports from the Prefects and the official employers' organizations. Not one factory operative was asked for his or her views, nor was there any canvassing of medical opinion. Moreover, the only investigation into conditions in the manufacturing areas that carried any weight during the legislative debates was the one by Louis Villermé. He did of course have a medical background, and the support of the Académie des Sciences Morales et Politiques. But again it was a discrete affair: very conveniently, there was none of the controversy that had surrounded The Commission for Enquiring into the Employment of Children in Factories earlier during the 1830s in Britain.

In the final analysis, the impulse to reform must therefore be sought in the minds of a small group of middle-class reformers. What then were their motives? Were they trying, in the words of one French historian, 'to introduce a little humanity into the brutal play of economic

---

[30] Sewell, *Work and Revolution in France*, *passim*; Roger Magraw, *France 1815–1914: The Bourgeois Century* (London, 1983), pp. 91–106; Christopher Johnson, *Icarian Communism in France, 1839–1851* (Ithaca, NY, 1974), *passim*; Lasserre, *La Situation des ouvriers*, pp. 212–29.

[31] Armand Cuvillier, *Un journal d'ouvriers: 'L'Atelier', 1840–1850* (Paris, 1914), p. 187.

forces'? Or was it less a matter of humanity, and more one of seeking conditions for a 'rational exploitation of child labour', which would ensure the physical survival and the 'moralization' of the workers?[32] One might conclude that there is a grain of truth in both of these interpretations, for enlightened self-interest stands out as the main driving force behind the reformers. The *patronat* of Mulhouse was explicitly concerned about the quality of its labour force. Jean-Jacques Bourcart urged his colleagues to petition for factory legislation by saying:

The principal advantage to be drawn from this law will be the health of the children and all the workers in industry as well as their greater moral development. The master will have a choice of robust workers; he will have workers who are more intelligent and easier to guide. France, when necessary, will find *men* amongst them, defenders of the fatherland, whilst if she fails to take energetic measures, she risks only finding in our working class, after a certain number of years, miserable wretches, feeble and depraved creatures, incapable of upholding the glory of their country.[33]

The threat to the military strength of the nation from abuses of child labour was taken up by all later reformers, for it was too persuasive an argument amongst conservative *notables* to be ignored. Reform-minded employers were aware that their attempts to improve the productivity of labour by reducing hours of work for children and allowing more time for primary instruction would take time. The law was therefore essential in their scheme of things, to ensure that all firms operated under the same conditions in the employment of children.[34] Otherwise, there was always the possibility that far-sighted entrepreneurs would be driven out of business in the interim period by competitors with lower labour costs.

It is tempting to add, by way of parenthesis, that industrialists in Alsace appeared at first sight better placed than their rivals in other regions to pursue such a long-term strategy within the confines of a law. If this case could be proved, then one could argue that beneath all the talk of humanity and productivity, reformers in the Société Industrielle de Mulhouse had a more sinister aim: to use factory legislation as a means of curbing the output of competitors, or even bankrupting some of them, and thus enhancing their own position on the market. This line of

---

32 Evrard, 'Le Travail des enfants', 14; Douailler and Vermeren, 'Les Enfants du capital', 15–23.
33 Bourcart, 'Proposition', 327–8.
34 In 1837, and again in 1840, employers from Mulhouse were emphatic that *all* industries should be covered by the child labour law, with the exception of family workshops in which parents were employing their own children; AN, F^{12} 4705–4706.

argument has been advanced in the British literature, and it is of interest to test the hypothesis in the French context.[35] Labour was after all relatively abundant in the east, which made it possible to envisage employing extra children for a relay system. In the Nord, by contrast, there was a long series of anguished complaints about labour shortages, which helps account for opposition to a Factory Act. Typically, in 1840 the Conseil des Prud'hommes of Lille asserted that there were not enough children in the town to form *brigades*.[36] Also, the average size of mill in Alsace was large by French standards. In the cotton spinneries, the average number of operatives per mill during the 1840s was 290 in the Haut-Rhin, compared to 167 in the Vosges, 151 in the Aisne, 119 in the Nord, 100 in the Aube and 81 in the Seine-Inférieure.[37] This made compliance with factory legislation potentially less onerous, since the larger mills could more easily set up a school on their premises, and organize the paperwork required by

[35] Howard Marvel has suggested that the 1833 Factory Act in Britain was 'designed to have differential impact on textile production. The group standing to gain was the large urban manufacturers who relied on steam engines to drive their machinery. Such steam-powered mills not only employed relatively fewer very young children, but were less susceptible to production interruptions than were the water-powered mills.' See his 'Factory Regulation: A Reinterpretation of Early English Experience', *Journal of Law and Economics*, 20 (1977), 379–402. We have only given serious consideration to this type of interpretation in the context of inter-regional competition, since a literal application does not fit the French case. In the first place, many of the big industrialists belonging to the Société Industrielle de Mulhouse came from the small towns and villages of the Haut-Rhin: J.-J. Bourcart, for example, was from Guebwiller. The most implacable opponents of factory legislation, it might be noted, came from the great conurbation of Lille-Roubaix-Tourcoing. In the second place, within the Haut-Rhin, the structure of the textile industry revealed by the 1839–45 Industrial Enquiry gives no support to the assertion that the large mills employed relatively fewer children than the small ones. The seven cotton spinning mills located in Mulhouse were all steam powered, and relatively large: the average (mean) number of spindles per mill was 24,781, compared to the 13,875 for the mills in the rest of the department (medians: 13,000 and 9,800). Yet they had a higher proportion of child labour than the country mills: 40.1 per cent of operatives under sixteen, on average in the former, compared to 28.9 per cent in the latter (medians: 39.5 and 29.4 respectively). Taking the total of forty-seven spinning mills in the department as a whole, and ignoring the rural–urban difference, produces a similar divergence from the British experience. The top quartile of mills (from 17,000 to 84,000 spindles) contained only one mill that was exclusively steam powered, and three others that relied on water wheels alone. In the bottom quartile (300 to 7,920 spindles), the mills were more oriented towards water power, but it cannot be said that they were more reliant on child labour. The statistical evidence is ambiguous. The median percentage of children in the small mills was 32.1, compared to 29.7 in the large mills; but the respective means were 26.6 and 30.7. Statistique de la France, *Industrie*, 1847–52, vol. 1, pp. 136–43.

[36] AD Nord, M 613/5, letter to Minister of Commerce from Lille Conseil des Prud'hommes, 14 September 1840. See also Stearns, *Paths to Authority*, p. 40.

[37] Statistique de la France, *Industrie*, 1847–52, vol. 1, pp. 80–1, 148–9, 170–1, 208–9, 224–5; vol. 3, pp. 90–1.

bureaucracy. However, other considerations make it difficult to pursue this line of argument very far. First, the textile industries in Alsace relied on child labour more heavily than most of their rivals, and so could least afford to dispense with its services. In the cotton-spinning mills of the Haut-Rhin, no less than one in three of the operatives were children under sixteen, compared to one in four in the Seine-Inférieure, and one in five in the Nord. And in the calico-printing works, although working hours were shorter than in most industries, young children were recruited in droves. The following figures from Mulhouse, collected during the early 1840s, will illustrate the point:[38]

Industry	Number of mills	Number of children aged			Percentage of children
		8–10	10–12	12–16	under 12
Calico-printing	7	268	251	359	59.1
Cotton-spinning	13	28	209	702	25.2
Wool-spinning	2	4	22	210	11.0
Weaving (power loom)	8	–	13	298	4.2

Secondly, the spinning industry in the east was heavily reliant on water power, which made the fixed working day for children required by law a potential liability. The stoppages that occurred with water wheels caused by flooding, freezing or drought created pressure to make up for lost production with additional hours afterwards. Steam-powered mills were less at the mercy of the elements, and so were able to work more regularly through the year. The Industrial Enquiry begun in 1839 found forty steam engines in the *filatures de coton* of the Haut-Rhin, but also forty-eight water wheels. In the spinning industry of the Nord the position was very different, with fifty-five steam engines, and no water wheels at all.[39] We must therefore return to the straightforward conclusion that the manufacturers of the Société Industrielle de Mulhouse pushed for factory legislation to compel other manufacturers to follow their lead on a particular long-term policy for child labour.

A long-term perspective was also evident in the thinking of liberal

---

[38] AM Mulhouse, F VI Ea 1.
[39] This Enquiry listed water wheels and steam engines, but gave no information on their horsepower.

reformers like Louis Villermé, Adolphe Blanqui and Charles Dupin. The latter appealed to the Chamber of Deputies for support by proclaiming: 'It is a question of improving the health, the strength, the physical condition and the moral and religious life of the generation which providence has destined to succeed us on our native land.'[40] Although not directly involved as employers of children themselves, these men were concerned about the survival of the existing economic and social system.[41] Their researches made them painfully aware of the ravages that unrestricted competition could wreak on the physical and intellectual condition of labour, yet their faith in the liberal order remained largely unshaken.[42] The objective they set themselves was merely to curb some of the excesses provoked by industrial development. Thus Louis Villermé concluded his lengthy study of the textile workers with three very modest proposals, including the demand for a law to restrict the working hours of children. And children, as he noted elsewhere, were a special case, 'because too often victims of the debauchery and improvidence of their parents, they never deserve their misfortune'.[43] A hint that the same evidence on the plight of labour in industrial society could be used to develop a more radical critique of industrial society emerges in the work of Eugène Buret. However, during the 1830s it was the political right rather than the left which used the issue of child labour to attack the manufacturing interest. In the case of Villeneuve-Bargemont, for example, humanitarianism was tinged with a desire to stem the tide of industrialization. He was one of the reformers who wished to restrict all workers to a twelve-hour day, his aim being to take a first step towards modifying the rigours of competition between nations.[44] In sum, all of the participants in the debate were fired by the lofty vision of improving the quality of life for the industrial working class. But they also had interests of their own to promote, which paradoxically might conflict, yet still lead to agreement on the need for

---

[40] Dupin, 'Du travail des enfants', part 1, p. xii.
[41] To quote Guy Standing: 'It is commonly argued that the exploiting class benefits from super-exploitation (i.e. the worker receiving less than the cost of reproducing his or her labour power) because it means, definitionally, that more surplus product or surplus value is transferred than if workers were paid the equivalent of the cost of reproducing their labour power. However, it involves disadvantages which the State sooner or later has to recognize. And here the relevance of Poulantza's distinction between the State acting in the long-term interest of capital against the immediate perceived interest is brought out most forcefully.' See his 'State Policy and Child Labour', 620.
[42] See Coleman, *Death is a Social Disease*, *passim*.   [43] Villermé, *Discours*, p. 59.
[44] Buret, *De la misère, passim*; Villeneuve-Bargemont, *Discours, passim*; for discussion of the way factory reform in Britain came to be seen as a 'symbolic focus for a broader contest between competing conceptions of social order', see W. G. Carson, 'Symbolic and Instrumental Dimensions of Early Factory Legislation: A Case Study in the Social Origins of Criminal Law', in Roger Hood (ed.), *Crime, Criminology and Public Policy* (London, 1974), pp. 107–38.

factory legislation. Industrialists were concerned to improve conditions for the reproduction of labour; doctors wished to encourage public health; what might be called the liberal establishment of the July Monarchy in the Académie des Sciences Morales et Politiques hoped to restrict abuses that threatened the social and political order; whilst opponents of the industrial bourgeoisie saw an opportunity to resurrect some of the old, paternalist forms of legislation.[45]

[45] This parallels in important respects the alliance between High Tories and Radicals in Britain; see Ward, *Factory Movement, passim.*

••

Chapter 9

The experiment in practice, 1841–70

The difficult birth of the 1841 law gave a hint of the obstacles to come during the period of enforcement. The crusading fervour of the reformers had exposed the complacent attitude to child labour of Ministers in the Government, and the opposition to State intervention of many industrialists. The passage of the law did at the outset provoke a flurry of activity within the administration. A body of Inspectors was created, and a campaign of enforcement launched at both the national and the municipal levels. Nonetheless, the early experience of social legislation was fraught with difficulties, against which successive régimes made little headway.

The period of illusions and disappointments, 1841–3

In August of 1841 the Minister of Commerce requested Prefects to draw up lists of firms covered by the 1841 law, and others to which it might usefully be extended. The Prefects in turn consulted the Mayor of each commune, and examples of their replies survive in all of the major manufacturing areas.[1] The Minister then set about organizing a system of inspection. He chose to ignore the considerable pressure for salaried Inspectors, on the lines of those established in Britain by the 1833 law. Instead he opted for voluntary, unpaid Commissions of Inspection, recruited mostly from the *notables* of industry, commerce and the liberal professions. The twelve members of the Commission covering the *arrondissement* of Colmar, for example, included three manufacturers, three doctors, two lawyers, a landowner, a former merchant and a retired army officer. Between them they occupied four *mairies*, three places on the

---

[1] AN, F¹² 4706, circular of 14 August 1841; AN, F¹² 4708, 'Classement des industries par catégories', 1841–3 (an incomplete series by department). Fragments of similar lists in the provinces include: AD Ardèche, 15 M 3, replies to a circular dated 15 February 1842; AD Haut-Rhin, 10 M 4, 'Etat des établissements industriels, arrond. de Colmar', n.d.; AD Nord, M 611/7, 'Enquête', 1842; AD Vosges, M 279, 'Tableau des manufactures'.

Conseil Général and one on the Conseil d'Arrondissement.[2] The Minister
made it clear to his subordinates that he wanted the Commissions to act
with circumspection. In the first instance, he did not expect the rigorous
and complete execution of a law that would inevitably clash with personal
interests. The Commissioners were to rely on persuasion and conciliation,
overcoming resistance by the 'authority of their language and character'.[3]
Only in October 1843 did he demand a firmer application, circulating a
model *procès-verbal* for taking offenders to court.[4]

This régime worked in a few areas, where factories employing children
were not numerous and where employers were well disposed towards the
law. In the Meurthe, for example, the Commissions were able to cope
with the handful of glassworks and textile mills covered by the law. Even
before they started work, the owner of the *cristallerie* at Baccarat was
sending most of his ninety-four child workers to school during the
evening, and keeping them for less than twelve hours per day. Subsequently the Commissioners reported that he made every effort to obey
the law. The Dieulouard spinning mill at Belleville had equally co-
operative owners, who sent all of their juvenile employees to school in
shifts during the working day. Recalcitrant employers were soon brought
to heel by regular inspections and the occasional court case: in February
1843 the Prefect could report five *procès-verbaux* from the *arrondissement* of Nancy, and, a year later, four more. The fines levied were all
derisory, of 5 francs or so, but the impression remains that the law was
being enforced throughout the 1840s.[5] Parts of the Haut-Rhin were also
amenable to pressure from the Commissions. In the *arrondissements* of
Belfort and Colmar, the big textile mills scattered around the countryside
experienced few problems in recruiting labour, and were often prepared
to set up their own schools. Towards the end of 1844, the Prefect himself
visited the spinning mills around Colmar, and was impressed by the
organization of a two-shift system for children which allowed work and
school to be combined within the limits set by the law.[6] These, however,
were the highspots in a general morass.

When the Ministry of Commerce first took stock of the law in 1844,
only twenty-four Prefects declared themselves satisfied with its progress,

2 AD Haut-Rhin, 10 M 4, 'Registre des délibérations de la commission d'inspection sur le
   travail des enfants, arrond. de Colmar', 9 March 1842. Numerous further examples can
   be found in AD Nord, M 613/2, and AD Seine-Maritime, 10 MP 1362.
3 AD Vosges, M 277, letter from Cunin-Gridaine to Prefect, 25 November 1841. The same
   conciliatory approach was tried in Britain between 1833 and 1836; Maurice W. Thomas,
   The Early Factory Legislation (Leigh-on-Sea, 1948), pp. 75–6.
4 AN, F¹² 4706, circular to Prefects of 13 October 1843.
5 AD Meurthe-et-Moselle, 10 M 27.
6 AN, F¹² 4712, letters from Prefect of the Haut-Rhin to Minister of Commerce, 15
   February 1844 and 29 October 1844.

and most of those were from agricultural departments in the west, centre and south. The other fifty admitted that the law was either not being enforced at all, or meeting with resistance on substantial issues.[7] The Rhône and the Nord were two important manufacturing areas where the progress of the law was almost entirely blocked. In the former, the Prefect blamed the inactivity of the Local Commissions for the lack of results. This might have been expected in Lyons, where the dispersed structure of the silk industry provided little scope for the 1841 law to make an impact. But even in the *arrondissement* of Villefranche, the appeal to 'friends of the working class' fell on deaf ears. The Commissioner for Tarare claimed to find no evidence of abuses in his areas, but the Sub-Prefect remained sceptical: in a verbal report, the industrialist concerned stated that even if he had found irregularities, he would not have drawn attention to the fact, since he was unwilling to take hostile action against his colleagues.[8] In Flanders, passive resistance from the *patronat* threatened to paralyse the efforts of the local administration. The Prefect complained in 1841 that the Chambers of Commerce and Conseils des Prud'hommes delayed replying to his requests for information on employers of child labour, and then took the line that enforcing the law was not one of their attributes. Two years later he was pleading the weakness of his position before the Minister of Commerce:

You know ... how far political considerations dictate a strategy of reserve and caution for the administration this year. Here, where manufacturing industry has developed to such an extent that the principal wealth of the country is in its hands, and where elections of the Government's own choice have brought it most of the municipal and administrative posts, the intrusion of a law considered harmful to industrial interests is bound to receive little sympathy.[9]

It was only in the summer of 1843 that the Commissions of Inspection began to assemble in the Nord. Roubaix stood out as the area where opposition to the law was most determined. Industrialists there trotted out the familiar arguments on the difficulty of restricting hours for children in the spinning industry when the *rattacheurs* always worked beside an adult. In October 1844, the Commission for the town resigned

---

[7] AN, F¹² 4706, 'Notes sur le travail des enfants dans les manufactures, usines et ateliers', 1844. In September 1844, the Minister sent a confidential circular to the Prefects, admitting that the Local Commissions had met with serious difficulties. He let it be known that he was considering modifications to the 1841 law, especially concerning the minimum age and working hours. His aim was therefore to assess the opinions of manufacturers on these issues, without giving away the intentions of the Government.

[8] AD Rhône, 10 M, letter from Chambre de Commerce of Lyons to Prefect, 13 August 1841; letter from Sub-Prefect of Villefranche to Prefect, 3 October 1843.

[9] AN, F¹² 4712, letter from Prefect of the Nord to Minister of Commerce, 5 December 1843.

en bloc. Their letter of resignation accused the new law of having the opposite effects to those intended, producing idleness and corruption instead of 'moralization'. They asserted that the announcement of the law in Roubaix had caused one third of the children in the spinning mills to be discharged. Moreover, insisting on the instruction of the young was, they alleged, to deprive them of their daily bread. In the end the Prefect only had his way by using Commissioners from Lille to start the inspections.[10]

Elsewhere the Commissions often found parts of the 1841 law enforceable without much difficulty, notably the minimum working age of eight, the ban on night work, the posting of the law in the factories and the issue of *livrets* to child workers. The sticking points were the length of the working day and compulsory schooling.[11] In Normandy, the Prefect noted during the summer of 1843 that there was barely any distinction between the hours worked by children aged eight to twelve and those of twelve to sixteen: both were likely to put in a thirteen- to fourteen-hour day. Manufacturers in Elbeuf threatened to dismiss all the younger children if the law was applied to the letter: a trump card that would be played in various parts of France. The Local Commission pronounced itself 'Terrified by the disturbances which the immediate suppression of the wages of approximately 300 children would bring to the poor families of our area', and so proposed as an interim measure a twelve-hour day for children over ten years of age. As for instruction, the Commission in Elbeuf found many young children refusing to attend school, and a shortage of free places. In Rouen the Commission was overwhelmed by the immensity of the task facing it. Towards the end of 1843 they sent twelve *procès-verbaux* to the Prefect, observing, 'Our aim in drawing them up has been to provide an authenticated statement of the unfortunate work régime in our factories (in general), rather than to start legal action against the few people whose establishments we entered at random.' With three to four hundred mills in the area operating under the same conditions, the Prefect decided to drop the charges.[12] To the south, in the Vivarais, inspections showed the young *dévideuses* of the silk mills habitually working from 4.00 in the morning until 8.00 at night, with three hours off for breaks. One of the Commissioners for the canton of Privas acknowledged that this breached the ban on work before 5.00 in

---

10 *Ibid.*, containing an extensive correspondence between Prefect and Ministers; AD Nord M 613/5, letter from Mayor of Roubaix to Prefect, 11 October 1844; and the reply, 15 November 1844.

11 Precisely the same difficulties emerged in Britain, following the first attempts to enforce the 1833 Act; Thomas, *Early Factory Legislation*, p. 78.

12 AN, F¹² 4713, diverse reports from the Seine-Inférieure; AD Seine-Maritime, 10 MP 1362, report from the Comité Cantonnal d'Inspection, Elbeuf, 21 July 1843; and letter from the President of the Rouen Commission to the Prefect, 27 November 1843.

the morning. However, he justified the practice on the grounds that the girls themselves preferred to start early. He also noted with an air of resignation the lack of instruction amongst the juvenile workers. Among those over the age of twelve, none could write, and only a minority were able to read.[13] Even in Mulhouse, there was 'resistance and inertia'. The spinning mills and calico-printing works were accused of hesitating before the sacrifices involved in organizing two relays of children, yet the Local Commissions were reluctant to take severe action.[14]

The law was faltering in an atmosphere of suspicion and hostility. In each town there was a feeling amongst manufacturers that other regions were tolerating abuses. The Mayor of Saint-Quentin alleged in April 1842 that in Lille, Amiens, Rheims, Mulhouse, Rouen and even Paris, 'under the eyes of the Government', industrialists were not obeying the law.[15] A year later the Société Industrielle de Mulhouse petitioned the Minister of Commerce for a change in the 1841 law. It argued that the eight-hour limit for children under twelve was incompatible with the needs of various industries, and called for 'inspecteurs fonctionnaires publics et salariés par l'état'.[16] The Commissions of Inspection were generally recognized to be a weak link in the system. Their members were prepared to dispense wisdom in the benevolent atmosphere that prevailed in the early days, but when they encountered hostility and resistance they lacked the heart to take their peers to court. An observer in Yvetôt vividly described this trajectory. In his area of Normandy, the announcement of the law had frightened employers into making a number of changes, including the enforcement of schooling for children under twelve and a limitation on the working hours of those under sixteen. The first inspections had gone well, with the members of the Commission pontificating on the need for a little more humanity in the treatment of the young. The industrialists promised to do everything that was asked of them. But then they said to themselves:

The Commission is composed of a doctor, a lawyer, one is a relative of mine, another a friend. These Messieurs were willing to take on the work out of charity. They have spoken of the law and what it requires, but as for *procès-verbaux*, they won't draw them up. They will not risk making enemies for the pleasure of dragging us before the courts; that is a rôle they will not relish. A doctor and a

---

[13] AD Ardèche, 15 M 3, 'Rapport de Crouzet, notaire à Privas, l'un des Inspecteurs du travail des enfants dans les manufactures pour le canton de Privas', drawn up for Prefect, n.d. (c. 1843–4).

[14] AN, F12 4712, letter from Prefect to Minister of Commerce, 15 February 1844.

[15] AN, F12 4709.

[16] AN, F12 4704.

lawyer want to keep their clients ... And then there are the municipal elections ... No, we have nothing to fear from them.[17]

At this point, the Commissioners became discouraged, met less frequently and resigned in droves. Their venerable, not to say gerontocratic, character tended to militate against them after a while. The Mayor of Blâmont, in Lorraine, reported in January 1845 that of the three members of his Commission, one had been dead for two years, another had been confined to bed over a long period by serious illness and the third was too old to make any visits.[18]

The impact of the Weights and Measures Inspectors, 1843–7

The response from Paris was to stiffen the Commissions with a *fonctionnaire*: the Vérificateur des Poids et Mesures.[19] Since his job involved making regular visits to factories and drawing up *procès-verbaux* from time to time, he appeared an ideal candidate to a régime that abhorred the idea of creating additional public servants. Writing to inform a Vérificateur in the Ardèche of his new responsibilities, the Minister of Commerce made it clear that the 1841 law contained no provision for paying its Inspectors, and that no extra money for expenses would be forthcoming. What the Minister counted on was the loyalty of his employees: 'Later on I will look into ways of taking into account the extra work which will, in any case, provide you with an opportunity to show me your zeal.'[20] Although there was some criticism that such minor officials lacked authority to deal with big industrialists, reports soon came in from various parts of the country praising their ardour and devotion to duty. A few did indeed act with exceptional determination and moral courage, taking on almost single-handedly the task of enforcing the law in their *arrondissements*.

Prominent amongst these was the Vérificateur Lachave from Troyes. Drafted in as secretary of the Local Commission during the summer of 1843, he soon breathed life into a listless campaign effort. His first important conflict, absurdly enough, was with another member of the Commission: Fontaine-Gris. In June of 1844 Lachave started legal

---

17 AD Seine-Maritime, 10 MP 1362, report of Weights and Measures Inspector, *arrondissement* of Yvetôt, 20 November 1847.
18 AD Meurthe-et-Moselle, 10 M 27, letter to Sub-Prefect of Lunéville, 19 January 1845.
19 AN, F¹² 4773ᴬ; the original plan, in September 1843, was to add the Vérificateurs to the Commissions in seven departments where the 1841 law was encountering difficulties. By March of 1844 there were sixty-eight of them at work in twenty-two departments.
20 AD Ardèche, 15 M 3, letter from Minister of Commerce to Perchet, 12 February 1845. Eventually most Vérificateurs received payments of between 100 and 200 francs for their work as Factory Inspectors; see the dossier in AN, F¹² 4773ᴬ.

proceedings against this cotton manufacturer, accusing him of denying his child workers sufficient time for rest and schooling. At this stage, the administration gave Lachave no support. The Commissioner of Police declined to press charges; the other members of the Commission rounded on him, treating him as an 'imposter', and the Prefect could only see the political capital that was being made of the affair. The latter informed Paris in December 1844:

> Monsieur Fontaine-Gris is, by his social and industrial position, one of the most important men in the town of Troyes. A member of the Conseil Supérieur des Manufactures, he has also served over several years as President of the Chamber and Tribunal of Commerce, and for a long time the municipal council has not had a more enlightened member. His essentially conservative political opinions have made him enemies, whose influence has perhaps been felt in the drawing up of the *procès-verbal* we are discussing. It is not that I am accusing Monsieur Lachave of having knowingly been the instrument of passions aroused against Monsieur Fontaine, but I do regret that this agent reported an infringement or minor offence without prior warning, in an area where I am certain Monsieur Fontaine had made most pressing recommendations.[21]

The Minister sided with the Prefect, and agreed that the organization of the Commission in Troyes be left unchanged. Not until July 1846 did a new Prefect rebuke Fontaine-Gris for flouting the law. The official described it as particularly serious in view of the public offices he held: Fontaine-Gris was at the time sitting on the Conseil Général des Manufactures in Paris as it discussed revisions to the 1841 law! Even then his social position stood him in good stead, for the Prefect offered to waive legal charges if he undertook in writing to obey the law. In the meantime, Lachave maintained his pressure on the manufacturers, regularly visiting factories and bringing offenders to court. Although obliged by ill-health to retire from public service, he continued his duties as a Factory Inspector. In November 1844 he secured his first conviction, when the cotton spinner Kottebaur was fined 5 francs for making children under twelve work on Sundays. By November 1847 he had brought seven employers to court, and the Prefect regarded this as a suitable display of firmness.[22]

Perchet, from the *arrondissement* of Privas, was another Vérificateur whose exceptional efforts have left their mark in the official records. He reported visiting 143 silk mills in his part of the Vivarais during 1845, and finding over 700 children. His stance was far more aggressive than that of his predecessors on the Local Commission. He noted the widespread practice of slowing down the clocks to obtain up to two hours extra work per day, which he attempted to counter by warning the labour force to be

21 AN, F^{12} 4709, letter of 13 December 1844.
22 AN, F^{12} 4709, and AD Aube, M 2283.

on its guard. He insisted that conditions in the dormitories be improved, with a maximum of two girls to a bed, a change of sheets every fifty days, and regular sweeping of the floors. He also took fifteen offenders to court, securing convictions in all cases. None of the fines exceeded 5 francs, but by 1847 the Prefect was reporting that, despite its large concentration of mills, Privas was the area of the department where the law was best enforced.[23] Unfortunately, both Troyes and Privas were secondary centres for manufacturing: generally speaking, in the more important areas, the Vérificateurs made less of an impact.[24]

The influence of the 1841 law on practice in the workshops was limited during the 1840s, but should not be written off entirely. In the first place, it had the unintended effect of driving some of the younger children, under the age of twelve, out of the factories. This was partly a matter of industrialists not wishing to be bothered with the problems of organizing relays of children and seeing to their education, but there was also a willingness among the more forward-looking industrialists to be rid of their most immature workers. The extent of the exodus is not clear. Observers in the Seine-Inférieure, the Nord, the Aisne, the Somme, the Haut-Rhin and the Vosges were amongst those who drew attention to it, but their figures were fragmentary. The Prefect of the Somme, for example, noted that the number of children under the age of twelve employed in Amiens fell from 401 in 1842 to 216 in 1844, following the decision by a big linen mill owner to use only the older children. Similarly, the Prefect of the Vosges recorded a decline in the number of under-twelves working in the *arrondissement* of Saint-Dié, from 148 in 1844 to 34 in 1847.[25] In the second place, the law stimulated a number of initiatives to provide school places for factory children. Early efforts to apply the law soon revealed the acute shortage of educational facilities in the manufacturing areas. The usual response in the cities was for the Commission of Inspection, the Mayor and the manufacturers to organize special classes for factory children. These schemes encouraged some school building, but they invariably met with a stormy passage during their execution. In Mulhouse, evening classes had first been organized by the municipality, without much success, in the early 1830s. The 1841 law

23 AD Ardèche, 15 M 3.
24 For interesting parallels concerning the drawbacks of using existing officials (as opposed to specialized Inspectors) to enforce new social legislation see Oliver MacDonagh, *A Pattern of Government Growth, 1800–1860: The Passenger Acts and their Enforcement* (London, 1961), pp. 77, 89. The work shows customs officers paying little attention to their responsibilities for enforcing the 1828 and 1835 Acts.
25 AN, F¹² 4713, letter from Prefect of Somme to Minister of Commerce, 4 October 1844; AN, F¹² 4714, letter from Prefect of Vosges to Minister of Commerce, 28 December 1847.

gave them brief impetus, as children flocked in to obtain a certificate stating that they had some elementary instruction behind them. But the numbers soon dwindled: after a fourteen-hour day, the children had little appetite for learning. In 1843, the Mayor therefore proposed that classes be held in the daytime, between 8.00 a.m. and 6.00 p.m. His idea was that each child would attend school twice a week for two-hour classes. The juvenile labour force was to be organized into relays, with one extra child being hired to cover for eight already employed. Two schools were eventually set up, one in Mulhouse and one in the *faubourg* of Dornach, but they did not live up to expectations. No more than a third of the children registered ever turned up to class, and there were complaints that very little was being learned. The 1848 Revolution provided the oppor-tunity to suppress the whole system.[26]

In Lille, there was the same disastrous experience with evening classes, both teachers and pupils being drained of energy by 9 o'clock at night. The Prefect of the Nord stepped in with a decree of May 1844, requiring *classes de fabrique* to be held for one hour at midday. Factory children were liable to a fine if they missed their class, and more than six absences over a period of two months could lead to exclusion from the workshops. Despite new schools opened by the Christian Brothers and the Town Council, the project put severe pressure on resources in Lille. For example, the *école communale* in the Rue de la Deule was found to be handling 280 pupils in 1846, which was clearly beyond the capacity of one teacher. Such overcrowding in the special classes was not conducive to learning. Kolb-Bernard, President of the Commission of Inspection in Lille, informed the Prefect that

bad behaviour during class, a refusal to take part in the lessons given by the teacher, a habitual and systematic indiscipline, and the most unpardonable outrages against the heads of school and the clergy who come to give religious instruction: all these facts have unfortunately taken place on a large scale, and encouraged a general disposition to indiscipline in these schools.[27]

The manufacturers resented the loss of working hours, claiming that a shortage of labour prevented them organizing relays of children. As in Mulhouse, the system limped along until the Second Republic dealt it a severe blow.[28] In Troyes, too, the classes suffered from the combination of

---

26 AN, F^{12} 4712, extract from a letter from the Mayor of Mulhouse to the Sub-Prefect of Altkirch, 26 January 1844; Raymond Oberlé, 'Le Travail des enfants-ouvriers et leur instruction à Mulhouse au XIXe siècle', *Actes du Quatre-Vingt-Cinquième Congrès National des Sociétés Savantes, Chambéry-Annecy, 1960* (Paris, 1961), 539–57; *idem*, *L'Enseignement à Mulhouse*, pp. 75–9.

27 AD Nord, M 611/11, letter of 4 July 1845.

28 AN, F^{12} 4712, letter from Prefect of Nord to Minister of Commerce, 21 December 1844; AD Nord, M 611/8, letter from Kolb-Bernard to Prefect 5 September 1846; Lasserre, *La*

hostility from employers and turbulent behaviour from children. Some of the manufacturers in the town docked 10 centimes from wages for time spent at school, whilst the children treated their classes as a place to let off steam after the rigours of work. In 1846 a local newspaper reported that the girls in particular were running riot. The school for boys run by a Monsieur Simmonet was said to be enjoying some success, but the nuns in charge of the girls were not up to their job. Twice a week the police had to be called to carry off the most rebellious pupils to the cells.[29]

Finally, the law had a marginal influence in shortening the working hours of children. As we have already noted, in some parts of northern and eastern France the Commissioners were able to give manufacturers a nudge towards employing children under sixteen for a maximum of twelve hours a day, and occasionally even towards organizing two relays of children in the youngest age category. Doubtless some employers were already following this régime before the law came into operation, and others made promises they had no intention of fulfilling. Yet the law evidently did give a lead, and by a combination of persuasion and coercion caused a minority of employers to ease the burden on their child workers.[30] The problem remained of trying to accommodate various groups of labour within a factory working different hours. The eight-hour limit imposed on children under twelve was particularly unpopular since it was neither a full nor a half working day. Cotton spinners in Lille and Rouen were vehement in their opposition to this part of the law. They reiterated their claim that each adult worker needed to have a *rat-tacheur* beside him all the time his machinery was in operation.[31] The Commission of Inspection in Lille bowed to such pressure, and as a 'temporary' measure, allowed the younger children to work for twelve hours. In Normandy, practice on the shop floor was little different. The Commission for Darnétal presented a sorry picture after its inspection of 1847. Amongst the fifty-one firms it visited, a handful of calico-printing works employed young children for eight hours a day, but the mainstream of spinning mills and power-loom weaving sheds kept all their

Situation des ouvriers, pp. 161–3; Pierre Pierrard, 'L'Enseignement primaire à Lille sous la monarchie de juillet', *Revue du Nord*, 220 (1974), 1–11; *idem*, 'Un grand bourgeois de Lille: Charles Kolb-Bernard, 1798–1888', *Revue du Nord*, 48 (1965), 393–4.

29 *L'Aube*, 28–9 March 1846; AN, F^{12} 4709, letter from Prefect of the Aube to Minister of Commerce, 9 February 1846.

30 See above, pp. 180–1; reports showing the progress of the 1841 law, or lack of it, can be found in AN, F^{12} 4709–13.

31 AD Seine-Maritime, 10 MP 1362, letter from Prefect to Minister of Commerce, 4 May 1844; AD Nord, M 611/8, 'Pétition collective relative au règlement sur le travail des enfants dans les manufactures', 20 August 1845.

workers going, no matter what their age, for a thirteen-and-a-half-hour day.[32]

Towards new legislation, 1847–51

Aware of general dissatisfaction with the 1841 law, the Government set in motion the machinery to provide a replacement. In 1845 the lawyer Pinède was sent to England to report on developments in the Factory Acts. At the same time, the General Councils on Commerce and Industry were asked to draw up reports on possible modifications.[33] The result was a *projet de loi* from the Ministry of Commerce, presented to the Chamber of Peers in February 1847. The Minister Cunin-Gridaine faithfully represented the interests of the bigger manufacturers. To meet their criticism that the 1841 law gave small workshops an unfair advantage, he proposed that the new law be applied to all industrial enterprises. And to smooth out the differences in working hours within the labour force, he was prepared to raise the minimum age of entry into the workshops to ten, but to allow all children under sixteen to work a full twelve-hour day. In these respects he followed the recommendation of the General Councils, but conspicuously absent from his bill was their scheme for a salaried Inspectorate. He had the effrontery to suggest that the existing Commissions had everywhere 'shown proof of zeal, intelligence and devotion'.[34]

As in the 1830s, the legislature took an independent line. First, the Peers rejected the proposed extension of the law to all firms, on the grounds that it would be impractical. Charles Dupin, resuming his rôle as secretary of the Special Commission examining the bill, agreed that comprehensive coverage was a desirable long-term aim. But he argued that for the present it risked making the law ineffective, given that the existing, very limited legislation was proving difficult to enforce. The Peers therefore voted to include only workshops with a total of ten employees, or those with five or more workers in the protected categories. Secondly, they reasserted the graduated working hours of the 1841 law. This decision followed an impassioned plea from Dupin, urging them not to return to the level of the 1802 British Act, with its twelve-hour day for young children. Thirdly, they agreed on a system of salaried Inspectors, paid by the State. And finally, concerned over the plight of mothers in the manufacturing areas,

---

[32] AD Nord, M 611/8, report from Lille Commission to Prefect, 5 February 1844; AD Seine-Maritime, 10 MP 1362, report from Committee of Inspection for cantons of Darnétal, Boos, Clères and Buchy, 31 December 1847.

[33] AN, F¹² 4707, 'Mission économique en Angleterre de M. Pinède, avocat du Ministère', 1845; and Conseils Généraux de Commerce, de l'Agriculture et des Manufactures, session for 1845–6.

[34] *Le Moniteur*, 19 February 1847.

they voted to extend the measures applicable to children over twelve years of age to all women workers.[35] These were promising developments, which marked an important step forward from earlier practice. However, they were stopped in their tracks by the 1848 Revolution. Under the Second Republic, the French body politic moved on to schemes far more grandiose than child labour reform. Although clearly sympathetic to such an issue, the new régime ran out of time before it could make any impact.[36]

What the Second Republic did at least have to its credit was legislation that complemented and rounded off the work of the 1841 law. First, on 9 September 1848, the National Assembly set a legal maximum of twelve hours' work per day throughout the manufacturing sector. Although watered down by Léon Faucher in a decree of May 1851, the measure was of some benefit to children, in so far as it reinforced a movement towards a shorter working day.[37] And secondly, on 22 February 1851, the Assembly passed its law on apprenticeship. A scheme to regulate the arrangements between masters and apprentices had originally been mooted within the July Monarchy administration during the 1840s. In August 1848 Peupin had followed this up with a detailed *projet de loi* for the Constituent Assembly. The usual soundings from the Chambers of Commerce were taken the following year, but the bill fell foul of the changing political climate. Enthusiasm for State intervention in the economy quicky waned after the turmoil of 1848. When a new, and ultimately successful, project was presented by the Ministry of Commerce in 1850, it was extremely cautious in its approach. The 1851 law did not insist on a written contract between master and apprentice; instead it allowed the alternative of verbal agreements to continue. It required the master to be of good character, but it did nothing to guarantee his technical competence, nor did it limit the number of apprentices he could take. When it came to the obligations of the two parties, it merely required the master to treat his charges 'as a good father' and to teach them their trade 'progressively and completely', whilst apprentices were to show 'fidelity, obedience and respect'. There was some effort to improve conditions, with a ban on work that was unhealthy or beyond the physical capacity of the young. Also, working hours were limited: a maximum of ten per day if the apprenctice was under fourteen, twelve if he was under sixteen. Yet even here the impact of the law was weakened by dropping the original plan for

[35] AN, F[12] 4707.   [36] See Weissbach, 'Qu' on ne coupe le blé en herbe', pp. 164–74.

[37] Levasseur, *Histoire des classes ouvrières*, vol. 2, pp. 400–1. In Britain, a Ten Hour Act had finally been passed in 1847, after years of popular agitation. It fared little better than its French equivalent, being effectively 'demolished' in 1850 by a test case in the courts. See Thomas, *Early Factory Legislation*, pp. 290–313; Ward, *Factory Movement*, pp. 346–72.

special Inspectors, and leaving supervision to the Conseils des Prud'hommes. The outcome was that practice in the workshops continued much as before. Enquiries in 1853 and 1877 revealed the majority of contracts still to be on a verbal basis, with all the risks of misunderstandings that this entailed. They also indicated the problem of apprentices breaking agreements before their time had expired to be no nearer to a solution than before. The 1851 law doubtless gave apprentices some defence against a brutal or rapacious master, but it missed the opportunity of giving a positive stimulus to an ailing institution.[38]

Into the doldrums, 1851–70

With the establishment of the Second Empire, the impetus from the centre toward child labour reform was lost entirely. There was some movement behind the scenes, with various schemes for reform circulated within the Ministry of Commerce, but no practical results followed.[39] The lack of commitment from the Imperial régime was most tellingly exposed by its reluctance to devote State funds to enforcing the 1841 law. In 1858 the Minister floated a scheme for the organization of a network of seven Divisional Inspectors in the thirty-two most industrial departments, capped by an Inspector General. The costs would be shared equally between central Government and departmental funds. All too predictably, the Conseils Généraux in a majority of the departments concerned refused to vote the necessary resources, claiming that factory inspection was a charge for the State. As a rule, it was the smaller manufacturing areas that resisted the ministerial wishes. Some baulked at the cost: the Orne, for example, resented being expected to pay the same as the Seine-Inférieure. Others saw no need to replace the existing system of unpaid Commissioners. The Minister must have had a sneaking sympathy for the Conseil Général of the Aisne when they asserted:

Your Commission starts by repudiating absolutely the departmental character of the expenditure on this scheme. Besides, it considers that the same result could be achieved by more certain and more economical means; and that the zeal and activity of the Primary School Inspectors could be utilized. We would then avoid the creation of a new category of public officials. It would only be fair to increase the salary of the Primary Schools' Inspectors by a modest amount, appropriate to the extra work that the new functions would involve.[40]

[38] AN, F^{12} 4830–1; Levasseur, *Histoire des classes ouvrières*, vol. 2, pp. 432–3; Guinot, *Formation professionnelle*, pp. 106–7, 114–19; Weissbach, 'Qu' on ne coupe le blé en herbe', pp. 175–81.
[39] See AN, C 2873, report for the Emperor by Tallon, 27 November 1867.
[40] AN, F^{12} 4773^A.

Undeterred by this rebuff, the Minister returned to the fray the following year with the idea of charging industry itself for the Inspection service. In a circular of June 1859, he asked the Prefects whether the Commissions of Inspection in their departments were able to enforce the 1841 law, and whether industrial firms could pay for a salaried Inspectorate. The replies were unanimous in condemning the unpaid Inspectors of the Commissions as inadequate for their job. But only a minority supported the proposed alternative. This time it was the industrial departments of Normandy, Flanders and Alsace that raised objections, seeing the scheme as excessively complicated or potentially unpopular.[41] The final gesture from the Empire, in December 1868, was to draft the Mining Engineers as Child Labour Inspectors.[42] This again avoided the expense of a new body of officials, but it produced a poor compromise. The odd Ingénieur could not conceal his contempt for the extra tasks foisted on him; others complained of being overwhelmed by two demanding jobs.[43]

New initiatives during the 1850s and 1860s, such as they were, came from the provinces. At this period, Lille rather than Mulhouse made the running. The exceptionally obstructive tactics adopted by *notables* in the Nord during the 1840s and early 1850s provoked the Prefect into creating a special Departmental Inspector. The Conseil Général voted a salary of 1,500 francs for the post, and in April 1852 the successful candidate, Frederic Dupont, was officially nominated. Dupont was a man of some substance: a lawyer by training, he had been notary and Mayor at Pont-à-Marcq, and a member of the Local Commission of Inspection from 1844. His *règlement d'attributions* required him to report on conditions in establishments covered by the 1841 law; to draw up *procès-verbaux* where necessary; to advise on precautions against industrial accidents; and to consider himself directly responsible to the Prefect. During his first year in office, he visited 546 firms, and, after allowing a period of grace, he drew up 110 *procès-verbaux*.[44] Subsequently he wrote regular reports on his visits to all parts of the department, and was particularly active in encouraging special classes for factory children. The local administration was well satisfied with his efforts, raising his salary to 3,000 francs in 1858, and to 5,000 francs during the 1860s.[45] Two other

---

41 AN, F^{12} 4773^A.

42 AN, F^{14} 12343, 'Extrait des Régistres des délibérations du Conseil Général des Mines', 5 December 1868; report for the Emperor, by De Forcade, Minister of Commerce, 8 December 1868.

43 In 1869, for example, the Mining Engineer in Lille complained to his superiors that he had 800 to 900 factories to visit under the 1841 law, but only 60 to 80 days per year available for visits. Inspection, he concluded, would be illusory: AD Nord, M 611/15.

44 AN, F^{12} 4773^A, letter from Prefect of the Nord to Minister of Commerce, 30 July 1853. Dupont unfortunately refrained from giving information on convictions.

45 AD Nord, M 611/15, letter from Dupont to Prefect, 1 August 1860.

departments followed suit: by 1867, the Seine and the Seine-Inférieure were spending 11,000 and 3,000 francs respectively on full-time Inspectors. A further six departments went half way, allocating somewhere between 1,000 and 1,600 francs per annum to an existing official for duties as a Factory Inspector.[46]

Elsewhere, the inspection service inherited from the July Monarchy either limped along as best it could, or collapsed entirely. A survey taken amongst the Prefects in 1867 revealed a sorry picture: the official summary of the results showed inspection in the departments to be 'non-existent', 'irregular', 'insufficient', 'incomplete', 'illusory', 'disorganized', 'without guarantees' and only occasionally 'satisfactory' or 'recently organized'. In the Rhône, there were no inspections; in the Eure, the Prefect admitted that the Commissions existed in name only; and in the Aisne, they had long ceased functioning.[47] As in the 1840s, a few of the Commissions and Vérificateurs des Poids et Mesures had some success in their attempts to enforce the law. Thus in 1859 the Prefect of the Vosges acknowledged that the Vérificateurs alone were responsible for inspections in his department. At the very end of the Empire, his colleague in the Meuse reported that the 1841 law was generally well observed in his area, on account of the efforts made by the Local Commissions.[48] But these, it must be emphasized, were exceptions to the rule.

All types of Inspector had to operate in an environment that continued to be hostile: the battle to persuade the population to accept factory legislation was far from over in the 1850s and 1860s. A circular from the Procureur-Général in Rouen, warning of his intention to enforce the 1841 law, provoked a public outcry in 1852. The Commissioner of Police gave notice of the 'deplorable effects' such a move would bring, notably the alienation of the local people from the Government: 'Never, say the manufacturers, has industry been more harassed and less protected; our struggle with foreign competitors will become impossible if the Government persists in this persecution, and if it does not act quickly enough to restrain the deadly zeal of those who serve it.' A few years later, during the disastrous cotton famine of the 1860s, the Prefect himself reined back

---

[46] AN, C 2873, Tallon, report for the Emperor, 1867. See also AN, F^{12} 4773^A, for correspondence between the Minister of Commerce and the Prefects in 1853 and 1866, as the Minister tried to persuade other departments to organize a departmental inspection service.

[47] AN, F^{12} 4723, 'Enquête sur le travail des enfants dans les manufactures: resultats généraux de l'application de la loi du 22 mars, 1841'.

[48] AD Vosges, M 277, letter from Prefect to Minister of Commerce, 27 July 1859; AN, F^{12} 4718, letter from Prefect to Minister of Commerce, 21 March 1870.

on the application of the law, worried that he might exacerbate a difficult position for industry.[49]

A long-running crisis in the silk-throwing industry of the Vivarais obliged the administration there to tread no less cautiously.[50] In 1858 the Prefect of the Ardèche informed the Minister of Commerce: 'Public opinion appears generally disposed to favour everything concerning the production and manufacture of silk, which is hardly surprising when it is realized that the industry constitutes one of the principal sources of wealth in the region.' No money could be expected from the Conseil Général for a Departmental Inspector, and even the courts were showing an 'invincible repugnance' for punishing industrialists who exceeded statutory working hours. The Prefect concluded sombrely, 'the administration, to its great regret, is therefore bound to act in this matter with the greatest circumspection, taking care to resolve a situation which offers numerous and serious difficulties'.[51] A series of incidents confirmed his assessment of the atmosphere in the region. The police agent for Villeneuve-de-Berg and a local bailiff found themselves coming under a hail of stones late one night when they were investigating the working hours of a silk mill. They only escaped from their six or seven unknown assailants by firing off their carbines.[52] More orderly, but also more tenacious, was the campaign by the silk mill owners to have the 1841 and 1848 laws interpreted 'in a broad sense'. Their demand was for an extension of the twelve-hour day in the silk industry so that its factory girls could return home early to the outlying villages on Saturday afternoons. In 1859, for example, the 'Spinners and Throwers of the Ardèche' petitioned the Minister of Commerce to be allowed to continue with a working day which began at 3.00 a.m. and ended at 7.00 p.m.: sixteen hours, divided by a total of three hours and twenty minutes of rest.[53] In other parts of the country, Factory Inspectors risked finding their efforts blocked by the realities of power, even during periods of prosperity. A former Primary School Inspector from the Oise complained that when he was on a Commission during the late 1850s, the Prefect refused to follow up any of the thirty

49 AD Seine-Maritime, 10 MP 1362, letter from Commissaire Central de Police de la Ville et de l'Arrondissement de Rouen to Prefect, 10 July 1852; AN, F¹² 4719, letter from Prefect to Minister of Commerce, March 1862.

50 On the plight of the silk industry in the Vivarais, see AD Ardèche, 15 M 3, letter from the Directeur de la Condition Publique des Soies to Prefect, c. January 1858.

51 AN, F¹² 4773, letter from Prefect of the Ardèche to Minister of Commerce, 27 February 1858.

52 AD Ardèche, 15 M 4, letter from Commissaire de Police de Villenueve-de-Berg to Prefect, 18 December 1856.

53 *Ibid.*, letter from Les Filateurs, Mouliniers du Département de l'Ardèche to Minister of Commerce, 23 May 1859. Other requests and petitions from the 1850s and 1860s can be found in this dossier.

procès-verbaux he prepared for fear of compromising good relations with the big manufacturers.[54]

The Second Empire witnessed some changes affecting working-class children. By the late 1860s, according to both the Prefects and the Mining Engineers, the twelve-hour day was becoming the norm. There were various exceptions, such as the silk throwing mills of the Ardèche, where a thirteen-hour day was still common. But, as the Prefect of the Seine-Inférieure reported, 'In general, children work a twelve-hour day like the adults.'[55] Also, a number of industries saw the proportion of children in their labour force decline. Between the Industrial Enquiries of the 1840s and the 1860s, this occurred in the cotton-spinning industries of Normandy, Alsace and the Vosges, the woollen cloth industry of the Champagne and also in the *indiennages* centred on Mulhouse and Rouen.[56] Finally, the percentage of the child population attending primary school continued to increase: from 51 per cent of those aged five to fourteen years in 1851, to 68 per cent in 1866, according to Toutain.[57] In 1860 the Inspector Dupont noted an excess demand for primary school places in Roubaix. He concluded that many parents preferred to do without the wages their children could earn, in order to obtain the certificate which would allow an exemption from any part-time schooling after the age of twelve.[58]

It is difficult to see these changes in working hours, levels of child employment and school participation rates owing much to the 1841 law. After its initial impact during the 1840s, all our evidence has pointed to the law losing most of its bite in the embattled atmosphere of early industrial capitalism. More important was the influence of the labour market, and other underlying social and economic forces. The shift towards a twelve-hour day in the mills was the result of a complex interplay of forces, with the labour movement, partially supported by the

[54] AN, F[12] 4773[A], 'Note relative au travail des enfants dans les manufactures, par M. Gandon, Chef de bureau au Ministère de l'Instruction Publique', 8 November 1867.
[55] AN, F[12] 4723, 'Enquête sur le travail des enfants', 1867; AN, F[12] 4724, 'Situation des établissements industriels, au point de vue de l'observation de la loi du 22 mars, 1841', 1869–73.
[56] Statistique de la France, *Industrie*, 1847–52; *idem*, *Industrie*, 1873. The percentage of children in the labour force of the cotton spinning industry of Seine-Inférieure fell from 27 to 22; in the Vosges, it fell from 29 to 14; in the cloth industry of the Marne, the decline was from 13 to 2 per cent (though in wool spinning the proportion remained constant at 19 per cent); in calico printing, both the Haut-Rhin and the Seine-Inférieure experienced a decline from 28 to 22 per cent. The latter industry was very clearly influenced by the introduction of mechanization: in 1869, Dollfus-Mieg, of Dornach, gave two sets of figures: 46 per cent of his labour force in hand printing was under sixteen, compared to only 24 per cent in the workshops printing *au rouleau*. See above, pp. 106–7.
[57] Toutain, *La Population de la France*, p. 227.
[58] AN, F[12] 4719, report of 16 December 1860.

State after 1848, pressing for shorter working hours, whilst employers gradually came round to the view that productivity could be enhanced through more concerted effort. Children therefore benefited from a general movement on the shop floor, affecting all workers. Where efforts were made to apply special reductions in hours for them alone, the outcome was less satisfactory. As in the 1840s, an eight-hour day for children under twelve, or for those aged twelve to fifteen who were required to attend school, proved almost impossible to attain. In the spinning mills of Normandy, Flanders and Alsace, for example, young children notoriously worked a full day beside the adults, with at best an hour or two off per day (or per week) for school.[59]

The declining proportion of child labour in various industries was also only marginally influenced by administrative action. The 1841 law did not set out to drive children from the workshops, though this was a likely side-effect. The extent of this pressure can be gauged from a comparison of the position in the cotton industries of the Haut-Rhin and the Nord. In the former, the percentage of children in the labour force dropped sharply in a short space of time, probably concentrated in the 1840s. In the Nord, the use of child labour was never so lavish, and it remained firmly entrenched at one fifth of the total employed:

	1839–45	1861–5
Haut-Rhin	31.5	19.7
Nord	18.4	18.7

Yet the Nord was a department whose record in enforcing factory legislation was second to none during the 1850s and 1860s. Shortages of child labour were what made the difference. In Alsace, these were rarely mentioned, and industrialists were more willing to bow to pressure for change from the law. In Flanders they were something of an obsession amongst industrialists. The Inspector Dupont confirmed their emphasis from time to time. In 1860, for example, he noted that children were difficult to recruit for mill work, on account of stiff competitition from the smaller workshops. Later in the decade he reported from Roubaix that

59 See in particular AN, F[12] 4723, replies of Prefects to Enquiry on the application of the 1841 law, 1867.

much spinning machinery was idle for lack of piecers, the children finding work in the newer weaving sheds better paid and less tiring.[60]

The growing impact of the primary schools on the child population was, in principle, supported by the 1841 law, and it had a number of achievements to its credit. The efforts of the Departmental Inspector and the local administration in the Nord to provide extra school places during the Second Empire, and to compel industrialists to send their child workers to special classes, are worthy of acknowledgement. An Enquiry of 1867 revealed the Prefects in a few departments to be satisfied with measures being taken to secure the education of working children. In the Allier, Ardennes, Doubs, Loir-et-Cher and Maine-et-Loire, for example, employers were said to be either setting up their own classes, or allowing children to attend local schools. Far more common, though, were Prefects who stressed the neglect of this part of the 1841 law. According to their reports, in the Ardèche, the numerous silk mills completely ignored their legal obligations; in the Creuse, the majority of children did not go to school, since neither parents nor employers were interested; and in the Loire, children were employed without any concern to secure their instruction. The obvious conclusion is that children employed in the workshops were prominent among those who spent little or no time in school.[61] And even where manufacturers did follow the letter of the law, their juvenile employees all too often had nothing much to show for it at the end. The Lille Chamber of Commerce explained during the 1860s that factory children attending class at midday could lose up to half an hour on their journey from work to school and on the calling of the attendance register: a task that had to be taken seriously, since absentees were liable to a fine. This left the *instituteur* with only thirty minutes or so to instruct up to 200 children of various ages and abilities. 'One can understand that the teaching given under these conditions cannot be serious.'[62]

Conclusion: the 1841 law reconsidered

The 1841 law is invariably written off by historians as a dead letter. This is an exaggeration, which does not give due credit to the efforts of various

---

[60] AN, F¹² 4719, report of 16 December 1860; AM Roubaix, F II c 2, letter to Prefect, 12 March 1866. See also AN, F¹² 5722, Chambre de Commerce de Lille, *La Question du travail des enfants* (Lille, 1867), *passim*.

[61] AN, F¹² 4722, 'Enquête sur le travail des enfants. Résumé des renseignements fournis par les Préfectures au Ministère de l'Instruction publique concernant l'exécution des dispositions relatives à l'instruction primaire', 1867; AN, F¹² 4723, 'Enquête sur le travail des enfants dans les manufactures; état numerique par département', 1867.

[62] AN, F¹² 4722.

Prefects, Mayors and Inspectors.[63] However, there is no denying that the law failed to make much headway in the face of indifference or even outright resistance from parents and industrialists. The reason, according to most authorities, is that the original drafting of the law was fatally flawed. It was too limited in scope, covering only a small minority of workshops. It was unnecessarily passive in its acceptance of existing practices, setting the minimum working age of eight. And it was wretchedly feeble in its enforcement procedures, refusing to insist on a properly funded professional Inspectorate, and allowing first offenders to appear before a Justice of the Peace rather than a Tribunal de Police Correctionnelle.[64]

These criticisms cannot be sustained. Their weakness is to ignore the mammoth nature of the task facing reformers during the 1840s. The decision to concentrate on the minority of larger firms certainly missed out whole tracts of French industry, and it was open to the charge of unfair discrimination. But directing attention to the workshops most readily identifiable for inspection was a realistic strategy during the early stages of the reform campaign. Attempts to enforce the law on the thousands of small *ateliers* that were either concentrated in a big city like Paris or Lyons, or dispersed across the countryside of, say, Normandy or Flanders, would have risked stretching any inspection service beyond its limits, rendering the law impotent. As the Minister Villemain observed, 'On commence par le possible.'[65] Leaving the minimum working age at eight also appeared to betray a lack of determination, given that many industrialists at the 1837 Enquiry had signalled their willingness to accept a slightly later age. The reasons behind this strategy were indeed conservative: a reluctance to disturb vested interests, and a belief in the benefits of child labour for the *classes laborieuses*. The Minister of Commerce, Cunin-Gridaine, made his beliefs perfectly clear to the Chamber of Peers in January 1841:

63 The fate of the 1841 law has been well covered in the local studies. See especially: Lasserre, *La Situation des ouvriers*, pp. 158–68; Pierrard, *La Vie ouvrière'*, pp. 170–8; Kahan-Rabecq, *L'Alsace économique*, vol. 1, pp. 197–206; Francis Hordern, 'L'Evolution de la condition individuelle et collective des travailleurs en Alsace au XIXᵉ siècle, 1800–1870', unpublished thesis, University of Paris, 1970, pp. 249–55; Vidalenc, *Le Département de l'Eure*, pp. 496–8; Lequin, *Les Ouvriers de la région lyonnaise*, vol. 2, pp. 5–6, Elie Reynier, *Histoire de Privas*, vol. 3, *Epoque contemporaine, 1789–1950* (Privas, 1951), pp. 171–5; Monique Baudoin, 'Le Travail des enfants', 31.

64 Guéneau, 'La Legislation restrictive', 501–2; Evrard, 'Le Travail des enfants', 12–13; Touren, *La Loi de 1841*, pp. 108–17; Weissbach, 'Qu'on ne coupe le blé en herbe', pp. 143–4.

65 *Le Moniteur*, 1840, p. 2495, cited by Levasseur, *Histoire des classes ouvrières*, vol. 2, p. 128, n. 8. It should be remembered that the early British Factory Acts only applied to cotton and then to the other textile industries: not until the 1860s did they cover a broad range of industrial employments.

We should not forget that the admission of children into the workshops from the age of eight is a means of supervision for the parents, a start on apprenticeship for the child, and a source of income for the family. At that age, a regular and modest occupation favours the development of physical strength, and when the work can be reconciled with the time necessary for rest and instruction, the greatest difficulty has been overcome. From another perspective, the habits of order, discipline and work have to be acquired early, and most industrial jobs require a speed and dexterity of hand that can only be obtained by long experience, and that cannot be started too early.[66]

However, with hindsight, the decision to regulate rather than abolish child labour had its advantages. Twentieth-century experience has indicated that the policy of banning the practice altogether is likely to drive working children underground. The State then has very little chance of improving conditions for its younger citizens.[67] In France, by contrast, the records show that there was some move, particularly during the 1840s, to eliminate the very young from the labour force, and to encourage the primary instruction of children remaining in the workshops.

Finally, as far as the inspection system was concerned, contemporaries soon realized that the voluntary, unpaid members of the Local Commissions were the weakest link in the enforcement system. Justices of the Peace were not always much more useful, given their tendency to impose fines well below the maximum of 15 francs per offence.[68] However, the main obstacle at this period was the reluctance of Inspectors to prosecute employers, or even to make routine visits to the factories. A salaried Inspectorate, appointed by and responsible to the central Government, was the obvious answer. But what was clear in 1847 was not necessarily so in 1841, and it is absurd for historians to prescribe measures without taking into account the forces working against their implementation. The principle of paid Inspectors was, after all, raised in several quarters during the 1830s, only to be rejected by the legislature. A charitable interpretation would suggest that during the 1830s and 1840s the French admin-

---

66 *Le Moniteur*, 13 January 1841.
67 Rodgers and Standing, 'The Economic Roles of Children: Issues for Analysis', in Rodgers and Standing, *Child Work*, p. 39; Victoria Goddard and Benjamin White, 'Child Workers and Capitalist Development', *Development and Change*, 13 (1982), 471; Standing, 'State Policy and Child Labour'.
68 Data which could be used to compare the number of violations of the 1841 law recorded by the Inspectors with the number of prosecutions and convictions do not exist, it need hardly be said. A dossier to centralize information on prosecutions in each department exists in the Archives Nationales, but the entries are sparse: AN, F^{12} 4715. However, we have already noted examples of Prefects discouraging Inspectors from drawing up or proceeding with *procès-verbaux*. And, although fines in the range of 50, 150 or even 300 francs were mentioned, the 'going rate' appears to have been closer to 10 francs or less. Information drawn from reports on the execution of the 1841 law in AN, F^{12} 4712 and 4714; AD Nord, M 613/14; AD Vosges, M 279 and 284; AD Ardèche, 15 M 3–4.

istration was struggling, in all good faith, to evolve a solution to the delicate problem of enforcement. The British experience with the early Factory Acts might have pointed the way to full-time Inspectors, but there was always the counter-argument that the scale of child labour abuse in industry was of a different order on the two sides of the Channel. Besides, in the French case, a strong current of feeling against bureaucratic intervention in the economy came into play: a reaction, dating from the Revolution, to the *étatisme* of the *ancien régime*. From this perspective, the French body politic emerges unready to countenance a new set of public officials in 1841, and would have to discover from its own experience why the British came to appoint Factory Inspectors with Althorp's Act.[69] During the interim period, France took the traditional path of entrusting the administration of the law to members of the local oligarchy: a system of 'ad hoc and quasi-amateur instruments of Government' already established in such areas as poor relief, education and public health.[70] Although the Local Commissions of Inspection were not a success, they were at least slightly more effective than the Justices of the Peace and paid informers relied upon by the pioneering British Acts.

This was only part of the story, however, for there were also powerful forces at work determined from the outset to limit the impact of any child labour legislation. Under the *monarchie censitaire*, a narrow suffrage based on various forms of property gave the industrial and commercial interest considerable political weight which Governments could ill-afford to ignore.[71] The 1840 Enquiry showed a large majority of them, as represented on the employers' organizations and Conseils Généraux, firmly set against a salaried Inspectorate. Manufacturers resented the prospect of 'curious, disturbing, obtrusive, upsetting, even vexatious investigations' in their establishments, which they had been accustomed to ruling as a private fief.[72] The majority in the legislature was also, as we have seen, concerned to safeguard the productive capacity of French industry as much as to protect child labour from abuse. Hence Cunin-Gridaine readily accepted that special Inspectors would be an unnecessary burden for the taxpayer and for industry. He pledged that the administration would tread warily, taking upon itself 'the cares and as I might almost say, the embarrassment of enforcement'. Without committing

69 See P. W. J. Bartrip and P. T. Fenn, 'The Conventionalization of Factory Crime – A Re-assessment', *International Journal of the Sociology of Law*, 8 (1980), 176–7; and *idem*, 'The Evolution of Regulatory Style in the Nineteenth Century British Factory Inspectorate', *Journal of Law and Society*, 10 (1983), 202–3.

70 See MacDonagh, *Passenger Acts*, p. 117.

71 This point is made in Charles de Freycinet, *Souvenirs, 1848–1878*, 2nd edn (Paris, 1912), p. 88. See Standing, 'State Policy and Child Labour', *passim*.

72 This jaundiced, though essentially accurate, summary of the manufacturers' position, was given by de Gérando in the Chamber of Peers: *Le Moniteur*, 11 March 1840.

himself to any specific formula, he did say that the Inspectors would be chosen from 'elements of the honourable notability', which the voice of the people put before the Government. Turning to the penalties for breaking the law he soft-pedalled further, refusing to accept that industrialists could be hauled before the Tribunal de Police Correctionnelle and charged with a *délit*. Such a system, he feared, would lead to a loss of respect from the workers. He therefore proposed that first offenders be limited to the accusation of a *contravention* before a Tribunal de Simple Police.[73] Only when the failure of this whole approach was manifest beyond doubt would the *grands notables* of the Orleanist régime accept that a more rigorous inspection service would be necessary.

A more plausible explanation for the cloud that hangs over the reputation of the 1841 law is that it ran far too long a course. Originally envisaged as a *loi d'experimentation*, it was thought to be testing the water in a difficult new area. Had it been replaced in 1848, as so nearly happened, it would surely have appeared as a useful foundation for further factory legislation, akin to the pioneering 1802 Act in Britain. In the event, the cause of child labour reform succumbed to the heavy swings of the pendulum that shook French politics during the mid-nineteenth century, and the 1841 law remained in force for thirty-three years.[74] Governments under the July Monarchy were doubtless half-hearted in their commitment to factory legislation, and their failure to follow up the 1841 law with *règlements d'administration publique* was rightly condemned by Charles Dupin in 1847.[75] Yet the principal culprits remain the political leaders of the Second Empire, who repeatedly hesitated to act on the issue, and so wasted twenty potentially fruitful years.

[73] *Ibid*. For a discussion of a class bias in British factory legislation, see W. G. Carson, 'The Conventionalization of Early Factory Crime', *International Journal of the Sociology of Law*, 7 (1979), 37–60.

[74] J. T. Ward writes of the British factory movement: 'Throughout the agitation, the greatest danger was the extraordinary fascination exerted by the almost meaningless word "Radical"; Whig Reform, Owenite Socialism, Chartism and, sometimes, Trade Unionism, all distracted attention, at different times': *Factory Movement*, p. 419. Such 'distractions' as republicanism and socialism may have retarded the progress of factory legislation in France, but we would not wish to imply that the political left had the wrong priorities.

[75] AN, F¹² 4704, report to Chamber of Peers, 29 June 1847.

Chapter 10

1874: child labour legislation comes of age

The last quarter of the nineteenth century saw a more forceful intervention by the State in the lives of children than had hitherto been attempted. The *loi Roussel* of 1874 regulated the practice of putting infants out to wet-nurse. The *lois scolaires* of the 1880s, associated with the name of Jules Ferry, made schooling free and compulsory for all children aged between six and thirteen. More direct curbs on the power of fathers over their offspring came with laws passed in 1889 and 1898. The former permitted the State to deprive parents of their authority if they were compromising the welfare of their children through habitual drunkenness or scandalous ill-treatment. The latter made it possible for minors who had been criminally abused within their families to be handed over to the *assistance publique* or to guardians from a charitable society.[1] This was the context for the child labour law of 19 May 1874, which is the focus for the final two chapters of this book. The new Act went some way to meet the criticisms levelled at its predecessor of 1841. But it was one thing to pass ambitious legislation, quite another to transform the customs of a large sector of the population. The 1874 law and its network of Inspectors had to contend with a whole range of forces on the labour market, which affected the willingness of employers and parents alike to see children move from the workshops to the primary schools. This chapter will trace the origins of the 1874 law, and consider the strategies used to enforce it.

The origins of the 1874 law

The 1874 *loi sur le travail des enfants et des filles mineures dans l'industrie* was a long time in brewing. Debates over the 1847 bill had made it clear to everyone that the 1841 law needed replacing, but a whole series of projects and enquiries had to be paraded before new legislation finally

[1] André Armengaud, 'L'Attitude de la société à l'égard de l'enfant au XIXe siècle', *Annales de démographie historique* (1973), 306–7; Donzelot, *The Policing of Families*, pp. 82–4.

emerged. The Conseil Général de l'Agriculture, des Manufactures et du Commerce produced a detailed scheme for a child labour law in 1850, borrowing heavily from the proposals put forward by Dupin and his colleagues in the Chamber of Peers at the end of the July Monarchy. This promptly disappeared from view in the reactionary political climate of 1851. Rouher, as Minister of Commerce, revived the issue in 1855, having become aware of the need for paid Inspectors. He, too, failed to translate words into action, finally giving up in 1862. The Minister who came closest to putting a child labour law on the statute book was Forcade la Roquette. In 1867 he went through the established procedure of launching enquiries, studying the latest examples of foreign legislation and formulating a *projet de loi*. The Conseil d'Etat stalled at first, reluctant to countenance the expenditure on salaried Inspectors. The Ministry persevered nonetheless, with the result that in the spring of 1870 the Conseil approved a revised bill, which Louvet, a new Minister of Commerce, presented in the Senate. Once again, political events intervened, with the outbreak of War and the sudden collapse of the Empire interrupting all thoughts of child labour reform.[2]

Public opinion in the meantime had been kept simmering by a series of polemical works directly or indirectly concerned with child workers. Armand Audiganne, with his book *Les Populations ouvrières et les industries de la France*, followed in the footsteps of Louis Villermé, visiting the industrial regions during the 1850s, and commenting on the predicament of labour. Jules Simon was also influential, his *L'Ouvrier de huit ans* providing a methodical investigation of child labour and factory legislation. Their efforts were supported by the Society for the Protection of Apprentices and Factory Children, founded in 1866 and active in campaigning for a new law.[3] The main lines of argument during the 1860s were much as they had been in the 1830s and 1840s, with warnings of physical and moral degeneracy striking down the working-class population. Where the debate took a new tack was in the heightened emphasis given to education, and, in particular, vocational training. Although the decline of apprenticeship had aroused a good deal of discussion during the first half of the century, the peculiar circumstances of the Second Empire gave the problem a new urgency.

The Saint-Simonian pretensions of the Imperial régime had stimulated

---

[2] AN, F¹² 4706, Charles de Freycinet, 'Commentaire de la loi du 22 mars 1841', c. 1868; AN, F¹² 4722, M. Heurtier, Conseiller d'Etat, 'Rapport fait à la section de l'Agriculture, du Commerce, des Travaux publiques, et des Beaux-arts, sur un projet de loi relatif au travail des enfants dans les manufactures', 8 June 1868; AN, C 2873, Tallon, 'Rapport à sa Majesté', 27 November 1867; Weissbach, 'Qu'on ne coupe le blé en herbe', pp. 201–48.
[3] Audiganne, *Les Populations ouvrières*; Simon, *L'Ouvrier de huit ans*; *Société de Protection des Apprentis et des Enfants des Manufactures: Bulletin*, 1 (1867).

an interest in the links between education and economic development.[4] In 1855 the Minister of Education asked his officials to assess the influence of the primary schools on the wealth of their districts. The replies gave some encouragement to continue with factory legislation and State education, despite a number of contradictions and dissonances. Several Primary School Inspectors in the manufacturing areas confidently assumed that the education system was making a positive contribution. The Inspector in Lunéville, perhaps influenced by practice in the model establishment at Baccarat, could write: 'It is readily understandable that hands directed with intelligence produce more than those left to their own devices, and that the ignorant labourer has less appetite for work, less precision, less concern for the future, and more of an inclination to consume straight away the fruits of his labour.'[5] His colleague in Rouen echoed this view. Although concerned over the effects of industrial development on school attendance, he concluded that workers with some primary education behind them generally outshone their peers in skill, intelligence and judgement.[6] A handful of Inspectors were sceptical of any links, or at least of the chances of a watertight case emerging from the evidence available. The Inspector in Lille, for example, wrote: 'As for the worker, destined to exercise purely mechanical functions, he will hardly become more skilful from being educated. It is not as a worker that he needs instruction, but as a reasonable and intelligent being.'[7] Others were at pains to prescribe limits to the education of the proletariat. The view from Troyes was that to prepare children for industrial work, they needed to be taught the three Rs, a little history and geography, singing, technical drawing and geometry for surveying. The Inspector here was wary of stirring ambitions that could not be satisfied. While not denying the risk of giving insufficient education, he preferred to stress the dangers of extending it beyond the 'true needs' of the people. Given their modest condition, instruction which could not be used in daily life was likely to be more of a torment than a means of improving one's lot.[8]

The signing of a free trade treaty with Britain in 1860 gave a further, more pressing incentive to improve the quality of labour. The official deputation to the 1862 Exhibition in London, acutely aware of the threat from British competition, demanded that industrial education in France be taken in hand and developed by the State. An Enquiry followed, which consulted a small and not particularly representative group of educational

---

[4] See Anderson, *Education in France*, p. 193; Guinot, *Formation professionnelle*, pp. 121–2.
[5] AN, F^{17} 9239.   [6] AN, F^{17} 9333.
[7] AN, F^{17} 9330. See also AN, F^{17} 9335, report from the *arrondissement* of Saint-Dié (Vosges).
[8] AN, F^{17} 9322.

specialists and industrialists.[9] One of their conclusions was that the 1841 law needed to be extended to the whole of manufacturing industry, and that school attendance be made compulsory for working children until the age of sixteen. There was also a feeling that there should be some kind of *rapprochement* between the school and the workshop, though no consensus emerged on the form this would take. Working-class leaders, represented by Gaumont and Guemid of the journal *L'Enseignement professionnel*, wanted to see elements of the workshop introduced into the schools. They considered that apprenticeship had been reduced to 'disguised domesticity', giving some practical teaching, but ignoring completely the applied sciences. In any case, the division of labour in modern industry made proper teaching redundant, since each worker was required to learn only one stage of manufacturing. Their remedy was a school for twelve- to fifteen-year-olds, which combined primary instruction and experience with a whole range of tools.[10] This approach grew out of the world of the skilled artisan, but it is doubtful whether it offered much that would be of use to a factory worker, and it certainly found little favour with the industrialists on the Enquiry. The Mulhouse Chamber of Commerce observed patronisingly:

A few minds, seduced by theories which are more brilliant than solid, have thought it important to create apprentices' workshops for working-class children, where the principles of handling the tools of each industrial speciality would be taught. As a result, the worker would only enter the manufacturing workshop when he had learnt his trade in a school. We need hardly stress the immense difficulties and the enormous costs that the large-scale implementation of this system would involve, especially when applied to factory industry, working as it does with the aid of machinery.

The Chamber asserted that children from working-class families could not afford to spare the time for full-time education. It was also doubtful whether the schools would be able to predict the future needs of industry, and it contrasted the artificial atmosphere of the classroom with the habits of real work on the shop floor.[11] Industrialists on the Enquiry preferred to see the school in the workshops, as in the ironworks at Le Creusot or the big textile mills of Alsace. A solid foundation of primary instruction would benefit both industry and the individual worker: as Bourcart of Guebwiller insisted: 'Exercising the intelligence of the worker is an indirect but sure route to raising the grade and hence the value of his

[9] Guinot, *Formation professionnelle*, pp. 134–6; Anderson, *Education in France*, pp. 193–204.
[10] Ministère du Commerce, *Enquête sur l'enseignement professionel* (2 vols., Paris, 1864), vol. 1, pp. 141–2. See also Corbon, *De l'enseignement professionnel*, pp. 119–44; and Georges Duveau, *La Pensée ouvrière sur l'éducation pendant la Seconde République et le Second Empire* (Paris, 1948), *passim*.
[11] Ministère du Commerce, *Enquête sur l'enseignement*, vol. 2, p. 768.

labour.'[12] But the industrialists had doubts on the extent to which additional subjects such as chemistry, physics, history, geography and technical drawing should be taught to working-class children since there was always a shortage of jobs available for graduates of 'intermediate' schools. As for the technical training necessary for any particular trade, they preferred to see it carried out in the workshops.[13]

Defeat at the hands of the Prussians in 1871 provided the final spur to action on child labour reform. The school system of Protestant Germany had long been admired in France, and it was only natural to assume that some of the discipline and technical competence of the invading army stemmed from this quarter. The time was ripe to prepare a new generation of French people for struggle on the industrial and military fronts. A short bill consisting of five articles was submitted to the National Assembly by the manufacturer Joubert in June 1871, and was duly referred to a special committee. A year later Eugène Tallon reported back urging the Assembly to adopt a more detailed project.[14] This met with some opposition, for issues such as the rights of the State to protect adult workers or to create new posts in the civil service remained contentious. Nonetheless, the passage of the law was relatively swift, as if in recognition that some such measure was long overdue.[15]

A new law, a new Inspectorate

The law of 19 May 1874 stipulated that children and female minors aged sixteen to twenty-one (*filles mineures*) could not be employed in the 'manufactures, fabriques, usines, mines, chantiers et ateliers' except under certain conditions. No attempt was made to define what was meant by factory or workshop, since this avoided the ticklish problem of how far the State could intervene in family affairs. The minimum working age was raised from eight to twelve, though in a number of industries, to be specified by *règlements d'administration publique*, the minimum would be ten. Children under twelve were to be limited to six hours of work per day, divided by a rest, as opposed to the eight hours allowed by the 1841 law. Young people aged between twelve and sixteen continued to be restricted to twelve hours a day, divided by rests. Night work was forbidden to children, and also to females under twenty-one, though, as

12 *Ibid.*, vol. 1, p. 265.
13 *Ibid.*, vol. 1, evidence from Marguerin, Directeur de l'Ecole Municipale Turgot, Paris, pp. 28–9; Bader, Directeur de l'Ecole Professionnelle de Mulhouse, pp. 248–9, 261–4; Aimé Gros, manufacturer from Wesserling and Deputy, pp. 363–70.
14 Eugène Tallon had a short and generally undistinguished political career. A lawyer from Riom, he was first elected to the legislature in February 1871. He sat on the centre right with the Orleanists, and went out of office in 1876: A. Robert, E. Bourloton and G. Cougny, *Dictionnaire des parlementaires français* (4 vols., Paris, 1891).
15 This paragraph is indebted to Weissbach, 'Qu'on ne coupe le blé en herbe', pp. 250–78.

before, time lost through an accident or *force majeure* could be made up between 9.00 p.m. and 5.00 a.m. for a limited period. Sundays and holidays were not to be worked by children and *filles mineures*. However, in workshops with a 'continuous fire', children could be employed during the night and on Sundays and holidays. Underground work in the mines was covered by child labour legislation for the first time, with children under twelve, female minors and adult women excluded from it.[16] The education clauses in the law required children under twelve to attend school, for a minimum of two hours per day if classes were held within the factory, whilst those under fifteen were restricted to six hours of work per day if they could not produce a certificate to prove they had received elementary primary instruction. Formalities to guarantee compliance with the law included: a *livret* for each child giving the name, date and place of birth, domicile and time spent at school; a register of child workers for each workshop; and the display of a notice giving details of the law. Enforcement of the law was to be in the hands of fifteen Divisional Inspectors, nominated and paid by the State. They would be supported by the unpaid local Commissions inherited from 1841 law. In addition, a Commission Supérieure was to be formed, with three sets of duties: to ensure the 'vigorous and uniform' application of the law; to advise on special regulations; and to draw up lists of candidates for the Divisional Inspectorate. Finally, the penalties for breaking the law were stiffened. As before, it was employers and not parents who were liable to be punished. But henceforth they would appear before the Tribunal de Police Correctionnelle at their first offence, and could be fined between 16 and 50 francs. The fine was to be imposed for each person employed illegally, up to a maximum of 500 francs.[17]

The Ministry of Commerce promptly followed up the law with a series of *règlements d'administration publique*. In March of 1875 the industries permitted to employ children under twelve were specified, including all of the major branches of textile production, plus glassmaking and paper milling. In May of the same year, boys of twelve to sixteen were granted an exemption from the ban on working during the night or on Sundays in four industries: paper, sugar refining, glass and metallurgy. Other *règlements* listed the conditions under which young males could be employed in the mines, and the dangerous or excessively heavy work considered unsuitable for children.

The 1874 law was as 'bourgeois' in origin as its predecessor. Working-

---

[16] An Imperial decree of 3 January 1813, concerning the policing of mines, had stipulated: 'It is forbidden to allow children under the age of ten to go down or to work in the mines.' The 1841 law, however, did not apply to the mining industry, as a circular from the Minister of Commerce reminded Prefects in June 1854.

[17] Recidivists were to be fined between 50 and 200 francs for each offence, with a maximum total of 1,000 francs.

class leaders were beginning to focus their attention on the problems of child labour during the 1860s, particularly as they affected education, but pressure from below remained shadowy. The law was passed in a period when the labour movement was on the retreat, reeling from the bloody repression that followed the Paris Commune. From 1867 onwards, during the gestation period, the Government consulted only the Prefects, employers' organizations and Mining Engineers on the drafts of its new law.[18] The Third Republic also persisted with the strategy of controlling as opposed to suppressing child labour, for its exemptions to the minimum working age of twelve were generous. By continuing to grade working hours according to age, and demanding that industrial employment for children be combined with schooling, it risked meeting the same kind of opposition that had made enforcement difficult for earlier régimes. At the same time, the law broke new ground, notably in paying attention to health and safety at work, in starting to protect adult labour and in creating a centralized Factory Inspectorate.

Those framing the 1874 law had evidently paid heed to the strengths and weaknesses of earlier British Factory Acts.[19] The French were keen to emulate the British Factory Inspectors' reports, which they had always read respectfully and quoted at each other. The Divisional Inspectors were to write annual reports on their activities, and these would form the basis for a general survey by the Commission Supérieure. On the other hand, to avoid the charge that the Divisional Inspectors were ignorant of industrial affairs, Article 17 of the law required candidates to fulfil at least one of three conditions: an engineering qualification, three years' experience as a Child Labour Inspector or five years in the management of an industrial firm employing 100 or more workers. Of the first fifteen Inspectors nominated in 1875, nine were civil or mining engineers, three were from industry and three owed their position to experience of inspection under the 1841 law.[20] There was also no repetition of the extensive police, judical and executive powers which had caused so much trouble when given to the British Inspectors in 1833. The French Inspectorate was, from the start, a tightly-controlled bureaucracy. The new officials were paid a modest salary of 5,000 or 6,000 francs a year, according to their grade, plus travelling and administrative expenses.[21] None achieved the celebrity

---

18 AN, F[12] 4722, for the replies to a questionnaire sent to the Chambers of Commerce, Conseils des Prud'hommes and Chambres Consultatives in 1867. AN, F[12] 4723, for Prefects' reports on the application of the 1841 law; AN, F[12] 4724–26, statistics and reports from the Mining Engineers; AN, F[12] 4727, preparation of the 1874 law.

19 See Ursula Henriques, *Before the Welfare State* (London, 1979), p. 106; Thomas, *Early Factory Legislation*, ch. 7; Bernice Martin, 'Leonard Horner: A Portrait of an Inspector of Factories', *International Review of Social History*, 14 (1969), 412–43.

20 AN, F[12] 4773[A–B]. Two of the engineers, Maurice and Delaissement, had been Child Labour Inspectors also.

21 This salary may be compared to the £1,000 (25,000 francs) paid to the four British Inspectors in 1833.

status and political influence of Leonard Horner in Britain, nor were they allowed to impose fines or draft regulations in their day-to-day work. Article 18 of the law gave them the right of entry to all workshops, and access to all the registers, *livrets*, school attendance sheets and internal regulations required by the law. They were empowered to draw up *procès-verbaux* in the case of violations, consulting the Local Commissions whenever they found dangerous or unhealthy working conditions.

Challenge and response: the inspection service

The 1874 law took an important step forward in creating a salaried Inspectorate, but the extension of protection to children in all industrial workshops also multiplied the workload of the enforcement agencies. Fifteen Divisional Inspectors, together with the Local Commissions, whose awkward position in the workshops had already been well exposed under the previous régime, were soon revealed to be under severe pressure at various points. The Comité Consultatif des Arts et Manufactures divided up the country into fifteen divisions on the basis of statistics collected during the 1860s. As they admitted in their report, these sources of information were incomplete.[22] Two sets of problem emerged from their attempt to match the demands of the law with the resources available for inspection.

First, there were several districts where the sheer number of workshops threatened to swamp the inspection service. This was particularly the case in the cities of Paris and Lyons, where myriads of small workshops were hidden in obscure tenements and back streets. The Comité Consultatif had assumed the total number of children covered by the law in the capital to be approximately 7,600, dispersed around 3,300 firms. Its estimate proved to be absurdly inaccurate. Maurice, the Divisional Inspector, put the total of children closer to 25,000 in his first report, and later enquiries showed him to be substantially correct.[23] The Seine department was at least given its own Divisional Inspector. Lyons and the Rhône were grouped with six other departments to form the fifteenth *circonscription*. Not surprisingly, a new Inspector was warned in 1880 that his was the toughest division, on account of its size, the variety of industries, the number of workers and the character of its inhabitants.[24] He soon found himself struggling with 12,000 small workshops in the city, as well as the dispersed industries of Saint-Etienne and Grenoble, and outlying trades in the Auvergne, the Dauphiné and Savoy. Even without a metropolis to cope with, Inspectors in the more important manufacturing areas faced an

---

[22] AN, F^{12} 4773^A, report of 2 December 1874.
[23] AN, F^{12} 4731, Maurice (Seine, 1st), 3 November 1875.
[24] AN, F^{12} 4755, Delattre (Lyons, 15th), 27 April 1880.

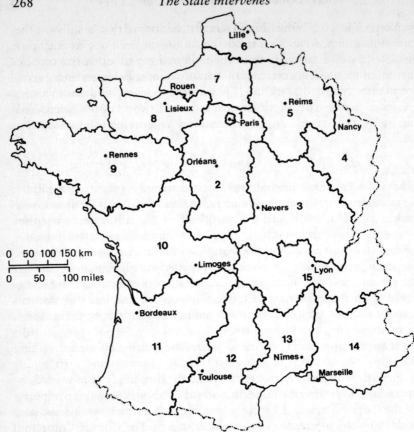

Map 5 Administrative divisions of the Inspecteurs du Travail des Enfants,
1875–85

Source: AN, F^{12} 4773^{A}.

awesome task. The incumbent at Rouen sounded a note of desperation in
1879, with his estimate of 11,000 establishments and 43,000 people liable
to inspection. The previous year, he noted, the number of visits had
totalled 2,200.[25]

A second type of problem confronted Inspectors in the less-developed
regions of the south and west. In this case it was a matter of attempting to
make regular visits to firms thinly dispersed over a large area. In 1881 the
Inspector based in Bordeaux complained that he could travel from six in
the morning until late at night, and still only see three or four factories.[26]
Poor communications and a general lack of amenities aggravated the
position. The silk-throwing industry of the Vivarais, with its 400 mills and
locations high in the mountains, sorely tried the stamina of officials. The
Inspector Estelle evidently saw himself venturing into a savage country

25 AN, F^{12} 4740, Colombier (Rouen, 7th), 6 January 1879.
26 AN, F^{12} 4748, Doll (Bordeaux, 11th), 15 January 1881.

from his residence in Nîmes. His first report mentioned that he still bore the scars from falling down a ramp outside an isolated mill one wet night. A year later, in 1876, he wrote that he had suffered a terrible dog-bite coming out of another, and since there had been no doctor or pharmacist in the area, he had been obliged to drag himself with a bleeding leg to the town of Vals.[27]

Contact between Inspectors and the industrial population was rendered uneven by these obstacles. A Parliamentary Enquiry of 1882 included a question for employers and workers on whether they were visited by the inspection service. The replies covered the whole range of possibilities. At one extreme, there was for example the operative from a woollen mill in Normandy who reported that the Inspector visited regularly, concentrating on the instruction and working hours of children.[28] The owner of a weaving shed at Saint-Génis-l'Argentière, in the Lyonnais, was also reassuringly specific in stating that M. Delattre inspected his establishment from time to time.[29] An employee from a silk mill in the same division was less satisfied: he admitted that inspections took place, but he considered them too rare.[30] This led to the other extreme: a quarry worker from the Nièvre could write, 'Monsieur, one is free to work ten hours or twelve hours, or even fifteen hours if one has the inclination and the courage.'[31]

The principal support for the Divisional Inspectors envisaged by the 1874 law was a network of unpaid Local Commissions. Article 20 charged the Commissions with the duties of attending to the execution of the law, supervising the inspection service and drawing up reports for the Prefects. Article 22 recommended that their membership include where possible a State or civil engineer, a Primary Schools' Inspector and, in mining districts, an Ingénieur des Mines. In principle, this measure had much to recommend it, even leaving aside the low cost which so appealed to Governments. Members of the Commissions could shoulder some of the burden of visiting workshops, and their detailed local knowledge was of potential value to an Inspector. Lyons was one obvious example of a manufacturing centre where the Divisional Inspector might have benefited from 'inside' assistance. In 1881 an observer wrote of the numerous workshops in the silk industry:

These *ateliers* are installed in five- or six-storey houses, and the life inside is so intimate that none of the activities can be perceived from outside. Even the closest neighbours do not know whether the children belong to the house or are outsiders.

27 AN, F[12] 4753, Estelle (Nîmes, 13th), 30 September 1875 and 14 October 1876.
28 AN, C 3370[3], Saint-Aubin (Seine-Inférieure).
29 AN, C 3369[2], Rhône.   30 AN, C 3332, Pradès (Ardèche).
31 AN, C 3365, Saint-Léger-des-Vignes (Nièvre).

Many of these small workshops are concealed in courtyards or on upper floors, which allows them to avoid surveillance without difficulty.[32]

Yet the Commissions in the Rhône department failed to respond to the demands made upon them. Most did not convene, and those that did were either indecisive or too close to the manufacturers to be of use.[33] In other words, the old problems associated with the Commissions under the 1841 law were re-surfacing.

Elsewhere in France, there was always the occasional Commission that took its responsibilities seriously. In the *arrondissement* of Troyes, for example, the members were praised for their 'devotion and zeal' by the Prefect. In 1879, they visited 240 firms, and noted 1,025 offences against the law. And in 1881, they founded a Société de l'Enfance Ouvrière, to reward children who worked well and attended school regularly.[34] For the most part, though, the arrival of a Divisional Inspector was not enough to rouse the Commissions from their torpor. Where they did meet, there was always the chance that they would confine themselves to a perfunctory discharge of formalities. Minutes for the *arrondissement* of Nantua in the year 1888 recorded:

Monsieur le Sous-Préfet, having declared the session open, called upon the members of the Commission to make it known if they had any observations to formulate, concerning the execution of the child labour law of 19 May 1874 in the factories of the *arrondissement*, and if they had received any complaints or demands from interested parties. Following the negative response from the Commission, and having made it known, from information collected, that in 1887 the Tribunal de Police Correctionnelle of Nantua had not passed any judgement for offences against the law of 19 May 1874, the Sous-Préfet declared the session closed.[35]

Divisional Inspectors occasionally regretted that industrialists were allowed to sit on the Commissions. Blaise, in Limoges, reflected that they were well placed to give useful information, but that their prestige and manifest reluctance to act against other employers tended to paralyse the

---

32 AD Rhône, 10 M, letter from Chépié, Departmental Inspector, to Divisional Inspector, 8 January 1881. The same point is made in AN, F¹² 4750, Delaissement (Toulouse, 12ᵗʰ), 15 March 1877.

33 AD Rhône, 10 M, note from official in Prefecture (signed H.G.) n.d.; AN, F¹² 4755, Delattre (Lyons, 15ᵗʰ), 21 February 1883.

34 AN, F¹² 4736, Delaissement (Rheims, 5ᵗʰ), 29 July 1881; AN, F¹² 4739, Delaissement (Rheims, 6ᵗʰ), 1885; AN, F¹² 4767, letter from Prefect of the Aube to Minister of Commerce, 20 September 1884; AN, F¹² 4772, Prefects' reports on the Local Commissions, 1879–84. Other departments where the Commissions were reported to be active included the Marne, Jura, Gard and Bouches-du-Rhône.

35 AN, F¹² 4772, letter from Prefect of the Ain to Minister of Commerce, 12 April 1889.

efforts of their colleagues.[36] But this was only one of several reasons for the widespread failure of the Commissions to function effectively: their membership was after all dominated by professional men drawn from education, the law and medicine, together with a sprinkling of retired merchants and engineers. The obvious conclusion was that factory inspection was both too onerous and too sensitive a task to be left to amateurs.

Governments attempted to remedy deficiencies in the original inspection system by providing additional personnel. The Central Inspectorate was boosted by a Presidential decree of 27 May 1885, which increased the number of *circonscriptions* from fifteen to twenty-one. In the same year, the budget was more than doubled, rising from 125,000 to 280,000 francs. The service would henceforth include an Inspector General at the summit, paid 12,000 francs a year, twenty-four Divisional Inspectors, paid between 5,000 and 7,000 francs a year according to their grade, and three clerks attached to the Commission Supérieure.[37] At the departmental level, the policy was to encourage Conseils Généraux to appoint and fund their own Inspectors. An element of flexibility could then be introduced into the system, concentrating resources where they were most needed. The department of the Seine had already led the way, with an impressive response to its predicament. In 1878 the Conseil Général dismissed the 100,000 francs allocated by the Ministry of Commerce to child labour inspection as derisory, voting 20,000 francs of its own to support a Departmental Inspector and to help the Local Commissions.[38] Even this sum was recognized to be inadequate in a department with over 145,000 workshops and factories, and so in April 1879 it established a corps of fourteen male and female Departmental Inspectors. By 1883, the budget for child labour inspection in the Seine had risen to 136,000 francs a year. The money was divided between an indemnity to the Divisional Inspector, a salary of 4,000 francs for its Principal Inspector, 3,000 francs apiece for twenty-two male and female Inspectors and 2,000 francs each for four supplementary Inspectors, and finally various allocations for travel, office and stationery expenses. The Inspectors were recruited from the ranks of the liberal professions, including several doctors and school-teachers, plus an architect, a former naval officer and a lawyer. Candi-

---

[36] AN, F[12] 4746, Blaise (Limoges, 10th), 1 February 1876. See also AN, F[12] 4750, Delaissement (Toulouse, 12th), 27 February 1878. A note in the Prefecture of the Rhône went as far as to say, 'The Commissions will never do anything. They are composed of industrialists, each as reprehensible as the others': AD Rhône, 10 M.

[37] AN, F[12] 4773[A].

[38] AN, F[12] 4731, letter from Prefect of Police in Paris to Minister of Commerce, 10 April 1878.

dates had to be over thirty and under forty-five years of age, to be willing to concentrate solely on their inspection duties and to have lived in the capital for at least four years. They were also required to pass a written and an oral examination on the application of the 1874 law and its *règlements d'administration publique*.[39] According to the Divisional Inspector, they were well respected by the local population, and they played a vital rôle in bringing the 1874 law to the small workshops: by the mid-1880s, the inspection service was visiting approximately 25,000 firms a year, which was over half of the total for the whole of France.[40] Other manufacturing departments took similar measures, either supporting full-time Inspectors, or supplementing the income of existing officials to cover their inspection duties. None of them, however, approached the scale of activity initiated in Paris. The Rhône appointed a Departmental Inspector in 1879, and in 1884 was voting 7,500 francs for the inspection service. Of this, 4,000 francs was paid to Chépié, the former silk manufacturer who did the inspections, 1,800 francs went to his secretary, and the rest covered expenses. The Nord and the Seine-Inférieure both had two full-time Inspectors, voting 6,000 francs and 10,300 francs respectively for the service in 1886.[41]

Departmental Inspectors were often singled out for praise by the Divisional Inspectors who supervised their activities.[42] Nonetheless, there were inherent weaknesses in the system. To begin with, the coverage was arbitrary. A survey in 1887 found twenty-five departments providing their own Inspector, five giving a small subsidy to the Local Commissions or for stationery and fifty-five doing nothing at all. The latter were by no means all departments where child labour was insignificant: their number included the Aisne, Ardèche, Ardennes, Drôme, Eure, Gard, Hérault and Vosges. Even where there was an Inspector, the post was always subject to the whims of the Conseil Général. During the 1880s, the Aude, Haute-Garonne, Indre-et-Loire, Isère and Rhône all suppressed their schemes, following the resignation or removal of an Inspector.[43] A second flaw was in the calibre of the personnel selected. The Departmental Inspectors had

---

39 AN, F[12] 4731, Maurice (Seine, 1st), 1 February 1880; AN, F[12] 4773[A], personnel in departmental inspection service.

40 AN, F[12] 4730, Laporte (Seine, 1st), 31 December 1882. Ministère du Commerce, *Rapport sur l'application de la loi du 19 mai 1874 pendant l'année 1884* (Paris, 1885), p.13.

41 AN, F[12] 4773[A]; AN, F[12] 4743, letter from Prefect of the Nord to Minister of Commerce, 30 October 1875; AD Seine-Maritime, 10 MP 1367, note on Departmental Inspector Dutertre.

42 For example: AN, F[12] 4736, Delaissement (Rheims, 5th), 29 July 1881; AN, F[12] 4739, Delaissement (Rheims, 6th), 1885; AN, F[12] 4740, Blaise (Rouen, 7th), 20 February 1884; AN, F[12] 4746, Blaise (Rouen, 10th), 25 January 1886; AN, F[12] 4750, Delaissement (Toulouse, 12th), 27 February 1878; AN, F[12] 4755, Delattre (Lyons, 15th), 21 February 1883.

43 AN, F[12] 4773[A].

often retired from other work: they were men of some social standing, who were prepared to work for the low salaries on offer. As with the members of the Local Commissions, the risk was that ill-health or senility would curtail their activities. In 1887, the two Inspectors in the Nord were confined to bed for long periods, one following a road accident, the other with his fevers, 'a sad after-effect of his military campaigns in Africa'. A year later there were complaints from the Loire that the inspection service was being compromised by the old age of the local official.[44] Thirdly, there was the problem of the ambiguous position of the Departmental Inspectors in the administration. Strictly speaking, they were subordinate to the Divisional Inspector, but it was impossible to ignore the fact that their funding depended on the goodwill of the Prefect and the Conseil Général. They therefore risked being caught between two conflicting hierarchies,[45] and, more seriously, were open to the charge of partiality. Blaise, the Divisional Inspector in Rouen, noted the tendency of his departmental colleagues to turn a blind eye to industrial accidents, and the lack of independence vis-à-vis the industrialists of one of them in particular: 'They are often paid by the people they have to inspect and prosecute, and are faced with the alternatives of failing in their duty or upsetting influential members of the Conseil Général, who voted the credits for their position.'[46] Similarly, Gouttes in Saint-Etienne reported the reluctance of Departmental Inspectors to prosecute offenders, when the Conseils Généraux were full of big industrialists.[47] A new law in 1892 implicitly recognized the faults in this hybrid system by instituting a single hierarchy of eleven Divisional Inspectors and ninety-two Departmental Inspectors nominated and paid by the State.

Challenge and response: towards an enforcement policy

The 1874 law on child labour, like that of 1841, was a deliberate attempt to modify some of the established practices of industrialists and working-class parents. The long campaign to promote child labour reform was in itself evidence that attitudes to the employment and schooling of children were evolving. But inevitably there were forces of inertia and resistance, which came to the surface when the attempt was made to translate

---

[44] AN, F^{12} 4742, Delattre (Lille, 8th), 20 March 1887; AN, F^{12} 4764, Gouttes (St-Etienne, 21st), 1888.

[45] AN, F^{12} 4755, Delattre (Lyons, 15th), 21 February 1883, concerning difficulties over the Departmental Inspector in the Isère.

[46] AN, F^{12} 4740, Blaise (Rouen, 7th), 20 February 1884, and annual report for 1884; AN, F^{12} 4746, Blaise (Rouen, 10th), 25 January 1886.

[47] AN, F^{12} 4764, Gouttes (St Etienne, 21st), 29 January 1888. See also AN, F^{12} 4744 Jaraczewski (Amiens, 9th), 1888.

sentiments into action. When the Divisional Inspectors first made their rounds, many employers confessed that they hoped the 1874 law would suffer the same fate as its predecessor. Others proclaimed it impossible to fulfil, or against their basic interests.[48] But the majority were probably busy men who, without bearing the law any particular good or ill-will, had other priorities. In 1876, the Inspector at Nevers reported that negligence was more of a problem than hostility among the small employers: 'the least preoccupation which does not bring a profitable return leaves them strongly indifferent'. Two years later, his colleague in Rouen also talked of 'absolute indifference', whilst Delaissement in Toulouse stressed the influence of self-interest, carelessness, forgetfulness and ignorance rather than outright opposition.[49] Parents could not be counted upon to support the law either, even though it purported to protect their offspring, and deliberately refrained from exposing them to prosecution. The Divisional Inspector in lower Normandy, for example, noted that feelings were running high in the principal manufacturing centres over the application of the 1874 law. His annual report for 1876 explained that 'the prospect of a fall in the working hours of children, and especially in the incomes earned for their families, had slightly irritated unenlightened minds'.[50]

Persistent opposition to the law naturally came from those industrialists who felt their livelihood most threatened by its application. The legislature had taken their sensitivities into account to a certain degree by providing for exemptions to the minimum working age of twelve. Those branches of industry pleading most vehemently to be allowed to employ young children gave some warning of future friction points. The Chambre Consultative des Arts et Métiers, evaluating the depositions with the Ministry of Commerce, isolated various types of argument.[51] First, it raised the possibility that apprenticeships had to be started early in certain trades, such as glassmaking, spinning and the hand-printing of textiles. However, it was consistently sceptical on this line of argument. It proved more receptive to the plea from a small number of industries that they provided simple, undemanding work for children. Spinning was the most important of these, with the familiar proposition that the *rattacheurs* and *bobineurs* had to be young children with a small stature and supple fingers. Papermaking was included, the stacking of newly made sheets and the manufacture of envelopes being considered light, discontinuous work.

[48] AN, F^{12} 4736, Doll (Rheims, 5th), annual report for 1875; AN, F^{12} 4748, Jacquemart (Bordeaux, 11th), 31 December 1875.

[49] AN, F^{12} 4734, Villenaut (Nevers, 3rd), annual report for 1875; AN, F^{12} 4740, Colombier (Rouen, 7th), 14 February 1877; AN, F^{12} 4750, Delaissement (Toulouse, 12th), 15 March 1877. See also AN, F^{12} 4753, Estelle (Nîmes, 13th), 12 April 1879.

[50] AN, F^{12} 4743.   [51] AN, F^{12} 4727.

Finally, running like a red thread through all of the discussions, was the problem of labour shortages. Glass manufacturers, the Chamber asserted, could probably train children from the age of twelve. The real difficulty for the *verriers* was the recruitment of child labour. With glassblowers reserving the best jobs for their own offspring, the industry offered only dead-end jobs for the children of outsiders. In the case of spinners, the Chamber emphasized the problem of having to find large numbers of child workers in one locality. It quoted the Lille Chamber of Commerce, with its estimate that 20 to 30 per cent of the labour force in the linen mills were children.[52] There was also the silk industry of the Ardèche: 40 per cent of its operatives were thought to be children, on account of the acute shortage of adult women available for factory work.[53] The paperworks too were recognized to have recruitment problems, with the need to find labour near their rural water mills.

The Divisional Inspectors subsequently confirmed this analysis. Where labour was abundant, they had little difficulty in enforcing a minimum working age of twelve. The Inspector based in Nevers informed his superiors in 1876: 'Leaving aside a few rare local circumstances, the managers and owners have enough applicants for work to be able to choose their young personnel exclusively from children over twelve years of age, particularly as they admit themselves that children below this age can rarely perform useful services.'[54] Aubert, in Lisieux, reiterated this point by contrasting conditions in the *arrondissements* of Louviers and Andelys with those in the other districts under his supervision. Most of lower Normandy, in areas such as Caen and Bayeux, was dominated by agriculture and handicraft production. A surplus of labour meant that children under twelve were rarely employed, the *patrons* preferring the strongest, oldest and best-educated youths. In the valleys of the Epte and Andelle, by contrast, the rapid expansion of cotton spinning and weaving had overstretched the resources of the local labour market. The minimum age and educational requirements of the 1874 law were therefore frequently ignored, and manufacturers talked only of the obstacles they had to negotiate.[55] Resistance to the law provoked by labour recruitment problems was reported from various regions in the glassworks, canning factories, sugar refineries and paper mills. Moreover, in the southern

[52] Statistics assembled by the Mining Engineers in 1869 did not support this estimate: they showed 19 per cent of the operatives in the linen mills to be children, including only 2 per cent of the total who were under twelve. Moreover, nearly half of the mills in Lille managed to do without children: AN, F^{12} 4724.

[53] This proportion *was* confirmed by the Mining Engineer: in 1873, he found 363 *moulinages de soie* in the Ardèche, employing 1,266 children under twelve, and 3,453 aged twelve to fifteen, equivalent to 38.6 per cent of the total labour force: AN, F^{12} 4726.

[54] AN, F^{12} 4734; see also AN, F^{12} 4744, Dechaille (Nantes 9th), 7 January 1879.

[55] AN, F^{12} 4742–3.

departments of Ardèche, Drôme, Isère and Vaucluse, the silk-throwing industry continued its campaign against the rigorous enforcement of child labour legislation throughout the 1870s and 1880s. The straitened circumstances of the industry at this period were responsible for a note of desperation in their claims. During the mid-1880s, for example, the Moniteur des Soies claimed that the actions of the Divisional Inspector were destroying the industry, driving labour into the smaller workshops and depriving it of apprentices.[56]

These varying pressures from the market place to evade or ignore the law sooner or later brought a confrontation with the Factory Inspectors. A few industrialists, or groups of industrialists, were prepared to risk a head-on collison. The silk manufacturers of the Vaucluse managed to have the Divisional Inspector called off his rounds by the Prefect, after widespread agitation in 1877 from an industry in the depths of a crisis.[57] Delattre, the owner of a woollen mill in the Nord, mounted a more personal offensive in 1879, after a Departmental Inspector warned him to end night work for his juvenile and young female employees. His first response was to fire off a letter to the Sub-Prefect at Douai, claiming that the lack of population in his district made it impossible for him to comply. Only foreigners would benefit from this 'absurd law', he concluded. Support was forthcoming from the 'fathers of families and workers' in his mill, with a petition asking that their sons and daughters be allowed to continue to work nights, and so maintain their wages. The President of the Société Industrielle de Fourmies also intervened, claiming that children from the poorest families needed a wage, and that the six-hour limit on those under twelve was a 'great nuisance' for industrialists. When threatened with prosecution, Delattre sent home his 500 employees, creating discontent in the surrounding villages, and causing the Prefect to suggest a withdrawal of legal action.[58] However, this approach could only bring a short-term respite from the law, for the central Government could not tolerate such forthright challenges to its authority.

The alternative strategy was one of covert resistance to the law and its Inspectors. It is difficult to avoid the conclusion that deception took place on a massive scale. The hard-pressed inspection service could not guarantee to visit each workshop even once a year, and during a short stay could not necessarily investigate all aspects of children's employment. The presence of an Inspector in a town or village was also easily signalled, giving employers time to take emergency measures. In the countryside, this was often obvious to Inspectors. Estelle mentioned lookouts posted at the entrance to silk mills in the Hérault and Ardèche, who gave a warning when he appeared on the high mountain roads.[59] In the towns, news doubtless travelled quickly on the grapevine. The Divisional Inspector in Rheims complained of its modern medium, the telephone system:

I had just visited one big factory, and was preparing to go and visit another belonging to the same Company, when the Manager of the first politely offered to announce my arrival to his colleague by telephone, so that I could see him immediately. I could hardly refuse without giving away my desire to appear without warning. The second Manager could in any case have been warned without my approval. I therefore accepted and a quarter of an hour later, when I arrived at the second factory, the man was waiting for me. I expressed a desire to see the workshops, but the Manager replied that the workers had just left. I insisted and found a few youths leaving or preparing to leave. The inspection was necessarily incomplete – I cannot prove that the order was given for the workers to leave a little before the end of the day, to stop me noting breaches of the law, but I have my suspicions.[60]

Where advance warning proved impossible, a second line of defence was to keep the Inspector talking in the office for a while. Muffled voices were sometimes heard shouting things like: 'Save yourselves, children, save yourselves, the Inspector is here!'[61]

Hiding or evacuating children during an inspection was the most blatant form of fraud, easily practised in the smaller workshops. The occasional slip-up in the escape routine gave Inspectors an inkling of what was going on behind their backs. Their reports gave a long list of children glimpsed as they disappeared into storerooms, private apartments or the surrounding countryside. In 1876, two members of the Local Commission for the *arrondissement* of Valenciennes became detached from the main group while inspecting a jute mill. Stumbling into an obscure part of the works, they discovered a young child of seven or eight years hidden in a storeroom. And as late as 1892 a Departmental Inspector for the Seine-Inférieure found an eight-year-old trying to hide away in a glass-works.[62] More gruesome evidence of cheating the Inspectors came to light in Tourcoing when an explosion demolished a woollen mill and the adjacent dyeworks. Three children were killed, and four others were injured in the incident. Yet earlier visits by Delattre had never found any

---

[59] AN, F¹² 4753, Estelle (Nîmes, 13ᵗʰ), 14 October 1876.
[60] AN, F¹² 4739, Delaissement (Rheims, 6ᵗʰ), 20 February 1888.
[61] AN, F¹² 4736, Doll (Rheims, 5ᵗʰ), 9 January 1877. The incident took place in a *fabrique de boulons* in the Ardennes.
[62] AN, F¹² 4738, Nadeau (Lille, 6ᵗʰ), February 1876; AN, F¹² 4747, Blaise (Rouen, 10ᵗʰ), 8 July 1892. See also: AN, F¹² 4736, Doll (Rheims, 5ᵗʰ), 29 July 1881; AN, F¹² 4748, Doll (Bordeaux, 11ᵗʰ), 13 June 1882; AN, F¹² 4750, Hegelbacher (Toulouse, 12ᵗʰ), 15 January 1881; AN, F¹² 4752-3, Estelle (Nîmes, 13ᵗʰ) January 1879 and 19 October 1878. For British examples, see Thomas, *Early Factory Legislation*, pp. 103–4.

juveniles in these establishments, which, as he put it, 'proves once again the ease with which industrialists can make them disappear when they see the inspector'. In this case, he was unable to prosecute because the employer had been blown up with his mill.[63]

'Tacit understandings' between employers and operatives to give misleading answers to questions posed by the Inspectors were no less effective. Cases of excess working hours and night work for children were notoriously difficult to prosecute because of a general reluctance to testify in court. The Divisional Inspector Chambard appeared to have a firm case against a cotton spinner from the Haute-Saône, after his employees let it be known that the machinery in his mill never stopped turning for twelve and a half hours per day. But in court they went back on their word, and an acquittal followed.[64] Other Inspectors were doubtful about the replies they received from children they interviewed. When the law first appeared, Aubert complained of fraudulent manoeuvres by industrialists in lower Normandy aimed at keeping their youngest child employees. Their tactics, he alleged, relied on his indulgence during the initial visit, and a long delay before he could return. They therefore feigned complete ignorance of the law and ordered children to say that they were over twelve years of age, working without a *livret*: 'The children, whose wages were threatened and who preferred to stay in the workshops than to go to school, willingly lent themselves to these false declarations.'[65] Barral, based at Grenoble, also found himself unconvinced by the embarrassed responses from mill girls to his questions on their working hours.[66] There remained the simple expedient of only complying with the law on the day of inspection: a ploy that was particularly difficult to detect. Children under twelve, for example, might work six hours a day for the benefit of a passing Inspector, before returning to a normal working routine with the rest of the labour force. Interestingly, the Conseil des Prud'hommes at Romilly-sur-Seine (Aube) explained the failure of local hosiery manufacturers to reply to a Parliamentary Enquiry of 1882 in terms of 'opposition to [their] particular interests concerning minors'. The 1874 was a dead letter in the town, the Conseil revealed: the industrialists, warned in advance of the arrival of an Inspector, were always able to put themselves in order at the required moment.[67]

63 AN, F[12] 4742, Delattre (Lille, 8th), 18 July 1885.
64 AN, F[12] 4765, Chambard (Nancy, 5th), 12 December 1892.
65 AN, F[12] 4742, Aubert (Lisieux, 8th), 30 July 1875.
66 AN, F[12] 4761, Barral (Grenoble, 19th), 16 January 1888.
67 AN, C 3338, President of the Conseil des Prud'hommes, Romilly-sur-Seine, 21 November 1884. See also AN, F[12] 4736, Doll (Rheims, 5th), 20 April and 10 October 1878.

Faced with large pockets of ignorance, hostility and indifference from vested interests, and aware of the dangers of regional disparities in the application of the law, the Inspectors needed a uniform policy to guide them through their day-to-day affairs. The strategy chosen for them was one of gradual reform, following the precedent set by the British Factory Inspectorate after 1833, and the early attempts at enforcement of the 1841 law.[68] When they first made their rounds, the Divisional Inspectors concentrated on spreading knowledge of the law and showing industrialists the benefits it could bring. Their early reports emphasized a tactful and conciliatory approach, in the attempt to avoid conflict over an unpopular law. Maurice, in Paris, anticipated opposition from the glass manufacturers, after his experience with the 1841 law. He therefore called a special meeting for them in 1875, to explain the new legislation. The response was predictably gloomy, with talk of closing down plants for lack of child labour. The Inspector made an effort to calm their fears by granting six months' grace before the law would be enforced rigorously.[69] Doll, in the Ardennes, tried to win over the labour force by stirring their patriotic feelings. Whilst visiting the workshops in Rethel: 'I told them that the Prussians could all read and write, and that those, like the brutes I had in front of me who were rotting in their ignorance, could only be bad Frenchmen and bad soldiers, who would run away on our day of revenge.'[70] During the early stages of enforcement, the Inspectors were also prepared to tolerate many unlawful practices. The requirement that children under twelve, and those aged twelve to fifteen who lacked a primary education certificate, should only work six hours a day was recognized to be a source of friction. Many a compromise or temporary accommodation was therefore made. Maurice allowed these categories to work a full day, on the understanding that they attended school during the evenings. Blaise, in Rouen, was content with two hours off for schooling instead of a proper half day in the spinning mills, admitting that he did not wish to impose a severe reduction in children's wages, and that he accepted the difficulty in recruiting two relays.[71] Children from excep-

---

[68] See Thomas, *Early Factory Legislation*, p. 75; Bartrip and Fenn, 'The Evolution of Regulatory Style', 204.

[69] AN, F[12] 4731, Maurice (Seine, 1st), 1 November 1878.

[70] AN, F[12] 4736, Doll (Rheims, 5th), annual report for 1876. See also AN, F[12] 4743, Aubert (Lisieux, 8th), 30 December 1877; AN, F[12] 4750, Delaissement (Toulouse, 12th), 5 March 1877; AN, F[12] 4753, Estelle (Nîmes, 13th), 30 September 1875.

[71] AN, F[12] 4731, Maurice (Seine, 1st), 28 March 1876 and 31 December 1877; AN, F[12] 4740, Blaise (Rouen, 7th), annual report for 1880. See also AN, F[12] 4733, D'Estienne d'Orves (Orleans, 2nd), 12 April 1876; AN, F[12] 4736, Doll (Rheims, 5th), 30 April 1876; AN, F[12] 4743, Aubert (Lisieux, 8th), 30 December 1877; AN, F[12] 4745, Duchaille (Rennes, 9th), 18 September 1875; AN, F[12] 4748, Jacquemart (Bordeaux, 11th), 31 December 1875; AN, F[12] 4750, Landois (Nantes, 12th), 1 January 1886.

tionally poor families were occasionally permitted to work illegally. In 1879, a Divisional Inspector yielded to the entreaties of a tearful widow from the Ardèche, and allowed one of her five children to work from 4.30 a.m. to 7.00 p.m., even though the girl was under twelve. Durassier made a similar concession in Nantes, tolerating the irregular employment of a young boy on the grounds that he was 'the son of a widow, whose situation was precarious in the extreme'.[72]

A fundamental part of this gradualist approach to enforcement was the sparing use of legal action by the Inspectors. Their visits regularly uncovered literally thousands of breaches of the law, but for the most part they attempted to rectify them by persuasive rather than coercive methods. In 1876, covering the 6th Division, Nadeau found 3,836 children failing to attend school, 14,181 young people under fifteen without a primary education certificate working over six hours a day, forty-nine children under twelve in the same predicament, 310 children and *filles mineures* working nights, another 1,041 of these two categories working on Sundays or holidays, plus 1,229 infringements of the regulations on *livrets* and registers of child labour. From this total of 21,016 offences, he drew up twelve *procès-verbaux*. By 1884, the total number of offences recorded had fallen to 8,903, countered by eleven *procès-verbaux*.[73] Some disparities between the prosecution policies of Inspectors is indicated by the statistical evidence. Between 1875 and 1879, Inspectors in the Seine drew up 379 *procès-verbaux*, while their colleagues in the 15th Division, based on Lyons, managed only one. During the same period, Nadeau in Lille initiated thirty-four prosecutions, compared to the 150 started by Colombier in Rouen. And Doll, in Rheims, drew up twenty-six *procès-verbaux* in 1876, but none in the next three years, while Delaissement in Toulouse began with a conciliatory line that rarely involved legal action, but then announced a firm stance and prepared twenty *procès-verbaux* in 1879.[74] The most embarrassing inconsistency occurred in the 4th Division. During the early 1880s, the Minister repeatedly wrote to Nancy criticizing the lack of rigorous enforcement procedures by successive Inspectors. In 1886 he sent in Boyer from the

72 AN, F¹² 4753, Estelle (Nîmes, 13ᵗʰ), 14 October 1879; AN, F¹² 4744, Durassier (Nantes, 9ᵗʰ), 22 April 1883.
73 AN, F¹² 4739. Unfortunately, comparisons between the number of offences recorded and prosecutions cannot be made at the national level, for the Ministry of Commerce did not require Inspectors to provide such information. For British figures on this point, see Bartrip and Fenn, 'The Conventionalization of Factory Crime', 179–80; W. G. Carson, 'White-Collar Crime and the Enforcement of Factory Legislation', *British Journal of Criminology*, 10 (1970), 383–98; Bartrip and Fenn, 'The Evolution of Regulatory Style', 205–6.
74 Ministère du Commerce, *Rapport sur l'application de la Loi du 19 mai 1874 pendant l'année 1884* (Paris, 1885), p. 13.

Seine, presumably with instructions to take a firm line. The result was a jump in the number of prosecutions from zero in 1885 to twenty-one in 1886: and complaints from the industrialists that the new Inspector was too quick to take them to court![75] Even taking these disparities into account, however, the fact remains that the Inspectors used the courts as a last resort: their first reaction to an offence was always to issue a warning, and only when this had been ignored at least once would they prosecute.[76] During the 1870s and 1880s, the total number of *procès-verbaux* prepared by the Child Labour Inspectorate settled in the range of 200 to 300 a year.

Conclusion: a middle-class conspiracy?

The deficiencies in the inspection service, together with the indulgent treatment of industrialists by the administration, might be taken as evidence that the Third Republic was no more serious about enforcing child labour legislation than previous régimes. The 1874 law could then be dismissed as another piece of window dressing, intended to head off the reform movement, but not to force the pace of change on the shop floor. Michel Foucault, we might note, has argued that a class bias crept into the legal system under capitalism. On the one hand, the typical working-class crimes of pilfering and theft, 'the illegality of property', were rigorously pursued by the police and punished in the ordinary courts. On the other, middle-class crimes such as fraud and tax evasion, 'the illegality of rights', were dealt with in special courts, which permitted accommodations and reduced fines. The bourgeoisie, then, had 'the possibility of getting round its own regulations and its own laws', and flourished accordingly.[77] In the case of the 1874 law there were of course no special courts but there was certainly a reluctance in some 'bourgeois' quarters to see industrialists turned into criminals.

The most explicit evidence of this attitude comes from the occasional intervention, at various levels, to rescue employers who had fallen foul of the Inspectorate. At the very summit Ministers of Commerce were not averse to using their position to protect offenders from the due process of

[75] AN, F¹² 4735. For discussion of similar disparities in Britain, see Thomas, *Early Factory Legislation*, pp. 259–63; Ursula Henriques, 'An Early Factory Inspector: James Stuart of Dunearn', *Scottish Historical Review*, 50 (1971), 29–30; P. W. J. Bartrip, 'British Government Inspection, 1832–75: Some Observations', *Historical Journal*, 25 (1982), 621–2; Bartrip and Fenn, 'The Evolution of Regulatory Style', 213–14.

[76] AN, F¹² 4731, Maurice (Seine, 1ˢᵗ), 1 February 1880; AN, F¹² 4740, Colombier (Rouen, 7ᵗʰ), 14 February 1877; AN, F¹² 4746, Landois (Limoges, 10ᵗʰ), 22 June 1883; AN, F¹² 4752, Estelle (Nîmes, 13ᵗʰ), 22 December 1876.

[77] Foucault, *Discipline and Punish*, p. 87, cited by Carson, 'The Conventionalization of Early Factory Crime', 37.

law. Pouyer-Quertier, the conservative Deputy from Rouen, was one of the first to benefit. In 1876, the Inspector Colombier reported that the Filature de la Foudre was more out of step with the law than any other mill in his division. Two visits and an audience with Pouyer-Quertier himself had not stopped four children working without a *livret*, six others under twelve working a twelve-hour day without any schooling, and sixty-seven young people of twelve to fifteen, who lacked an educational certificate, working a full day. The Minister advised his Inspector not to draw up the seventy-seven *procès-verbaux* that should have followed: instead, he demanded a special report for the Commission Supérieure. Pouyer-Quertier stayed out of the courts.[78] Connections in high places also stood a Monsieur May in good stead when he was threatened with prosecution. The death of a thirteen-year-old girl at his button factory in Beauvais ' l to a *procès-verbal* from the Divisional Inspector. However, a note in the Ministry revealed this industrialist to be a judge in the Tribunal of Commerce for the Seine, and a personal friend of the Minister. May explained to the Head of the Industrial Bureau, during a visit to Paris, that the Inspector had cleared his establishment shortly before the accident, and that he was keen to see the law enforced. The Minister handled the affair with some finesse, writing to the Divisional Inspector in November 1884:

It is left to your appreciation as to whether, given these explanations, the *procès-verbal* you have drawn up should be pursued. Perhaps you will be of the opinion that, under these conditions, there is room for taking into account the good will of this industrialist, especially when the public prosecutor in Beauvais has made enquiries, and absolved him of responsibility for the accident in question.

Blaise took the hint, and a week later reported that he had abandoned the prosecution.[79]

A more impersonal 'accommodation' occurred in 1887, following the discontent aroused by the litigious début of Boyer in the 4th *circonscription*. A first wave of prosecutions in Dijon came to court, and were badly received in the local press. *Le Progrès de la Côte d'Or* accepted that the fines had been lenient, but left no doubts that the industrialists should never have been in court in the first place. It considered the offences very minor, and the preliminary warnings inadequate. A second wave of prosecutions in Besançon created a storm. The Mayor claimed that he had not yet started issuing *livrets* for children (after thirteen years!), and the Local Commission testified that it had not made any inspections for several years. The Prefect of the Doubs was no less hostile to the new

[78] AN, F[12] 4741.   [79] AN, F[12] 4740.

Inspector. He informed the Minister of Commerce that the 'very honour-able industrialists' should have received a warning first, and implied that the rashness of the Inspector was bringing the 1874 law into disrepute. Despite the dubious nature of some of these arguments, the Minister advised Boyer to drop the cases at issue: only six of the thirty-two *procés-verbaux* he prepared in 1887 ever resulted in court action.[80]

At a lower level, public prosecutors often refused to press charges connected with the 1874 law. Several Divisional Inspectors complained that their efforts were being hampered by lack of support from this direction. Nadeau suffered two such rebuffs while in Lille, protesting in vain against decisions by prosecutors in Dunkirk and Boulogne. Review-ing the latter case, the Procureur-Général at Douai observed that the 1874 law was generally ignored in the district, making it inequitable to isolate four 'honourable industrialists': manufacturers who kept children under twelve in their workshops for over six hours a day.[81] Landois in Limoges reported in 1883 that three of the six *procès-verbaux* he had drawn up the previous year had been withdrawn by the prosecutors, on the grounds that the manufacturers involved had subsequently fallen into line with the law.[82] Plassiard in Nancy was scandalized when charges against a foreman were dropped 'out of consideration for the industrialist' concer-ned. He reported in 1881:

A foreman, married and father of several children, seriously abused several young married women in a short space of time. He sent them on some sort of pretext to carry things to an isolated workshop where the noise of the looms and machinery prevented any cries being heard. The unfortunate women did not have the courage to complain, because the reception of their work and that of their husbands was in the hands of the foreman.

An anonymous letter eventually exposed the incidents but in the end the foreman was not even dismissed.[83] Doll, whilst in the 11th *circonscrip-tion*, carried on what can only be described as a running battle with the local *parquets*. To begin with, in 1882, he stated that he had initiated prosecutions against all of the glass manufacturers in Bordeaux, but that the Procureur refused to proceed. The prosecution service took the line that the 'most honourable people' in Bordeaux, including members of the Tribunal and Chamber of Commerce, could not be hauled up in court. Doll concluded sourly, 'As long as the courts make common cause with

[80] AN, F^{12} 4735. Pleas for Ministerial intervention were not always successful: see AN, F^{12} 4731, for the failure of the Deputy Camille Sée to secure assistance for his acquaintance Raby, a manufacturer of walking sticks near Paris, in 1877; and AN, F^{12} 4740, for the hostile reception given to the cotton spinner Gresland, from Bondeville-lès-Rouen, when he attempted in 1883 to have a *procès-verbal* withdrawn.
[81] AN, F^{12} 4742.   [82] AN, F^{12} 4746.   [83] AN, F^{12} 4735.

delinquents, it will be difficult to obtain serious results in these departments.' A year later, he was complaining that the *substituts* were not accepting his reports unless they had been verified by *gendarmes*, who invariably missed the most blatant violations of the law. He became increasingly exasparated over the course of the 1880s. In 1884 he alleged that the Procureurs were throwing his *procès-verbaux* into their wastepaper baskets. And in 1887 he outraged the Minister of Commerce by writing that 'The Procureurs of the Republic will never summons an industrialist for having children without a certificate.'[84]

For employers unfortunate enough to end up in court, there was always the chance of a light fine, or even an outright acquittal. Maurice complained that in 1880 only 44 per cent of his prosecutions in the Paris region had resulted in a conviction. He therefore felt obliged during the following year to take only the most serious cases to court.[85] However, in general, the Commission Supérieure pronounced itself well satisfied with the conviction rate. In 1886, for example, 275 *procès-verbaux* produced 205 convictions, sixteen acquittals, thirty-seven cases dropped and eighteen pending. This meant that where a decision had been reached, 80 per cent of the reports had produced a verdict of guilty.[86] The Inspectorate spent more time lamenting the token fines of 1 franc or so which the courts were frequently content to impose. These were anything but a deterrent; as Doll drily observed, 'In Bayonne, a manufacturer of espadrilles, condemned for the first time to a 1 franc fine, has naturally continued to take children unable to read and write. At 1 franc a time, one can permit oneself such a luxury.'[87] Similar complaints poured in from Lyons, Saint-Etienne, Lille, Dijon, Orleans, Lisieux and Nantes.[88]

In some areas, the courts did give the Inspectors a good deal of support. Blaise observed considerable disparities within his division: in 1881 he concluded that similar offences were far more severely punished in Beauvais, Péronne and Montdidier than in Rouen, Le Hâvre, Dieppe and Neufchâtel.[89] In Paris, a number of heavy sentences were recorded. During the early 1880s, for example, a glassmaker who repeatedly broke the law received a series of 1,000 franc fines; a foreman who assaulted an Inspector was sent to prison for eight days; another who attacked a female

---

84 AN, F[12] 4748 and 4755.   85 AN, F[12] 4730.

86 Ministère du Commerce, *Rapport sur l'application de la loi du 19 mai 1874 pendant l'année 1886* (Paris, 1887), p. 31.

87 AN, F[12] 4748.

88 AN, F[12] 4755, Delattre (Lyons, 15th), 2 February 1882; AN, F[12] 4761, Jacques (Lyons, 20th), 1889; AN, F[12] 4764, Gouttes (St-Etienne, 21st), 29 January 1888; AN, F[12] 4743, Delattre (Lille, 8th), 19 January 1889; AN, F[12] 4735, Boyer (Dijon, 4th), 1886; AN, F[12] 4733, Linares (Orleans, 2nd), 1881; AN, F[12] 4743, Aubert (Lisieux, 8th), 1884; AN, F[12] 4750, Landois (Nantes, 12th), 23 November 1886.

89 AN, F[12] 4740.

Inspector was fined 200 francs; and a master launderer who grossly abused a *dame inspectrice* received both the eight days in prison and a 100 franc fine.[90] Chambard in Limoges also felt by 1885 that magistrates were realizing the need for severe fines, after a long period of indulgence.[91] Elsewhere, the Inspectors risked humiliation at the hands of the legal profession. At Le Mans, the Inspector Delattre found himself out on a limb during his attempt to prosecute five manufacturers in 1885. The court first annulled 294 of the 325 charges he had laid. It then expressed its utter contempt for his prosecution of a shoe manufacturer who had failed to display a poster of the 1874 law: 'it is regrettable that the accused, whose establishment is well ordered and where children are the object of particular care and supervision, should be obliged to justify himself before the court on the reproaches directed at him, with regrettable lack of consideration, by the author of the *procès-verbal*'.[92] The sentence was two fines of 1 franc each. Detailed statistics assembled between 1875 and 1884 by Nadeau in the 6th Division provide the best overall view of sentencing policy in the courts. His seventy-four *procès-verbaux* led to seventy-one convictions: a very high rate of 96 per cent. However, two-thirds of convicted offenders received minimum fines for each offence, the average total being only 69 francs. Relatively stiff fines of 100, 150 or even 500 francs were registered from time to time, particularly after industrial accidents. More commonly, fines of 1 franc, 5 francs or 15 francs were the response to excessive working hours for young children, or negligence of the education clauses. Thus in September 1880 a cotton spinner from Fives-Lille was fined 1 franc after a girl of thirteen, who was working twelve hours a day despite being without an educational certificate, had a finger crushed by uncovered gearings.[93]

As for the Divisional Inspectors, their policy of gradual enforcement did not necessarily mean that they were allowing their class loyalties to outweigh their duty to protect children.[94] They were keenly aware that there were too many workshops in the country for a close surveillance to be possible. In 1884, they and their subordinates visited 48,000 firms, with 200,375 children and *filles mineures*. The following year, with the number of Inspectors increased from fifteen to twenty-one, the respective

---

[90] AN, F^{12} 4730.   [91] AN, F^{12} 4754.

[92] AN, F^{12} 4773^B, extract from the *Gazette des Tribuneaux*, 19 July 1885.

[93] AN, F^{12} 4739. See A. E. Peacock, 'The Successful Prosecution of the Factory Acts, 1833–55', *Economic History Review*, 2nd ser., 37 (1984), 197–210; and P. W. J. Bartrip, 'Success or Failure? The Prosecution of the Early Factory Acts', *Economic History Review*, 2nd ser., 38 (1985), 423–7.

[94] For discussion of this strategy of 'negotiated compliance' in Britain, see Bartrip and Fenn, 'The Conventionalization of Factory Crime', 178–85; and *idem*, 'The Evolution of Regulatory Style', *passim*.

figures rose to 60,800 and 240,778.[95] In these circumstances, and indeed even with many more Inspectors, the law simply could not be applied without the goodwill of the majority of employers. It was for this reason that the Inspectors relied heavily on moral persuasion, trying to avoid stirring up unnecessary resistance by brusque action. Delaissement, in Toulouse, accepted that the number of industrialists who would obey the law spontaneously was very limited, but he was convinced that the rest could be led into compliance. He therefore appealed to the good side of human nature, on the assumption that 'things are only done well when they are done voluntarily'.[96] Doll preferred an appeal to the self-interest of employers: lectures which showed that 'the more they have intelligent and educated workers, the more their industrial production will increase', were, in his view, far more effective than prosecutions.[97] The latter, being costly in time and uncertain in outcome, were held in reserve for use against serious opposition. And there was always the hope that the occasional example of a heavy fine, or even the humiliation of a big industrialist by an appearance in court, would have a salutory effect in a particular locality.[98]

It follows that a middle-class conspiracy to emasculate factory legislation, along the lines perceived by Marx in relation to the first British Factory Acts, was out of the question by the 1870s. Too much pressure for change had built up both inside and outside the manufacturing sector to allow complete neglect of the enforcement procedures. A professional Factory Inspectorate was in place, and its independence of the industrial interest was never called into question. Nonetheless, unlike thieves and pilferers, employers breaking the 1874 law did not have to face the police, and they were given a great deal of latitude by the administration as they tried to come to terms with its requirements. Abuses of child labour were proscribed by the law, yet there is a suspicion that much of the population did not consider, say, the employment of illiterate fifteen-year-olds for twelve hours a day, as 'really' criminal behaviour.[99] This ambiguous attitude can partly be explained by the nature of social legislation. The State was after all attempting to modify practices that had long been accepted as normal. There were also the costs of the law to be set against the benefits of protecting children. The legitimate anxieties of industrialists over the competitiveness of their enterprises, and of families over their incomes, were taken into account, even if they were not ultimately admissible.

95 Ministère du Commerce, *Rapport sur l'application de la loi du 19 mai 1874 pendant l'année 1885* (Paris, 1886), pp. 30–1.
96 AN, F¹² 4750, Delaissement (Toulouse, 12th), 15 March 1877.
97 AN, F¹² 4736, Doll (Rheims, 5th), 1876.
98 See, for example, AN, F¹² 4743, Aubert (Lisieux, 8th), 1876; AN, F¹² 4752, Estelle (Nîmes, 13th), 22 December 1876.
99 See Carson, 'White-Collar Crime', 384–5.

••

Chapter 11

The curbing of child labour in industry, 1874–92

Our final task is to examine the impact of factory legislation on the evolution of child labour practices during the last quarter of the nineteenth century. With the 1874 law at last providing for a reasonably effective inspection service, the stage was set for a serious confrontation between the State and employers who resisted or ignored the reform movement. A number of important questions arise for the historian: How did the laws making primary education free and compulsory affect child labour? Which sections of the 1874 law provoked the most hostility? Were large-scale enterprises more amenable to pressure from Factory Inspectors than small ones? And what was the overall position when the 1874 law was superseded by new factory legislation in 1892? Fortunately, the documentation available to help provide some answers is abundant. All of the quarterly and annual reports drawn up by the Divisional Inspectors for the Minister of Commerce have survived in the national archives.[1] Although unlikely to provide a full account of events, being vulnerable to the widespread fraud committed in the workshops, this source does leave us with a mass of detail on the implementation of the law. It can be complemented by the findings of various Enquiries into the condition of the proletariat during the 1870s and 1880s, and by the occasional working-class autobiography.

School versus work

The triumphant consolidation of the primary school system during the early years of the Third Republic was the major force undermining the employment of child labour in industry at this late stage in the reform campaign. Persuading the mass of the population to attend school was, as we have already seen, a protracted process. By the late 1870s, few children in France escaped the classroom entirely. Jules Ferry estimated in 1881

[1] AN, F^{12} 4730–64.

that over 600,000 young people aged between six and thirteen were not attending school, but many of these were probably eleven- or twelve-year-olds who had left early. The *loi Duruy* of 1867 had given a considerable boost to the schooling of the poor, by helping the municipalities finance free places. From the position in 1837, when less than one third of primary school children had been admitted free, the proportion rose to 57 per cent in 1876–1877. The rôle of the *lois scolaires* of the 1880s was therefore less to round up new recruits for the education system, and more to encourage a longer and more regular period on the school benches.[2] The result was that time available for work during childhood became increasingly compressed. Children might continue to help their parents in a family enterprise, or earn a little pocket money with casual work from time to time, but it was the school that loomed ever larger in their daily lives.[3] After the 1882 *loi Ferry*, a number of reports from the Divisional Labour Inspectors show that thirteen was beginning to be accepted as the normal age at which children should start work.[4]

The 1874 law made its own contribution to the schooling of the people. The aim of securing part-time education for all working children under the age of twelve, and for those aged twelve to fifteen whose primary instruction was incomplete, met with the approval of many industrialists. The larger ones in particular were well placed to comply with the law, for they were in a position to establish their own factory schools. These institutions could provide a convenient solution to the various problems encountered by industry, such as harmonizing work schedules with a school timetable, moving large numbers of children to and from their classes or even finding a school near enough to the workshops. Successful examples can be traced back to earlier periods in the nineteenth century. The Schneiders first set up a primary school and an *école supérieure* for their employees at Le Creusot in 1837. The curriculum was more extensive than that laid down for State schools at this period, comprising the three Rs, grammar, geometry, drawing, surveying, history and geography. By 1873 the original establishment had blossomed forth into four separate schools and one advanced class, with a total of over 2,000 pupils.

---

[2] Ministère de l'Instruction Publique et des Beaux-Arts, *Statistique de l'enseignement primaire*, vol. 2, pp. cx–cxi, cxxiii; Maurice Gontard, *L'Œuvre scolaire de la Troisième République* (Toulouse, 1965), pp. 88, 200; Prost, *Histoire de l'enseignement*, pp. 91–102.

[3] A handloom weaver from Prétot-Vicquemare (Seine-Inférieure), for example, informed a Parliamentary Enquiry of 1882 that children worked three to four hours a day when they went to school: AN, C 3370[3]. On casual work for young children in Paris during the 1890s, see Untrau, 'J'avais dix ans', 105–16.

[4] See, for example, AN, F[12] 4730, Laporte (Seine 1st), 21 December 1884; and AN, F[12] 4742, Aubert (Lisieux, 8th), 28 March 1884; Ministère du Commerce, *Rapport sur l'application de la loi du 19 mai 1874 pendant l'année 1884* (Paris, 1885), p. 3.

Those in the *groupe spéciale* were prepared for the Ecoles des Arts et Métiers, or for a post in the company offices. The rest went into the workshops, with the best jobs being reserved for boys who had performed well at their studies.[5] The school attached to the glassworks at Baccarat dated back to 1827. The régime there was strict: all children under the age of twelve were expected to attend, and in the rare cases where they missed classes, parents were seen by the management.[6] Similar ventures were to be found in the Anzin coal mining company, the spinning mill at Barentin and the Bonnet silk mill at Jujurieux, to name only the most famous.[7] The Divisional Inspectors had some success after 1874 in encouraging more of these factory schools and other special classes for working children in a particular locality. The total rose from 276 in 1875 to a peak of 714 in 1881, before a slow decline set in with compulsory schooling legislation.[8] A number of 'model' establishments were highlighted by the Inspectors, with the schools forming part of a more general paternalist régime. For example, Dechaille in Rennes was impressed by the welfare schemes in the cotton-spinning mill of a M. Gustave Denis et Fontaine Daniel (Mayenne). He found subsidised housing, a relief fund, a nursery and a well-equipped school. The industrialist, he had no hesitation in stating, was the first to profit from this 'ensemble de soins intelligents'.[9] The Inspector Aubert in his turn praised the efforts of the municipality in Louviers, which organized a series of two-hour classes for factory children. After attending some of the sessions, he reported that the behaviour of the pupils was excellent, and that many showed signs of a lively intellect.[10]

There was also a feeling among some observers that child labour legislation was giving working-class families more of an incentive to invest

5 Felix Courtois, 'Les Ecoles du Creusot, 1787–1882', *Mémoires de la société éduenne*, 21 (1893), 129–57.
6 AD Meurthe-et-Moselle, 10 M 30, letter from Mayor of Baccarat to Sub-Prefect of Lunéville, 1 December 1872; François Renaud, 'La Cristallerie de Baccarat: de ses origines à la fin du XIXᵉ siècle', unpublished thesis, Diplôme des Etudes Supérieures, University of Nancy, 1947, pp. 93–4.
7 AN, C 3019, Compagnie des Charbonnages d'Anzin (Nord), 1872; AN, C 3020, Bodin, Filateur de Lin et de Coton, Barentin (Seine-Inférieure), 1872; Turgan, *Les Grandes Usines*, vol. 7, p. 221.
8 Ministère du Commerce, *Rapport sur l'application de la loi du 19 mai 1874 pendant l'année 1884* (Paris, 1885), p. 12.
9 AN, F¹² 4744, Dechaille (Rennes, 9ᵗʰ), 27 January 1877.
10 AN, F¹² 4742, Aubert (Lisieux, 8ᵗʰ), 3 January 1878. Other favourable assessments of the instruction given in factory schools or special classes can be found in AN, F¹² 4733, Linares (Orleans, 2ⁿᵈ), 6 February 1882; AN, F¹² 4734, Villenaut (Nevers, 3ʳᵈ), 15 December 1877; AN, F¹² 4735, Plassiard (Nancy, 4ᵗʰ), 25 May 1876, and Durassier (Dijon, 4ᵗʰ), 7 February 1886; AN, F¹² 4740, Blaise (Rouen, 7ᵗʰ), 1880; AN, F¹² 4742, Aubert (Lisieux, 8ᵗʰ), 31 December 1875; AN, F¹² 4748, Aubert (Lisieux, 11ᵗʰ), 31 December 1885.

time in primary education. During the 1880s, the President of the Local Commission at Raon-l'Etape, in the Vosges, proclaimed enthusiastically:

Far from being an obstacle to instruction, the presence of these factories in the region only serves to increase the pressure on families to send their children to school. From the moment employers only admit children with a certificate, regular attendance at class becomes a question of self-interest for the parents, and obedience to the law a new necessity. This requirement from industrialists has the further advantage of arousing competition within the school itself. Obliged to produce proof of instruction before they can enter the factory, children are no longer content with the ordinary certificate, countersigned by the Mayor. Instead, they aspire to the *certificat d'études*, which is obtained by public examination, and which gives them a stronger position in the eyes of the employer.[11]

However, statistics drawn up by the Divisonal Inspectors reveal the limits to this new-found confidence in formal education. In 1886, across the country as a whole, two-thirds of young people aged twelve to fifteen, protected by the law, had the certificate of primary instruction (as opposed to the more demanding *certificat d'études primaires*). Of the remainder, approximately one half was attending school part time, whilst the other half was not. In a number of industrial departments, the school system was well entrenched among working children – or at least among those covered by the Inspectors. The Rhône, the Loire, the Seine-Inférieure, the Oise and the Ardèche all had exceptionally high propor-tions of young people with a certificate, and a correspondingly low proportion deprived of schooling. The Aube, the Marne, the Eure, the Drôme and the Vaucluse also appeared to be having some success in providing school places for children, even if their record on certificates was poor. On the other side of the coin, there were whole tracts of the country where the schools left little imprint. The west, predictably, emerged as an area where only a small minority of children in industry had a certificate, and where the rest had only a slim chance of continuing with their schooling. A similar pattern was to be found in various departments of the centre and south-west, notably the Haute-Vienne, Vienne, Charente, Charente-Inférieure, Dordogne and Lot. Then there was the Nord, which emerged as an area still struggling to accommodate its huge contingent of child workers: less than half of them had their certificates and another quarter, 4,129 strong in number, did not attend school.[12]

---

11 AD Vosges, M 287, letter from Dufour, President of the Second Commission to Sub-Prefect of St-Dié, 28 December 1883. See also AN, F[12] 4735, Plassiard (Nancy, 4th), 31 January 1879; AN, F[12] 4750, Delaissement (Toulouse, 12th), 10 January 1879, AN, F[12] 4766, Villenaut (Dijon, 3rd), 27 February 1877; AD Meurthe-et-Moselle, 9 M 35 letter from Delaissement to Prefect of Marne, 10 March 1888.
12 Ministère du Commerce, *Rapport sur l'application de la loi du 19 mai 1874 pendant l'année 1886* (Paris, 1887), *passim*. These figures provide only a broad indication of

The old obstacles to mass schooling had not entirely disappeared from the industrial regions by the 1870s and 1880s: a shortage of school places, poverty and pressure from the workplace. In 1879, Nadeau admitted that the *écoles communales* in the Nord were unable to accommodate all of the children under twelve who presented themselves, and so, in the more populous areas, young people of thirteen to fifteen were automatically turned away. From Toulouse, Delaissement stressed the problems of distance between schools and workshops, whilst in 1882 the glass workers of Lyons complained that although there were plenty of schools nearby, their children did not have time to attend them.[13] A similarly bleak outlook can be glimpsed from official correspondence in the Meuse. During the early 1880s, a manufacturer of lapis lazuli wrote, in an apparently reasonable tone, to ask the Divisional Inspector whether it was worth spending money on the education of three child employees, given their general lack of progress. 'They make no real effort to profit from the lessons given', he asserted, and the only alternative he could envisage was sending them off to a life of begging and vagabondage. A few years later the Inspector was warned that a certain apprentice girl of thirteen in Verdun rarely went to school. Her employer was allegedly not obstinately resisting the law, but 'suffered' to see any girl losing two hours of work every day. A letter from the woman in question confirmed this assessment for she wrote: 'The young girl has not attended the Congregational School for two months. To begin with she was ill, then we had a heavy work load. We have consulted the schoolmistress, who tells us that the progress of the child was almost non-existent, given her limited memory.'[14] In Bordeaux, the rope-makers took a more aggressive stance when required to fall into line with the law. The Inspector, Doll, found himself the centre of unwelcome attention when he visited Rousseau, the most prominent of the *cordiers*:

For a quarter of an hour, I could not make myself heard, as M. Rousseau held the floor: 'The Inspector is nothing but a bad citizen, who wants the children to attend school, without worrying about whether they eat or not; M. Doll lunches and dines every day, but the children he exploits do not always get a square meal. And we will see whether an Inspector can penetrate the workshops at any time' – as for Rousseau himself, he would not give a centime for the instruction of his young apprentices, etc. etc.[15]

reality for they were liable to fluctuate wildly according to the findings of the Inspectors in any given year. They were also vulnerable to the deceptions mentioned below, pp. 292–4.

[13] AN, F^{12} 4765, Nadeau (Lille, 6th), 3 November 1879; AN, F^{12} 4750, Delaissement (Toulouse, 12th), 8 March 1876; AN, C 3369^{1}, 100e Société de Secours Mutuels de Lyon, Verriers et Tailleurs de Cristaux, 1882.

[14] AD Meurthe-et-Moselle, 10 M 12, letter from Deschamps to Divisional Inspector, 31 October 1881, letters from B. Frinon, 7 March 1889, and Mlle Don, 12 March 1889, to Divisional Inspector.

[15] AN, F^{12} 4748, Doll (Bordeaux, 11th), 5 January 1880.

Even schoolteachers were sometimes reluctant to admit factory children to their classes. There were reports from Normandy that *instituteurs* in the *écoles communales* resented the daily intrusion of an uncouth horde from the mills. Dressed in tatters, reeking of machine oil, and full of obscenities, they were difficult to discipline, let alone teach. 'Respectable' parents opposed the contamination of their offspring by such undesirables, hence the temptation to refuse admission to working children, or to discharge them as soon as possible.[16]

More pernicious for the Inspectors was the potential for manipulating the institution of the law: a young person holding a certificate of instruction might be illiterate, and a pupil at a factory school starved of teaching. A circular from the Minister of Public Instruction in 1875 stipulated that certificates should only be given after a serious examination, when the pupil could show proof of his or her elementary instruction.[17] This was taken to mean competence in reading, writing, elementary arithmetic and the metric system. Yet the wording of some certificates revealed simple ignorance of these requirements. In 1880, the Divisional Inspector at Orleans complained of certificates stating that children had spent four or five years at school and could read and write a little, or even that they had not managed to learn anything. Later in the decade, Delattre sent in two certificates from the Rennes area, worded as follows:

S.C.J.M.   *St Brienne, 1 March 1884*
Marie Louise Huet remained at the Sacre Cœur School for five years. She is a good child.

      H. Corbin
      R^{se} du S.C.

I certify that Yvonne Laurent attended classes at La Providence for several years. During the short time that she was in my class, her work and her conduct left nothing to be desired.

      Mère St Yves,
      10 August 1883.[18]

Other certificates were issued too easily. For example Chépié, the Departmental Inspector for the Rhône, exposed the false assessment on a certificate issued to an eleven-year-old in Lyons. The boy had supposedly

---

16 AN, F^{12} 4741, Colombier (Rouen, 7th), 10 July 1875; AN, F^{12} 4743, Aubert (Lisieux, 8th), 31 December 1882; AN, F^{12} 4747, Blaise (Rouen, 10th), 10 July 1887; AN, F^{12} 4765, Blaise (Rouen, 7th), 29 June 1880.

17 AN, F^{12} 4765.

18 AN, F^{12} 4733, Linares (Orleans, 2nd), January 1880; AN, F^{12} 4744, Delattre (Nantes, 9th), 1884. See also AN, F^{12} 4746, Blaise (Limoges, 10th), 1 February 1876; AN, F^{12} 4755, Delattre (Lyons, 15th), 21 February 1883; AN, F^{12} 4765, Blaise (Rouen, 7th), 10 April 1882.

mastered the three Rs before starting work with a ropemaker. Investigation by the Inspector suggested that the young lad had barely started to learn to read, write and calculate, and that he was receiving no encouragement from his parents to attend school. The Inspector from the Academy at Lyons felt bound to admit that the 1874 law had been broken.[19] The background to such lapses is not difficult to perceive. Colombier observed from Rouen in 1878:

Three years' experience has taught me that, pressured no doubt by parents, eager to be rid of such turbulent and undisciplined children as soon as possible, and yielding perhaps to the influence of a manufacturer with whom it was in his interest to be tactful, the teacher all too easily grants a certificate to children who do not merit one.[20]

Needless to say, neither the Inspectors nor anyone else was in a position to determine the extent of this tacit conspiracy to produce 'certificates of ignorance'.[21] All that could be done was to issue a series of circulars from the Ministry of Public Instruction reminding teachers of their duties and the formalities they were obliged to follow.[22]

The realization that factory schools could be used to elude rather than obey the 1874 law only came gradually to the Inspectorate. During the 1870s, private schools owned and run by industrialists were generally welcomed, and as we have seen there were plenty of examples that operated within the spirit of the law. But after 1882 in particular, disillusionment set in as the scope for abuse became clearer. Since the employer was in complete control of his own establishment, it was always possible for him to shorten or interrupt classes, and to skimp on teaching staff and materials. Delattre was a Divisional Inspector who viewed the *écoles de fabrique* with a notably jaundiced eye. He went as far as to assert in 1885 that during his visits to 500 firms in the Nord, he had not seen one single child in a school. When he made an inspection in the morning, school was supposedly held in the afternoon; but when he appeared in the afternoon, school was always in the morning. Tables and benches in the classrooms were frequently covered with a thick layer of dust, or used exclusively for meal breaks. And where classes were held, especially in the evenings, the familiar problem of children being too tired to benefit from

---

[19] AD Rhône, 10 M, letters from Chépié to Prefect, 22 July 1882, Commissaire de Police to Secrétaire Générale pour la Police à Lyon, 3 August 1882, and Inspecteur d'Académie de Lyon to Prefect, 10 August 1882. The same abuse is reported in AN, F[12] 4733, Linares (Orleans, 2nd), March 1881; AN, F[12] 4752, Estelle (Nîmes, 13th), 31 January 1878 and 10 January 1880; AN, F[12] 4765, Colombier (Rouen, 7th), 19 June 1878.

[20] AN, F[12] 4764, Colombier (Rouen, 7th), 19 June 1878.

[21] *Ibid.*, Blaise (Rouen, 7th), 10 April 1882.

[22] *Ibid.*, circulars of 20 February 1877 and 20 May 1882.

them re-appeared.[23] Other Inspectors provided their own criticisms. Gouttes, at Saint-Etienne, reported a suspiciously large number of schools on holiday when he visited, and a common failure to produce exercise and reading books for the pupils. He also noted the tendency to slot classes into rest periods, so that children could work a full day.[24] The Local Commission for Neuilly, on the outskirts of Paris, was no less sceptical:

All the big glassworks have a school. In some they frankly admit that it is useless, that it is never attended. In others, we are shown tables covered in dust, and handed old stocks of powdery exercise books: there is writing and sums; they are shown triumphantly to visitors, with a 'There you are!' There is no name or date, but appearances are safeguarded.[25]

Finally, Blaise in Rouen regretted the use of clerks instead of proper teachers to run the classes, these employees being more attentive to the financial interests of their bosses than the education of the children. There were indeed several reports of unqualified, retired or incompetent teachers ending up in factory schools, for it was difficult to recruit an *instituteur breveté* into a position that carried no exemption from military service or entitlement to a State pension.[26]

The school and the working-class child

The impression remains that the school system had more success in capturing the bodies than the souls of working-class children. Evasion of the 1882 law obstinately persisted during the late nineteenth and early twentieth centuries. In the towns the drift to regular attendance at primary school was irresistible, but a wholehearted commitment to the principle of an extended formal education during childhood proved more difficult to achieve. This was hardly surprising when the schools tended to restrict themselves to a narrowly academic curriculum, accompanied by a heavy-handed dose of moral and civic education.[27] The links between the schools and the world of industry were almost non-existent. There was the occasional example of a 'school in the workshops', as at Le Creusot,

---

23 AN, F[12] 4743, Delattre (Lille, 8th), May 1881 and January 1886; and AN, F[12] 4766, special report on private industrial schools, 31 January 1888; see also his comments from the west, in AN, F[12] 4745, Delattre (Nantes, 9th), 20 October 1884 and April 1885.

24 AN, F[12] 4764, Gouttes (St-Etienne, 21st), 8 January 1887 and 29 January 1888.

25 AN, F[12] 4731.

26 AN, F[12] 4765, Blaise (Rouen, 7th), 27 September 1882. A series of reports and enquiries concerning factory schools can be found under this and the *cote* that follows it: AN, F[12] 4765, application of the 1874 law, articles 8 and 9, 1874–93; and AN, F[12] 4766, private industrial schools, 1877–97.

27 See the chapter entitled 'Schools for the Republic' in Sanford Elwitt, *The Making of the Third Republic* (Baton Rouge, 1975), pp. 170–229.

where teaching was related directly to the needs of manufacturing. Parents and children could then presumably sense a progression from theoretical studies, in such disciplines as maths and technical drawing, to vocational training in the workshops. But this was the exception rather than the rule in the *écoles de fabrique*. The alternative of the 'workshop in the school' also failed to take off. The Third Republic did make an effort to ensure that children left school with some initiation into manual work. The 1882 law required primary schools to teach 'The elements of natural, physical and mathematical sciences, their application to agriculture, hygiene, the industrial arts, manual work, and the use of the tools of the principal trades.' Paul Bert, as Minister of Public Instruction, explained quite reasonably that the aim was not to train children for a particular trade, but to make them aware of the practical dimension to scientific teaching. This initiative was successfully followed up in Paris, where sixty-eight schools had their own workshops in 1883, but in the provinces it came to nothing.[28] Other initiatives to make teaching more interesting included 'lessons about things', with visits to farms and factories, and examination of rocks and plants, and also a greater interest in stimulating the powers of reasoning and observation of children. However, these had to struggle against the dead weight of tradition, which relied on learning by heart, and emphasized basics such as grammar and arithmetic, necessary to pass the *certificat d'études*.[29] Much of course depended on the teacher. If schooling was a pleasant interlude in a hard life for some children,[30] others found it an arid experience, which, basic literacy and numeracy apart, was irrelevant to their environment.

Children attending school part-time under the aegis of the 1874 law were particularly poorly served. A circular of 20 February 1877 from the Minister of Public Institution made explicit the limitation of their curriculum to the three Rs, the metric system and religious instruction.[31] Mastery of these elements was not always assured. Doll, for example, complained of children from a cotton-spinning mill in Troyes whom he had known for three years and who 'knew absolutely nothing': two hours per day in a Christian Brothers school had proved entirely fruitless.[32] Even where children were gaining their *certificats d'instruction*, it was not necessarily anticipated that much had been achieved. All that the Divisional Inspector

---

[28] Guinot, *Formation professionnelle*, pp. 146–8; Bertrand Gille, 'Instruction et développement economique en France au XIXe siècle', *Annales cisalpines d'histoire sociale*, series 1, no. 2 (1971), 95–101.

[29] Gildea, *Education in Provincial France*, pp. 260–4; Jacques Gavoille, *L'Ecole publique dans le département du Doubs, 1870–1914* (Paris, 1981), pp. 245–6, 266–8.

[30] See, for example, Georges Dumoulin, *Carnets de route* (Lille, 1937), pp. 18–26; and Jacques Caroux-Destray, *Un couple ouvrier traditionnel* (Paris, 1974), pp. 53–5.

[31] AN, F^{12} 4765.   [32] AN, F^{12} 4736, Doll (Rheims, 5th), 22 September 1875.

Linares could come up with was, 'It is always something to have been to school, where one learns to obey the law, know the rules, and hear duty and physical and moral order spoken of, instead of turning only to vagabondage.'[33] To emphasize the low priority given to formal education under the 1874 law, after 1882 children who had acquired their *certificat d'études primaires* at the age of twelve were dispensed from the obligation to attend school. In other words, the more academically successful were given the dubious privilege of leaving school a year before the statutory norm.[34]

Children who pursued a full-time education before starting work had a more varied curriculum, including some history, geography and science. Yet even here there is evidence of resentment and alienation. The 'Enquête Spuller' opened a can of worms during the 1880s when it invited comments from workers on their education. A silk weaver from Lyons mentioned that 'to his great regret' he had attended a Christian Brothers school until the age of nine. A wool spinner from Saint Aubin (Seine-Inférieure) described education in his milieu as limited to reading, writing and 'very little else'. And from Oissel, also in Normandy, a representative of the cotton-spinning industry reported that the operatives attended primary school, though many did not profit much from it.[35] The Enquiry made it clear that in the textile areas, most workers were thought to be able to read and write, but few had a *certificat d'études* when they left school. The memoirs of René Michaud, recalling a childhood in Paris on the eve of the First World War, laid stress on a growing impatience with school as the time for an apprenticeship drew nigh. At the age of twelve, he felt humiliated when parked 'like some brat in a nursery'. Playing truant and escaping from the police was an early affirmation of independence. His widowed mother was not supportive, for she had more pressing concerns than academic qualifications like the *certificat d'études*:

For what was the interest in possessing this 'parchment'? She did not have one, and nor did most of those around her, and they were working. She could not understand the importance my schoolmaster attached to it, because in any event her son would be a worker: what she expected from me was the pay packet which would improve the family's daily fare.[36]

---

[33] AN, F[12] 4733, Linares (Orleans, 2nd), 29 January 1879.

[34] This issue caused dissension between the Minister of Instruction and the Commission Supérieure. The former assumed that the 1882 law abrogated the 1874 law as far as education was concerned, whilst the latter gave priority to child labour legislation. Eventually it was agreed that children of twelve with the *certificat d'études* could work full time: AN, F[12] 4765.

[35] AN, C 3369[3], 'Tisseurs d'étoffe de soie', Lyons; and AN, C 3370[3], Seine-Inférieure.

[36] René Michaud, pp. 52–3. The same attitude is documented in Caroux-Destray, *Un couple ouvrier*, p. 55.

His failure cost him a job as a printer, but he took his relegation to employment with a box manufacturer in good heart: working and earning were after all a sort of liberation.[37] The inhabitants of Belleville, a working-class quarter on the northern edge of Paris, also presented a turbulent image of life in and around the schools that had little in common with the model of civic virtue proposed by the Third Republic. For a young boy, entering the school system meant contact with older youths taking the *certif*. This opened a whole new world of smoking in the streets, brawling and petty theft, inspired no doubt by the legendary street gangs of the city, the 'Apaches'. And if full-time work was out of the question, except in the cases where parents were prepared to defy the law, there was every incentive to run errands for shopkeepers as a way of making a little pocket money.[38]

A cursory academic education in the primary schools might have been more palatable if specialized institutions for further vocational training had been developed.[39] Experiments in this field can be traced back to the 1820s, and they gained momentum from the 1870s as the crisis of the old apprenticeship system continued apace. Apprenticeship schools attempted a more methodical and reasoned approach to training the young, instead of the haphazard accumulation of skills beside a seasoned craftsman. The school attached to the Chaix printing works was one such, founded in 1862. It provided a four-year course for young people who had completed their primary instruction. Subjects with which a printer needed some acquaintance were taught, such as history, geography and foreign languages, and there was in addition practical instruction from foremen in the works. Other examples included a Municipal School of Watchmaking

---

[37] Other autobiographies are no less revealing. Jeanne Bouvier observed that after her eight months in school, 'The baggage of knowledge that I carried off, although thin, was sufficient for me to enter the factory immediately.' *Mes mémoires*, p. 55. Jean Guéhenno remembered a yawning gap between the life portrayed in his school books and the life going on around him in Fougères: *Changer la vie* (Paris, 1961), p. 133. And Marc Bernard stressed the rowdiness of many of his classes in Nîmes, plus the alternating spells of rage and gaiety which gripped one of his teachers, a de-frocked priest; *As Little Children* (London, 1949), pp. 159–61, 193.

[38] Untrau, 'J'avais dix ans', *passim*. See also Alain Cottereau, 'Les Jeunes contre le boulot: une histoire vieille comme le capitalisme industriel', *Autrement*, 21 (1979), 197–206; Carter Jefferson, 'Worker Education in England and France, 1800–1914', *Comparative Studies in Society and History*, 6 (1964), 345–66; Michelle Perrot, 'Dans la France de la Belle Epoque: "Les Apaches", premières bandes de jeunes', in special issue of *Cahiers Jussieu: Les Marginaux et les exclus dans l'histoire* (1978), pp. 387–407; Gerard Jacquemet, 'Belleville ouvrier à la Belle Epoque', *Le Mouvement social*, 118 (1982), 61–77; Lenard R. Berlanstein, *The Working People of Paris, 1871–1914* (Baltimore, 1974), pp. 146–7; and Faure, 'Enfance ouvrière', 13–35.

[39] This paragraph is indebted to Guinot, *Formation professionnelle*, pp. 129–31, 149–52, 165; and I. Christin, 'L'Enseignement technique', in Pierre Chevallier (ed.), *La Scolarisation en France depuis un siècle* (Paris, 1974), pp. 77–114.

in Besançon, a Hosiery School in Troyes, the Elbeuf Industrial Society School of Manufacturing and a series of municipally run courses for the various luxury trades in Paris. The State took a hand in 1880, with a law on manual schools of apprenticeship. A series of what became known as Ecoles Pratiques de Commerce et d'Industrie resulted, which were designed to promote the training of skilled workers. Again, though, these promising schemes served only to point the way to what could have been achieved had politicians, employers and parents acted with more vision. A favoured minority of managers and technicians benefited, but the rank and file was neglected. An Enquiry of 1906 found that 90 per cent of the labour force left school without any technical instruction. The State, still wedded to *laissez-faire* principles, hesitated to take any bolder initiatives, whilst employers persisted in thinking that the young 'should move quickly from school to the workshop', as the *chef d'atelier* of a weaving shed put it.[40] Parents also continued to insist on earnings from an early age. In 1876 a Divisional Inspector pondered the failure of a power-loom weaving school at Saint-Quentin to attract working-class pupils. Free teaching was not enough, for parents complained that during the three-month course nothing could be earned. In the local workshops, by contrast, children were paid after a few days' work. He concluded that parents were sacrificing the education of their children to the desire for immediate earnings.[41]

The importance of the school system, then, was that it provided an acceptable alternative to child labour. The threat of widespread 'vaga-bondage' which had plagued early efforts to drive children from the workplace was thereby avoided. It also of course encouraged the move towards universal literacy, and gave children from working-class back-grounds some insight into the wider world around them. At the same time, it was only partly successful in solving a problem first perceived during the 1830s: convincing a large section of the industrial population that a long period of formal education was both necessary and useful. The *certificat d'études* formalized the long-standing division between *le bon ouvrier* and the 'donkey'. The former were skilled, relatively well-off and passionately involved in industry. The latter, massed in their big battalions, were destined to be herded into dead-end jobs in industry and the service sector. Strength or stamina rather than skill was the requirement for their work, and the atmosphere surrounding them at home and at work was scarcely conducive to intellectual enquiry. Doubtless this division was partly inherent to industrial society with its demand for a cadre of technicians and skilled workers, and a proletariat of machine minders and general

---

[40] AN, C 3369[1], 'Chef d'atelier de tissage mécanique velours et pluches', L'Abresle (Rhône).
[41] AN, F[12] 4736, Doll (Rheims, 5th), 8 November 1876.

labourers. However, J. P. Guinot is persuasive in arguing that more could have been done to upgrade the skills of the labour force, encourage a more positive attitude to work among machine operatives and enrich the lives of the working class. As evidence, he cites the ground lost by the French luxury trades to foreign competition around the turn of the century. He also points to the short-sightedness of parents whose materialism caused them to neglect the future benefits of investing in education and vocational training. Decisions that might be excusable on grounds of poverty during the 1840s were not necessarily so in 1900, given the general rise in living standards.[42]

Health and safety at work

The 1874 law made a bold attempt to prevent children being employed on work which was dangerous, beyond their strength or pernicious for their health. Article 13 established a provisional list of industries from which children under sixteen should be excluded, and this was quickly followed by a more comprehensive classification in the *règlement d'administration publique* of 14 May 1875. Most of the industries concerned had never employed many children, but henceforth it was formally laid down that the young should not work with a whole range of explosives, corrosives and poisons. Article 14 of the law required workshops to be kept clean and well ventilated, and all moving parts of machinery were to be covered during normal working. The *règlement* of 13 May 1875 was more specific: children were banned from greasing or cleaning machinery that had not been switched off, from pushing timber towards a circular saw, from using cutting machinery, from stirring molten glass (under the age of fourteen) and from operating steam cocks. Limits were also set to the loads they could carry, and they were given some protection from exploitation as sources of energy. In no circumstances could they be employed on pedal-operated machines or on the turning of horizontal wheels. Otherwise, with vertically-operated wheels, for example, they were allowed a maximum of half a day's work divided by at least one hour of rest. Finally, a special section on *travaux souterrains* prohibited children under twelve, and all females, from going down into mines and quarries. A *règlement* of 12 May 1875 went on to ban face-work for boys aged twelve to sixteen, limiting them to supporting rôles with wagons and ventilation systems. This was all well and good. But the problem remained

---

[42] Guinot, *Formation professionelle*, pp. 171–2. Cf. Faure, 'Enfance ouvrière', 34, which argues that many working-class families in Paris had only recently arrived in the city, and had little in the way of skills to pass on to their children. He suggests that a secure employment offered more for the future than an educational qualification.

for Inspectors that, even in the late nineteenth century, most branches of industry were quite unable to provide secure, hygienic conditions for labour.

Reports from the Divisional Inspectors during the 1870s and 1880s showed that conditions in the workshops had not changed radically since the mid-nineteenth century. There was the same recognition that large, purpose-built factories were better to work in than small, improvised ones. There were the familiar problems of dust, dampness and high temperatures in the textile mills. And in the domestic industries, the need to use one confined space as workshop, kitchen and bedroom continued to produce its own form of squalor. Delattre, in Lille, was appalled that young people could be permitted to work for twelve hours in the over-heated, foul atmosphere of a glassworks or a spinning mill. Blaise wrote indignantly from Rouen of children imprisoned in the hot, dusty environment of a cotton mill, when the air could only be changed gradually for fear of ruining the yarns. In similar vein, Aubert described childen from the spinning and weaving industries of lower Normandy as small, pale and spindly, though he was inclined to blame poor housing as much as time spent in the mills.[43] A new twist to old problems emerged in Paris with the *loueurs de force*: entrepreneurs who sub-divided their factories into a series of small workshops, each with its individual power source. A special report drawn up for the Minister of Commerce in 1878 stressed the difficulty of supervising child labour in these establishments when so many of the tenants only occupied them for a few days at a time. The majority of the *ateliers* were given over to metal polishing, a job supposedly prohibited to children on account of the dust hazard. The report went on to single out the working of horn and bone for creating an exceptionally noxious atmosphere. Ten years later the Divisional Inspector drew attention to the growing use of celluloid in these workshops, for the manufacture of *articles de Paris*. A catastrophic fire in a large *usine de force motrice* exposed the dangers of working with this highly inflammable substance. The polishers were obliged to work in tiny cells with a naked gas flame for light and a cast-iron stove for heat. Yet the Inspectors were powerless to intervene, since most of the children worked beside their parents, and so fell outside the scope of the 1874 law.[44]

---

[43] AN, F¹² 4743, Delattre (Lille, 8th), 15 January 1886; AN, F¹² 4747, Blaise (Rouen, 10th), 10 July 1887; AN, F¹² 4742, Aubert (Lisieux, 8th), 5 December 1875; AN, F¹² 4748, Aubert (Lisieux, 11th), 31 December 1885.

[44] AN, F¹² 4731, 'Rapport à Monsieur le Ministre du Commerce sur la situation du travail des enfants dans les ateliers où on loue de la force motrice', 24 March 1878, by Maurice, Divisional Inspector of the Seine; AN, F¹² 4730, Laporte (Seine, 1st), 1887. See also AN, F¹² 4734, Laporte (Nevers, 3rd), 31 December 1879, for a reference to *loueurs de force motrice* in the Ain, used particularly by comb makers. The convention of excluding family workshops from the coverage of the 1874 law is discussed below, n. 101.

Industrial accidents were a further scourge for child workers that time had done little to ease. The smaller, more cramped mills in particular still bristled with uncovered gearings, belts and transmission shafts that grabbed and mutilated the unwary. Self-actors continued to crush the little *rattacheurs* who were too slow to leap out from under the *chariots*, and wagons down in the mines and quarries regularly overturned on their youthful *rouleurs*. The habit of cleaning machinery when it was still in operation proved difficult to break, for, with a piece-rate system of payment, there was money at stake. And children were, as ever, victims of their own curiosity and playfulness. Each year a number of them paid for this with their lives. Thus J. Delahousse, an eleven-year-old boy employed in a paper mill, was caught and mangled by a transmission shaft as he climbed a ladder to look out of the window. Jules Toupet, aged fifteen, tripped and fell as he ran across a sugar refinery in the Aisne, ending up in a vat of boiling liquid. And then there was Auguste Chalmandrier, who came to grief when he wandered from his machine to watch the cylinders being changed on a rolling mill. One of the men ordered him to clear off, but he evidently came back soon after. Somehow the machinery must have violently seized him, for the horrified workers suddenly realized that he was coming through the rollers. His body mightily compressed, the unfortunate youth expired a quarter of an hour later in great agony.[45]

Divisional Inspectors were hampered in their efforts to investigate mishaps by a lack of information. The 1874 law, unlike its British counterpart of 1844, did not require employers to notify the Inspectorate of an industrial accident. Indeed, there was every incentive to mount a cover-up. All too often Inspectors complained that they had only learned of an incident through newspaper reports.[46] They were also reticent in pursuing industrialists through criminal or civil law. According to Jules Perin, a lawyer attached to the Society for the Protection of Apprentices and Child Workers, a basic principle of French law was that employers were responsible for the safety of their workers. Articles 319 and 320 of the Penal Code punished as a misdemeanour any action causing involuntary injury to others. Furthermore, Articles 1382 and 1383 of the Napoleonic Code required compensation for all damage inflicted.[47] In practice, there was often no legal reckoning, the rashness and dis-

[45] AN, F¹² 4739, Nadeau (Lille, 6ᵗʰ), 31 December 1883; AN, F¹² 4740, Nadeau (St-Quentin, 7ᵗʰ), 5 March 1885; AN, F¹² 4735, Boyer (Dijon, 4ᵗʰ), 1 September 1890.
[46] See, for example, AN, F¹² 4738, Nadeau (Lille, 6ᵗʰ), December 1875; AN, F¹² 4740, letter from Departmental Inspector for the Seine-Inférieure to his Divisional Inspector, 14 March 1884, and Blaise (Rouen, 7ᵗʰ), 8 March 1884. Cf. P. W. J. Bartrip and P. T. Fenn, 'The Administration of Safety: The Enforcement Policy of the Early Factory Inspectorate 1844–64', *Public Administration*, 58 (1980), 87–102.
[47] Perin, *Le Travail des enfants*, p. 12.

obedience of the victims being held to exonerate the employer from all responsibility. During the early 1880s, less than half of the accidents that came to the attention of the Divisional Inspector for the Nord and Pas-de-Calais resulted in a *procès-verbal*. In Paris, the proportion was closer to a third. The majority were blamed on the victims, the usual reasons given being infringements of safety regulations, disobedience of orders or impetuousness.[48] Few concessions were made to immaturity when Inspectors were considering the behaviour of children involved in accidents. Take the example of Eugène Thuillier, who lost part of a leg while working at the age of thirteen in an ironworks. An investigation by the Departmental Inspector for the Oise found that the boy had been working on a twelve-hour shift, from 6.00 p.m. to 6.00 a.m. His job, entirely within the law, was to manoeuvre red-hot bars of iron with a rod as they moved between the various levels of a rolling mill. The accident occurred at 11.15 p.m. The Inspector found against the victim, mercilessly noting his momentary lapse of concentration:

Thuillier was not paying attention to his work; he had even turned his back on the rolling mill while he chatted to the young Ducrotoy, his neighbour. When he spun round again, he put his foot on a white-hot bar. This wrapped itself around his left leg, and dragged him by the rotational force of the cylinders (420 r.p.m.) against the edge of the mill. The shock caused his leg to be cut off 5 centimetres above the ankle, leaving the left foot on the ground, still shod in its boot.[49]

Industrialists did sometimes volunteer to cover the medical expenses of accident victims, or to pay out a lump sum to their families. But this fell far short of the twentieth-century solution: a compulsory insurance scheme to cover all industrial accidents. A significant step in this direction had to await a law of 1898.[50]

The Inspectorate was nonetheless able to make some headway in improving this dangerous working environment for children. There is some evidence that industrialists were becoming more safety-conscious during the late nineteenth century, partly in response to the 1874 law. A number of Divisional Inspectors mentioned a willingness to improve the design and lay-out of machinery. Marteau, for example, noted from eastern France that new carding machines and self-actors had all of their moving parts covered, and that transmission shafts were being installed under floors or high up near the ceilings. Blaise was impressed by the efforts of a Society for the Prevention of Accidents in Rouen, which managed to encourage preventive measures among the bigger industrial

[48] AN, F^{12} 4739 and 4730.
[49] AN, F^{12} 4740, report from Departmental Inspector of the Oise to Divisional Inspector, 24 January 1884.
[50] Jean-Pierre Dumont, *La Sécurité sociale toujours en chantier* (Paris, 1981), p. 36.

enterprises at least. And Laporte, in Paris, assured the Minister that manufacturers were fencing in wheels, belts, gearings and so forth, though he felt bound to add that the imprudence of children often rendered such measures useless.[51] The Inspectors were seconded in their efforts by insurance companies. When an employer took out a policy to cover his workers against industrial accidents, the companies usually insisted upon a range of security measures.[52] The impact of these changes cannot be measured from the sources available. The number of accidents affecting children recorded in official statistics rose steadily, from 46 in 1876 to 212 in 1886. However, it is not unreasonable to conclude that this reflected a more effective surveillance by the Divisional Inspectorate rather than a deterioration of conditions on the shop floor.[53]

State intervention also had some influence in rescuing children from the extremes of physical exertion at work. In Paris the Divisional Inspector considered the ban on *surcharges* to be the part of the 1874 law most warmly received by the population at large. The sight of a young lad struggling under a heavy load, or sitting exhausted at the side of the road, was guaranteed to arouse general indignation to the point where the police would inevitably be called in. This 'collaboration of the crowd' produced a high number of recorded incidents in the department of the Seine: 552 in all between 1875 and 1881. In the latter year, these included three boys under twelve years of age found carrying loads between 53 and 84 pounds, and fifteen boys of fourteen to sixteen years carrying between 44 and 159 pounds. Over half of the seventy-two infringements that year resulted in legal action, and fines of up to 25 francs.[54] Elsewhere, the Inspectors intervened in mines, quarries, textile mills, rope manufactures, porcelain, glass and tileworks to prosecute employers overloading child workers.

In the mining industry, for example, the ban on underground work for young children and females was easily enforced, for the custom had long been to employ these categories of labour at the pit-heads. Indeed, during the 1870s and 1880s several Inspectors noted a drift towards fifteen or sixteen as the minimum age for work in the underground galleries.[55]

---

[51] AN, F^{12} 4736, Marteau (Nancy, 5th), 1 January 1886; AN, F^{12} 4746, Blaise (Rouen, 10th), 25 January 1886; AN, F^{12} 4730, Laporte (Seine, 1st), 1881.

[52] AN, F^{12} 4730, Laporte (Seine, 1st), 1886; AN, F^{12} 4748, Aubert (Lisieux, 11th), 31 December 1885; AN, F^{12} 4750, Landois (Nantes, 12th), 28 January 1885; AN, F^{12} 4755, Pellet (Lyons, 15th), 31 December 1884.

[53] In 1884 the Divisional Inspector in Paris was prepared to assert that the number of accidents in his area was gradually declining: AN, F^{12} 4730.

[54] AN, F^{12} 4730, Laporte (Seine, 1st), 1881.

[55] AN, F^{12} 4734, Villenaut and Pellet (Nevers, 3rd), 1876 and 1883 respectively; AN, F^{12} 4735, Plassiard (Nancy, 4th), 13 July 1875; AN, F^{12} 4755, Pellet (Lyons, 15th), 31

Occasional examples of overwork did, however, remain to be challenged. Hegelbacher claimed to have imposed an entirely new régime for children in one iron-ore mine in Languedoc:

At the Rancié mine, the weight carried by children often used to exceed the almost incredible figure of 88 pounds. Accidents were frequent, notably sprains caused by children falling in steep, uneven galleries. Today, the loads have been reduced to the regulation figures of 22 to 33 pounds, and the accidents have completely disappeared.[56]

In Limoges, famous for its fine porcelain, the Inspectors were no less optimistic. During the 1880s, they encouraged the abandonment of the old horizontal wheels on the *tours français* and the pedals on the *tours anglais*, customarily operated by children. In their place came a pedal mechanism which the potter could operate himself.[57] A further example of technical progress helping to ease the plight of children was the mechanical hoist, increasingly used in various factories towards the end of the century.[58]

When it came to encouraging hygiene in the workshops, the Inspectorate was practically impotent. Some factories did make the most of existing ventilation techniques, and were able to avoid the extremes of hot and cold temperatures. But others, probably the majority, were too old or too cramped for any real hope of improvements. And this of course includes the thousands of 'sweatshops' in the garment trades, which employed countless young women in atrocious circumstances. The occasional, marginal influence was all that was possible for the Inspectors in this sphere. The banning of children from work with noxious substances had some effect. In the china works of Bordeaux, for example, the Inspector was able to have juveniles removed from the dusty workshops which prepared the raw materials and also from the glazing shops.[59] There was the odd example of a prosecution for neglecting hygiene. Thus in 1884, a mill owner from the Ardèche was fined 5 francs for expecting his employees to work in a stifling heat, the result of refusing to open any

December 1884; AN, F[12] 4759, Pellet (Nîmes, 17th), 14 January 1886; AN, F[12] 4764, Gouttes (St-Etienne, 21st), 8 January 1886.

56   AN, F[12] 4750, Hegelbacher (Toulouse, 12th), 24 January 1882. See also AN, F[12] 4736, Delaissement (Rheims, 5th), 25 August 1880; AN, F[12] 4744 Jaraczewski (Amiens, 9th), 14 January 1888; AN, F[12] 4745, Delattre (Nantes, 9th), 14 January 1888; AN, F[12] 4745, Delattre (Nantes, 9th), April 1885; AN, F[12] 4750, Delaissement (Toulouse, 12th), 27 February 1878; AN, F[12] 4759, Pellet (Nîmes, 17th), 15 January 1887.

57   AN, F[12] 4746 Blaise (Limoges, 10th), 15 January 1878; AN, F[12] 4754, Leseur (Limoges, 14th), 17 January 1887. See also AN, F[12] 4771, memoir on porcelain manufacturing, by the owner of the Manufacture de Foëcy (Cher), 25 September 1874.

58   See, for example, AN, F[12] 4734, Pellet (Nevers, 3rd), 31 December 1882; and AN, F[12] 4748, Jacquemart (Bordeaux, 11th), 31 December 1875.

59   AN, F[12] 4748, Jacquemart (Bordeaux, 11th), 31 December 1875.

windows.[60] There was too a concerted effort by various Inspectors in southern France to make the lodgings attached to the silk mills more habitable. During the 1870s, Jeanne Bouvier had experienced at first hand the squalor of a poorly-run mill in the Drôme. The beds consisted of four planks nailed together, with a sack of wood shavings for a mattress, a meagre issue of blankets and sheets that were almost never changed. The dormitory, following the usual practice, was in the attic of the building. But in this particular case there was no proper flooring, and the roof was so low that the girls barely had enough room to sit up in their beds. Soon after this experience she moved to Vienne, and better lodgings, with good, clean beds, adequate lighting and heating during the winter months.[61] The Inspectors claimed to be nudging employers towards the latter type of régime. In 1886 Gouttes reported from Saint-Etienne that beds were being regularly powdered to get rid of vermin, sheets were being changed every two months (instead of every six), mattresses better kept than before and toilets separated more distinctly from the sleeping areas.[62]

Finally, it is worth noting that the 1874 law included a section to promote the moral welfare of child workers. Article 15 held employers responsible for morality and public decency in their workshops. This was little more than a pious hope. Most importantly, the law was quite unable to influence the major area of anxiety among reformers: the weakening of parental influence as production moved from the home to the factory. Working girls continued to have a dubious reputation in 'respectable' circles. Delaissement wrote from Toulouse in 1875 that the morality of juvenile labour left much to be desired:

I have even heard an honourable industrialist confess to me that if someone presented him with a chaste young girl, of good conduct and really worthy of interest, he would, in all conscience, have to refuse her, in order to avoid exposing her to contact with the workers. And yet his workshop is relatively well ordered.[63]

A few years earlier, in 1869, the Mayor of Colmar had gone as far as to suggest a strong overlap between the worlds of prostitution and the cotton mills. He listed 100 or so prostitutes in his town, but added another 150 or 200 factory girls, 'much more difficult to supervise', who regularly swelled their ranks.[64] Some of this, and similar talk of illicit liaisons behind machines or even in the toilets, may simply reflect over-heated middle-

[60] AN, F[12] 4753, Estelle (Nîmes, 13th), 12 October 1884.
[61] Bouvier, *Mes mémoires*, pp. 61–4.
[62] AN, F[12] 4764 Gouttes (St-Etienne, 21st), 1 July 1886. See also AN, F[12] 4752, Estelle (Nîmes, 13th), 31 January 1878.
[63] AN, F[12] 4750, Delaissement (Toulouse, 12th), 8 March 1876.
[64] AM Colmar, D2, letter from Mayor of Colmar to Prefect of Haut-Rhin, 16 March 1869 (on display in the Musée Bartholdi, Colmar, 9 September 1980).

class imaginations. But however intense their concern, Inspectors were painfully aware that irregular sexual encounters, say between a foreman and a young woman worker he was blackmailing, were necessarily infrequent and opportunistic. They therefore had scant chance of identifying the culprits.[65] And unlike security and hygiene measures, there were few precautions that could realistically be recommended. The use of nuns to supervise young girls at work was one possible solution, widely adopted in the silk mills of the Midi. But the Inspectors recognized it to be potentially oppressive, and it was only applicable to the exceptional circumstances of this 'feminine' industry. A separation of males from females in the workshops was considered alien to French customs, and so unenforceable as a general prescription. Hence the Inspectorate had to be content with such minor interventions as having the odd obscene graffiti removed from factory walls, excluding young girls in Paris from work with condoms, and dealing with a handful of rogue employers reputed to be actively 'debauching' the children in their care.[66]

Limits on working hours

Protecting children from excessively long working hours had been a crucial part of the reform campaign from the time of Jean-Jacques Bourcart and Louis Villermé onwards. The 1841 law had already tackled the problem with its system of grading working hours according to age. The 1874 law did not attempt to go much further than its predecessor in this area, maintaining the twelve-hour limit for young people of twelve to sixteen years, and reducing the maximum permitted for children under twelve from eight to six hours. As might be expected, the successes and failures of the earlier régime tended to recur during the final quarter of the nineteenth century. The long-standing drift towards a shorter working day for all types of labour, regardless of age, continued to be an encouraging development for the Inspectorate. Our study of the labour market has already shown ten or eleven hours being increasingly accepted by employers at this period. Indeed, an official Enquiry of 1891–1893, drawing data from 3,000 of the larger industrial companies in France, concluded that ten and a half hours was the national average.[67] This of course left many young people over the age of twelve, perhaps even the

---

65 Information from AN, F[12] 4735, Plassiard (Nancy, 4th), 2 April 1881, AN, F[12] 4748, Aubert (Lisieux, 11th), 31 December 1885; AN, F[12] 4750, Delaissement (Toulouse, 12th), 27 February 1878.

66 AN, F[12] 4753, Estelle (Nîmes, 13th), 14 October 1876; AN, F[12] 4730 Laporte (Seine, 1st), 1883, and 31 December 1882; AN, F[12] 4731, Maurice (Seine, 1st), 13 January 1879.

67 Office du Travail, *Salaires et durée du travail dans l'industrie française* (5 vols., Paris, 1893–7), vol. 4, Table IV, pp. 38–9. See above pp. 129–32.

majority, working comfortably within the legal limit. Villenaut, based in the Nivernais, described the twelve-hour maximum as 'so modest that it is easily observed', while Doll, when in Bordeaux, made much the same point in his own particular fashion. Betraying his northern prejudices he accused workers in the south of putting in as few hours a week as possible:

The bar is so tempting, the workshop so tiresome, that none of them works on a Sunday, to be like everyone else, nor a Monday, to avoid being taken for a clerk or a civil servant, nor a Tuesday, if they have any credit left. Serious work starts again on Wednesdays, generally for eight hours, ten at the most, never twelve. Often, when making my rounds on a Monday I have to try four or five workshops before I find anybody.[68]

On the other side of the coin, there remained two intractable problems for the Inspectorate to confront: the persistent hold of exceptionally long · working hours in certain branches of the textile industry; and the general resistance to half-time working for children under twelve or young people under fifteen whose primary education was unfinished.

Article 3 of the 1874 law stated that from the age of twelve, children 'could not be employed for more than twelve hours per day, divided by rests'. This wording gave rise to considerable confusion, and ultimately proved unsatisfactory as a measure for curbing excessive working hours. The authoritative *Practical Manual* on the law, written by Eugène Tallon in his capacity as member of the Commission Supérieure, interpreted it to mean that the rest periods had to be taken from within the twelve hours. All time spent in the workshops would therefore count towards the twelve hours, so that if a young person started work at 6.00 a.m., he or she would have to stop by 6.00 p.m.[69] Several of the Divisional Inspectors made it clear in their reports that this was their understanding of the law. However, they were not always successful in imposing it on manufacturers. The latter were inclined to argue that the law allowed twelve hours of actual work, with rest periods coming as an addition. In 1886, the Commission Supérieure felt compelled to admit that, as the law stood, this interpretation would have to be permissible. Although this ruled out the thirteen and a half hours of *travail effectif* found during the 1840s, it still left the way open for a punishingly long working day. It also created an

[68] AN, F^{12} 4734, Villenaut (Nevers, 3rd), 30 December 1876; AN, F^{12} 4748, Doll (Bordeaux, 11th), January 1855. Other references to adults and young people (over twelve) working less than twelve hours a day include: AN, F^{12} 4730, Laporte (Seine, 1st), 31 December 1881 and 1886; AN, F^{12} 4733, Linares (Orleans, 2nd), 29 January 1879; AN, F^{12} 4735, Durassier (Dijon, 4th), 7 February 1886; AN, F^{12} 4744, Durassier (Nantes, 9th), 1 February 1882; AN, F^{12} 4748, Aubert (Lisieux, 11th), 31 December 1885; AN, F^{12} 4762, Perbost (Lyons, 20th), 9 July 1892.

[69] Eugène Tallon, *Manuel pratique et commentaire de la loi du 19 mai, 1874, sur le travail des enfants et des filles mineures dans l'industrie*, 3rd edn (Paris, 1885), pp. 77–9.

unfortunate legal loophole: employers hauled before the courts could always argue that however long a child spent on the shop floor, their period of work never exceeded twelve hours.[70]

The extent of abuse is not easy to determine. Cheating was notoriously rife in this area, and working hours tended to fluctuate with the seasons, the trade cycle and, in the water-powered mills, the interruptions caused by droughts and freezing water. In the textile industry of northern and eastern France, a working day that began at 5.00 in the morning and ended at 7.00 in the evening was common: twelve hours of work, but fourteen hours in and around the workshops.[71] There were many examples of shorter working days. Calico printing remained substantially below this level, and in the Rouen area, the Divisional Inspector observed the cotton and woollen mills to be holding to ten or eleven hours a day, even as they came out of a recession during the late 1870s.[72] Yet, in some areas at least, there was always the threat of demands for even greater exertions from time to time. In 1876, manufacturers in the cotton-weaving industry of lower Normandy were rumoured to be pressing for a twelve-and-a-half-hour day, as they struggled to fulfil their orders. And in 1892, the owner of a weaving shed in the Vosges was denounced by one of his employees for a breach of the 1848 and 1874 laws. The Divisional Inspector informed his superiors:

The industrialist, wishing to make up for time lost during a water shortage, compelled his operatives to work until 10 o'clock at night. One of them, not wishing to comply with his demands, refused on the grounds of tiredness to go beyond twelve hours of work. Badly treated by her employer, she complained to the Gendarmerie, who made the necessary enquiries.[73]

The inspection service was, for the most part, reduced to a grudging acceptance of these practices. A close scrutiny of the *procès-verbaux* drawn up by Nadeau in the Nord and Pas-de-Calais between 1876 and 1884 revealed an almost total absence of prosecutions involving the working hours of children over twelve, unless they arose in connection with industrial accidents or breaches of the educational clauses. The only exceptions were from 1884, when Nadeau used both the 1848 and 1874 laws to prosecute two linen spinners for imposing a thirteen-hour day on

---

[70] Ministère du Commerce, *Rapport sur l'application de la loi du 19 mai pendant l'année 1886* (Paris, 1887), p. 12; AN, F^{12} 4742, Delattre (Lille, 8th), 12 April 1886; AN, F^{12} 4754, Leseur (Limoges, 14th), 31 January 1888.

[71] For example, AN, F^{12} 4735, Plassiard (Nancy, 4th), 30 September 1875 and 31 January 1879; AN, F^{12} 4743, Delattre (Lille, 8th), 15 January 1886; AN, F^{12} 4736, Doll (Rheims, 5th), 1875.

[72] AN, F^{12} 4740, Colombier (Rouen, 7th), 15 January 1880.

[73] AN, F^{12} 4742, Aubert (Lisieux, 8th), 28 May 1876; AN, F^{12} 4765, Chambard (Nancy, 5th), 22 December 1892.

all of their workers.[74] His successor Delattre could only recommend a change in the wording of the law. Echoing the findings of Villermé in the 1830s, he complained of twelve-year-olds who were obliged to get up at 4.00 in the morning, so that they could walk the 3 or 4 kilometres into work and who were unlikely to be home before 9.30 at night. With little time for sleep, and inadequate food and clothing, these unfortunate children became puny physical specimens, looking closer to ten than twelve years of age.[75]

This leaves the special case of the silk industry in southern France, which proved no less obstinate after 1874 than before in its defiance of Child Labour Inspectors. By the early 1870s, the *moulinages de soie* of the Vivarais, Cévennes and Dauphiné appeared to have reined back on some of their more extreme abuses. There was no more talk of fraudulent manoeuverings with the clocks, and the Mining Engineers reported a twelve-hour day rather than the thirteen current at mid-century.[76] This was the régime put forward to the 'Enquête Spuller' in 1882, with the familiar 5.00 a.m. start and 7.00 p.m. finish.[77] However, the Divisional Inspectors soon discovered that some of the old habits died hard. The source of conflict was, as before, the desire to extend working hours on weekdays. With the extra hours in hand, the young girls lodging at the mills could then stop early on Saturdays and go home for the weekend. Five days a week, the custom was to work a full thirteen hours of *travail effectif*, often starting at 4.00 or 4.30 in the morning. This was the kind of routine that Jeanne Bouvier recalled, from the time she entered a silk mill in the Drôme at the age of eleven. The year was 1876, and she was required to work from 5.00 a.m. till 8.00 p.m., with two hours off for meals: *la soupe* at 8.00 in the morning, *le dejeuner* at midday.[78] A succession of Divisional Inspectors in the south-east, to their credit, took the bull by the horns and issued numerous warnings and *procès-verbaux*. The results of their campaign were uneven. Besides the various reports indicating a reduction in hours must be set the findings of an official Enquiry mounted between 1891 and 1893. It could still point to examples of young girls from the *internats* spending up to fourteen hours a day in the mills.[79]

---

[74] The law of 16 February 1883, which increased the number of Divisional Inspectors, also required the Inspectors and the Local Commissions to enforce the law of 9 September 1848 on working hours.

[75] AN, F¹² 4739 and 4743.

[76] AD Ardèche, 15 M 4, reports from the Ingénieurs des Mines, 28 February 1870, 22 July 1871 and 12 November 1873.

[77] AN, C 3331–3.   [78] Bouvier, *Mes mémoires*, pp. 56–64.

[79] Information from AN, F¹² 4734, Laporte (Nevers, 3ʳᵈ), 31 December 1879; AN, F¹² 4752–3, Estelle (Nîmes, 13ᵗʰ), 30 September 1875, 30 January 1876, 22 December 1876, 14 January 1883; AN, F¹² 4755, Pellet (Lyons, 15ᵗʰ), 31 December 1884; AN, F¹² 4761,

At the hub of the silk industry, in Lyons, the Inspectorate struggled against even greater odds, given the huge number of workshops they had to cover. The Departmental Inspector, Chépié, observed crisply in 1880 that in silk-weaving and related industries, the law was completely disregarded.[80] The reeling and finishing workshops were particularly prone to exploiting their child workers, holding them to somewhere between twelve and fifteen hours of *travail effectif* a day. The employers claimed that a combination of low wages, frequent stoppages and the pressing demands of the merchants made it impossible for them to adhere to the law.[81] In 1891, a distressed father wrote to the police in order to denounce the conditions of employment for his child, an apprentice reeler. He complained that the master kept his charges at work from five in the morning until eleven at night, reducing them to a 'dreadful physical condition'.[82] In the same year, the Divisional Inspector prosecuted a *maîtresse dévideuse* for overworking two girls aged thirteen and fourteen years. The so-called apprentices were found to have been working from 5.00 a.m. until 10.00 p.m., with two rests: fifteen and three-quarter hours of actual work.[83] There was no suggestion that such prosecutions were doing much to encourage a general compliance with the law.

Modifying the half-time system so that children under twelve could only work six rather than eight hours per day did not make it any more palatable to the industrial population. Under the 1841 law, manufacturers had frequently complained that eight hours was more than half a day's work, making it difficult to organize two shifts of children. The new law quickly called this bluff. Even with the lower limit, there was no move towards the use of *relais*. Working-class parents for their part were equally unenthusiastic, not wishing to see a decline in the family income. The requirement after 1874 that young people aged twelve to fifteen who lacked an education certificate should also work a maximum of six hours per day aroused even greater hostility. The numbers involved were more substantial, causing employers to baulk at the prospect of losing time at work from an important section of their labour force. Inevitably, market forces pushed the majority of employers and parents alike into some form of breach with the law. How far they were prepared to go depended largely on their attitude to primary schooling. In the minority of 'model'

Barral (Grenoble, 19th), 1 October 1885; AN, F[12] 4764, Gouttes (St-Etienne, 21st), 1888; AD Ardèche, 15 M 3, report of Local Commission, *arrondissement* of Tournon, 1876, and letter from Prefect to Minister of Commerce, 5 June 1884.
[80] AD Rhône, 10 M, letter from Chépié to Delattre, 30 April 1880.
[81] AN, F[12] 4755, Delattre (Lyons, 15th), 12 February 1881 and 2 February 1882; AD Rhône, 10 M, letter from Chépié to Delattre, 1 June 1880.
[82] AD Rhône, 10 M, letter from J. Lihelmann to the Sécrétaire Général de la Police, 2 January 1891.
[83] AD Rhône, 10 M, *procès-verbal*, by Jacques, 22 May 1891, against Mme Monreynaud.

establishments, which organized their own factory school or classes in the local *école communale*, the law was scrupulously obeyed. Typical of these was the cotton and spinning mills at Gisors, in the Hon valley. It was large, with a total of 800 operatives when Aubert visited it in 1876, and it had its own qualified teacher. All of the children under twelve had two hours in class each day, and none worked over six hours.[84] More commonly, children were allowed some time off for school, but the six-hour limit went by the board. And there was always the possibility that schooling would be ignored entirely, so that children would work the same hours as adults.

The worst culprits were the glassworks and the spinning mills, both of which employed large numbers of very young children. The *verreries* were almost a law unto themselves, with their isolated rural locations, and their reputation for assembling what Inspector Doll labelled 'The most appalling collection of undisciplined good-for-nothings, drunks and idlers that it is possible to imagine.'[85] Reports from Paris, Normandy, Flanders, Lorraine, the Lyonnais and the Bordelais all mentioned children under twelve being subjected to anything between eight and twelve hours of gruelling work per day.[86] The spinning mill owners were more inclined to pay lip service to the authority of the law. But some of the Inspectors were sceptical of their intentions. Thus Delattre wrote from the Nord during the 1880s that industrialists talked of implementing a six-hour day, but he personally was convinced that they were imposing at least eight, and in the majority of cases, ten to twelve hours.[87] The Inspectorate was well aware of the strength of feeling aroused by the six-hour limit, and to begin with they were prepared to compromise. Bargains were struck, which would, for example, allow an extension of working hours in return for regular schooling. But eventually the Inspectors all took a firmer line including the

[84] AN, F12 4742, Aubert (Lisieux, 8th), 31 March 1876. Other references to the six-hour limit being adhered to can be found in AN, F12 4733, Linares (Orleans, 2nd), 4 October 1878; AN, F12 4735, Plassiard (Nancy, 4th), 31 January 1879; AN, F12 4752, Estelle (Nîmes, 13th), 16 January 1884; AN, F12 4754, Leseur (Limoges, 14th), 17 January 1887; AN, F12 4755, Gauthier (Lyons, 15th), 30 December 1876; AN, F12 4761, Barral (Grenoble, 19th), 9 January 1889.

[85] AN, F12 4736, Doll (Rheims, 5th), 1875.

[86] AN, F12 4730 Laporte (Seine, 1th), 21 December 1883; AN, F12 4733, Linares (Orleans, 2nd), 6 February 1882; AN, F12 4735, Plassiard (Nancy, 4th), 16 February 1884; AN, F12 4740–1, Colombier (Rouen, 7th), 3 January 1876 and 6 January 1879; AN, F12 4743, Aubert (Lisieux, 8th), 1876; and Jacques (Lille, 8th), 1892; AN, F12 4746, Blaise (Rouen, 10th), 25 January 1886; AN, F12 4748, Jacquemart (Bordeaux, 11th), 31 December 1875 and 6 January 1879. Glass manufacturers themselves sometimes corroborated these reports; see, for example, AN, C 3370³, Graville Ste-Honorine (Seine-Inférieure), 1882; and AD Meurthe-et-Moselle, 10 M 1, letter from L. Guernier and E. Bailly, Verrerie de Croismare, to Divisional Inspector Marteau, 1 December 1885.

[87] AN, F12 4742, Delattre (Lille, 8th), 22 October 1886. See also AN, F12 4736, Doll (Rheims, 5th), 20 April 1878.

prosecution of offenders.[88] The hours and education of young children were after all at the very heart of the reform campaign. Rarely, it seems, did this policy of harassing industrialists lead to a two-shift system. But several Inspectors claimed quite plausibly that it was encouraging them to dispense entirely with the services of very young or ill-educated children.[89]

Besides working hours, the 1874 law set out to regulate night and Sunday work for children. The policy of making the law acceptable by accommodating industrial interests was pushed to its limits here. Section II of the law began with the principle that children under the age of sixteen could not be employed at night, on Sundays or on official holidays. But this was later modified in two ways. First, periods of interrupted production could be compensated for over a limited period with night work, using children of twelve years and above. And secondly, industries using furnaces in a continuous process, such as basic metallurgy and glassmaking, were given a permanent dispensation from the general rule. These prohibitions were extended to girls aged between sixteen and twenty-one, but, in the case of night work, for their employment in factories only. This latter qualification was widely regretted by the Inspectorate. Few such girls were found working in *la grande industrie* at night, but in the small workshops of the garment trades, they were continually expected to work late when orders were pressing. The Inspectors could only sit back and describe their scandalous conditions of employment. Crowded into small, gas-lit rooms, and dosed up with frequent cups of coffee, the girls had to keep going with as little as four or five hours of sleep a night.[90] All that could be achieved was the occasional intervention with a big company. Those raised few problems. In 1876, the Anzin Mining Company and the le Creusot Ironworks were found to be employing *filles mineures* on their night shifts. Both complied with the order to change the rosters for these women over a set period.[91]

As far as children were concerned, the 1874 law could be accused of ducking out of some of the most difficult problems. By allowing the *usines à feu continu* to work young people through the night, the glassmaking

88 60 per cent of the seventy-six *procès-verbaux* drawn up by Nadeau in the 6th *circonscription* between 1875 and 1884 included charges on this count: AN, F¹² 4739.
89 AN, F¹² 4734, Villenaut (Nevers, 3ʳᵈ), 30 December 1876; AN, F¹² 4744 Durassier (Nantes, 9ᵗʰ), 1 February 1881; AN, F¹² 4748, Jacquemart (Bordeaux, 11ᵗʰ), 25 May 1877; AN, F¹² 4750, Delaissement (Toulouse, 12ᵗʰ), 10 January 1879.
90 AN, F¹² 4730, Laporte (Seine, 1ˢᵗ), 1889; AN, F¹² 4734, Fache (Nevers, 3ʳᵈ), 25 February 1886; AN, F¹² 4746, Landois (Limoges, 10ᵗʰ), 25 January 1882; AN, F¹² 3750, Landois (Nantes, 12ᵗʰ), 1888; AD Meurthe-et-Moselle, 10 M 12, letter from Departmental Inspector to Delaissement, 8 December 1882. See also Richard Waddington, *Rapport à la Chambre au nom de la Commission chargée d'examiner le projet de loi sur le travail des enfants et des femmes dans les usines et manufactures* (Paris, 1888), pp. 14–21.
91 AN, F¹² 4734, Villenaut (Nevers, 3ʳᵈ), 30 December 1876; AN, F¹² 4738, Nadeau (Lille, 6ᵗʰ), April 1876.

industry was given free rein to take a heavy toll from a substantial part of its labour force. To quote the Inspector Pellet, writing from Nevers in 1881, 'It is truly distressing to see them [children under twelve] waste away from the effects of heat and the arduous work to which they are subjected.'[92] Industries where production was largely seasonal, notably sugar refining and canning, were also given considerable latitude by the Inspectors. In Brittany, the Inspector Dechaille concluded that the local sardine canning industry would be crippled if it was deprived of the night and Sunday work of children. Bearing in mind the poverty of the region, as well as the need to process the fish as soon as it was landed, he allowed the industry to set its own work rhythm, and concentrated his efforts on promoting school for the children during the winter.[93] Where the Inspectorate did make more of an impact was in discouraging Sunday work. Tradition in the small workshops was that apprentices came in during the morning to clean up. Some of the textile mills followed suit, and called in children to help maintain their machinery and boilers. Various reports indicated some success in establishing Sunday as a day of rest – helped, it might be added, by the general decline in apprenticeship.[94]

The age of admission to the workshops

Raising the minimum working age for children proved to be a relatively straightforward matter. The 1874 law was running with the tide in this respect, for both industrialists and parents were coming round to the view that young children were more usefully occupied in the schools than in the workshops. The generous provision which allowed industries relying heavily on child labour to start their employees at ten years of age instead of twelve eased the transition. From the beginning, it was extremely rare for the Inspectorate to find a child of less than ten years of age at work. The odd case turned up from time to time in a textile mill or a glassworks during the 1870s, but there was little difficulty in persuading employers to part with them.[95] Ropemaking was an industry that relied more sys-

[92] AN, F¹² 4734, Pellet (Nevers, 3ʳᵈ), 31 December 1881.

[93] AN, F¹² 4745, Dechaille (Rennes, 9ᵗʰ), 15 September 1875. On sugar refining, see AN, F¹² 4735, Plassiard (Nancy, 4ᵗʰ), 18 January 1876; AN, F¹² 4743, Aubert (Lisieux, 8ᵗʰ), 30 December 1877; AN, F¹² 4744, Jaraczewski (Amiens, 9ᵗʰ), 22 January 1889.

[94] Information from AN, F¹² 4730, Laporte (Seine, 1ˢᵗ), 1887; AN, F¹² 4734, Villenaut and Pellet (Nevers, 3ʳᵈ), 1876 and 1882 respectively; AN, F¹² 4741, Colombier (Rouen, 7ᵗʰ), 10 July 1875; AN, F¹² 4744, Dechaille (Rennes, 9ᵗʰ), 24 July 1876.

[95] Examples from the textile industries in AN, F¹² 4736; Doll (Rheims, 5ᵗʰ), 1875; AN, F¹² 4738, Nadeau (Lille, 6ᵗʰ), April 1876; AN, F¹² 4741, Colombier (Rouen, 7ᵗʰ), 10 July 1875; AN, F¹² 4743, Aubert (Lisieux, 8ᵗʰ), 31 December 1876; AN, F¹² 4753, Estelle (Nimes, 13ᵗʰ), 19 October 1878 and 12 April 1879. For the glassworks, see AN, F¹² 4735, Plassiard (Nancy, 4ᵗʰ), 16 February 1884; AN, F¹² 4740, Colombier (Rouen, 7ᵗʰ), 6 January 1879; AN, F¹² 4748, Jacquemart (Bordeaux, 11ᵗʰ), 31 December 1875.

tematically on children under twelve, or even under ten. The Inspector Colombier found eighty such establishments at Abbeville, each employing a handful of children to turn wheels for twelve to fourteen hours a day. Nearly all were under twelve, with the youngest being a mere six and a half years of age. Work that exercised only the arms, and a complete disregard for elementary instruction, combined to produce a child population that was both weak and illiterate: Colombier reported twenty 'idiots' in the total of 200 children. But even in this branch of industry a few *procès-verbaux* against the most blatant offenders was sufficient to remove under-age labour from the *ateliers*.[96]

Children aged ten to twelve in the exempted industries were more of a problem, for the Inspectors increasingly came to see them as a regrettable anomaly in the 1874 law.[97] Most were concentrated in spinning, weaving, silk throwing, paper and glass manufacturing. They were, however, a declining force. In 1876, there were 7,780 of them in the official records, equivalent to 6.5 per cent of the juvenile and young female population protected by the law. Ten years later, their number had fallen to 2,478, a mere 1 per cent of the total.[98] Technical progress helped make many redundant, though legislation also served to fuel the growing disillusionment of employers with their youngest workers. The legal obligation to organize a six-hour day and part-time schooling was considered impractical by large numbers of employers, and so they closed their workshops to the under-twelves. After 1882, the *loi Ferry* had the further effect of keeping most children in the schools until the age of thirteen.[99] The ground was therefore well prepared for the 1892 law, which confirmed thirteen as the minimum working age in industry. This did not prevent some determined rearguard actions to hold on to under-age child labour. The glass industry was the outstanding centre of resistance. In 1895, the Commission Supérieure could still report 129 offences in the *verreries* for offences concerning the age of admission, encouraged by an initial tolerance of children hired under the 1874 régime.[100]

Not all child workers under the age of twelve were protected by the 1874 law. Besides those employed in agriculture and commerce, the law scrupulously avoided regulating children working beside their parents in a

[96] AN, F^{12} 4741, Colombier (Rouen, 7th), 9 December 1875; AN, F^{12} 4740, Blaise (Rouen, 7th), 1880.
[97] See, for example, AN, F^{12} 4740, Blaise (Rouen, 7th), 26 January 1882; AN, F^{12} 4747, Blaise (Rouen, 10th), 25 January 1886; AN, F^{12} 4764, Gouttes (St-Etienne), 21st), 1888.
[98] Ministère du Commerce, *Rapport sur l'application de la loi du 19 mai 1874 pendant l'année 1885* (Paris, 1886), p. 6.
[99] These points were reiterated each year in the reports of the Commission Supérieure.
[100] Ministère du Commerce, *Rapports sur l'application pendant l'année 1894 des lois règlementant le travail* (Paris, 1895), p. xiii.

family workshop.[101] Handloom weavers, framework knitters, lace-makers, embroiderers, seamstresses, ropemakers, cobblers and metal workers were often dispersed in this form of production, and benefited from the legal exemption. During the 1880s, for example, children still began to help their parents in the weaving shops from the age of seven or eight onwards.[102] Even where the law did apply, the sheer number of small workshops in a manufacturing town could, as we have already seen, provide a measure of *de facto* immunity from the attentions of the Inspectorate.[103] Hosiery in the lower Champagne, carding in upper Normany and silk reeling in Lyons were, in the eyes of the Inspectors, nests of corruption which went their own way with scant regard for the requirements of the law.[104] Charitable establishments run by the Catholic Church provided a different type of anomaly in the 1874 law, which the administration was slow to recognize. In principle, the legislature had proposed to regulate conditions in the variously described *ouvroirs*, *maisons de refuge*, *orphelinats* and *ateliers de charité* where industrial work was geared to profit, leaving to their own devices those concentrating more on vocational training. Both were to be supervised by the Divisional Inspectors, but, in the event, access was often fiercely resisted.[105] Only in 1888 did the Ministry of Commerce take a firm stand on the issue, with a circular instructing the Inspectors to make regular visits. From then on, nearly all of the religious houses readily conformed to the 1874 law.[106]

The existence of an unprotected sector of the economy raised problems for the Inspectorate. There was the possibility that it would act as a refuge for under-age or illiterate children sent away from firms eager to comply with (or avoid) the 1874 law. Indeed, there was always the risk that it would permit unfair competition on the market, as the unregulated workshops flourished at the expense of rivals burdened with the expense involved in child welfare measures. Instead of curtailing child labour, legislation would then have the perverse effect of relocating it, possibly in inferior conditions. There is some evidence from the inspection service that this happened under the 1874 law. Work in agriculture and market

---

[101] A circular from the Ministry of Commerce, dated 29 May 1875, explicitly stated that the 1874 law should stop at the threshold of the family; Levasseur, *Questions ouvrières*, p. 435.

[102] Numerous examples can be found in the 'Enquête Spuller', of 1882.

[103] See above, pp. 267–8.

[104] AN, F^{12} 4740, Blaise (Rouen, 7th), 26 January 1882; AN, F^{12} 4736, Delaissement (Rheims, 5th), 13 January 1883; AN, F^{12} 4755, Gauthier (Lyons, 15th), 23 April 1878.

[105] Tallon, *Manuel pratique*, ch. 3.

[106] For the background, see Louis-Henri Parias (ed.), *Histoire générale de l'enseignement et de l'éducation en France*, vol. 3, *De la Révolution à l'école républicaine* (Paris, 1981), pp. 199–203.

gardening was one obvious outlet for children excluded from industry, mentioned by Divisional Inspectors in Picardy and Brittany.[107] This shift did not give rise to any particular alarm in official circles. The movement of children from industrial to commercial employment could also be seen in a positive light, as a form of social mobility.[108] However, there was a dismal side to this development. In Paris the Inspectors noted a tendency for parents to seek out work for their children which did not require a long apprenticeship. This led them to accept dead-end jobs in the service sector, such as telegraph boy in the postal service, or groom in the stables of a hotel, club or department store.[109] Most ominously of all for the interests of the children was the drift within industry itself, from large to small workshops. In Rheims, the Divisional Inspector cited ropemakers, dyers, finishers, launderers and stonemasons as the most common employers of fugitives from the factories, prepared to take on an illiterate child for a few sous a day.[110] And in Troyes, the Local Commission asserted in 1879: 'the parents, who know very well that in the big mills the law is better observed, cannot accept the idea of their children working less than ten or eleven hours a day, and so find jobs for them in the small workshops, thereby increasing the earnings from their labour'.[111]

A deliberate attempt to exploit anomalies in the 1874 law came to light in Limoges during the 1880s. The Divisional Inspector Leseur drew attention to a recently established rag depot, which, he alleged, put out its preliminary sorting work to 200 or so family workshops as a way of circumventing the law. Children were of course prohibited from working in the *dépôts de chiffons*: sorting rags was notoriously unhealthy work, which Leseur linked to an unpleasant skin disease among the local population.[112]

As in England, most of the allegations of distorted competition stemming from anomalies in child labour legislation were concentrated in the clothesmaking industry.[113] However, parallels between the two countries

---

107 AN, F[12] 4744, Jaraczewski (Amiens, 9th), 22 January 1886; AN, F[12] 4744, Durassier (Nantes, 9th), 22 April 1883.

108 This was a point made by the Inspector Aubert, linked to the spread of popular instruction: AN, F[12] 4743, Aubert (Lisieux, 8th), 31 December 1879.

109 AN, F[12] 4730, Laporte (Seine, 1st), 21 December 1883; Ministère du Commerce, *Rapport sur l'application de la loi du 19 mai 1874 pendant l'anée 1885* (Paris, 1886), p. 6. On the same problem of 'boy labour' in dead-end jobs across the Channel, see J. R. Gillis, *Youth and History* (New York, 1974), pp. 125–8.

110 AN, F[12] 4736, Doll (Rheims, 5th), 31 December 1895.

111 AN, F[12] 4772, letter from the President of the Commission for the *arrondissement* of Troyes to Prefect of the Aube, 18 July 1879.

112 AN, F[12] 4754, Leseur (Limoges, 14th), 17 January 1887. The disease he referred to was 'a kind of favus'.

113 See James A. Schmiechen, 'State Reform and the Local Economy: An Aspect of Industrialization in Late Victorian and Edwardian London', *Economic History Review*,

did not go very far, for the peculiarly Catholic institution of the *ouvroir* was the main source of conflict. Laporte mentioned 'a certain emotion' among Parisian manufacturers who claimed to be obeying the law, while nearby religious houses blatantly overworked young children and skimped on their education. Besides the garmentmakers, manufacturers of funeral wreaths and bleachers in the eleventh *arrondissement* claimed to be suffering unemployment in the face of ruthless competition from such seemingly unworldly institutions as the Dames de Saint Michel and the Ouvroir Sainte Eugénie.[114] Echoes of these clashes reverberated in the provinces, as far afield as Flanders, Normandy, Brittany, the Orléannais, the Champagne and Provence. In Troyes, Doll was told by a factory owner that since part of his labour force was attached to a convent, the education of the young girls was not his responsibility. Yet closer investigation revealed that none of the children in question had a *livret* or *certificat d'études*, and two of them 'knew absolutely nothing'. Tavernier faced similar problems in Marseilles. An agreement he had made with the local ropemakers in 1880 was being jeopardized by the activities of a *corderie* on the premises of a local Congregation. The employer once again claimed that his contract with a religious establishment exempted him from the 1874 law, and he duly employed orphans of seven to ten years on his wheels for a whole day at a time.[115]

The extent of this type of displacement, so important for the success or failure of State intervention on behalf of child workers, is unknown – and, given its illicit nature, probably unknowable. Most of the evidence comes from the Divisional Inspectors, relying in part on the word of industrialists, who had their own vested interests to defend. There are grounds for playing down the overall scale of the phenomenon, however. Most of the outlets for children refused entry to the factories were tending to shrink in the late nineteenth century, particularly agriculture and the family workshops. Many of the handicraft trades were not interested in taking on young or illiterate children, since skill and physical strength were essential to them. It is also worth reiterating the point that French child labour legislation was relatively mild, deliberately aiming to mini-

---

2nd ser., 28 (1975), 413–28; *idem, Sweated Industries and Sweated Labour: The London Clothing Trades, 1860–1914* (London, 1984), ch.6. See also Jenny Morris, 'State Reform and the Local Economy', *Economic History Review*, 2nd ser., 35 (1982), 292–300.

[114] AN, F[12] 4730, Laporte (Seine, 1st), 21 December 1883, 21 December 1884, 31 December 1885 and 1886.

[115] AN, F[12] 4736, Doll (Rheims, 5th), 1878; AN, F[12] 4754, Tavernier (Marseilles, 14th), 22 January 1881. Information also from AN, F[12] 4733, D'Estienne d'Orves (Orleans, 2nd), 13 October 1875; AN, F[12] 4742, Aubert (Lisieux, 8th), 30 March 1877, and Delattre (Lille, 8th), 22 October 1886; AN, F[12] 4744, Delattre (Nantes, 9th), 1884; AN, F[12] 4754, Lagard (Marseilles, 14th), 29 December 1884.

mize disruption for employers. This, then, leads us back to the triumph of the primary school system under the Third Republic, and the near-universal acceptance of full-time education for children up to the age of thirteen. By the 1890s, regular employment for the very young was fast becoming seen as an anachronism, that would soon disappear entirely.

Conclusion

The 1874 law was superseded by new labour legislation in 1892. This gave formal recognition to changes affecting child workers that had occurred over the previous two decades. In raising the minimum working age to thirteen, it confirmed that the employment of pre-adolescent children in industry was no longer acceptable to French society. In dropping all part-time schooling clauses, it took for granted that children would have completed their primary education when entering the workshops. And in regulating the working hours of adult women, it gave a hint of the declining importance of child labour as a focus of attention. The 1892 law had manifestly been drafted with a view to rectifying past errors. Charitable establishments were specifically mentioned in the list of institutions to be covered. Medical certificates could be demanded by the Inspectors when they suspected that a job was beyond the strength of a particular child. Industrial accidents which led to injuries had to be declared to the local Mayor within forty-eight hours, and a doctor's report on the state of the victims prepared. Maximum working hours were clearly stated in terms of *travail effectif*. A certain flexibility was introduced into the definition of night work, to allow for seasonal influence or the peculiar circumstances of certain industries. And, most importantly, to complement the existing network of Divisional Inspectors, each department was to have its own Inspector, nominated and paid by the State.[116]

These modifications did not guarantee the new law an easy passage. At the outset, there was the resistance from glass manufacturers, and also from a few brick and ropemakers, when called upon to yield up their child workers under the age of thirteen.[117] The policy of varying legal working hours according to the age and gender of labour caused more widespread dissent. The maximum permitted for juveniles under the age of sixteen was ten hours a day; and for girls under eighteen and adult women eleven hours a day. A Ministerial Circular to the Divisional Inspectors dated 19

---

116 For useful commentaries on this law, see Béziers, *La Protection de l'enfance ouvrière*, *passim*; Lina Marini, *L'Inspection du travail* (Paris, 1936), pp. 57–68; and Judith F. Stone, *The Search for Social Peace* (Albany, NY, 1985), pp. 123–34.
117 Ministère du Commerce, *Rapports sur l'application, 1894*, p. xiii.

December 1892 admitted, from all the experience accumulated since 1841, that this would be difficult to enforce. In the Vosges, for example, the employers' organizations spelt out the usual objections to having various categories of labour putting in different hours, notably the disruption it would cause to work schedules. Meanwhile, their operatives in some of the cotton mills refused to leave their machines after eleven hours, insisting on working the extra hour. The law was vilified by the workers as an affront to their liberty and as anti-democratic. From Remiremont, there were ominous reports of soldiers stationed in the local barracks hanging around the factory gates to await young girls let out an hour before their mothers. The Sub-Prefect solemnly observed that one of the first effects of the law would be a rise in illegitimacy rates: 'Youth, when left to itself, soon embarks on love affairs, which always have the same outcome.'[118] Elsewhere in France, as the Commission Supérieure reported in 1894, the ten-hour day for children under sixteen proved almost impossible to implement.[119]

Such widespread dissatisfaction provoked a further, decisive intervention from the legislature. Its law of 30 March 1900 stipulated that young people under the age of eighteen, and women workers, be limited to ten hours of *travail effectif* per day. The new law insisted that in workshops where men, women and children were employed together (*les ateliers mixtes*), adult males be held to the same hours as the protected categories of labour. The result, predictably enough, was a further rash of strikes, and more wholesome dismissals from the workshops of juvenile workers under eighteen.[120]

118 AD Vosges, M 289.
119 Ministère du Commerce, *Rapports sur l'application, 1894*, p. xvi.
120 Levasseur, *Questions ouvrières*, pp. 442–5.

Conclusion

The 1830s and 1840s were the decades when French people first became aware that a new urban and industrial society was emerging in their midst – and they were not a little alarmed by what they saw. Villeneuve-Bargemont wrote of the 'English' industrial and political system that was being introduced into his own country. He identified its key features as the concentration of capital, production that knew no bounds, competition that was equally unlimited and the replacement of human labour by machinery.[1] The origins of this form of production could be traced back to the late eighteenth century, but as in Britain, it took a few years before the wholesale implications of economic development came into focus.[2] Contemporary observers certainly appreciated the material advantages to be gained from mechanization and competitive markets, but some of them were more concerned at the heavy burden placed on the proletariat. In retrospect, the labour policy of entrepreneurs during the early nineteenth century does indeed appear extremely crude. In the words of Eric Hobsbawm, an 'extensive' exploitation of labour was the order of the day, with long hours and low wages being seen as the way to profitability. Mesmerized by the spectacular levels of output that could be achieved with their new machines, the first generation of industrialists never considered the further increases in productivity attainable through improving the quality and organization of their operatives. Labour was treated as simply another commodity on the market, being driven hard lest it fall back into its supposedly 'natural' idleness. Hence the sad saga of fifteen-hour days in the mills, subsistence-level wages and Draconian work regulations.[3] The working class, deprived of bargaining power by

[1] *Discours*, p. 3.
[2] See, for example, J. F. C. Harrison, *Learning and Living, 1790–1960* (London, 1961), pp. 5–20; and David Roberts, *Paternalism in Early Victorian England* (London, 1979), pp. 31–2; on the 'condition of England question', raised by Thomas Carlyle.
[3] Eric J. Hobsbawm, 'Custom, Wages and Work-Load', in his *Labouring Men*, 2nd edn (London, 1968), pp. 344–70.

an overcrowded labour market and by a hostile legal system, had little choice but to knuckle down to the grim régime on offer.

This was the context for the campaign to reform child labour practices in industry. The plight of factory children featured prominently in the contemporary perception of the evils of industrial society. Juveniles were the cheapest and most docile section of the workforce, and so they fitted in all too easily with the labour strategy of the early industrialists. Reformers had no shortage of ammunition when they accused employers of imposing an entirely new work pattern with the machines, which jeopardized the health of children and left little time for schooling. The whole future of French society was thought to be in danger, with the weakening of its military defences, and the undermining of its moral and political cohesion, such as it was, by the new 'barbarians' of the slums. Of course, these polemics conveyed at best a partial view of what was happening to children at this period. A more measured account would have pointed to the growing burden of labour also evident in the countryside from the middle of the eighteenth century onwards, both in the domestic work-shops of the 'proto-industrial' sector and on the farms. It would stress the generally poor physical shape of village children and deeply entrenched obstacles to formal education in peasant society. It might also draw attention to the contrasting régimes in, say, the calico-printing works and the spinning mills, or silk-reeling shops in Lyons and the *ateliers* of hightly-paid artisans in Paris.

Nevertheless, the weight of our evidence has indicated an intensification of work for children employed in many of the factories and 'sweatshops' of the capitalist system during the first half of the nineteenth century. Even an essentially conservative observer like Louis Villermé could not fail to be shocked by the long hours of enervating toil inflicted upon the young in these types of establishment. Moreover, the unprecedented concentration of labour helped draw attention to *la condition ouvrière*. Contemporaries were tantalized by the sights and sounds of huge water wheels, tall factory chimneys, clattering machinery and ragged brigades of workers that emerged from behind the walls of the textile mills. Similarly, the forbid-ding exteriors of tenements in the crowded working-class areas of the towns aroused the curiosity of investigators like Dr Gerspach and Adolphe Blanqui, determined to expose the fate of labour in the domestic workshops. This new régime on the shop floor, it might be added, was grafted on to a society which already harboured glaring inequalities. These could still leave the children of the poor undernourished, exception-ally vulnerable to various diseases, and illiterate, before they ever came near to a workshop.

Ironically, it was precisely at the period when this growing consciousness of the drawbacks to capitalism caused child labour to become a political issue that the underlying conditions in industry began to change once again. In 1840, Eugène Buret wrote hopefully:

Our reason refuses to believe that while politics and philosophy combine so actively to enfranchise and ennoble all men, the worst effects of slavery, such as vice and ignorance, should be fatally maintained and even reintroduced by industry. These entire populations, which I see struggling painfully with machines, following their tireless movements and imitating their mathematical precision, cannot be eternally condemned to such an existence. My heart persists in the hope that their present fate is a temporary suffering, by means of which they will purchase a better future.[4]

In a limited sense, time bore him out. Broadly speaking, from the middle of the nineteenth century onwards, industrialists gradually shifted to a more 'intensive' use of labour, with the realization that yielding to working-class demands for shorter hours and higher wages might actually improve productivity. At the same time, they began to experiment with the manipulation of piece-rates, on the assumption that money incentives to hard work might be more effective than a policy of repression.[5] In this climate, with its emphasis on the quality of labour, children came to be seen as more of a hindrance than a help. They lacked the stamina necessary to cope with the speeding up of machinery, and they were not likely to be 'bought out' by sophisticated bonus systems. The growing disenchantment with child workers was revealed in complaints from employers over their lack of application and the poor quality of their output. School then stood out as the most suitable place for working-class children. From the *instituteurs*, the industrial lobby hoped, they would acquire a basic instruction in the three Rs, and, most importantly, learn the discipline and values that would make them 'good' workers. This was the 'herdsman's viewpoint' on education, which, as C. A. Anderson has observed, ruling groups are so often inclined to assume.[6]

And then there was the continuing influence of mechanization on the composition of the labour force. Whether, in the early stages of French industrialization, this form of technical progress caused an increase or a decrease in the proportion of children in the manufacturing sector is impossible to determine. We have tended to stress the qualitative changes in children's work, with the extra efforts required of them, rather than the

---

[4] *De la misère*, vol. 1, p. 73.
[5] See, for example, Stearns, *Paths to Authority*, pp. 57–61; William M. Reddy, *The Rise of Market Culture* (Cambridge, 1984), pp. 113–27; Hobsbawn, 'Custom, Wages', *passim*.
[6] C. A. Anderson, 'Patterns and Variability in the Distribution and Diffusion of Schooling', in C. A. Anderson and M. J. Bowman (eds.), *Education and Economic Development* (London, 1968), p. 314.

quantitative change in the number of jobs available. In other words, rather than accept the conventional view that mechanization allowed a substitution of female and child labour for that of adult males, we have stressed the elements of continuity with the past. Great traces of industry did after all remain largely in the hands of men, and children in particular were still limited to their traditional rôle of assistant to an adult worker. But in the maturer industrial society emerging after 1850, the steady shift towards capital-intensive forms of production tended first and foremost to exclude the young from the industrial labour force. Their simple tasks were often the easiest to mechanize, leaving a core of skilled craftsmen and machine minders to continue with the essential human inputs.

By giving pride of place to underlying economic forces in explaining what might be called the 'rise and fall of child labour' during the nineteenth century, we have inevitably given less prominence than is usual to the efforts of reformers, politicians and administrators. It is worth emphasizing that the injustices affecting children were deep-rooted in the economic system, and could not be rectified merely by administrative or judicial intervention. What was needed was a long period of economic development, which, among other things, could bring a clearer margin over subsistence for working-class budgets, improved diet and living conditions, some reduction in the power of landed and industrial *notables* – and a greater tolerance of legislation on child labour and compulsory schooling. In this perspective, the outlook for child labour reformers in low-income countries today appears distinctly gloomy. The message would seem to be to wait patiently for the trickle-down effects of development – and these of course have all too often obstinately refused to materialize. Certainly the European historical experience points to the lengthiness of the period necessary to emancipate children from the abuses of child labour, and the futility of reformist activity which fails to take into account the pressures on the industrial population. Yet, limiting the sphere of political action need not cause us to deny a 'margin of liberty' to its actors, which gave them the opportunity to force the pace of change for children. The French reformers in effect adopted a gradualist strategy, requiring two or three generations of them to attempt to curb abuses in the employment of children, before compulsory primary schooling virtually ended the whole practice. From an early stage in industrialization, then, these campaigners had a useful rôle to play. Without the *exposés* of a Jean-Jacques Bourcart or a Louis Villermé, the trials and tribulations of child workers would have remained buried from view. Without the critique of *laissez-faire* prepared by intellectuals like Simonde de Sismondi and Eugène Buret, the challenge to existing practice on the shop floor would have been difficult to mount. And without the sustained efforts of bodies such as the Société Industrielle de Mulhouse, and individuals such as Daniel Le Grand and Charles Dupin, the law would have remained aloof from the problems of child labour. At a later stage, concentrated in the final quarter of the nineteenth century, Ministers of Commerce, Prefects and Child Labour Inspectors came to the fore. These administrators had the vital function of publicizing legislation, persuading industrialists of the benefits of reform and, in the last resort, taking blatant offenders to court.[7] Fatalism, in the form of unquestioning acceptance of market forces or parental authority, is therefore not the answer to the problem of child labour in a developing economy.

There remain the children themselves, too often depicted as passive victims of the economic system. Many did indeed suffer: from isolation and boredom in the fields; from dangerous or unhealthy work on the shop floor; and from a lack of interest in their intellectual development. But their resilience was also in evidence, given support by their families and the cultural traditions of peasant and working-class communities. The stress throughout this study has been on the adaptability of the popular culture during the nineteenth century, rather than on some deep-seated crisis. Children were therefore able to offer some resistance to the pressures exerted by employers, schoolteachers – and Child Labour Inspectors. Odd glimpses have emerged of them turning the factory into a playground; running amok when expected to face school on top of a long working day; dabbling in strike action; and scorning the oppressive authority of *notables* from both Church and State. Behind the pale, sickly figure of the factory child there lurked Gavroche, in open rebellion against the 'bourgeois' order.[8]

[7] We are indebted here to Alexander Fyfe, 'The International Campaign against Child Labour – Problems and Prospects', Paper given at a Conference on 'The History of Child Labour and Apprenticeship', University of Essex, May 1986.
[8] Victor Hugo, *Les Misérables*, transl. Charles E. Wilbour (2 vols., London, 1958), vol. 2, *passim*.

Bibliography

For ease of reference, the bibliography is divided into the following sections:

I Manuscript sources

II Published primary sources
1. Official publications
2. Discussions of child labour and education issues
3. Novels and autobiographies

III Secondary works (selected)
1. General works on the economic, social and cultural history of France
2. Works on childhood, child labour and education
3. Books and articles used for comparative purposes

I MANUSCRIPT SOURCES

ARCHIVES NATIONALES

Series BB[18]: Ministry of Justice
BB[18] 1423 Surveillance du travail des enfants dans les manufactures (règlement-ations, contraventions), 1844–71

BB[18] 1666 Grèves dans le ressort de Riom occasionnées par la violation de la loi sur la durée du travail dans les usines; application de la loi sur le travail des enfants dans l'industrie, 1863–5

BB[18] 1715 Inexécution dans le département de l'Aisne des règlements sur le travail des enfants dans les manufactures, 1865

Series C: Chamber of Deputies
C 943–69 Enquête sur le travail agricole et industriel en France: exécution du décret du 25 mai 1848

C 2873 Enfants dans les manufactures

C 3018–23 Enquête sur la situation des classes ouvrières, 1872–5

C 3326–73 Enquête sur la situation des ouvriers de l'agriculture et de l'industrie en France: Commission des Quarante-quatre sous la présidence de Jacques-Eugène Spuller (sampled)

Series F⁹: military recruitment
F⁹ 159 Aube, An VIII – 1833
F⁹ 218 Meurthe
F⁹ 227–8 Nord
F⁹ 240 Haut-Rhin
F⁹ 248 Seine-Inférieure

Series F¹²: commerce and industry
F¹² 1338–9 Filatures de coton, lin, chanvre, 1721–An VIII
F¹² 2335–6 Enquête sur l'enseignement technique, 1863
F¹² 2357–8 Procès-verbaux et notes de la Commission d'enquête sur la fabrication et le commerce des dentelles et broderies, 1851–7
F¹² 2366–7 Projets de lois relatifs aux manufactures, régime industriel, An IX–1867
F¹² 2368–9 Mémoires divers sur la fabrication du papier et la condition des ouvriers papetiers, 1806–43
F¹² 2370–4 Mémoires, lettres, pétitions, relatifs au salaire, 1849–69
F¹² 4617 Accidents au travail, 1841–92
F¹² 4704–6 Préparation et exécution de la loi de 1841, 1837–47
F¹² 4707 Mission de Pinède en Angleterre, 1845; préparation et exécution de la loi de 1847, 1844–58
F¹² 4708 Inspection du travail, 1841–55
F¹² 4709–14 Rapports des inspecteurs du travail, 1841–66
F¹² 4715 Contraventions, 1841–71
F¹² 4718–19 Correspondance avec les Préfets relative au travail des enfants, 1855–71
F¹² 4722–3 Enquête sur le travail des enfants, 1867
F¹² 4724–6 Statistique, 1869–73
F¹² 4727 Préparation de la loi du 19 mai 1874 et règlements d'administration publique
F¹² 4730–64 Application de la loi de 1874 sur le travail des enfants et, à partir de février 1883, de celle du 9 septembre 1848 sur le travail des adultes
F¹² 4765 Application de la loi de 1874, articles 8 et 9, 1874–93
F¹² 4766 Ecoles industrielles privées, 1877–97
F¹² 4767–70 Commissions locales d'inspection, articles 20–2 de la loi de 1874
F¹² 4771 Réponses des Préfets à la circulaire du 14 décembre 1875 demandant des renseignements sur le fonctionnement des Commissions locales
F¹² 4772 Rapports des Commissions locales, 1880–5
F¹² 4773ᴬ⁻ᴮ Inspection du travail des enfants: personnel
F¹² 4830–3 Apprentissage industriel: loi du 22 février 1851: préparation et exécution, 1841–90

Series F^{14}: public works

F^{14} 12343 Législation de l'inspection du travail des enfants dans les manufactures, 1841–75

Series F^{15}: assistance

F^{15} 2458 Emploi des enfants des hospices dans les manufactures, An V–An XI

Series F^{17}: education

F^{17} * 80–160 Enquête sur la situation des écoles primaires, 1833 (sampled)

F^{17} 9306–20 Rapports des Inspecteurs sur les écoles primaires, 1832–55

F^{17} 9321–35 Inspection des écoles primaires: rapports et affaires diverses, 1855–6

F^{17} 9371 Rapports des recteurs sur l'état de l'enseignement primaire, 1811–37

F^{17} 9373 Correspondance avec les Préfets sur la situation générale de l'enseignement primaire, 1854–7

F^{17} 12203 Etat des enfants en âge de recevoir l'instruction qui ne fréquentent pas les écoles, 1847

Series F^{20}: statistics

F^{20} 103 Bureau de statistique: tableaux statistiques divers, 1787–1811

F^{20} 506–7 Mouvement de la population, 1853

F^{20} 518 Mouvement de la population, 1854

F^{20} 527 Mouvement de la population – nomenclature des causes de décès 1856

Series AD

AD XIX S18–21 Rapports, comités de patronage, 1879–93, Préfecture de Police, Seine

ARCHIVES DÉPARTMENTALES

Ardèche

10 M 63–4 Population et état civil; dénombrement; 1836–56

14 M 5–7 Industrie, 1806–1938

14 M 10 Rapports et correspondance sur la situation industrielle du département, 1856–86

14 M 20–2 Statistiques industrielles, 1814–41

15 M 1 Enquêtes: questionnaires; livrets

15 M 3 Application et Commissions locales des lois du 22 mars 1841 et 19 mai 1874, 1842–1937

15 M 4 Inspection départementale du travail: rapports du Préfet, 1849–73

T 175 Instruction primaire: affaires diverses, 1840–53

T 211–13 Instruction primaire: situation des écoles, 1835–45

Aube

M 2282–3 Travail des enfants dans les manufactures

M 2330–1 Statistiques industrielles, 1815–40

M 2344 Industrie: statistiques et enquêtes

Drôme
4 E 114/19–20 Registres des décès: Dieulefît, 1837–69
4 E 348/11 Registres des décès: Taulignan, 1851–69
10 M 1–2 Travail des enfants
10 M 4 Inspection du travail
34 M 115–16 Listes nominatives de recensement, Dieulefît, 1851–91
35 M 335–6 Listes nominatives de recensement, Taulignan, 1841–1936
10 T 21 Exécution de la loi du 28 juin 1833
10 T 23 Statistiques, états de situation, rapports d'inspection
10 T 25 Comités supérieurs
10 T 27 Ecoles primaires: fréquentation
10 T 36 Pièces générales de l'enseignement primaire

Isère
162 M 1 Industrie et travail; documents concernant l'organisation du travail; Enquête sur le travail agricole et industriel, arrond. de Grenoble, 1848 (on microfilm)

Meurthe-et-Moselle
2 E Registres des décès (sampled)
6 M 15–16 Recensements: circulaires et instructions, An VIII–1856
6 M 103–25 Recensements, 1851–6 (sampled)
9 M 35 Cours spéciaux créés en application de la loi du 19 mai 1874
10 M 1 Etats des établissements visités dans les Vosges, la Meurthe-et-Moselle, la Haute-Saône, le territoire de Belfort, le Haut-Rhin; rapports d'inspection, 1885–92
10 M 10–12 Statistiques des établissements visités par l'inspecteur du travail des enfants, 1878–92
10 M 27–30 Enquêtes sur le travail des enfants dans les manufactures, 1837–40; application des lois du 22 mars 1841 et 19 mai 1874, 1841–1936

Nord
M 547/1 Enquête sur le travail agricole et industriel, 1848 (on microfilm)
M 611/1–20 Travail des enfants dans les manufactures
M 613/1–18 Travail dans l'industrie. Travail des enfants. Inspection, personnel, rapports, contraventions
M 614/6–14 Accidents

Haut-Rhin
5 E 337 Mulhouse: registres des décès, 1850–6
5 M 2 Santé: conseils d'hygiène et de salubrité, 1803–73
6 M 7 Recensement de 1856
6 M 110–12, 124 Recensement de la population: Munster, Mulhouse et Thann
6 M 22 Recensement de la population: Munster, 1851
9 M 21 Effectif des ouvriers employés dans les manufactures, 1808–50

9 M 22–3 Etats nominatifs des ouvriers employés dans les manufactures du Haut-Rhin, 1822

10 M 1 Apprentissage, 1807–53; salaires, 1800–70; livrets, 1804–66

10 M 2–3 Durée du travail dans les manufactures, 1845–70

10 M 4–5 Travail des enfants dans les manufactures, 1828–70

10 M 10 Accidents au travail, 1803–70

10 M 11 Moralité et instruction des classes ouvrières, conseils aux ouvriers, 1807–66

Rhône

10 M Travail des enfants (unclassified)

Seine-Maritime

6 M 106–8 Recensement de la population, 1851: cantons d'Elbeuf et Grand-Couronne

6 M 122 Tableau général de la population, 1856

6 MP 742–3 Mouvement de la population, 1847–59

6 MP 5150 Statistique industrielle

6 MP 5156–7 Statistique des salaires industriels; statistique sommaire des industries principales

10 MP 1361–70 Industrie et commerce: travail des enfants dans les manufactures

144 TP 2 Ecole Bachelet, rue du Vert-Buisson, Rouen: registre d'inscription, de classification et de retribution scolaire, 1853–90

Vosges

M 250–1 Contrats d'apprentissage: loi du 22 février 1851

M 275–9 Travail des enfants

M 280–5 Application de la loi du 22 mars 1841: rapports d'inspection par communes, et par arrondissement, 1841–73

M 286–9 Travail des enfants et des filles mineures employés dans l'industrie: loi du 19 mai 1874

M 292 Travail de la dentelle et broderie dans les écoles, 1853–8

ARCHIVES MUNCIPALES

Caudebec-lès-Elbeuf

Registres des décès, 1851–5 (unclassified)

Mulhouse

F I Aa 17–18 Dénombrement de 1856

F VI Ea 1–18 Travail des enfants, 1839–71

Roubaix

E I a Registres des décès, 1851–5

F I a Dénombrements, 1851, 1856

F II c 1 Travail et salaires

F II c 2 Travail des enfants dans les manufactures

R I a 2 Instruction primaire: écoles libres, 1816–27

R I ba 2 Institutions actuelles, 1830–81

Troyes
F 613 Durée de travail, 1824–84
F 614 Travail des enfants dans les manufactures
F 707 Livrets des enfants

II PUBLISHED PRIMARY SOURCES

I. OFFICIAL PUBLICATIONS

Chambre de Commerce de Paris. *Statistique de l'industrie à Paris, résultant de L'Enquête faite par la Chambre de Commerce pour les années 1847–8*, Paris, 1851

Dumas, M. J. *Rapport présenté à M. le President de la République au nom de la Commission Supérieure du Travail des enfants et des filles mineures dans l'industrie*, Paris, 1878

Ministère de l'Agriculture. *Statistique agricole de la France: résultats généraux de l'enquête décennale de 1882*, Nancy, 1887

Ministère du Commerce. *Enquête sur l'enseignement professionnel*, 2 vols., Paris, 1864

Rapports sur l'application de la loi du 19 mai 1874, Paris, 1885–7

Rapports sur l'application de la loi du 2 novembre 1892 pendant l'année 1893, Paris, 1894

Rapports sur l'application pendant l'année 1894 des lois règlementant le travail, Paris, 1895

Ministère de l'Instruction publique et des Beaux-Arts. *Statistique de l'enseignement primaire*, vol. 2, *Statistique comparée de l'enseignement primaire, 1829–77*, Paris, 1880

Office du Travail. *Salaires et durée du travail dans l'industrie française*, 5 vols., Paris, 1893–7

Statistique de la France. *Industrie*, 4 vols., Paris, 1847–52

Industrie: résultats généraux de l'enquête effectuée dans les années 1861–5, Nancy, 1873

Mouvement de la population en 1851, 1852 et 1853, Strasbourg, 1857

Mouvement de la population, 1851–7, Strasbourg, 1857–61

Population, résultats généraux du dénombrement de 1866, Paris, 1869

Résultats du dénombrement de la population en 1856, Strasbourg, 1860

Territoire et population, Paris, 1855

2. DISCUSSIONS OF CHILD LABOUR AND EDUCATION ISSUES

'Accidents occasionnés par les appareils mécaniques dans les ateliers industriels', *Annales d'hygiène publique et de médecine légale*, 43 (1850), 261–89

Audiganne, A. *Les Populations ouvrières et les industries de la France*, 2 vols., Paris, 1860

Bigot de Morogues, P. M.-S. *Recherches des causes de la richesse et de la misère des peuples civilisés*, Paris, 1834

Blanqui, Adolphe. *Des Classes ouvrières en France pendant l'année 1848*, Paris, 1849

Bonneff, Léon and Bonneff, Maurice. *La Vie tragique des travailleurs*, Paris, 1908

Bourcart, Jean-Jacques. *Du travail des jeunes ouvriers dans les manufactures, usines ou ateliers*, Paris, 1840
  'Proposition sur la nécessité de fixer l'âge et de réduire les heures de travail des ouvriers des filatures', *Bulletin de la Société Industrielle de Mulhouse*, 1 (1828), 325–8

Bruno, G. *Le Tour de la France par deux enfants*, 13th edn, Paris, 1878

Bugniot, l'Abbé. *Les Petits Savoyards: ou l'exploitation de l'enfant par l'homme*, Chalon-sur-Saône, 1863

Buret, Eugène. *De la misère des classes laborieuses en Angleterre et en France*, 2 vols., Paris, 1840

Carnot, Hippolyte. *Lettre à Monsieur le Ministre de l'Agriculture et du Commerce sur la législation qui règle, dans quelques états de l'Allemagne, les conditions du travail des jeunes ouvriers*, Paris, 1840

Corbon, Anthimé. *De l'enseignement professionnel*, Paris, 1859

'Discussion entre MM. Blanqui, Passy, Dunoyer, De Beaumont, Franck et Mignet sur ce qu'il faut entendre par l'organisation du travail et sur les effets de la loi qui règle le travail des enfants dans les manufactures', *Séances et travaux de l'Académie des Sciences Morales et Politiques*, 8 (1845), 189–202

Dupin, Charles. *Du travail des enfants qu'emploient les ateliers, les usines et les manufactures*, 2 parts, Paris 1840 and 1847

Dupont, J. B. *Mémoire sur les moyens d'améliorer la santé des ouvriers à Lille*, Paris, 1826

Duruy, Victor. *L'Administration de l'Instruction publique, de 1863 à 1869*, Paris, n.d.

Gérando, Joseph-Marie de. *De la bienfaisance publique*, 4 vols., Paris, 1839
  Des progrès de l'industrie considerés dans leurs rapports avec la moralité de la classe ouvrière, Paris, 1841

Gerspach, Jean. *Considérations sur l'influence des filatures de coton et des tissages sur la santé des ouvrier*, Paris, 1827

Guépin, A. and Bonamy, E. *Nantes au XIXe siècle*, Nantes, 1835

Le Play, Frederic, ed. *Les Ouvriers des deux mondes*, 5 vols., Paris, 1857

Leroy-Beaulieu, Paul. *L'Etat moderne et ses fonctions*, 2nd edn, Paris, 1891
  Le Travail des femmes au XIXe siècle, Paris, 1873

Lhoste, Gréau and Pigeotte. 'Rapport fait au conseil de salubrité établi près de l'administration municipale de la ville de Troyes sur les accidents auxquels sont exposés les ouvriers employés dans les filatures de laine et de coton', *Annales d'hygiène publique et de médecine legale*, 12 (1834), 5–25.

Lorain, P. *Tableau de l'instruction primaire en France*, Paris, 1837

Michelet, Jules. *Le Peuple*, Paris, 1974

Penot, Achille. *Statistique générale du département du Haut-Rhin*, Mulhouse, 1831

Perin, Jules. *Le Travail des enfants employés dans les manufactures*, Paris, 1869

Reybaud, Louis. *Le Coton*, Paris, 1863
  Etudes sur le régime des manufactures: condition des ouvriers en soie, Paris, 1859
Simon, Jules. *L'Ecole*, 3rd edn, Paris, 1865
  L'Ouvrier de huit ans, 4th edn, Paris, 1867
Simonde de Sismondi, J.-C.-L. *Nouveaux principes d'économie politique*, 2 vols., Paris, 1819
Tallon, Eugène. *Manuel pratique et commentaire de la loi du 19 mai, 1874, sur le travail des enfants et des filles mineures dans l'industrie*, 3rd edn, Paris, 1885
Thouvenin, Dr. 'De l'influence que l'industrie exerce sur la santé des populations dans les grands centres manufacturiers', *Annales d'hygiène publique et de médecine légale*, 36 (1846), part 1, 16–46, part 2, 277–96; and 37 (1847), part 3, 83–111
Turgan, Julien. *Les Grandes Usines: études industrielles en France et à l'étranger*, 18 vols., Paris, 1866–89
Villeneuve-Bargemont, Alban de. *Discours prononcé à la Chambre des Députés*, Metz, 1841
  Economie politique chrétienne, Brussels, 1837
Villermé, Dr Louis R. *Discours sur la durée trop longue du travail des enfants dans beaucoup de manufactures*, Paris, 1837
  Tableau de l'état physique et moral des ouvriers employés dans les manufactures de coton, de laine et de soie, 2 vols., Paris, 1840
Waddington, Richard. *Rapport à la Chambre au nom de la Commission chargée d'examiner le projet de loi sur le travail des enfants et des femmes dans les usines et manufactures*, Paris, 1888

3. NOVELS AND AUTOBIOGRAPHIES

Audoux, Marguérite, *Marie-Claire*, Paris, 1910
Balzac, Honoré de. *Les Paysans*, Paris, 1970
Bardin, Angélina. *Angélina, une fille des champs*, Paris, 1956
Benoit, Joseph. *Confessions d'un prolétaire*, Paris, 1968
Bernard, Marc. *As Little Children*, London, 1949
Besson, P. *Un Pâtre du Cantal*, Paris, 1914
Blasquez, Adelaide. *Gaston Lucas, serrurier*, Paris, 1976
Bouvier, Jeanne. *Mes mémoires*, Paris, 1983
Carlès, Emilie. *Une soupe aux herbes sauvages*, Paris, 1977
Chaulanges, Martial. *La Terre des autres*: vol. 1, *Les Mauvais Numéros* (Paris, 1971); vol. 2, *Le Roussel* (Paris, 1972); vol. 3, *Les Rouges Moissons* (Paris, 1975)
Coignet, Jean-Roch. *Les Cahiers du Capitaine Coignet*, 1799–1815 (Paris, 1883)
Dumoulin, Georges. *Carnets de route*, Lille, 1937
Existence, G. 'Village', *Les Œuvres libres*, 221 (1939), 257–85
Gascar, Pierre. *Le Meilleur de la vie*, Paris, 1964
Grafteaux, Serge. *Mémé Santerre*, Paris, 1975

Grenadou, Ephraim and Prévost, Alain. *Grenadou: paysan français*, Paris, 1966
Guéhenno, Jean. *Changer la vie*, Paris, 1961
Guillaumin, Emile. *La Vie d'un simple*, Paris, 1905
Hélias, Pierre-Jakez. *Le Cheval d'orgueil*, Paris, 1975
Hugo, Victor. *Les Misérables*, transl. Charles E. Wilbour, 2 vols., London, 1958
Jamerey-Duval, Valentin. *Mémoires*, Paris, 1981
Michaud, René. *J'avais vingt ans: un jeune ouvrier au début du siècle*, Paris, 1967
Nadaud, Martin. *Léonard, maçon de la Creuse*, Paris, 1977
Noiret, Charles. *Mémoires d'un ouvrier rouennais*, Rouen, 1837
Perdiguier, Agricol. *Mémoires d'un compagnon*, Paris, 1943
Pergaud, Louis. *La Guerre des boutons*, Paris, 1963
Phillippe, Charles-Louis. *Charles Blanchard*, Paris, 1913
Reboul, Jules. *La Vie de Jacques Baudet, 1870–1930*, Privas, 1934
Renard, Jules. *Poil de carotte*, Paris, 1965
Restif de la Bretonne, Nicolas. *Monsieur Nicolas*, Paris, 1932
Rey, Raymonde Anna. *Augustine Rouvière, cévénole*, Paris, 1977
Sand, George. *La Mare au diable*, Paris, 1962
Sylvère, Antoine. *Toinou, le cri d'un enfant auvergnat*, Paris, 1980
Truquin, Norbert. *Mémoires et aventures d'un prolétaire à travers la révolution*, Paris, 1977
Zola, Emile. *The Earth*, transl. D. Parmee, Harmondsworth, 1980
  Germinal, transl. L. W. Tancock, Harmondsworth, 1954
  L'Assommoir, New York, 1962

III SECONDARY WORKS (SELECTED)

I. GENERAL WORKS ON THE ECONOMIC, SOCIAL AND CULTURAL HISTORY OF FRANCE

Beauroy, Jacques, Bertrand, Marc and Gargan, Edward T., eds. *The Wolf and the Lamb: Popular Culture in France from the Old Regime to the Twentieth Century*, Saratoga, Cal., 1977
Benoit, Martine. 'Les Couvents ateliers au XIXe siècle', *Le Peuple français*, 22 (1976), 22–6
Bercé, Yves-Marie. *Fête et révolte*, Paris, 1976
Bernot, Lucien and Blancard, René. *Nouville: un village français*, Paris, 1953
Beteille, Roger. *La Vie quotidienne en Rouergue avant 1914*, Paris, 1973
Bougeatre, Eugène. *La Vie rurale dans le Mantois et le Vexin au XIXe siècle*, Meulan, 1971
Brékilien, Yann. *La Vie quotidienne des paysans bretons au XIXe siècle*, Paris, 1966
Caroux-Destray, Jacques. *Un couple ouvrier traditionnel*, Paris, 1974
Carrier, Hervé. 'Le Manichéisme urbain–rural: quelques stéréotypes de la société heureuse', in Hervé Carrier and Emile Pin, eds., *Essais de sociologie religieuse*, Paris, 1967, pp. 147–65
Castan, Yves. *Honnêteté et relations sociales en Languedoc, 1715–80*, Paris, 1974

Causse, Henri. 'Un industriel toulousain au temps de la Révolution et de l'Empire: François-Bernard Boyer-Fonfrède (1767–?)', *Annales du Midi* (1957), 121–33

Chapiseau, Félix. *Le Folk-lore de la Beauce et du Perché*, 2 vols., Paris, 1902

Charrié, Pierre. *Le Folklore du Bas-Vivarais*, Paris, 1964
  Le Folklore du Haut-Vivarais, Paris, 1968

Chassagne, S., Dewerpe, Y. and Gaulupeau, Y. 'Les Ouvriers de la manufacture de toiles imprimées d'Oberkampf à Jouy-en-Josas, 1760–1815', *Le Mouvement social*, 97 (1976), 39–88

Chatelain, Abel. *Les Migrants temporaires en France de 1800 à 1914*, 2 vols., Lille, 1976
  'Migrations et domesticité féminine urbaine en France, XVIIIe–XXe siècle', *Revue d'histoire économique et sociale*, 47 (1968), 506–28

Chevalier, Louis. *Labouring Classes and Dangerous Classes*, London, 1973

Cholvy, Gérard. 'Société, genres de vie et mentalités dans les campagnes françaises de 1815 à 1880', *L'Information historique* (1974), 155–66

Coleman, William. *Death is a Social Disease*, Madison, Wisc., 1982

Corbin, Alain. *Archaisme et modernité en Limousin au XIXe siècle, 1845–80*, 2 vols., Paris, 1975
  Les Filles de noce, Paris, 1978

Crubellier, Maurice. *Histoire culturelle de la France, XIXe–XXe siècle*, Paris, 1974

Darmon, Jean-Jacques. *Le Colportage de librairie en France sous le Second Empire*, Paris, 1972

Désert, Gabriel. 'Une société rurale au XIXe siècle: les paysans du Calvados, 1815–95', 2 vols., unpublished thesis, University of Paris I, 1971

Desrousseaux, A. *Mœurs populaires de la Flandre française*, 2 vols., Lille, 1889

Dolléans, Edouard and Dehove, Georges. *Histoire du travail en France*, 2 vols., Paris, 1953

Donzelot, Jacques. *The Policing of Families*, transl. R. Hurley, London, 1980

Drouillet, Jean. *Folklore du Nivernais et du Morvan*, 5 vols., La Charité-sur-Loire, 1959–65

Dubosq, Guy, Plongeron, Bernard and Robert, Daniel, eds. *La Religion populaire*, Paris, 1979

Duveau, Georges. *La Vie ouvrière en France sous le Second Empire*, Paris, 1946

Fabre, Daniel and Lacroix, Jacques, *La Vie quotidienne des paysans du Languedoc au XIXe siècle*, Paris, 1973

Foucault, Michel. *Discipline and Punish*, Harmondsworth, 1977

Fournel, Paul. *L'Histoire véritable de guignol*, Paris, 1981

Fraysse, C. *Le Folklore du Baugeois*, Bauge, 1906

Galarneau, Claude. 'La Mentalité paysanne en France sous l'Ancien Régime', *Revue d'histoire de l'Amérique français*, 14 (1960), 16–24

Garrier, Gilbert. *Paysans du Beaujolais et du Lyonnais, 1800–1970*, 2 vols., Grenoble, 1973

Guillaume, Pierre. *La Population de Bordeaux au XIXe siècle*, Paris, 1972

Hémardinquer, J.-J., ed. *Pour une histoire de l'alimentation*, Cahiers des Annales, 28, Paris, 1970

Hilaire, Yves-Marie. *Une chrétienté au XIXe siècle? La vie religieuse des populations d'Arras, 1840–1914*, 2 vols., Lille, 1977

'La Pratique religieuse en France de 1815 à 1878', *L'Information historique*, 8 (1963), 57–69

Hufton, Olwen. *The Poor of Eighteenth-Century France, 1750–1789*, Oxford, 1974

'Women and the Family in Eighteenth-Century France', *French Historical Studies*, 9 (1975), 1–22

'Women, Work and Marriage in Eighteenth Century France', in R. B. Outhwaite, ed., *Marriage and Society*, London, 1981, pp. 186–203

Jalby, R. *Le Folklore du Languedoc*, Paris, 1971

Kahan-Rabecq, M.-M. *L'Alsace économique et sociale sous le règne de Louis-Philippe*, 2 vols., Paris, 1939

Lasserre, André. *La Situation des ouvriers de l'industrie textile dans la région lilloise sous la Monarchie de Juillet*, Lausanne, 1952

Le Bras, Gabriel. *Etudes de sociologie religieuse*, vol. 1, *Sociologie de la pratique religieuse dans les campagnes*, Paris, 1955

Lehning, James R. *The Peasants of Marlhes*, London, 1980

Lequin, Yves. *Les Ouvriers de la région lyonnaise, 1848–1914*, 2 vols., Lyons, 1977

Leuilliot, Paul. *L'Alsace au début du XIXe siècle*, 3 vols., Paris, 1959–61

Levasseur, Emile. *Histoire des classes ouvrières et de l'industrie en France de 1789 à 1870*, 2nd edn, 2 vols., Paris, 1904

Questions ouvrières et industrielles en France sous la Troisième République, Paris, 1907

McBride, Theresa M. *The Domestic Revolution*, London, 1976

'Social Mobility for the Lower Classes: Domestic Servants in France', *Journal of Social History*, 8 (1974), 63–78

Mathé, R. *Emile Guillaumin, l'homme de la terre et l'homme de lettres*, Paris, 1966

Medick, Hans. 'The Proto-Industrial Family Economy: The Structural Function of Household and Family during the Transition from Peasant Society to Industrial Capitalism', *Social History*, 3 (1976), 291–315

Melucci, Alberto. 'Action patronale, pouvoir, organisation. Règlements d'usine et contrôl de la main-d'œuvre au XIXe siècle', *Le Mouvement social*, 97 (1976), 139–59

Merriman, John M., ed. *Consciousness and Class Experience in Nineteenth-Century Europe*, New York, 1979

Moch, Leslie Page. *Paths to the City*, Beverley Hills, 1983

Morineau, Michel. *Les Faux-semblants d'un démarrage économique: agriculture et démographie en France au XVIIIe siècle*, Paris, 1971

Muchembled, Robert. *Culture populaire et culture des élites dans la France moderne, XVe–XVIIIe siècles*, Paris, 1978

Perrin, Olivier. *Galérie bretonne*, 3 vols., Paris, 1835

Perrot, Michelle. 'Les Ouvriers et les machines en France dans la première moitié du XIXe siècle', *Recherches*, 32 (1978), 347–75

'Travailler et produire: Claude-Lucien Bergery et les débuts du management en France', in *Mélanges d'histoire sociale offerts à Jean Maitron*, Paris, 1976, pp. 177–87

Pierrard, Pierre. *La Vie ouvrière à Lille sous le Second Empire*, Paris, 1965
La Vie quotidienne dans le Nord au XIXe siècle, Paris, 1976

Plongeron, Bernard and Pannet, Robert, eds. *Le Christianisme populaire*, Paris, 1976

Poitrineau, Abel. *La Vie rurale en basse-auvergne au XVIIIe siècle, 1726–1789*, 2 vols., Paris, 1965

Ragon, M. *Histoire de la littérature prolétarienne en France*, Paris, 1974

Raison-Jourde, Françoise. *La colonie auvergnate de Paris au XIXe siècle*, Paris, 1976

Robert, G. *'La Terre' d'Emile Zola: étude historique et critique*, Paris, 1952

Rougé, Jacques-Marie. *Le Folklore de la Touraine*, Tours, 1931

Saint-Jacob, P. de. *Les Paysans de la Bourgogne du nord au dernier siècle de l'ancien régime*, Paris, 1960

Schmidt, Charles. 'Les Débuts de l'industrie cotonnière en France, 1780–1806', *Revue d'histoire économique et sociale*, 7 (1914), 26–55

Sébillot, Paul. *Coutumes populaires de la Haute-Bretagne*, Paris, 1886

Segalen, Martine. *Love and Power in the Peasant Family: Rural France in the Nineteenth Century*, Oxford, 1983

Séguin, Jean-Pierre. *Nouvelles à sensation: canards du XIXe siècle*, Paris, 1959

Seignolle, C. *Le Folklore de la Provence*, Paris, 1963

Sewell, William H. *Work and Revolution in France*, Cambridge, 1980

Stearns, Peter N. *Paths to Authority*, Urbana, Ill., 1978

Tardieu, Suzanne. *La Vie domestique dans le mâconnais rural préindustriel*, Paris, 1964

Thuillier, Guy. *Pour une histoire du quotidien au XIXe siècle en Nivernais*, Paris, 1977

Tilly, Louise A. and Scott, Joan W. *Women, Work and Family*, New York, 1978

Toutain, J.-C. *La Consommation alimentaire en France de 1789 à 1964*, Geneva, 1970
La Population de la France de 1700 à 1959, Paris, 1963

Trempé, Rolande. *Les Mineurs de Carmaux, 1848–1914*, 2 vols., Paris, 1971

Van Gennep, Arnold. *Le Folklore du Dauphiné*, 2 vols., Paris, 1932
Manuel de folklore français contemporaine, vol. 1, *Introduction générale et première partie: du berceau à la tombe*, Paris, 1972

Vanoli, D. 'Les Ouvrières enfermées: les couvents soyeux', *Les Révoltes logiques*, 2 (1976), 13–39

Vidalenc, Jean. *Le Département de L'Eure sous la monarchie constitutionelle, 1814–1848*, Paris, 1952

Vincent, Louise. *Le Berry dans l'œuvre de George Sand*, Paris, 1919

Weber, Eugen. *Peasants into Frenchmen*, London, 1979

Zonabend, Françoise. *La Mémoire longue*, Paris, 1980

2. WORKS ON CHILDHOOD, CHILD LABOUR AND EDUCATION

Abbadie d'Arrast, Mme Charles d'. *Causeries sur le pays Basque: la femme et l'enfant*, Paris, 1909

Allain, E. *L'Instruction primaire en France avant la Révolution*, Geneva, 1970; first publ. 1881

Anderson, R. D. *Education in France, 1848–1870*, Oxford, 1975

Ariès, Philippe. *Centuries of Childhood*, Harmondsworth, 1973

Armengaud, André. 'L'Attitude de la société à l'égard de l'enfant au XIXᵉ siècle', *Annales de démographie historique* (1973), 303–12

Aron, J. P., Dumont, P. and Le Roy Ladurie, E. *Anthropologie du conscrit français*, Paris, 1972

Artz, F. B. *The Development of Technical Education in France, 1500–1850*, Cambridge, Mass., 1966

Baker, Donald N. and Harrigan, Patrick J., eds. *The Making of Frenchmen*, Waterloo, Ontario, 1980

Baudoin, Monique. 'Le Travail des enfants dans les manufactures de l'Isère, 1841–1870', *Le Peuple français*, 23 (1976), 31

Béziers, Simone. *La Protection de l'enfance ouvrière*, Montpellier, 1935

Boudard, René. 'L'Enseignement primaire clandestin dans le Département de la Creuse entre 1830 et 1880', *Mémoires de la Société des sciences naturelles et archéologiques de la Creuse*, 33 (1959), 525–35

Bozon, Michel. *Les Conscrits*, Paris, 1981

Calvet, J. *L'Enfant dans la littérature française*, 2 vols., Paris, 1930

Chartier, Roger, Compère, Marie-Madeleine and Julia, Dominique. *L'Education en France du XVIᵉ au XVIIIᵉ siècle*, Paris, 1976

Chevallier, Pierre, ed. *La Scolarisation en France depuis un siècle*, Paris, 1974

Chombart de Lauwe, Marie-José. *Un monde autre: l'enfance*, Paris, 1971

Corbin, Alain. 'Pour une étude sociologique de la croissance de l'alphabétisation au XIXᵉ siècle: l'instruction des conscrits du Cher et de l'Eure-et-Loire, 1833–83', *Revue d'histoire économique et sociale*, 153 (1975), 99–120

Cotterau, Alain. 'Les Jeunes contre le boulot: une histoire vieille comme le capitalisme industriel', *Autrement*, 21 (1979), 197–206

'Méconnue, la vie des enfants d'ouvriers au XIXᵉ siècle', *Autrement*, 10 (1977), 117–33

Courtois, Félix. 'Les Ecoles du Creusot, 1787–1882', *Mémoires de la société éduenne*, 21 (1893), 129–57

Crubellier, Maurice. *L'Enfance et la jeunesse dans la société française, 1800–1950*, Paris, 1979

David, Jean-Philippe. *L'Etablissement de l'enseignement primaire au XIXᵉ siècle dans le département de Maine-et-Loire, 1816–79*, Angers, 1967

Demonet, M., Dumont, P., and Le Roy Ladurie, E. 'Anthropologie de la jeunesse masculine en France au niveau d'une cartographie cantonale, 1819–30', *Annales ESC*, 31 (1976), 700–60

Douailler, S. and Vermeren, P. 'Les Enfants du capital', *Les Révoltes logiques*, 3 (1976), 8–43

Duveau, Georges. *La Pensée ouvrière sur l'éducation pendant la Seconde Républi-que et le Second Empire*, Paris, 1948

Evrard, F. 'Le Travail des enfants dans l'industrie, 1780–1870', *Bulletin de la société d'études historiques, géographiques et scientifiques de la région parisienne*, 37 (1936), 1–14

Faure, Alain. 'Enfance ouvrière, enfance coupable', *Les Révoltes logiques*, 13 (1981), 13–35

Flandrin, Jean-Louis. 'L'Attitude à l'égard du petit enfant et les conduites sexuelles dans la civilisation occidentale', *Annales de démographie historique* (1973), 143–210

  'Enfance et société', *Annales ESC*, 19 (1964), 322–9

Fleury, Michel and Valmary, Pierre. 'Les Progrès de l'instruction élémentaire de Louis XV à Napoléon III d'après l'enquête de Louis Maggiolo, 1877–9', *Population*, 12 (1957), 71–92

Fohlen, Claude. 'Révolution industrielle et travail des enfants', *Annales de démographie historique* (1973), 319–25

Furet, François and Ozouf, Jacques. 'Literacy and Industrialization: The Case of the Département du Nord in France', *Journal of European Economic History*, 5 (1976), 5–44

  Reading and Writing, Cambridge, 1982

Gavoille, Jacques. *L'Ecole publique dans le département du Doubs, 1870–1914*, Paris, 1981

Gélis, J., Laget, M. and Morel, M.-F. *Entrer dans la vie: naissances et enfances dans la France traditionnelle*, Paris, 1978

Gildea, Robert. *Education in Provincial France, 1800–1914*, Oxford, 1983

Gontard, Maurice. *Les Ecoles primaires de la France bourgeoise, 1833–1875*, Toulouse, 1957

  L'Enseignement primaire en France da la Révolution à la loi Guizot, 1789–1833, Paris, 1959

  L'Œuvre scolaire de la Troisième République, Toulouse, 1965

Grew, Raymond, Harrigan, Patrick J. and Witney, James, 'The Availability of Schooling in Nineteenth-Century France', *Journal of Interdisciplinary History*, 14 (1983), 25–63

Guéneau, L. 'La Législation restrictive du travail des enfants: la loi française du 22 mars 1841', *Revue d'histoire économique et sociale*, 15 (1927), 420–503

Guinot, J. P. *Formation professionnelle et travailleurs qualifiés depuis 1789*, Paris, 1946

Heywood, Colin. 'The Market for Child Labour in Nineteenth-Century France', *History*, 66 (1981), 34–49

Jégouzo, Guenhaël and Brangeon, Jean-Louis. *Les Paysans et l'école*, Paris, 1976

Johnson, Douglas. *Guizot*, London, 1963

Le Roy Ladurie, E. and Bernageau, N. 'Etude sur un contingent militaire, 1868', *Annales de démographie historique* (1971), 311–17

Le Roy Ladurie, E., Bernageau, N. and Pasquet, Y. 'Le Conscrit et l'ordinateur. Perspectives de recherche sur les archives militaires du XIXe siècle français', *Studi Storici*, 10 (1969), 260–318

Le Roy Ladurie, E. and Zysberg, A. 'Anthropologie des conscrits français, 1868–87', *Ethnologie française*, 9 (1979), 47–67

Lynch, Katherine A. 'The Problem of Child Labor Reform and the Working-Class Family in France during the July Monarchy', *Proceedings of the Western Society for French History*, 5 (1977), 228–36

Marini, Lina. *L'Inspection du travail*, Paris, 1936

Mercier, Roger. *L'Enfant dans la société du XVIIIe siècle*, Dakar, 1961

Meyer, Philippe. *L'Enfant et la raison d'Etat*, Paris, 1977

Moch, Leslie Page. 'Adolescence and Migration', *Social Science History*, 5 (1981), 25–51

Moscovici, M. 'La Personnalité de l'enfant en milieu rurale', *Etudes rurales*, 1 (1961), 57–69

Oberlé, Raymond. *L'Enseignement à Mulhouse de 1789 à 1870*, Paris, 1961
  'Etude sur l'analphabétisme à Mulhouse au siècle de l'industrialisation', *Bulletin du Musée historique de Mulhouse*, 67 (1959), 99–110
  'Le Travail des enfants-ouvriers et leur instruction à Mulhouse au XIXe siècle', *Actes du Quatre-Vingt-Cinquième Congrès National des Sociétés Savantes, Chambéry-Annecy, 1960*, Paris, 1961, 539–57

Perrot, Michelle. 'Dans la France de la Belle Epoque: "Les Apaches", premières bandes de jeunes', in special issue of *Cahiers Jussieu: Les Marginaux et les exclus dans l'histoire*, Paris, 1978, pp. 387–407

Pierrard, Pierre. 'L'Enseignement primaire à Lille sous la Restauration', *Revue du Nord*, 217 (1973), 127–31
  'L'Enseignement primaire à Lille sous la monarchie de juillet', *Revue du Nord*, 220 (1974), 1–11
  'Le Patronat et le travail des enfants en 1848', *Economie et humanisme*, 117 (1959), 53–64

Poutet, Yves. 'L'Enseignement des pauvres dans la France du XVIIe siècle', *XVIIe siècle*, 90–1 (1971), 87–110

Prost, Antoine. *Histoire de l'enseignement en France, 1800–1967*, Paris, 1968

Querrien, Anne. 'Travaux élémentaires sur l'école primaire', *Recherches*, 23 (1976), 5–189

Rivet, Auguste. 'Aspects et problèmes de l'enseignement primaire en Haute-Loire pendant la première moitié du XIXe siècle', *Actes du 88e Congrès National des Sociétés Savantes, Clermont-Ferrand, 1963*, Paris, 1964

Rouard, D. 'Enfants au travail', *Le Monde de l'éducation*, 53 (1979), 9–18

Ruffet, J. 'La Liquidation des instituteurs-artisans', *Les Révoltes logiques*, 3 (1976), 61–76

Sandrin, Jean. *Enfants trouvés, enfants ouvriers, XVIIe–XIXe siècle*, Paris, 1982
  'Le Travail des enfants au XIXe siècle', *Le Peuple français*, 21 (January–March 1976), 12–16; and 22 (April–June 1976), 27–30

Schmidt, Charles. 'Notes sur le travail des enfants dans les manufactures pendant la Révolution', *Bulletin de la Commission de recherches et de publication des documents relatifs à la vie économique de la Révolution* (1910), 198–221

Snyders, Georges. *La Pédagogie en France au XVIIe et XVIIIe siècles*, Paris, 1965

Soreau, E. 'Notes sur le travail des enfants dans l'industrie pendant la Révolution', *Revue des études historiques*, 102 (1938), 159–63

Soudjian, Guy. 'Quelques réflexions sur les statures des jeunes Parisiens sous le Second Empire', *Ethnologie française* (1979), 69–84

Strumingher, Laura S. *What Were Little Girls and Boys Made Of?*, Albany, 1983

Thabault, Roger. *Education and Change in a Village Community: Mazières-en-Gâtine, 1848–1914*, transl. P. Tregear, New York, 1971

Tilly, Louise A. 'Linen Was their Life: Family Survival Strategies and Parent–Child Relations in Nineteenth-Century France', in Hans Medick and David Warren Sabean (eds.), *Interest and Emotion*, Cambridge, 1984, pp. 300–16

Touren, Suzanne. *La Loi de 1841 sur le travail des enfants dans les manufactures*, Paris, 1931

Tronchot, Raymond. 'L'Enseignement mutuel en France de 1815 à 1833', unpublished thesis, University of Paris I, 1972

Tudesq, André. 'Comment le grand patronat considère le travail des enfants en 1840', *Huitième colloque d'histoire sur l'artisanat et l'apprentissage*, Aix-en-Provence, 1964

Untrau, Martine. 'J'avais dix ans, j'habitais le 20ᵉ, c'etait 1900 . . .', *Autrement*, 10 (1977), 105–16

Vilar, P. 'Enseignement primaire et culture populaire en France sous la IIIᵉ République', in Louis Bergeron, ed., *Niveaux de culture et groupes sociaux*, Paris, 1967, pp. 267–87

Vovelle, Michel. 'Y a-t-il eu une révolution culturelle au XVIIIᵉ siècle? A propos de l'éducation populaire en Provence', *Revue d'histoire moderne et contemporaine*, 22 (1975), 89–141

Weissbach, Lee S. 'Qu'on ne coupe le blé en herbe: A History of Child Labour Legislation in Nineteenth-Century France', unpublished PhD thesis, Harvard University, 1975

Zind, Pierre. 'L'Enseignement primaire sous la Restauration dans l'arrondissement de Saint-Etienne', *Cahiers d'histoire*, 4 (1958), 359–72

3. BOOKS AND ARTICLES USED FOR COMPARATIVE PURPOSES

Anderson, C. A. and Bowman, M. J., eds. *Education and Economic Development*, London, 1968

Bartrip, P. W. J. 'British Government Inspection, 1832–75: Some Observations', *Historical Journal*, 25 (1982), 605–26

'Success or Failure? The Prosecution of the Early Factory Acts', *Economic History Review*, 2nd ser., 38 (1985), 423–7

Bartrip, P. W. J. and Fenn, P. T. 'The Administration of Safety: The Enforcement Policy of the Early Factory Inspectorate 1844–64', *Public Administration*, 58 (1980), 87–102

'The Conventionalization of Factory Crime – A Re-assessment', *International Journal of the Sociology of Law*, 80 (1980), 175–86

'The Evolution of Regulatory Style in the Nineteenth Century British Factory Inspectorate', *Journal of Law and Society*, 10 (1983), 201–22

Bowman, M. J. and Anderson, C. A. 'Human Capital and Economic Modernization in Historical Perspective', in F. C. Lane, ed., *Fourth International
Conference of Economic History, Bloomington, 1968*, Paris, 1973,
pp. 247–72

Carson, W. G. 'The Conventionalization of Early Factory Crime', *International
Journal of the Sociology of Law*, 7 (1979), 37–60

'White-Collar Crime and the Enforcement of Factory Legislation', *British
Journal of Criminology*, 10 (1970), 383–98

Finnegan, Ruth. 'Literacy versus Non-Literacy: The Great Divide?', in Robin
Horton and Ruth Finnegan, eds., *Modes of Thought*, London, 1973,
pp. 112–44

Geertz, Hildred. 'An Anthropology of Religion and Magic', *Journal of Interdisciplinary History*, 6 (1975), 71–89

Hoyles, Martin, ed. *Changing Childhood*, London, 1979

Hutt, W. H. 'The Factory System of the Early Nineteenth Century', in F. A. Hayek
(ed.), *Capitalism and the Historians*, London, 1954, pp. 160–88

Jefferson, Carter. 'Worker Education in England and France, 1800–1914',
Comparative Studies in Society and History, 6 (1964), 345–66

Johnson, Richard. 'Educational Policy and Social Control in Early Victorian
England', *Past and Present*, 49 (1970), 96–119

Laslett, Peter and Wall, Richard, eds. *Household and Family in Past Time*,
Cambridge, 1972

McKendrick, Neil. 'Home Demand and Economic Growth: A New View of the
Role of Women and Children in the Industrial Revolution', in N. McKendrick, ed., *Historical Perspectives*, London, 1974, pp. 152–210

Marvel, H. P. 'Factory Regulation: A Reinterpretation of Early English Experience', *Journal of Law and Economics*, 20 (1977), 379–402

Mause, Lloyd B. de, ed. *The History of Childhood*, London, 1974

Nardinelli, Clark. 'Child Labor and the Factory Acts', *Journal of Economic
History*, 40 (1980), 739–55

'Corporal Punishment and Children's Wages in Nineteenth-Century Britain',
Explorations in Economic History, 19 (1982), 283–95

Niemi, Beth and Lloyd, Cynthia. 'Sex Differentials in Earnings and Unemployment Rates', *Feminist Studies*, 2 (1975), 194–201

Peacock, A. E. 'The Successful Prosecution of the Factory Acts, 1833–55',
Economic History Review, 2nd ser., 37 (1984), 197–210

Pollock, Linda A. *Forgotten Children*, Cambridge, 1983

Richards, Eric. 'Women in the British Economy since about 1700: An Interpretation', *History*, 59 (1974), 337–57

Rimbaud, Christiane. *52 millions d'enfants au travail*, Paris, 1980

Rodgers, Gerry and Standing, Guy, eds. *Child Work, Poverty and Underdevelopment*, Geneva, 1981

Sanderson, Michael. 'Literacy and Social Mobility in the Industrial Revolution in
England', *Past and Present*, 56 (1972), 75–103

'Social Change and Elementary Education in Industrial Lancashire, 1780–
1840', *Northern History*, 3 (1968), 131–54

Smelser, Neil J. *Social Change in the Industrial Revolution*, London, 1959

Sommerville, John. *The Rise and Fall of Childhood*, Beverley Hills, Cal., 1982

Standing, Guy. 'State Policy and Child Labour: Accumulation versus Legitimation', *Development and Change*, 13 (1982), 613–20

Tanner, J. M. 'Sequence, Tempo and Individual Variation in the Growth and Development of Boys and Girls Aged Twelve to Sixteen', *Dædalus*, 100 (1971), 907–30

'The Apprenticeship of Women and Girls', *International Labour Review*, 72 (1955), 283–302

Thomas, Keith. 'An Anthropology of Religion and Magic II', *Journal of Interdisciplinary History*, 6 (1975), 91–109

Thomas, Maurice W. *The Early Factory Legislation*, Leigh-on-Sea, 1948

Thompson, Edward P. 'Time, Work-Discipline and Industrial Capitalism', *Past and Present*, 38 (1967), 56–97

'Wage Differentials Affecting Young Workers', *International Labour Review*, 122 (1955), 521–34

Wall, Richard. 'The Age at Leaving Home', *Journal of Family History*, 3 (1978), 181–202

Ward, J. T. *The Factory Movement, 1830–55*, London, 1962

White, Benjamin, ed. 'Child Workers', special issue of *Development and Change*, 13 (1982)

Index